PENGUIN BOOKS

MANY ROADS THROUGH PARADISE

Shyam Selvadurai's first novel, *Funny Boy*, won the WH Smith/Books in Canada First Novel Award and the Lambda Literary Award in the US. He is the author of *Cinnamon Gardens* and *Swimming in the Monsoon Sea*, and the editor of an anthology, *Story-wallah! A Celebration of South Asian Fiction*. His books have been published in the US, the UK and India, and translated into seven languages. His latest novel, *The Hungry Ghosts*, was shortlisted for Canada's prestigious Governor General's Award for Fiction and longlisted for the DSC Prize for South Asian Literature.

many roads through paradise

An Anthology of Sri Lankan Literature

Edited by
SHYAM SELVADURAI

PENGUIN BOOKS
An imprint of Penguin Random House

PENGUIN BOOKS

USA | Canada | UK | Ireland | Australia
New Zealand | India | South Africa | China | Singapore

Penguin Books is part of the Penguin Random House group of companies whose addresses can be found at global.penguinrandomhouse.com

Published by Penguin Random House India Pvt. Ltd
4th Floor, Capital Tower 1, MG Road,
Gurugram 122 002, Haryana, India

Penguin Random House India

First published by Penguin Books India 2014

10 9 8 7 6 5 4 3 2

ISBN 9780143423034

For sale in the Indian Subcontinent only

Typeset in Bembo by Eleven Arts, Delhi
Printed at Manipal Technologies Limited, India

www.penguin.co.in

FSC www.fsc.org MIX Paper | Supporting responsible forestry FSC® C043100

This is a legitimate digitally printed version of the book and therefore might not have certain extra finishing on the cover.

For Sunila Abeysekera,
much missed reader,
who loved Sri Lanka for its 'many roads'.

Contents

Acknowledgements

My many thanks to:

Tissa Jayatilaka, Neloufer de Mel, Vijita Fernando, Ranjini Obeyesekere, Yasmine Gooneratne, Lakshmi de Silva, Rajiva Wijesinha, Chelva Kanaganayakam and Cheran, who gave so generously of their knowledge and time in helping me track down works and authors. Especial thanks to Tissa Jayatilaka, Neloufer de Mel and Vijita Fernando who also lent me their books, always a precarious thing to do in Sri Lanka. Also a thank you to Mr Pathmanabhan Iyer who helped with securing rights to the works of some of the Tamil writers and read the manuscript.

I am grateful to the following anthologies and their editors. Their efforts made my task a little easier: *Lutesong and Lament: Tamil Writing from Sri Lanka* edited by Chelva Kanganayakam; *The Rapids of a Great River* edited by Lakshmi Holmström; *A Lankan Mosaic* edited by Ranjini Obeyesekere, Ashley Halpe and M.A. Nuhman; *Kaleidoscope: An Anthology of Sri Lankan English Literature* edited by D.C.R.A. Goonetilleke; *Sri Lankan Literature in English, 1948–1998: A 50th Independence Anniversary Anthology* edited by D.C.R.A. Goonetilleke; *Modern Sri Lankan Stories* edited by D.C.R.A. Goonetilleke; *Modern Sri Lankan Poetry: An Anthology* edited by D.C.R.A. Goonetilleke; *The Penguin Book of Modern Sri Lankan Stories* edited by D.C.R.A. Goonetilleke; *A Selection of Modern*

Sri Lankan Poetry in English edited by Rajiva Wijesinha; *Bridging Connections* edited by Rajiva Wijesinha; *Mirrored Images* edited by Rajiva Wijesinha; *An Anthology of Modern Writing from Sri Lanka (Poetry & Prose)* edited by Ranjini Obeyesekere and Chitra Fernando.

Finally, my thanks to Chiki Sarkar and Tara Khandelwal at Penguin India; Bruce Westwood and Lien de Nil at Westwood Creative Artists; and, as always, to Andrew Champion.

Introduction

Reading for My Life

Shyam Selvadurai

From my early childhood I had a passion for books, by which I meant British books, without any question that this was the only form of reading worth being passionate about. The chief source of books was my Aunty Bunny. A nurse and unmarried, she spent her off days off in our house, and we looked forward to her visits because she brought books with her. Better still was payday when she would take my brother, my sister and me by bus or taxi to the K.V.G. de Silva Bookshop in the Fort. The hushed atmosphere of the place with its high ceilings and slow-turning fans, the muffled honk of cars out on the roads of the Fort, are all part of that memory of early reading; when taking a book down from a shelf, I would, before I opened it, sniff the slight petroleum odour of its laminated cover. Then, after we had each chosen a book—almost always an Enid Blyton—it would be time for iced cakes and highly sweetened lime juice at the Pagoda Café, with its busy office crowd and ancient, grandly whiskered waiters in white sarongs and coats that somehow remained spotless. As I munched on my slice of ribbon cake or on a cream bun, I would, from time to time, lick my fingers with the assiduousness of a cat before lifting the flap of the brown paper bag on my lap to take a peek at my purchase. My feet, which did not quite reach the ground, would kick at the chair leg in excitement, as I glimpsed the illustrations in my book. Later that same day, after we'd had our evening bath and been powdered, we would troop into Aunty Bunny's room, each with our new book tucked under our arm. She would be stretched out on her bed and we would clamber on to the bed, jostling each other for the best place which was always just above Aunty Bunny's pillow. From there, the lucky one, smelling the fragrance of rose shampoo in her hair, got the fullest view of the book and its illustrations, as she read to us.

The pleasure of books did not end with reading; it spilt out into the rest of our lives too. In early evenings and on the weekends, we would construct those fictional worlds in our front garden. The tropical landscape would transform into the British moors or a storm-tossed island off the Cornish coast, araliya trees becoming willows or firs. We would crawl into tents made of coverlets and old curtains where we would snuggle under thin cotton bed sheets, pretending to shiver with cold in the thirty-degree heat. Pineapple or wood apple jam would serve as a substitute for gooseberry or raspberry jam, carefully cut circles of bread stand in for crumpets, Marmite a poor substitute for potted ham or chicken. My favourite for a long time was the Naughty Amelia Jane series. I was a timid and slightly anxious boy, and what wicked pleasure I got from this Terror of the Toy Cupboard, relishing her kicking and pinching the other toys, her snipping off the blonde tresses of the beautiful dolls, or the tail of the pink rabbit. And no matter how much the other toys tried to reform her, no matter how contrite she was by the end of the book, one was always guaranteed that, in the next book, Amelia Jane would do something outrageously naughty.

Looking back now, how strange these early reading experiences seem to me, their peculiarity being that they were so untouched by all the changes that had occurred in the country post-Independence. The British, by the early 1970s, had been gone twenty-odd years. In the 133 years they had ruled Sri Lanka, they had entrenched English as the language of government. English schools had produced a new elite, loyal to their colonial masters, an elite who privileged English culture, traditions and values, who believed, without much question, that the values of their masters were far superior to their own indigenous ones. Then, in 1956, only a few years after Independence, a new government swept into power under S.W.R.D. Bandaranaike, its mandate to do away with English as the ruling language. The Sinhala Only Act was passed in Parliament and Sinhala, the language of the majority, replaced English as the official language of the country. The Sinhalese would study Sinhala in school, the Tamils Tamil. Burghers, Muslims and those of mixed parentage could, if they chose to, study in the English medium, which would be gradually phased out as well.

By now Sinhala literature was well into a revival that had begun at the turn of the century. The written language, which had remained classical, began to change to meet the new social and technological realities of the twentieth century, becoming more supple and contemporary. The most prominent writer of this revival was Martin Wickramasinghe, with whose seminal work, *Gamperaliya* (*Uprooted*), the modern Sinhala novel was born. Strongly influenced by the nineteenth-century Russian writers, Wickramasinghe created skilfully crafted works of realism with stories that, in his words, 'examine the internal psychological and external social pressures that condition actions'. The writers who followed Wickramasinghe experimented with things like stream of consciousness, impressionism and free verse.

Like their Sinhala counterparts, Tamil writers too were in the middle of a revival by the 1950s, also grappling with how to make an ancient language fit modern realities, modern genres. While Tamil literature, like Sinhala, had to wriggle its way out from under the rock of colonialism, it had the added task of having to extricate itself from the dominance of south India, which had, long before colonialism, set the rules and boundaries for what Sri Lankan

Tamil writers wrote—works that made only the vaguest reference to the place where they were produced (that is, Jaffna, Sri Lanka), and were mostly imitations of south Indian literary masterpieces. Leading the revival of Tamil literature was the poet Mahakavi and a new set of poets who were his contemporaries. Like their Sinhalese counterparts, they were fluent in both their own and Western culture, being English educated. As such, they were able to take words, metres and themes from classical Tamil literature and meld them with a truly modern style, drawing on Western influences to make their work challenging and psychologically complex. Like their Sinhalese counterparts, Tamil writers drew on Western narrative models, but fused them with local subject matter, landscape, customs and traditions, as well as explored socially relevant concerns of the time such as caste, the abuse women faced in society, and the beginnings of nationalism.

The revival for Sri Lankan literature in English came much later. Until the 1970s, it remained trapped in its colonial past. So much so that, within the English departments of universities, there was sharp criticism of English-language writers, a ringing of the death knell on the literature, many feeling that the sooner its paltry offerings died out altogether the better it would be for the country. The main point of these critics was that writers in English needed to engage in a significant way with their milieu and the social and political issues of the day. It took the failed socialist youth insurrection of 1971, led by the Janatha Vimukthi Peramuna (JVP), to finally begin to change English literature in a substantial way. Many of the insurgents were either university students or graduates. Beneficiaries of the free education system, they had been schooled exclusively in Sinhala and found, upon entry into the job market, that they were unemployable because they did not know English—which they referred to as 'Kaduwa', the sword that divides the haves from the have-nots. English was the symbolic focus of their anger, as were the anglicized elite who, despite the changes in 1956, continued to dominate in the political and economic spheres.

The children of these elite, though they might have to study in their native language, often had access to supplemental private learning in English, and anyway the language of their homes was English, as it was in mine. Those who could afford it, Bandaranaike included, sent their children abroad to study. Faced with the tragedy of the insurrection—not just the numbers killed but also the way it had thrown into relief their privilege—English writers began to engage more meaningfully with the reality in which they found themselves. Soon, journals such as *New Ceylon Writing*, *Navasilu* and the *New Lankan Review* were providing forums, not just for the publication of English work, but for critical pieces that helped raise standards and expectations.

In school, because I was of mixed parentage, my father being Tamil, my mother Sinhalese, I had been allowed to enter the English medium. But mine was the last year of the English medium. Behind me, as I went through school, there were only the two languages and the students who were their products. Like those colonials who had stayed behind, I felt, as I made my way into the upper forms, my world of English books, films, music, etc., become an increasingly rarefied thing. People like me grew more and more isolated from the mainstream of the country, even as we became, paradoxically, more and more privileged, because facility with English was now an exceptional thing.

The primary focus of my reading during my teenage years was, as it is for all teenagers, sex. I read to come to some understanding of the changes in my body, to stimulate that heady rushing up of feelings and impulses. My earliest forays were into the tame Mills and Boon romances that I borrowed almost on a daily basis from my father's secretary. My father had only one rule for us children: between 3 and 5 p.m., we had to be at the club on the tennis court. I was a physically weak boy who hated sports, hated the heat and dust of the playfield, the constant humiliation of loss at the hands of my sister and even younger girls, and my father's 'Keep your eye on the ball, not the girls, Shyam!' I soon devised ways to avoid tennis, hiding in the bathroom until my father had gone to the club, whiting my shoes so they would not dry in time, breaking a racket string. Once my father's car would fade into the distance, my glorious afternoon of reading began. Armed with a tin of condensed milk, I would curl up in bed or crawl into the branches of the araliya tree to lose myself in those tales of seduction and passion, of women in peril saved by husky men. I would read the passages of consummation over and over again, trying to decipher through the flowery, evasive language what exactly was physically happening, not realizing in my innocence that I was identifying with the woman.

As I grew into my teens, I discovered the used bookstalls of Maradana, where I soon graduated from Mills and Boon to the novels of writers like Sidney Sheldon, Jacqueline Susann and Harold Robbins, with their more frank descriptions of sex that further enlightened me. Particularly memorable was Sheldon's *A Stranger in the Mirror*, which I read repeatedly with the assiduousness of someone swotting for an exam, marvelling at the hero Toby Temple's mythical libido, marvelling also at the way he and the heroine Jill Castle slept their way through continents, becoming porn stars, celebrity hosts, seducing to revenge, to punish, to savage. Just like with Amelia Jane, I took vicarious wicked pleasure in their exploits.

And while I was going through this time of growth and exploration, which took place entirely through the pages of Western books, the world around me had begun to darken. While the first decades of Independence had brought a national flowering on many fronts, these decades also saw the beginning of ethnic tension between the Sinhalese and Tamils, leading to the communal riots in 1956 and again in 1958, when many Tamils lost their lives, homes and livelihood. During the 1970s, ethnic tension continued to grow between the Sinhalese and Tamils. There were riots in 1977 and again in 1981 in which more Tamils lost lives and property. From the late '70s, the Liberation Tigers of Tamil Elam (LTTE) became the dominant Tamil political voice, demanding a separate state and resorting to increased violence in order to get this separate country. Finally, the tension boiled over in the July 1983 riots. That morning of 24 July, I got up early like I always did and went for a jog, this new non-competitive sport a sop to my father that finally freed me from the tennis court. I came home an hour later to learn that, just fifteen minutes away from where we lived, Sinhalese mobs had started a campaign of destruction. They were armed with electoral lists that allowed them to isolate Tamil homes, which they burnt, often murdering the families within. My family scattered, taking refuge in the homes of Sinhalese or Burgher friends. Over the next seven days, while Sinhalese thugs attacked Tamil homes and businesses all over the country, burning, looting and killing, I escaped from the terror of my reality into reading. I must have read a lot but the only book I recall now was *The Good Earth* by Pearl S. Buck, and the relief of disappearing into China at the turn of the century and the trials and tribulations of a Chinese farmer. By the time the riots were over, 3000 people were dead and 150,000 were homeless. Many Tamils fled to the North, but others, like us, left for Western countries.

It was in Canada that, finally, my deficit in reading caught up with me. I had taken the culture in which I grew up for granted but now, exiled from it, I wanted to know not only what it was that I had lost but also how things had come to where they had in our country. I found, almost amazed at this discovery, that I knew next to nothing about the world I had left behind, beyond my immediate lived experience. And so, ironically, in the very West that I had escaped to in my books, I found myself now trying desperately to find Sri Lankan books to read, a craving that could not be fed as there were none to be bought, so few to be found even in libraries. Michael Ondaatje's *Running in the Family* was the only Sri Lankan book that I read in those early years in Canada, but one book was simply not enough. Finally, I turned to Indian writers, whose physical and social landscapes were the closest simulacrum to what I had left behind, whose writing allowed me to see what had happened in Sri Lanka, in the context of similar happenings in the subcontinent. Anita Desai's *Clear Light of Day* was a revelation. Set in Old Delhi at the time of Partition and after, its protagonists, the Das family, were achingly familiar, being anglicized while at the same time living in their South Asian world; achingly familiar were the details of their lived lives, the very physical layout of their house, the way they dressed and talked and moved, that old gramophone with its creaking records which the brother played over and over again. Then there was the rising tension between the Muslims and Hindus that spilt over into rioting, the loss of Muslim neighbours, the ghostly, empty houses they left behind when they fled to Pakistan. After reading the novel, I knew that I too could be a writer, that I had something to say. Inspired by Desai, I began to write my first novel, which tried to examine what had happened in my country and how we had come to where we had—writing, as she had, from the point of view of the anglicized elite, staying true to the world I knew, as she had to her world. My protagonist, like me, read Western novels, acted in Western plays, but was firmly rooted within the social, physical and political landscape of Sri Lanka. I wrote to fill in what I couldn't find to read and was soon a published writer.

As the next three decades of war raged on, I, like my fellow Sri Lankan writers in all the languages, recorded with urgency the suffering, death and trauma that were unfolding in our country. Poems, short stories and novels came into being that depicted this new reality of thousands and thousands of people killed, the destruction of entire villages and streets, the abandonment of homes by thousands more. The massive displacement of Tamils to foreign lands gave birth to a new diasporic literature in Tamil, many of the most important Tamil writers, such as Cheran, Jayapalan and Muttulingam, now writing in exile. Hybridity enlivened their work as it did mine. As the years progressed, I returned often to Sri Lanka, even spending a year there in 1997. Now I was reading other

Sri Lankan writers, seeing the different ways they had recreated our world. I read the poetry of Vivimarie Vanderpoorten and Anne Ranasinghe not just for pleasure but also for inspiration. I laughed my way through Carl Muller's *Jam Fruit Tree*. I found myself turning to Sinhalese writers, reading Liyanage Amarakeerthi, Ajit Tilakasena and many others in translation, reading also the Tamil poets like Cheran and Jayapalan, and Tamil novelists and short-story writers in translation. I finally read Martin Wickramasinghe's seminal novel *Uprooted*. Wickramasinghe had, over the years, come to be consecrated by the Sinhala nationalists and I had expected that the work would be didactic and pious. Instead, I was delighted to find how complex it was, how deeply human and flawed the characters—delighted also by the period details of a lost world brought to life.

As the war continued, the social landscape of Sri Lanka changed. The old anglicized elite finally lost their political and economic grip on the country. They were steadily replaced by a new Sinhala-speaking elite both in the commercial and political spheres—until now, in post-war Sri Lanka, they dominate all spheres.

This should be a fulfilling of the promise of 1956, but the world outside Sri Lanka has, meanwhile, has changed. Globalization has come to mean that English is even more dominant than it was before, even more essential for advancement. It is now the language of commerce not just between the West and East but also within the East itself—the language in which the Chinese talk with Indians, Singaporeans with Middle Easterners. Too late there is an understanding in Sri Lanka that we were wrong to get rid of English, that we should have kept it on like the Indians did, their facility with English putting them ahead of us. Yet, by now, a lot of the infrastructure that could help develop a facility in English has been destroyed. On a basic level, there are hardly any qualified teachers to teach it.

The language policies of the 1950s have resulted in three solitudes—Sinhala, Tamil and English—across which there are hardly any connections, not just on a personal level but also less and less on an artistic level. The writers of the 1950s and '60s were schooled in the English medium and so shared this common language among themselves, and also a common body of Western literature from which they drew inspiration or against which they rebelled. Now Sinhala and Tamil writers cannot, for the most part, read each other and are often unaware of each other. Because many of them were educated monolingually, they can't read English well enough to see what is going on among English-speaking Sri Lankan writers. I wonder, too, how much access they have to the literatures of the world, which come to most readers through English translations. Translations of world literature into other languages often work off the English version, and I wonder about the quality of the works that are translated into Sinhala or Tamil.

Now the new elite are sending their children to international English-medium schools that prepare them for the London A-Levels or other foreign exams, which give them entry into foreign universities. The literary curriculums in these schools do not include much, if any, Sri Lankan literature. The students, who might one day run this country, do not study Sri Lankan history or geography. In the last decade, government schools have begun to offer English medium again. The syllabus in literature is not very different from the one I studied, with its primary focus on Western texts, though now a few Sri Lankan works are also included. Will a new fluency in English bring about a new flowering of culture and literature? Produce a new set of artists who, like their forbears in the 1950s and '60s, are fluently bilingual, who will borrow the best of both cultural streams and meld them into something new? Only time will tell.

Carrying this baggage of cultural and linguistic history then, I have put together an anthology in *English*. Some of the work has been written in English, some translated from Sinhala and Tamil. What can the anthology contribute at this moment in Sri Lanka's history? On a basic level, reading this anthology will allow Sri Lankan readers, who might be as ignorant of their literary heritage as I was growing up, access to a body of work that will fill a reading deficit in their lives. This anthology presents an opportunity to know a country and its various cultures in a holistic way by reading a multiplicity of literary voices. In a post-war situation, this anthology provides an opportunity to build bridges across the divided communities by allowing Sri Lankans access to the thoughts, experiences, history and cultural mores of their fellow countrymen, of which they have remained largely ignorant due to linguistic divides. To promote this ethos of unity, I have not, as many previous anthologies of Sri Lankan literature have done, divided the work by the three language streams. Instead, the work is grouped under four themes that are explained at the beginning of each section.

In a book of this size, it was impossible to include all the works I would have wanted to. Sometimes, I couldn't extract a short self-contained excerpt from a novel I liked. Novels, by their nature, move slowly and take many pages to build plot and momentum. A word about the novel excerpts I do include: novels, particularly at their beginning, develop many strands. I felt the reader would find it frustrating and dissatisfying to read the many strands going nowhere in an excerpt. So I have followed the *New Yorker* magazine's model when it publishes novel extracts, which is to make a coherent narrative arc by leaving out some of these strands. Like the *New Yorker*, I have not included ellipses where I have left out material. This way, the excerpt flows smoothly, without interrupting the narrative engagement of the reader.

For those readers interested in getting an even fuller vision of Sri Lankan literature, I have suggested some anthologies in the acknowledgments. There is a paucity of Sinhala and Tamil work in English translation and so I am aware that those I have included represent only a glimpse of a much larger body of work in both languages. When needed, I have provided a short commentary at the beginning of a prose piece or as a footnote at the end of a poem.

In closing, I would like to say that this has been a passionate labour of love and discovery. I hope that you too, as you read the anthology, share in this passion and, like I did, find your vision of what it means to be Sri Lankan expanded.

The Chariot and the Moon

The opening poem by Mahakavi sets the theme for this section, which is about social class and class conflict. Family, which is intrinsically linked to social class, is also one of the themes. As the section proceeds, class disparity and conflict intensify until the last few pieces, beginning with 'April, 1971' by Ashley Halpe, where the conflict boils over into the first and second JVP insurrections. The Janatha Vimukthi Peramuna (People's Liberation Front) was a Marxist–Leninist group that led two armed rebellions in Sri Lanka in an attempt to overthrow the ruling classes, the first in 1971 and again in 1987–89.

The Chariot and the Moon

Mahakavi

'Let's join the crowd
to pull the rope
and move the chariot,'
one said as he approached.

Earth, our mother,
gave birth to him,
to live a hundred years;
he came, eyes sparkling,
with sinewy arms,
to seek the grace of god.

He came,
a youth of lowly caste
a human being
kin to those
who spread their wings
to touch the moon
and return unscathed.

Translated by S. Pathmanathan

He came, bowed low
then touched the rope to haul.
'Stop,' said one,
'hands off,' barked another,
'get him,' cried a third,
'spare him not,' cried the fourth.

A stone hurled
a head split
teeth broken
blood spilt
the earth red
in the commotion
humans were massacred.

Abruptly
the moving chariot
stopped.
The Mother who created all
sat mute
watched in horror
this frenzied passion.

Behold, this kin of men
who spread their wings
to touch the moon,
now writhing in pain
on the reddened earth.

The Mahagedara
(From *Uprooted*)
Martin Wickramasinghe

This self-contained excerpt is from Martin Wickramasinghe's seminal novel Uprooted, *considered the starting point of modern Sinhala literature. Set in 1904 in the southern village of Kogalla, it is a loving depiction of the world Wickramasinghe grew up in, and whose changes he witnessed over time.*

To the villagers the house was the Mahagedara, the mansion, and the surrounding acres of parkland the Mahagedarawatte. The head of the Mahagedara household, Don Adirian Kaisaruwatte Muhandiram, was an elder of the land-owning class of village gentry, with a lineage going back many generations. The other inmates of Mahagedara are the Muhandiram's wife, two grown daughters and a son who was still a boy.

It was a day in April in the year 1904, a few days before the customary Sinhala New Year celebrations, a day for a special celebration at the Mahagedara, a family event, known in the circle of the Muhandiram's family and those of his close relatives, as

---

Translated by Lakshmi de Silva and Ranga Wickramasinghe

'The day for cooking in small pots and pans'. This special festivity, celebrated in no other house in the village, had a curious history.

It was the custom of the village potter to bring a pingo load of clay pots and pans to each of the three or four leading families in the village, a few days before the New Year. The potter was invited to partake of a meal of rice followed by sweetmeats. He was given gifts of uncooked rice, coconuts, chilies, salt, and home-made sweetmeats, which enabled him to enjoy the New Year meal with his own family in style. In his pingo load of pots, the potter included stacks of little toy clay pots for the children in the households he visited. It was six years ago to this day that Nanda, the younger of the Muhandiram' s two daughters, then in her early teens, had washed and cleaned a handful of rice and some vegetables, and cooked a meal in the toy pots. She had served little portions of the meal she had cooked, all by herself, to her family members, as well as her paternal uncle, and his wife and daughters, who were visiting them with gifts for the New Year. Nanda's playful effort to cook had led to this annual gathering held three or four days before the beginning of each Sinhala New Year. The event was organized by the Muhandiram's daughters together with his elder brother's daughters and daughters-in-law. To meet the expenses, fifty cents to a rupee was collected from each member of the two families. Although they continued to call the event 'Cooking in little clay pots', it had now become a family banquet cooked in very large pots, for nearly twenty people. Just as the word 'hunga' which in the past meant a little is now used by the villagers to signify a lot, Nanda's 'cooking in little pots' came to signify cooking in the large pots!

This year, the gathering of young people included, apart from the Muhandiram's own two daughters and son, the daughters, sons, and daughters-in-law of the Muhandiram's brother. The only person who was not a relative was a young man of twenty-five years. He visited the Mahagedara twice a week, to teach the Muhandiram's two daughters to read and write in English. Some villagers called him 'the Schoolmaster'. The Muhandiram's wife and daughters addressed him by his name, Piyal.

The expanse of white cloth that had been spread over reed mats laid on the floor of the Mahagedara hall bore two large flat oval dishes heaped with rice, surrounded by an array of dishes with curries. All the young people seated themselves cross-legged, on mats arranged at the edge of the white cloth, to partake of the food. Following tradition for the occasion, they partook of food served onto squares of banana leaf, instead of the customary porcelain plates. The elders did not join the young people. They knew that their presence would dampen the spirited exchanges and gibes, and flow of jokes and laughter of the young folk. Young village folk feel that it is improper to engage in repartee and tease each other in the presence of their elders.

It was the older of the Muhandiram's two daughters, Anula, who bustled around the guests, serving food, with the assistance of two servants, whilst the younger Nanda sat and ate with the others. Anula circled round the seated guests, a dish and spoon in her hand, bending and at times even kneeling in her eagerness to ply them with fish and vegetables. This gave her a greater pleasure than to sit and eat with the guests.

After the meal, all except the elders, divided themselves into two teams to play panchi. Each of the players of two groups alternately took turns to toss seven lead-filled little cowries held in the hollow of half of a small polished coconut shell, onto the polished convex surface of a larger inverted half of a coconut shell. After each toss of the cowries, those that had come to rest with the flat surface upturned scored a point. The points scored by each side were registered by moving one or more of a set of pawns along a pattern of squares outlined on a wooden board, towards a home base. The first team to take all the pawns to the home base won. Moving the pawns in the most advantageous way, and avoiding elimination by pawns of the opponents, requires foresight, experience and shrewdness. Piyal, who had experience and an intelligence sharpened by education, made the moves for one team. Anula, who made the moves on behalf of the other team, was equally adept and experienced. The other members of each team gave advice by approving or criticizing a particular move. As the game progressed, arguments and taunts exchanged between the opposing teams sometimes became heated. As the New Year approaches, there is hardly a household where the rattle of the cowries and the clatter they make when tossed onto the inverted coconut shell is not heard.

The fading light brought an end to the game of panchi. The Muhandiram's brother and his family departed in the gathering darkness, but the two nieces chose to stay behind to exchange gossip and banter with the others.

'Do you know, Kathirina does not stop playing panchi even three months into the New Year?' observed Anula.

'She started playing a full month before the dawn of the New Year!' responded Soma derisively.

'You may depend on it, she will stop only when she loses all her cash, and has to resort to pawning her gold hair-pin and her ear-studs.'

'Last year she mortgaged the anticipated crop of coconuts from her garden and lost even that money,' Piyal interjected.

'There have been years in which she claims to have won fifty or sixty rupees.'

'For Kathirina, panchi isn't a game, it's a form of gambling,' added Piyal.

'Both of you will play panchi till next New Year if father and mother let you!' Tissa taunted his sisters.

'We aren't addicted to gambling like Kathirina,' retorted Anula.

'We just play to amuse ourselves during the New Year,' added Soma.

'That is what Kathirina also says,' observed Tissa.

'She plays for the money.'

'Don't you take the money when you win?' responded Tissa sarcastically.

'Of course we do. But we don't play just to win money.'

'I can't believe that,' said Piyal.

'It must be because you don't play to win that all of you quarrel so much when you play panchi,' Tissa sneered.

'We are not interested in what Kathirina does. We don't pawn our jewellery and go from place to place to play panchi,' Soma rebuked Tissa.

Piyal rose and quietly made his way to the verandah. A coconut-oil lamp with four burning wicks hung in the hall. The verandah was brightly lit by an imported paraffin oil lamp with a glass chimney, mounted on the wall. The affluent villagers had replaced coconut oil lamps with paraffin oil lamps, particularly in the verandahs, where the wind often put out the naked flames of the wicks of the coconut oil lamp. Nanda wandered into the verandah to enjoy the coolness of the evening breeze. The breeze carried the fragrance from the flowers of the hendirikka and jasmine shrubs planted and tended by her mother. It was like stepping under a fragrant bower. The breadfruit tree, with its crown of leaves gleaming in the moon-light, towered above the distant boundary wall of stacked stone. Two servants sat under the tree, talking. The loud voice that carried to her ears was Sada's. Sada has been part of the Mahagedara household from his childhood. The Muhandiram's children treated him as one of the family. Sada did not hesitate to reprimand not only the Muhandiram's little son, but even the two grown-up daughters, if the need arose. Sada loved to show off his New Year clothes. He sported his new vest and sarong held up by the leather belt round his waist, and the silk scarf draped over his shoulder. Despite his forty-five years, Sada lit the fuse of the bunch of Chinese fire-crackers suspended from a tree out in the garden, and watched them explode, like a gleeful child.

As she stood on the verandah, Nanda could hear Sada talking about the silk sarong and scarf and the mesh cotton vest he had received from the Muhandiram as New Year gifts. Nanda wondered whether the voice of the other servant, a boy who had recently joined the household, was subdued because his New Year clothes were inferior to Sada's. She decided to buoy up his spirits with the gift of a packet of fire-crackers. It was the Muhandiram's wife and her grown-up daughters who saw to it that not only the family and their guests but also the servants had a thoroughly enjoyable time on the first day of the New Year.

'Nanda, here's the money you lost.' Piyal broke into Nanda's reverie. He held out a rupee coin on his open palm to Nanda.

'I don't want it!' Nanda slapped the palm with the coin. The silver coin dropped from Piyal's hand, emitting a musical tinkle as it hit the floor. Piyal bent down, picked up the coin from the floor and held it in his clenched fist.

'You lost, didn't you, Nanda?'

'Do we play only to win?'

'Of course we do. If you'd joined our team you would have won a rupee.'

'I joined the team of my choice. Why should I follow someone else's choice?'

Piyal saw that not so much as the hint of a smile had touched the corners of Nanda's lips. He changed his mind about offering the coin to Nanda a second time.

'If both sisters had not been in the same team, one would have been on the winning side.'

'I'll win back the rupee I lost another day.'

'And if you lose again?'

'I won't play any more.'

'This is your rupee, Nanda, take it.' He held the coin in his fingers, and proffered it to Nanda again.

'I don't want it.' She struck the hand, this time in anger. Piyal put the rupee in his coat pocket. He decided to change the subject of their conversation.

'Why hasn't your father come home yet?'

'Father went to give New Year gifts to my grandmother in Matara.'

'Isn't it time he was back?'

'Perhaps he was persuaded to stay and have dinner with my grandmother.'

'What did your father give you for the New Year?'

'I got two pieces of chintz and two jacket-lengths,' said Nanda, with a smile.

'Why won't you accept a New Year gift from me?'

'Why should I accept a gift from you?' Nanda's voice conveyed the disdain of a lady of high birth for a presumptuous stranger.

'But you accept the books I bring.'

'Only to read and return.'

'Have you read the book I gave you?'

'Which one?'

'*Robinson Crusoe*.'

'I found it difficult to read and understand that book. My knowledge of English is still inadequate.'

'What about the other book, *Grimm's Fairy Tales*?'

'I enjoyed reading that.' Nanda looked towards the gate in the stone boundary.

'If you take the trouble to read books, it's very easy to learn English,' said Piyal, trying to break through the wall of her indifference.

'Mother says it's quite sufficient if I learn enough English to sign my name and read a telegram.'

Piyal laughed.

'Yes, you can read a telegram with a limited knowledge of English. But it is not just to read telegrams, but to be able to read books that you should learn English.'

Nanda laughed in reply.

'We haven't the leisure to read books.'

'So you think your mother's advice is right?'

'What else!' retorted Nanda, responding to Piyal's taunt with her own.

'But hadn't you learnt to sign your name in English even before you started to learn English from me?'

She sensed that Piyal was leading up to something.

'Yes, all the young people in the village learnt to sign in English.'

'Is that because you think it is demeaning to sign in Sinhala?'

'That may be why you sign in English, Piyal,' Nanda ridiculed him.

Piyal realized that this crosstalk was getting him nowhere. All this while, he had been trying to prepare the ground to ask her a very personal question, but Nanda had parried all his attempts by leading him into fruitless debate. Piyal never thought to attribute this to family pride on her part. In the eyes of Nanda's family, who were descended from a class of land-owning village gentry of many generations, Piyal and his family were of lowly social status, although they were of the same caste. The Muhandiram and his wife had known Piyal's paternal grandfather, who was a vendor from whom they bought vegetables. They had seen him use a pingo, two baskets slung from the ends of a pole borne on his left shoulder, to carry his wares. Nanda was also aware of this, though only by hearsay. When in the company of others, Nanda was indulgent towards Piyal. This encouraged Piyal to hope that she was becoming fond of him. But when she was alone with Piyal, she acted as if she was conscious of Piyal's lowly origins in relation to the Kaisaruwatte lineage. Whenever Piyal attempted to probe her feelings for him, like a turtle that shrinks into its shell at the first sign of danger, Nanda would withdraw into the shell of her family pride, fearful of the consequences of acknowledging any feelings of affection for Piyal.

'Nanda, wouldn't you like to learn enough English to read good books?'

'No,' Nanda snapped rudely. 'A little English is more than enough for our purpose.'

Having failed to get her into a receptive frame of mind, Piyal finally got round to the question he had been hesitating to ask.

'Nanda, why didn't you at least send a reply to my last letter?'

Nanda's face changed as she heard his question. She had been facing him all this time. In the dim lamplight, Piyal could see that she averted her face from him.

'Your last letter? Was it the letter hidden inside the book?' she asked bluntly.

'Yes.'

'Have you forgotten that I told you I would not reply to any letters?'

'I said I would not write to you any more once you answered the question I asked. Did you read that letter?'

'Yes.' Nanda's voice was expressionless.

'If you can't answer me now, will you write and tell me?'

'No!' Her monosyllabic reply came out like the sharp, short explosive sound made by a hard berry shot from a child's toy bamboo pop-gun. After a moment, she added softly, 'Ask my mother.'

'Certainly, I'll ask your mother. But I must know first whether you agree, Nanda?'

'If mother agrees, I will also agree.'

Piyal's face lit up as he heard her words.

'What if she doesn't agree? Perhaps she won't like it.'

'If mother does not agree, why should I agree?' she murmured, with averted face.

'Why can't you, if you love me?'

Nanda did not attempt to hide her anger over Piyal's words.

'I love my mother,' she retorted.

Nanda's words left Piyal confused and uncertain. Afraid of provoking Nanda, he remained silent for a while.

'Then if your mother likes it, you are ready to accept what I propose in my letter, aren't you?'

'Haven't I already said so?'

'So if your mother is agreeable, you will marry me because you love me?'

'I don't know,' snapped Nanda angrily.

'Go, go inside, Punchi Nona, it's getting late, go into the house.' Sada admonished Nanda as he walked past them, heading towards the kitchen. Until he spoke, neither Nanda nor Piyal had realized that Sada had come within a few paces of the verandah.

Nanda smiled.

'Sada is very fond of my sister and me. Two days ago, we were watching a man who had drunk too much toddy on the village council road. Sada, who was quite a distance away came running back, sternly telling us to go inside immediately in a loud voice. Anu laughed and ignored Sada just to tease him.'

'Perhaps Sada is advising you to go in now because he thinks that I am also drunk.'

'No, it must be because you're a young man!' Nanda ran back to the hall, laughing. Piyal followed her into the hall, but he did not join the others in their conversation.

'It is getting dark. I must take your leave.'

'Piyal, what do you plan to do for the New Year?' queried Anula.

'Anything that comes to mind then.'

'Let's play cards.'

The ten-year-old Tissa's precocious knowledge of card games surprised and amused the adults.

'Where did you learn to play cards, Tissa?' inquired Anula.

'In Galle, at the boarding house.'

'Aha! So you have been studying to gamble! Don't you ever say that you play cards at your school boarding when mother is around.'

'I did not play cards. I just watched the others playing,' protested Tissa indignantly.

'So you learned to gamble by watching others play,' Soma interjected.

'What is wrong with that? Isn't panchi playing a kind of gambling?' Tissa's defense amused his sisters.

'Quite right,' agreed Piyal, making his exit.

'How can it be right? Panchi is just a game,' persisted Soma.

'Then so is playing cards.'

'Anyway, it is not a suitable game for small children.'

'You have to learn it young if you want to play well when you are a grown-up.'

'Don't try to be precocious, Tissa,' admonished Anula.

Three days later it was the Sinhala New Year. After an early breakfast, Sada dressed himself in his new silk sarong and vest, and tightened the leather belt around his waist. He stepped into the garden and lit a bundle of crackers. The exploding crackers heralded the New Year not only to the Mahagedara but also to the entire village. The sound of the crackers awakened Tissa. He jumped out of bed and grabbed two packets of crackers. Nanda had trailed behind Sada, and lit two bundles of crackers simultaneously.

'Look at this wench, behaving like a child,' exclaimed Anula.

Tissa listened joyously to the sound of the crackers lit by the others. He clutched his own crackers more tightly, fearful that they would drop out of his hand and explode before he could light them.

The auspicious time to start eating the first meal of rice in the New Year was just after two in the afternoon. The Muhandiram, his wife and children sat on reed mats, round a white cloth spread on the floor of the hall. The servants, male and female, knelt on the floor beside them. Each had his serving of milk rice on a square of singed plantain leaf, placed before him on the white cloth. When the auspicious moment arrived they all started to eat. After the auspicious meal, the servants left the hall. For this occasion, other than the Muhandiram and Matara Haminé, everyone, including the servants, was decked in the new clothes they had received. All joined in spending the rest of the day in festive enjoyment.

A crowd of women flocked to receive the 'first cent' for the year from Matara Haminé's hand. It was the giver of the first cent, not the value of the coin, that mattered, and giving a copper cent had become traditional. Excluding children, Matara Haminé was known to give a silver coin to everyone who came to her. Although many came in the firm belief that it was auspicious to receive a coin from Matara Haminé, there is no denying that some were more interested in the money itself.

'I was waiting to meet you.' Matara Haminé gave Kathirina a twenty-five-cent coin wrapped in a betel leaf.

Kathirina was a village woman, seven years younger than Matara Haminé. Matara Haminé believed her to be trustworthy and upright. Despite the poverty and hardships that she had to cope with, Kathirina was always dressed in a spotlessly clean cloth and jacket whenever she stepped out of her house. Her hard life was largely due to her husband who was addicted to liquor, although otherwise a villager of good repute. In Matara Haminé, Kathirina sought not only the patronage of a high-born lady, but also a mother's concern, and the understanding of a friend. Despite the life of hardship that was the lot of village women such as her, the forty-year-old Kathirina still retained traces of the good looks that had been hers when she was a young woman.

'Ané Haminé, I have not been able to come this way because my daughter had not recovered fully from her recent illness.'

'Is she well now?'

'Yes, Haminé. It was because of your help that we managed to keep her alive, and the merit for that will bless you. I will never in this or in future lives forget the help you gave me.'

It was not with the intent to flatter that Kathirina spoke in this way. She knew that Matara Haminé was not a vain lady susceptible to flattery. Rather, Kathirina spoke effusively to Matara Haminé to lighten the burden of the gratitude she felt, and to foster feelings of affection.

'Why didn't you bring your daughter here for the New Year?'

'Ané Haminé, Laisa is not quite fit yet. The Veda Mahattaya told us to be very careful, that she could have a relapse that would be dangerous for her health. Laisa was looking forward very much to paying her respects to you and the young ladies.'

Kathirina had come regularly on New Year's day, for more than fifteen years, to receive a silver coin from Matara Haminé. This year she had an added purpose.

'Haminé, I have to speak to you of another important matter today.'

'An important matter?' Matara Haminé echoed Kathirina's words, and called out to her daughter, Nanda.

'Nanda, put away these remaining coins in the wardrobe.'

'So you've finished giving away money!'

Matara Haminé laughed and turned to speak to Kathirina.

Nanda took the coins and the bunch of keys that her mother gave her and hurried into the bedroom.

'The Punchi Nona is resentful. She says I give money to each and every woman who comes here.'

'All the villagers will bless you with merit for your kindness. They say that even a cent from you will bring them prosperity.'

'They can't mean that.'

'There may be a few who do not mean it, but the majority of the women-folk are sincere,' said Kathirina. Kathirina hastened to raise the 'important matter' before Matara Haminé could say anything further.

'The important matter I broached is on behalf of the Schoolmaster.'

'The Schoolmaster? What Schoolmaster?'

'Piyal Mahattaya.'

'What is this about?' inquired Matara Haminé, her curiosity roused.

'About the Punchi Nona.'

'What Punchi Nona?'

'Haminé's Punchi Nona.'

'Do you mean Nandawathie Nona?'

'Yes.'

The nature of the important matter that Kathirina was trying to broach dawned at last on Matara Haminé. Matara Haminé had been slow in getting the drift of Kathirina's inquiries, because even the possibility that Kathirina would broach such a proposal was unthinkable to her.

'Who will give anyone in marriage to the likes of such fellows?'

Matara Haminé's vehement rejection was prompted by the affront to her pride in the Kaisaruwatte family lineage. Despite being bound to her proud family lineage, Matara Haminé never made use of it to humiliate or hurt the feelings of others of a lower status. Had the proposal been made by Piyal or his mother she would have avoided hurting their feelings by resorting to a plausible lie for not agreeing to the proposal. It was not to flaunt feelings of superiority that the elders of the Kaisaruwatte family clung to the traditions of their patrician lineage, but for self-preservation of themselves and their way of life, now declining in the face of social change. It was their inability to adapt to change due to the rigidity of their adherence to tradition that was also the cause of their decline. Extinction is the inevitable lot eventually of all living things where their inheritance has ceased to be of adaptive value in self-preservation.

To Kathirina, Matara Haminé's reaction was not totally unexpected, knowing as she did the family pride of the Mahagedara folk. She had even anticipated that a proposal regarding Piyal would anger Matara Haminé, so she had no difficulty in coming up with an appropriate response.

'Yes, they have no standing at all. Let alone proposing to marry into Haminé's family, they ought not to have even thought of it. It is because the Schoolmaster is such a good man and so learned that I just thought of telling you about it. It is because he asked me that I brought up this matter. Else, would the thought of such a proposal even enter my mind? Knowing their family background, would I have even thought of initiating such a proposal?'

'So Piyal did ask you to speak to me about the Punchi Nona?'

'Yes, Haminé. I said I couldn't do it, but he kept worrying me and . . .'

With her habit of introspection, Matara Haminé intuitively achieved levels of percipience usually associated with the most acute intelligence. She impatiently probed Kathirina's reluctance to complete whatever she had wanted to say.

'You said "because the Schoolmaster told me and . . ." Why are you reluctant to complete what you were saying, Kathirina?'

Kathirina squirmed and kept her eyes lowered. It was evident that she was reluctant to come out with whatever she had intended to say.

'Speak up, Kathirina, tell me everything.'

'Because the Punchi Nona had said she was agreeable . . .' Kathirina brought out the words reluctantly.

'The Punchi Nona said that she was agreeable! How dare you!' Matara Haminé berated Kathirina. She made no attempt to hide her dismay and anger.

'Don't be angry with me, Haminé. I just repeated what I was told, to make you aware of what the Schoolmaster said. After all, it is our duty to keep you informed of such things.'

The anger, and her curiosity to get to the bottom of all this, increased. She suppressed an overwhelming impulse to go immediately and confront Nanda, and berate her if there should be any truth in Kathirina's story.

'Don't repeat my disparaging reference to Piyal and his family to anyone. Both young ladies have taken lessons in English from him.'

Matara Haminé felt it would be unwise to hurt Piyal's feelings. As far as Matara Haminé was concerned, Piyal's status as English teacher to her two daughters had not been different from that of a paid employee. Although that was all there was to it, a humiliated Piyal could spread all manner of falsehoods to hurt Nanda. Such stories might be believed by many people, because Piyal had in fact been a regular visitor to the Mahagedara, albeit to teach English.

'Would I ever even dream of betraying your confidence, Haminé? I know how to convey your rejection of the proposal to the Schoolmaster so that he won't take it amiss. But, Haminé, there is no denying that the Schoolmaster is a good, well-bred young person.'

Kathirina continued to present her case, despite the lack of any encouragement from Matara Haminé.

'His father intended to make him a lawyer.'

'How do you know that?'

'His father had said so when he was alive.'

'He said it to you?'

'No, not to me, but the Schoolmaster once told me he could have studied and become a lawyer if his father had lived. The father had earned a lot and left it to the son when he died. The father had even taken a mortgage on the Government Official Nandias' house and land for three thousand rupees. With the accrued interest the debt has increased to nearly ten thousand.'

'Doesn't your mouth ache, Kathirina?' A smile curled the corners of Matara Haminé's lips.

'I am only mentioning the facts, not that I consider the Schoolmaster to be someone suited to your family.' Kathirina rose from the low stool on which she had been sitting. 'I know that if anyone else had spoken of this matter to you, that person would have been scolded and driven out. That is the only reason that made the Schoolmaster choose me.' Kathirina turned to depart.

'Don't repeat my disparaging remarks to Piyal. Why should we invite anyone's enmity?'

'Of course, Haminé. I know how to put it across. I will say it in a way that will further increase the esteem in which your family is held.'

'I expect you want to leave now, but do come again.' Matara Haminé rose from the chair.

Although Matara Haminé had waited impatiently to question Nanda the moment Kathirina departed, she suppressed the impulse, as she did not want to spoil Nanda's enjoyment of the New Year festivities. So it was not until three days later that Matara Haminé got down to questioning her daughter about Piyal.

'Has Piyal spoken to you about anything?' she asked Nanda.

They were in the bedroom occupied by Nanda and Anula. A satinwood wardrobe with carved patterns inlaid with ebony and ivory stood against the wall. Each of the double doors had four square panels. Each panel bore a flower of inlaid ebony. The ebony inlay work had been so delicately chiselled that the flowers seemed to be part of the satinwood itself. The four rounded ebony legs of the wardrobe had the smoothness of spherical brass pots. The upper and lower sections of the wardrobe were framed in ebony. No joints or discontinuities were visible, save for that revealed by the edge of the brass hinges which held the doors from within. The joinery was so skillfully concealed behind carved strips of ebony wood that it was as if a craftsman had hollowed out and constructed the entire wardrobe from a single enormous satinwood tree, and then polished it and embellished it with ebony carvings.

Nanda leaned against this satinwood wardrobe. Matara Haminé sat on the edge of the bed that stood against the wall at the far end of the room. The clean white pillow on the bed stood out against the drabness of the neatly woven mat of dried thunhiri sedge. The diligence and tidiness of the two sisters who occupied this room would have been apparent to even an outsider who entered the room.

Nanda promptly divined the reason for her mother's question. Although she had told Piyal that she would agree if her mother consented, she had never thought he would pursue the matter. Not in her wildest dreams would she have thought that Piyal would ask Kathirina to be an intermediary. Her response to Piyal's question had been mischievous banter.

'Yes, mother,' Nanda replied without hesitation.

'Did you say you would be willing, if I was?'

'Yes.'

'How could you discuss such matters with Piyal? How can you even think that we would consider a marriage proposal from such people?'

'I spoke without thinking, mother. I didn't think so far ahead. The words just came out. What I wanted to say was that I would never marry anyone without your approval.'

'Then Piyal must have spoken to you about this previously?'

'Piyal gave me some letters.'

To Matara Haminé, Nanda's words were like a thunderclap. Her eyes widened, elevating the eyebrows and bringing deep furrows to her smooth brow.

'No one in generations of our families has ever done anything so shameful. Let alone a nonentity like Piyal, a young girl of your breeding should not even think of exchanging letters with a young man even of our own social position, or even of a family related to ours.' Matara Haminé's voice carried the intensity of her anger and sorrow.

'I didn't exchange any letters, mother. Why do you have such doubts about me?' Nanda's eyes dilated in fear.

'You just admitted that Piyal gave you letters.'

'I said that he gave me letters, but when did I say I replied to them? He gave me two letters or so. I just threw them away . . . into the wardrobe. I have never replied to Piyal's letters.'

Nanda had lied when she said that she 'just threw the letters away' to mollify her mother. Her qualification that she threw them into the wardrobe was prompted by feelings of guilt.

Her heart had welled with strange feelings of delight when she read Piyal's letters praising her beauty and her ways. It was to savour these feelings, not romantic love for Piyal, that had prompted Nanda to hide the letters in a corner of the wardrobe instead of throwing them away.

Piyal, with his moustache trimmed to a barely visible thin black line above a small mouth bounded by thin upper and lower lips, and a blunt large wedge-shaped nose like a cashew fruit, could not be described as a handsome young man. It was his smile that made him attractive. The majority of men in the village combed back their hair and twisted it into a tight knot at the back of the head.

Piyal was one of the few young men in the village who followed the urban fashion of cutting and parting the hair.

Piyal had received his education in a school in the city of Galle, where the language of teaching and learning was English. He had become accustomed to the habit of wearing trousers in the city. In the village, he always dressed in sarong and banian, like the other young men. It was his custom to wear a coat over an open shirt when visiting another village. On visits to Galle town, or on special occasions such as a wedding, he would dress in shirt with neck-tie, and coat and trousers. Amongst the village women, he was known as 'the gentleman in cut and tailored clothes.'

Matara Haminé reflected that a girl looking for romance might be inclined to favour Piyal with more than a casual glance. Her doubts remained that despite her protestations, Nanda was not being entirely truthful in her denial that she had written to Piyal. She was aware of the longings, the feelings and the ways of girls in general, but she was not one who had developed her critical faculties to look for differences in motivation that might make them different from each other. Her habitual introspection prompted her to reflect on her own thoughts, feelings, and attitudes as a young girl, in judging the behavior of her two daughters. These were the reasons behind Matara Haminé's reluctance to believe Nanda's denial.

Matara Haminé had no doubts that if as a young girl she had received a letter from a young man, she would have been highly agitated, and she felt that this should have been Nanda's response to the letter from Piyal. A young girl thrown into such an emotional state by a letter from a young man would either love the youth in secret, or tear the letter and throw it away, to distance herself from him. Matara Haminé could conceive of no other response on the part of a young girl who secretly received a declaration of love from a young man. The changes that had transformed the village and the country she had known as a young girl did not enter into her reckoning. Matara Haminé had neither the knowledge nor the experience to conclude that, as the country and the village changed, the inhabitants too must change.

Piyal was an attractive young man in many ways, but contrary to Matara Haminé's suspicions, he had not stirred any special feelings for him in Nanda. Possibly Nanda's family pride, her awareness of the facts relating to Piyal's grandfather, and the familiarity resulting from seeing him so often had not encouraged a romantic attachment.

'Are you being truthful when you say that you did not send any letters to Piyal?'

'I did not send him letters, mother,' Nanda's tone was resentful.

'Why did you accept letters from Piyal?'

'I didn't think of long-term consequences of the kind you are thinking of, mother. It never even occurred to me that I was committing myself to anything. I took the letters, read them and threw them . . .'

'Threw them?'

'Yes, I threw them into the wardrobe! You keep interrupting me, mother. You don't even let me complete what I was going to say,' Nanda pouted sulkily.

'Piyal may have told Kathirina that he gave you letters.'

Scorn and anger swept like a dark shadow over Nanda's face and glowed in her eyes.

'I will ask Piyal.' Nanda's voice held a threat against the absent Piyal.

Matara Haminé, whose only wish was to bury the whole affair as if it were a dead rat, was alarmed by Nanda's tone. She tried to soothe her daughter's anger.

'Perhaps Kathirina does not know about the letters. I wondered whether she knew only because Piyal had told Kathirina that you were agreeable if I gave my consent. Anyway, it would be unwise to scold Piyal. Resentment may prompt him to get his own back by spreading false stories around the countryside.'

Nanda's simmering anger waned.

'I don't think he would have told Kathirina about the letters, mother. I know how to find out the truth of the matter from him. I got three letters from him. I will burn them now.'

Nanda opened the doors of the satinwood wardrobe inlaid with ebony. The fragrance that came from within was not from any perfumed notepaper used by Piyal. The young men of the village had not yet succumbed to the vanity of writing love letters on perfumed notepaper. The fragrance that spread through the room was from savanna, the dried roots of vetive grass that are kept in wardrobes not just for their fragrance, but also to preserve the clothes. Nanda thrust her hand into a corner of the middle shelf. She rummaged under the clothes and took out the three letters she had concealed. Matara Haminé watched in silence as her daughter burned the letters.

About two months after the New Year celebrations, Piyal left the village. During the two months, Piyal had visited the Mahagedara only on two or three occasions. Piyal's tutoring of the two daughters of the Muhandiram was discontinued. The rejection of Piyal's proposal was conveyed by Kathirina in a tactful manner, to avoid giving offence or hurt his feelings. She presented Matara Haminé's attitude in a manner to discourage Piyal from giving up all his hopes regarding Nanda, and from harbouring feelings of resentment towards Matara Haminé. Kathirina was not unaware of the possibility of some benefits to herself if Piyal continued to have such hopes.

Not even Piyal's mother knew for certain why Piyal decided suddenly to leave the village. He had left home, saying he was going to Colombo and would be back soon. Within two weeks he wrote to his mother telling her that since he had obtained a job, he would have to stay on in Colombo, and would be back on a visit in three or four months' time. When a villager inquired after Piyal, the mother would reply that he had got a job in Colombo.

Two weeks after Piyal left the village, Nanda was afflicted with a strange illness. It started with abdominal pains. After she got over this, there was constant welling up of phlegm in her mouth, accompanied at times by laboured breathing. The easing of these symptoms was followed by loud intermittent bouts of yawning.

It was not uncommon for villagers to supplement treatment by a practitioner of Ayurveda, the ancient system of traditional medicine, with the services of a village shaman, the yakadura, literally 'one who gets rid of bad spirits.' The inhabitants of the Mahagedara followed these traditional practices, and both an Ayurvedic physician and the yakadura were called in to treat Nanda.

Kathirina, who had seen Nanda the day she fell ill, had concluded that it was a mental state brought about by pining. When talking to Matara Haminé a few days later she thoughtlessly said as much. Matara Haminé was furious.

'Don't you ever dare speak such rubbish again!' she threatened Kathirina. 'Don't utter a word of such stupid nonsense to anyone! Do you hear me, Kathirina? If the Muhandiram comes to hear of this, he will be so furious that he will chase you out of the village. You know the Muhandiram's ways, don't you?'

'Ané, Haminé, I would never speak of it to others. The thought just slipped out because I was in your presence. I won't so much as think of it even in my dreams after this,' promised Kathirina.

Even after three months of continuous treatment, Nanda did not completely recover from her illness. Matara Haminé gave Kathirina travelling expenses and fees to travel to Heenatigala to consult a well-known soothsayer. Another woman was dispatched by Matara Haminé to a 'light-gazer' who read the future through the flame of a lamp placed before a circular patch of lamp-black. The Mahagedara folk used intermediaries like Kathirina and other village women bonded by loyalty to discreetly consult soothsayers and light-readers on confidential matters.

It was not knowledge of the missions undertaken by these women alone that led to the widespread belief among the villagers that Nanda's illness was due to possession by bad spirits. The visits to the soothsayer and light-reader only reinforced their belief. The large majority were convinced that the illness was due to bad spirits. That this sickness was due to a love-potion administered by the Schoolmaster to win the young lady's affections was a whispered secret earlier confined to two or three village women. It had now become an open secret in the village. Matara Haminé, who had at first scolded the women who voiced it, no longer argued with them. She herself was guided in such matters by her husband's beliefs.

Muhandiram Kaisaruwatte was not a disbeliever in 'Yantra-mantra-gurukam', the collective village idiom for amulets, incantations, spells and the like. Whether he spent time trying to decide whether they were true or not remains an open question. He was known for reticence, and for being very sparing of words. It was not uncommon to hear villagers comment that he had never been heard to laugh aloud. However, not only his wife, but the villagers as well, agreed that when he smiled, it gave a singular charm to his face.

When one of his children fell ill, the Muhandiram summoned the Ayurvedic physician, not because of an exclusive faith in Ayurvedic medicine, but because it was the accepted practice. When someone suggested that the patient would benefit from an exorcism he would summon exorcists. He rarely visited the temple for worship and treated religion, Ayurveda and exorcism with equal disinterest. This was not due to skepticism. He was disinterested because he had never acquired the curiosity to explore these areas of experience. His thoughts were of his wife, his children, and providing for their education, their food, clothing and daily needs, and providing for their future. His mind was almost exclusively preoccupied with these responsibilities, although he was by no means a selfish man.

Matara Haminé's favourite was Tissa. The Muhandiram loved all three alike, but his heart was most drawn to Nanda. It was after the light-reading that the Muhandiram came to accept the prevalent view that Piyal had given a love-potion to Nanda. Both he and Matara Haminé now took this to be a proven fact. Yet they never discussed the matter with anyone other than the Muhandiram's brother and his wife.

From the moment the Muhandiram came to believe that his daughter had been affected by a love-potion, he sought the services of more than one exorcist. At the same time, he got down a doctor from Galle to give Nanda the benefit of western medicine. The doctor was summoned at least once a week in the first month of her illness. The doctor diagnosed Nanda's illness as a form of hysteria and said she would get over it even without his treatment, with the lapse of time. Each time the doctor was brought down from Galle, it cost twenty-five or thirty rupees. He continued to treat her, as did the exorcists, and in time Nanda showed a remarkable improvement in her condition.

'She does not need any further treatment. With time, she will become completely normal,' said the doctor. He slipped his fee of fifteen rupees into a coat pocket.

To cure Nanda completely of her disease, however, the exorcists advised the performance of a series of rituals. For four months, hardly a week went by without an elaborate exorcist's ritual of masked dancing and chanting, the thovil ceremony, at the Mahagedara. Innovated rituals, with names the villagers had never heard before, were performed by the exorcists. Despite her distaste for it, Nanda, covered from head to foot in a white cloth, sat opposite the pideni, the stand carrying offerings to demon spirits, exposed to the stares of the exorcists. Although she had initially suppressed her resentment, she let it register openly in her expression after a while.

The respect and affection the villagers had for the Mahagedara family were evident during the ceremonies that were performed over these four months. The Mahagedara never lacked men and women to fetch or prepare all the items needed for the ritual. Where one would have sufficed to roll rags into the small torches used by the dancing exorcists, seven or eight would busy themselves with that task. Four or five men would set out to fetch banana-trunks and tender yellow palm-fronds for making the various adornments used in the ceremony. Another seven or eight would go in search of the special varieties of wild flowers and foliage required for the occasion. For some rituals, the exorcists would use only white flowers; for others they would insist on wild flowers of five different colours. To supply these flowers, the villagers had to roam the patches of jungle surrounding the village and even further afield.

The villagers who came to give their assistance during those rituals would not accept payment. The custom was to give them meals on such occasions. Not all partook of the food. Those who went home for meals did so unobtrusively and without the knowledge of the people of the Mahagedara. Nevertheless, on some days, the contents of half a sack of rice and sufficient vegetables, fresh fish and dry fish to go with it were cooked in the Mahagedara. The expenses borne by the Muhandiram during these four months were far more than that spent on the physician from Galle for all his visits. However, at the end of the four months Nanda was completely free of whatever affliction had taken hold of her. Though she regained her health, a residue of unusual behavior persisted. On any night when she heard the drumming that signaled an exorcising ceremony in a nearby village home, Nanda would get into bed quickly and keep yawning from time to time, until she fell asleep. In the morning, she would go about her affairs as usual. The villagers and exorcists alike saw in Nanda's behavior absolute proof of their belief that she had been possessed. Some took it as irrefutable evidence that Piyal had given her a love-potion. There was no one in the village to challenge this with a theory that the rituals constantly performed over a period of four months had conditioned Nanda, and implanted her unusual response to the sound of drumming at night in her subconscious mind.

By the time Nanda had fully recovered, the Muhandiram was faced with financial difficulties.

'Whatever the expenses, it's a great comfort that Nanda is well now,' he commented to his wife one evening.

'Yes, indeed. For the past seven months I was so anxious, I felt as if my mind was on fire.'

'Haminé, I have always told you not to take it so much to heart when a child falls ill. You don't listen to me. Now see how thin and frail you've grown during these seven or eight months.'

'What does it matter if I'm thinner? We saved Nanda, that is enough for me. Perhaps because the gods have looked after her, she has not grown haggard and lost her looks.' Matara Haminé's voice was reverently thankful.

'Haminé, I could not tell you earlier. I had to sell the plot of land in Imbulgahawatte too.'

Matara Haminé said nothing, but she sighed. She knew that the Muhandiram had been compelled to mortgage several small blocks of land which had belonged to her, to spend for Nanda's illness. Their possessions were now limited to the Mahagedara and the garden surrounding it.

'We must arrange a marriage for Nanda without delay,' proposed Matara Haminé. She had a lingering fear that Nanda's illness had resulted from forlorn love for Piyal.

'Jamis asked whether to bring a proposal from a clerk working in the Provincial Administrative Office in Matara. I told him to do so.'

'We must look for an upright young man from a family of good standing, whom we can accept into our family,' commented Matara Haminé.

The horoscope of the clerk from the Matara Kachcheri was brought by Jamis and sent together with Nanda's horoscope to two astrologers. Both said that the horoscopes were incompatible. 'Ralahamy, do not go ahead with this proposal' was the oracular advice of one of the astrologers whose opinion was sought by Kaisaruwatte.

Subsequently, horoscopes of three prospective suitors, the son of a registrar of marriages in Galle, the idle son of an old and respected family, and a successful and wealthy young land-owner, were sent to astrologers for evaluation of their compatibility with Nanda's horoscope. The astrologers concluded that only one of the three horoscopes was compatible with Nanda's. Kaisaruwatte liked the son of the registrar of marriages, but the astrologer swore that Nanda would spend her days as a widow if she married him. The horoscope that matched Nanda's was that of the successful young land-owner. Inquiries revealed that they were from a lowly social stratum. His paternal grandfather had made a living by selling betel leaves in the market-place. His father, who had been the owner of a small bakery, had made his money by supplying bread, meat, fish and other victuals to the labourers living on the plantations. The Muhandiram rejected this proposal.

Even more than Matara Haminé, it was the Muhandiram who was unhappy over their failure to arrange a marriage for Nanda. Aware that he was progressively becoming poorer, he had misgivings regarding the future. He resolved that he must free himself of the problem of Nanda's marriage early. If word were to get around of their straitened circumstances, it would become even more difficult to find a suitable young man for Nanda.

'I have not been able to send Tissa's boarding fees for six months,' said the Muhandiram whose mind was burdened by the thought of debt, and of the bleak future the family faced. 'I managed to send the school fees with difficulty. The clerk sent me a letter reminding me about the boarding fees. I will have to collect ninety rupees somehow in the next few days.'

'Poor little fellow! Will he have to leave the boarding house?' Matara Haminé asked anxiously.

'No, the clerk will not do that to me. But I must somehow send the money within the next day or two. The clerk knows I had to spend a lot on Nanda's illness. All the same, I feel it is very humiliating that we haven't been able to send the money. It is possible that the clerk will be reluctant to have Tissa return after the school holidays if we do not send the money, but I can't think of how I can find the money just now.' The Muhandiram glanced at his wife as if in expectation of a suggestion.

'We could pawn Anula's jewellery. What else can we do?'

'But that will anger Anula.'

'No, it won't. She is even more keen than any of us to give Tissa a good education.'

A sudden thunderstorm broke, accompanied by strong gusts of wind. Matara Haminé rose from the low chair in which she had been seated in the verandah, and hurried into the house. Drops of water splashed onto the floor in a corner of the hall. Matara Haminé looked up at the roof and saw the water dripping through a cracked tile. She fetched an empty brass spittoon from inside the house and positioned it on the wet floor, to catch the water dripping from the roof.

It was not only in the hall that water dripped onto the floor of the house through broken tiles, which had not been replaced for some time. The leaks in the roof had contributed to the hastening of the inevitable decay of the Mahagedara. It was believed that the massive walls of the Mahagedara were built during the time the Dutch ruled in the region. Due to their antiquity, such houses acquired a dilapidated appearance, if repairs were not undertaken every two years, unlike the newer village houses. For such a repair of the Mahagedara, at least two thousand or three thousand rupees would be needed. The last occasion on which such a repair had been carried out was fifteen years ago. The Mahagedara family could no longer afford to undertake such rehabilitation. So they had resorted to patching up the cracked plaster of the walls, and covering the blemishes by lime-washing, to keep up appearances.

Two years passed after Nanda's recovery from her illness, but the Muhandiram had still not found an acceptable suitor for Nanda. During the two years, Jamis had brought the horoscopes of more than seven eligible young men resident in the coastal towns of Galle, Matara and Weligama to the Muhandiram. Several of the horoscopes had been rejected because they were found to be incompatible with that of Nanda by the astrologers consulted by the Muhandiram. The others were of suitors of a social status or of a family lineage unacceptable to the Muhandiram and Matara Haminé. The one compatible horoscope of an acceptable young man was returned because his parents had insisted on a dowry of three thousand rupees.

Piyal visited Koggala only once in the six months following his sudden departure from the village. Angered and embarrassed by the village gossip that linked him to a love-potion given to Nanda, he laughed derisively and berated villagers who came to him with such tales. His far-seeing mother tried to dissuade him from arguing with the villagers to try to prove them to be wrong. She opined that Piyal should keep away from the village for the next year or two. Her worry was that frequent visits to Koggala by Piyal might provoke the Muhandiram to vent his anger on her son. Piyal's mother was aware that Muhandiram Kaisaruwatte could be vengeful. The villagers were aware of this flaw in Muhandiram Kaisaruwatte's character. They had much affection for Matara Haminé, but feared the Muhandiram.

To take revenge on an enemy, the Muhandiram would plan and lay his trap with cold calculation. Even the lapse of seven or eight years did not make him forget an affront to himself or his family, and the vengeful intent this provoked. When an opportunity for revenge presented itself, the Muhandiram would use it. He plotted to lead his victim into a trap that would enable him to frame charges in the courts of law. The collusion of the village police officer ensured his success.

Even after the lapse of a year and five months, Piyal had visited the village only thrice. On his first visit, he stayed only one night, but on the third occasion his mother allowed him to stay three days, encouraged by the fact that Nanda had fully recovered from her illness, and the gossip about the love-potion had lost currency in the village.

Whenever it came up, Piyal called the story of the love-potion an idiotic concoction. He would argue with the villagers that it was foolish to believe in these mantras and spells. He dismissed exorcists and shamans as a foolish lot who did not even have a good knowledge of the Sinhala language. Some of the villagers who listened to his arguments, and his condemnation of exorcists, began to believe that the Schoolmaster had indeed given Nanda a love-potion. The more he argued, the stronger grew their conviction.

Piyal had found a job as a clerk in the saloon bar of a large hotel in Colombo. He had succeeded in obtaining this employment with the recommendation of a teacher under whom he had studied in the English-medium school in Galle. Whilst holding this job, Piyal began to supply eggs, vegetables and fruit to the hotel on a regular contractual arrangement, with the approval of the management of the hotel. These contracts soon helped Piyal to earn profits amounting to three or four times his salary. Before long he organized his own network of suppliers of fruit and vegetables directly from Beliatta and Thihava, far south of Matara, and of eggs from places near Colombo, such as Negombo and Lunawa. Thereby he was able to increase his profits considerably.

Piyal was on friendly terms with a few Englishmen who patronized the bar of the hotel where he was employed. Piyal's fluency in English and pleasant manners soon won the confidence of some of these Englishmen. Piyal invited two of them to Weligama and took them fishing in Weligama Bay with the help of some fishermen he had befriended. Thereafter he was looked upon as a good friend by these Englishmen. With their assistance Piyal obtained contracts to supply victuals to army barracks and to another large hotel. After he negotiated these contracts, Piyal gave up his employment as a clerk.

Before two years had passed, Piyal had become a well-established supplier of provisions. He had accumulated capital amounting to thousands of rupees in cash. He had acquired a large old house in the Pettah, the old commercial sector of Colombo, to serve as both his office and store for supplies of provisions. Piyal, who had been employed as a clerk, was now the employer of three clerks and several labourers. By the skillful use of his capital, Piyal had grown to become a shrewd entrepeneur. When prices were low, he would buy and store rice and flour to the value of several thousand rupees, and often make very large profits from such forward purchasing.

Meanwhile, Piyal's home in Koggala was refurbished with chairs and couches, and tables of unusual design, not seen at the Mahagedara. New crockery services, vases and other such items were kept in a maha pettiya, the elegant strong-box of polished jak-wood, to be used and displayed when visitors came to the house. The house itself, though relatively modest in size, was frequently brightened with lime wash and paint. It stood out amongst the two or three other renovated houses seen in the village. A white-washed parapet boundary wall had been built four months ago. The two pillars on either side of the entrance bore the iron hinges for the two halves of a trellis-work gate. A polished brass nameplate, inscribed with the words 'Siri Nivasa' borne on one half, glittered in the morning sunlight like gold.

There were many village folk, men and women, who came to Piyal's house whenever he came to Koggala. The poorer amongst them never left without receiving a silver fifty-cent piece or twenty-five-cent piece. Some were served foreign delicacies that Piyal had brought from Colombo. On every occasion that Piyal came home, his mother would dispatch a tray of these delicacies and a length of tweed cloth to the Opisara Mahattaya. The Opisara was not unaware that Piyal's mother sent these gifts because she was afraid the Muhandiram might try to use him to wreak vengeance on Piyal. Not only did she send gifts to the Opisara Mahattaya, but she showed even greater deference than before to Matara Haminé. Piyal's mother was unaware that her son had now risen to a position in which he could enlist the support of officials at a much higher level to ward off any plots that the Muhandiram might hatch.

Our Valavu

(From *The Yaal Players: Memories of Old Jaffna*)

Vimala Ganeshananthan

The author of this piece found a few exercise books of her mother's writings, from which she shaped this exquisitely detailed memoir of life in Jaffna at the beginning of the twentieth century. This portrait of a tranquil, stable society gives us a chance to experience the Tamil north before it began its gradual descent into the nightmare of civil war.

I see in my memories the large house in *valavu*, the compound. The largest house in Karainagar was the one built by my paternal great-grandfather Pillai, a shortened form of a long name I presume? He was considered one of the richest villagers in the village. My great-grandfather being the only son inherited the entire twenty acres of land.

Grandfather was the eldest of four boys and a younger sister. The sister after her marriage moved to her in-laws' home and took with her the customary cash and jewels, the cash to help build a home in her in-laws' land. Grandfather's house was twenty yards away from our house, which too was built by him. Our house was of modest proportions though of the same design.

In my younger days in the village, I would spend more time in his house, enjoying his company. Grandmother, Manonmani, and a widowed niece Kamalam were the others there.

My grandmother had a tanned complexion and was slim and tall. She was an introvert, in absolute contrast to my grandfather who was very talkative and demonstrative in his affection.

Grandmother and her niece Kamalam ran the household efficiently and quietly. I would give my mother a dozen excuses to visit grandfather a dozen times a day. I would use the rear entrance as other family members often did when visiting grandfather or other uncles and aunts in the same compound. I would climb and tread the long but shallow four steps to reach the rear door which was kept open the greater part of the day. The door of heavy satinwood was very high, two paneled, and opened it seemed to space, air and breeze. The front door seen straight across from the rear one was invariably closed by a stout crossbar. Thieves were few, but the dust was plentiful, and would sweep through the tall doors, to be layered on the concrete floors. At first glance, the whole of the interior would look like an elevated rectangle of smooth cemented floor only. As I walked further in I would see a central rectangular-shaped drop, the courtyard from this floor to the sandy ground. The cemented part was twelve feet by four feet wide on the sides and a little less in breadth at the front and at the rear. The doors were at the front and rear. It was great fun to sit at the edge of the floor and dangle my legs over the courtyard. The courtyard was covered with fine sea sand that covered the brown earth beneath it. We as children went down into the courtyard, felt the sand with our feet and poured it through our fingers. It looked like white sugar. White sugar was first seen by us when it was brought by my maternal grandmother on her return from Malaya. She had five sons working there! Usually we used brown sugar or local jaggery to sweeten our hot drinks.

The courtyard was open to the sky, and the breeze poured in and swirled in the open spaces around it. The roof was high and a ceiling was unheard of. Compared to this spacious central section, the rooms, small and insignificant, opened onto the side floors that surrounded the central courtyard. These sides of the floor appeared like patios to the rooms. The door leading to each was narrow, not too high and two panelled. It opened into a small room with windows also of two panels. The room had a bed, a wooden box to keep fresh clothes in and a long wooden strip of wood with hooks, secured to a wall, to hang the used clothes. It seemed ascetic. There were six such rooms, four on the sides and two that opened onto the rear end of the courtyard.

Invariably, in each room a collection of palmyra leaf woven mats, each rolled on itself, stood in a corner. Sometimes a table was found in the room, but most often not. The house was termed *'Naatchara'* House, which meant it had four portions. Families were large and rooms were never in excess. Invariably two to three of same-sex siblings occupied one room. Curtains for doors and windows were never hung as they interfered with the flow of air and breeze, which was welcomed in the hot weather that became only hotter. Looking back, what struck me most was the paucity of furniture in that large cemented place. There were only the essentials—a square table and four chairs made of satinwood, heavy and squat, a few straight-backed rattan-covered chairs and of course the easy chair on which grandfather would loll when he was not in the garden. The rattan of that chair was replaced more often than that of the others.

One room at the back was always kept closed. Much later I was told the secret of that room. Any post-pubertal female who was considered unclean by the occurrence of her menstrual period was isolated in that room. Aunt Kamalam who had similarly used a room like this said she was not only considered unclean but temporarily low caste too, which meant that the kitchen and well were taboo to her. There was only a table with a plain wooden chair, a bed, a clay jug of water, an aluminum tumbler with a beaked rim and a few personal clothes. All these articles had to be washed at the end of the unclean period which was about four days. She would then be taken to the well and water poured on her by another relative. Till then, food and water were brought to that room and handed to her at the door. When she finally left it for her bath, the room was washed. The linen and clothes were washed by the washerman of the 'Kudimai', the lower householder caste. Incense was lavishly strewn on burning coals, held in long-handled brass bowls so as to drive out all uncleanliness and probably the mosquitoes too with it. This practice took many decades to be discarded. Even my cousins followed it.

The courtyard of grandfather's house opened to the sky. The smooth cemented portions were interrupted by pillars reaching to the beams of the roof. The pillars were of teak, square in shape and had designs cut into them. The pillars at our home were of concrete, and the very tall pillars found in the old houses of Karainagar were made of palmyra wood, smoothed and painted.

The house itself was built of coral stones plastered with mud and mortar and appeared like concrete. The courtyard was screened off on top by wire netting to keep out the ubiquitous crows. This courtyard was the heart of the home. The female relatives of every home in that compound would find excuses and dropped in to see grandmother, especially at midmorning, to have a chat. They brought their vegetables to be cooked by them for that day and the rice to be gleaned. They sat on the cemented platform and I would be mesmerized at the speed at which leaves were detached from the stems while they chatted. The leaves were cut finely by an outwardly curved knife fixed to a two-foot horizontal low bench designed to be sat on. The aunts, female cousins or even the niece of grandmother would sit demurely sideways with their legs stretched out and covered modestly by their saris. A similar device was used to scrape the coconut, but by a finely serrated steel knife attached to a similar bench. Scrapers and cutters fixed to a table were a thing of the distant future!

What a lot they gossiped while they cut and chopped the vegetables. Their gossip was sharp and unkind if it was about the number of proposals brought to a not so pretty girl, or of the puberty ceremonies of another female carried out on an inauspicious day. An hour or two was dawdled away chopping, scraping and gossiping. Then suddenly, they rushed back to their small, smoky kitchens built at the rear of their homes. Their deep wells were close to their kitchens.

In contrast to her house, grandmother's kitchen was small, dark and smoky. Cooking in the kitchen was considered a very temporary sojourn and the females just put up with it. A cemented raised platform with stones placed in triangles was the fireplace. There was space above it but there was no chimney. When they cooked, smoke swirled around the kitchen and was only taken away by the breeze brought through a small window and the door. The smoke billowed in the kitchen if two or three fireplaces were used at the same time. Firewood was used economically with coconut shells initiating the fire. Every kitchen had on its work table the scrapers and cutters made of steel. With constant bending, stretching and lifting things off the floor with bent knees, the women had straight, attractive backs. It was rare to see a fat aunt in the family. Only the old inactive ones became fat.

In the midst of the kitchen gloom there would be a glimmer and shine coming from brass utensils. They would be on a table stacked one inside the other, a set of them coming in different sizes. The chopped vegetables were usually strewn on palmyra-leaf woven and decorated winnowing fans or on brass platters. They were then taken out and washed in large brass bowls. It was taboo to wash fish and meat in these bowls. The gleaned rice would first be winnowed in a brass winnowing fan to blow off the finer grit, and washed in a brass shallow bowl with ridges to trap the smaller stones and dirt. My grandmother or Aunt Kamalam would swirl it around to trap the stones, and do it three times to perfection before she cooked it in a clay pot used only for rice. Another clay pot with water was always on a fireplace and was a ready source of drinking water. Whether boiled or not, the water was brackish. Soap took an age to lather and more water was needed to wash it off. Meat was cooked outside the kitchen and the utensils used for the cooking were stacked on a wooden rack outside the kitchen too.

All households had stacks of these brass utensils. They needed much effort to keep them glowing. Every so often, tamarind, salt and powdered brick would be briskly rubbed on them, left aside for an hour and then washed thoroughly. Once food was cooked the kitchen was left spotlessly clean. At the mealtime rice and curries were placed in appropriate-sized brass bowls, stacked and carried through the rear door of the house having crossed the rear verandah. If footwear was worn, which was rare, it was always left on the verandah. Grandfather's brass plate and tumbler were on the table all ready and bright for the meal. Many would eat their meals from banana leaves. Each leaf was cut to rectangular plate-size pieces, washed thoroughly and waved over the embers of a fire to make them lie flat on the table. Work was lessened using the leaves. Once a meal was over the leaves would be fed to the cattle in the stall. Aunt Kamalam was the hands and feet of my grandparents. She was a young widow. The small community was not harsh on her and she was not expected to shave her head, nor be covered in a white sari from head to foot. She, however, never wore bright or even dark, sober colours, but her saris were of pastel shades, or white with blue or green borders. These dull colours were considered inauspicious for celebratory ceremonies. She would go with the others to the temple, but no flowers adorned her hair and no red *'pottu'* on her forehead or on the hairline.

At any celebratory event like puberty and weddings she would be missing. I would look for her and find her far from the noise and bustle, getting the needed things ready for others to use. She had lost the position of standing behind the bride or circumbulating the brass tray which held the three lit wicks, the '*alathi*', a ceremonial ritual performed in front of the bridegroom or couple. I would see her, when everything was over, help to clear the things used and she did it so pleasantly and quietly.

Grandfather, in his ramblings of days gone by, would beam with pride as he recalled the educational advantages he gave his sons. My father was the eldest of his five sons. Grandfather had his education in the vernacular only in the village school founded by the American Mission. My father, Vedanayagam, who had his elementary education in the English school of the American Mission of the village, was bright enough and, more so, rich enough to be sent to the English school at Vaddukoddai. This was the premier school and the pride of the American Mission. This was first referred to as Batticota Seminary and boarding school—Batticota, an anglicized version of Vaddukoddai. This had been founded in 1823. The Methodist and Anglican missions had a head start in founding schools and building churches but they didn't spread their wings to the northwest of the peninsula or the islands in the northern waters. Their schools were in Jaffna town, its suburbs and villages.

Though American trade predated the work of the missions in Ceylon, Jaffna was not a recipient of this trade. The missionaries, Rev. Samuel Newell and his wife, were sent by the American Mission Board in New England. New England had a community of ardent protestants, probably the descendents of the Mayflower entourage. When Rev. Newell arrived in Colombo, Britain, its ruler, was not pleased as it was at war with the United States in upper Canada.

The Newells were sent away, but Rev. Newell returned alone in 1813, having lost his wife and daughter. Then he was asked by the governor to start the American Mission, as there was a paucity of protestant missionaries. In 1816, Rev. Newell travelled to Jaffna and set up the American Mission and its first church, which replaced the Dutch one, in Tellippalai, a conservative village.

Five other missionaries followed Rev. Newell, but they were not a welcome lot in Colombo. Governor Brownrigg diplomatically sent them all to the arid north. Their coming was like a monsoon downpour in the warmest and wrong month of the year! Jaffna blessed the British for sending the Americans north, and was in turn blessed by the coming of the Americans.

The Americans were not in search of spices like their foreign predecessors. Their search was for souls. They set out to win them by the Bible and bilingual education. They came to Jaffna when night meant lanterns and a journey meant bullock carts.

My father, who physically looked like my grandfather, was so unlike him in his speech and moods. He was taciturn and spoke when he was in a garrulous mood. When in such a mood he gave great details of his schooling. 'Thankfully the Batticota Seminary was right beside the road that went towards Jaffna. Karainagar was a boat journey away. Twenty minutes of rowing by the boatman, and one stepped onto this road, and within a few minutes' walk there stood the school of new buildings and paths. Vaddukoddai was a maze of lanes and neat small houses within fences or walls. Some houses abutted on the school buildings. The lanes meandered round the school. Small shops selling every type of merchandise jostled with the houses for space. Sometimes stepping out from a door of the school, it was only a step further to the door of a home, so close were they,' he recalled.

'There was much rapport and bonhomie between village and school from its very inception. Nothing happened in school which was not known by the villagers, and no village activities of any kind that were not known to the school.

'One of those five missionaries, Rev. Warren, was very keen on educating the students in both Tamil and English. He started bilingual schools in the west of Jaffna and in the islands. Their goal was "social reform, elimination of poverty and better lives for all." The village saw the American Mission give their utmost and best to the schools. Rev. Poor, the best known of those first five missionaries, founded the Batticota Seminary in 1823.'

My grandfather would then interrupt my father's flow of reminiscences with, 'Thank God for the paddy fields and the money left to me. I was able to pay the school fees of all my sons. Actually, Batticota Seminary started as a non-fee-levying school but couldn't afford to do so after a while.' The greater number of parents were not able to pay the fees. There were many bright students too in the feeder schools of the mission in the villages.

The American Mission made a great gesture by allowing parents who couldn't afford the school fees to mortgage their lands to the mission. The student's tuition was then free. The lands were to be redeemed by paying the school fees owed, when the young men got employment. Time was not stipulated, but the villagers' conscience made them pay promptly. They could not have hoped for more as so many of their sons had the great opportunity of education while their parents were allowed to live on the mortgaged land and till it.

The school in Vaddukoddai was in the midst of lush green paddy fields, tall sturdy palmyra, coconut palms and satinwood trees. The mahogany and flamboyant trees stood sentinel to small ponds. Colour was spread by the numerous and perennial hibiscus blooms. The Christian culture of the village had been brushed with the overlapping paints of Portuguese, Dutch and British rule. The ancient Portuguese Roman Catholic church became a Calvinist one of the Dutch, by the removal of statues, elaborate altar and structural religious decorations. This became the American Mission church and its ceiling was embellished with pinewood from New England. What the mission could not do for years as social reform was to make a dent in the caste system.

The school was a boarding school, with a few day scholars. The boarding had only Vellala caste students. The day students were a mixture of the Vellala and lower castes. The latter, willingly or not, took their place to study seated on the ground and this they did in the church too. Father spent eight years in Batticota Seminary. He would rattle off the medley of subjects that were taught there. Applied science, math, English, Tamil, Sanskrit, astronomy, music, art, theology, philosophy, a smattering of medical science and electricity—the latter was discovered only ten years earlier. The missionaries were keen that the students must know Tamil language and literature thoroughly. The final qualifying exam, when the student was seventeen, was the F.A., the First in Arts, which qualified a student to enter a university in India. The much recommended one was Madras University. There was great pride and rejoicing when the first student of Batticota Seminary to graduate was Charles Winslow Thamotherampillai.

By 1848 the American Mission had 105 Tamil schools and 16 English schools. Most of them were patronized by a majority of Hindus.

While the seminary marched on, the females were not forgotten. In 1816, only three females could read and write. Harriet Winslow made her appearance and without wasting time founded the girls' school at Uduvil, which was the first girls' school in Asia, and in 1824 she founded the Udupitty Girls' boarding school which again was the first girls' boarding school in Asia. Harriet Winslow did not have it easy. She met much opposition from the men. Females were considered the property of their husbands and their primary role was to be housewives and bear children. To entice the girls and their parents, they were offered gifts and a promise to give money for their dowries. In addition, they were given clothes for school wear.

The school started in a small way, but there was no turning back. The village of Uduvil ultimately had three schools: the mission station school, village school, and Uduvil boarding school.

Sir Emmerson Tennant, the Secretary in the British government, visited the schools in Jaffna and the Batticota Seminary. He was astonished at the knowledge exhibited by the students and ranked Batticota with any European university.

For all this march towards education, the winning of souls lagged behind. Of the ninety-six boarders only eleven were Christian. The American Board in New England thought that too much prominence was given to science and English, and little time to biblical instruction. The seminary seemed to be a stepping stone for employment. The seminary then wanted to admit only Christians and it was closed for a short time. The alumni and the village were shocked and upset at the turn of events and rallied round the school with financial help and other support. It was opened again in 1867. The seminary was renamed Jaffna College.

Conversions, however, still went on and the converts in Vaddukoddai took the names of missionaries or of their teachers, whom they admired, at their baptisms. There sprang up the Williams, Hensmans, Danforths, Mills, Taylors, Cloughs, Hooles, etc., among the Tamils. There was an instance where baptism was compulsory to sit the F.A., a foolish move that was revised later. There was no hesitation or compunction in a few Hindus to convert. After the exam or later, they cunningly or wisely reverted to their Hindu names. Having had a Christian surname denoting families of the same status, caste and village, they were reluctant to let go of it. Their American or biblical names were hyphenated to their Hindu or Tamil names. There popped up bizarre combinations like Jeremiah Balasingham or Clough Subramaniam or even Spencer Rajendram, all devout Hindus.

I was happy that father retained his original Hindu name after conversion. Grandfather would have died of anger and shame as he was a prominent member in the committee of the village temple and took his religion seriously. Ironically, typical Hindu and pure Tamil names have been retained in the Christian families such as the Casinaders, Subramaniams, Velummyilum, Sethukavalars or the different *Thambies* and *Aiyas* that ended their names. They added biblical or English names as their first names.

Even after leaving school, my father and my uncles kept in touch with the college and the changes there were conveyed to us.

When I lived in Karainagar, and not having reached the age of puberty, I was permitted to move around from *valavu* to *valavu*—compounds separated by fences. After puberty a girl had to be accompanied by a suitable family member. The adjacent compound and the *valavus* even further from ours were owned by relatives. A 'strip'—a portion of land called *thundu* in Tamil—was occupied by members of a particular caste, either of high- or lower-caste villagers. In fact, there was a strip occupied by members of our own extended family right next to the strip of land of another caste. These partitions were seen in almost every village. Everyone was safe to walk around in our village as everyone had some knowledge of his or her neighbour.

I would announce that I was going next door to uncle Kumar's. Uncle Kumar and his family lived next to us and within the common strip of land. My grandmother, who was so specific about relationships, would tell me that uncle Kumar was my *amman*, literally, the mother's brother. Amman, or maternal uncle, had a great and important part to play in the rituals at puberty and wedding ceremonies. My grandfather called after me and said, 'He'll be repeating all the wonders of the palmyra tree. He will ask you to name all its uses and products. So be prepared for a long visit.'

I saw my uncle's long fence that abutted ours, and I saw it winding along even before I spotted his house. The fence had been renewed and looked the loveliest fence of the neighbourhood. There was great activity when refencing the whole property. It was a palmyra frond fence, as he had so many groves of them in his compound. I watched with wonder as my uncle's labourers made this beautiful and artistic fence. The fronds and thick stems of the palms were held direct and up, lined with hardly a space between them. They were interwoven and tied with a rope made of horizontal strips of the stems of the fronds without a peekspace between the fronds. The fence looked like a row of slim dancers who held large green fans tinged with yellow.

The fence looked so pretty and new. These 'palmyra dancers' were seen going on for quite a distance and together made a sturdy barrier. Uncle Kumar had only to spend on his workmen. His compound with his palmyra groves surrounded his large solid house. The fence he had removed had lasted for two years. I saw that white ants had marched through the dried and now discarded old fence. The droopy disheveled old fronds had been stripped small and there was so much of these strippings on the ground. Some would have gone to feed the cattle and the others dumped in many of the compost pits scattered in his garden.

Uncle Kumar saw me in the lane, hailed me and suddenly disappeared from view. He had actually gone through his gate. I followed, but felt lost in the lane as I could not locate the gate to his compound. I trudged further forward a few more yards, but I still could not find the gate. I went back and forth and closely looked at the fence for a gate that he must have used. Finally I found it and felt a fool for not recognizing it. It was like all gates in our village, flush with the fence. It too had been made of palmyra fronds within a wooden frame and blended with the fence.

I entered the gate and found a huge mound of freshly cut palmyra fronds. He had harvested an excess of what he needed, almost the leaves of fifty palms, each palm having yielded fifty fronds. He was selling those he didn't need. My mind boggled at the sight of so many palmyra trees in his compound. Harvest of the palmyra fronds was done once in two years.

While he was bargaining and selling the excess fronds, others loaded them into long double bullock carts, like the ones my grandfather had. As I expected, he asked me to enumerate the uses of this palm and its products. He forgot that the palmyra was a sentimental plebian, a favourite of the north. Everyone knew everything about it. The coconut was a high-class 'horse' compared to the palmyra 'bull.' I had been told that the palmyra had a hundred and one uses, but it was too much to remember, since I was still young, but I remembered the edible things that came from it. The jams, cordials, yams and jaggery. He was disappointed that I had missed naming so many other products. He reminded me of the colourful baskets, boxes, winnowing fans, hats, fans and so on.

Uncle was well known for his degree of thrift even in that thrifty community. He would allow only two percent of his palms to be tapped for toddy. His relatives were always left disappointed during the toddy season! He would calculate the money he could make if the untapped blooms were left to become fruits and the fruits' pulp turned to jam and cordials. Most of the yams that came from germinating dried fruits were sold while the rest of the yams were boiled to eat or dried and turned into flour, an essential ingredient of a broth called *kool*. He was wealthy as he sold so much of the produce of the palmyra trees.

I tentatively asked him for some immature fruits. Very surprisingly he got a bunch of them brought down from the tree. My cousins and I relished scooping out the three 'eyes' in which there was a sweet jelly-like substance called *nongu*. I still remember its taste. In the corners of the compound were mounds of earth, long and rectangular in shape, that reminded me of the fresh burial mounds of the church yard. Dried palmyra fruits had been buried in these mounds to germinate and give out a bunch of underground yams that would be dug out later.

Grandfather's compound too had such mounds, but they were fewer. I trailed back home and all I could talk for days was about that beautiful fence. Everybody agreed that when new, the palmyra fence outdid a live fence in its loveliness.

The cockbird was a late riser in our village! The alarm was in the udder of the cow looked after by aunt Kamalam. At four thirty in the morning there would be a gentle moan from her cow that was affectionately named Ponni, though it was a white Sindh cow and not a golden one! If the moaning was ignored, louder and louder became the moans that followed. If still not heeded the cow bellowed, requesting immediate help to relieve the engorgement of milk in her udders. The calf, which was tied a little distance from his mother, clamoured to reach her. It had to wait its turn.

Kamalam jumped out of bed and wrapped a sari haphazardly over her long skirt and blouse. She as usual slept in the latter garments as nightdresses were unheard of. She tied her long black hair into a knot at her neck while she ran towards the cowshed. She hurriedly cleaned the already cleaned pails again, washed the udders and began her first chore of the morning. She deftly and quickly milked the udders of the cow alternately and very soon a pail or more was filled with milk. The calf, still young, nudged her shoulders while she milked, to get to its mother. The udders were never emptied as the calf had to be given its share of milk. With great joy the calf rushed to the mother after Kamalam had milked the mother. Every young and willing female of that large household were at the same task in the large cowshed with four or five cows in it. Each cow would be tenderly spoken to by its name. The calves were kept until they were weaned and then sold or kept if the mother was getting old. Kamalam took the pails brimming and frothing with milk to the rear verandah of grandfather's house.

Then she began her next chore. The villagers who had no cows bought the milk. Kamalam sold the excess milk. The villagers had brought clean utensils and bottles and had left them on the *thinnai*, the front porch, the previous evening. Kamalam cleaned them again and left them on the back verandah. She was so particular to clean the villagers' utensils as any souring of the milk would be promptly blamed on the drawn milk. After she took sufficient milk for the use of her household and ours, she poured the milk into a brass vessel with a beaked spout and filled the bottle upto a pint or more as requested. The purchasers ambled in and took their share of milk. Cash was paid promptly at the end of each month. She collected about ten rupees, a large sum it was at that time. Prompt payment was the rule as the northerners realized and appreciated the hard work that went into the production of grains, greens or milk.

My mother was given her share of milk and she boiled part of it in a large saucepan. While it was boiling she added the ground coffee and the brown sugar. Water was unheard of in the making of coffee. The milk was stirred and the thick cream that came to the surface was also stirred into the coffee. Each of us was given an enamel cup of steaming coffee. We enjoyed every sip. What a glorious taste it had. I can still taste it! Kamalam did the same and my grandfather relished his coffee. It tasted different! Coffee seeds had been ground with coriander seeds and then brewed. We did not care for that taste at all.

It was five in the morning and still dark. Soon the night was nudged away by the sun. I never saw a colour-tinged dawn. The sun rose suddenly, fast and hot. I saw the sun creep over the live fence. It sat awhile on the margosa trees at the edge of the *valavu*. Then it stealthily but quickly made bright the mango tree. The almost black palmyra of the dusk became brown, tall and distinct at the further end of the garden. In the blink of an eye the whole garden was bright and hot. The sunlight poured into every space and very soon the heat rose from the ground.

The men who walked the 'well sweep' descended from its height. They had been walking the well sweep since four in the morning to escape the hot, steamy sweaty mornings.

Kunchu, the old female domestic help, came with her *ekel* broom to sweep the ground before the heat made her physical work uncomfortable. Her *ekel* broom was a bunch of dry *ekels*, the midribs of the coconut frond, tied firmly at one end and splayed at the other. She swept the garden, bent over the broom as it had no long handle. *Ekel* brooms with long handles took time to arrive at our village. Kunchu swept the ground spotlessly clean, bereft of every dry leaf. She made piles of the dried leaves and refuse, gathered them painstakingly and deposited them into the nearest compost pit. Deep pits were dug in many parts of the garden. She collected the dung too from the cowshed and put it in these pits, and covered them with a layer of soil that was kept on the side of the pit when it was dug. Her daily work saw the pits filling with compost. Vegetation was so precious, even the dead ones. When swept, the compound was so white, clean and sandy that we sat on it.

Kamalam was still busy. She took a part of the milk to make buttermilk for a midday drink for grandfather, and I went there on time for it too! To make the buttermilk she poured some milk into a deep container. Into it she immersed a wooden churning rod which had a serrated oblong base. She held the rod between her two palms and rolled it to and fro, with speed and agility, churning the milk. I watched mesmerized and with admiration when she made the buttermilk. The cream rose to the top. She scooped out this yellowish tinged cream, which was left aside for days to become *ghee*—clarified butter. This was a great favourite in which vegetables were fried and lentils tempered. Ghee was also poured onto cooked lentils before eating. The lighter skimmed portion, *moor* or buttermilk, was poured into a brass container, and when sliced onions, cut green chillies and salt were added to it, it became a savoury tasty drink. Any visitor who came by was given this drink. Grandfather would drink a tumbler full of the drink with his lunch as well.

A little curd, saved from the previous day, was added to some of the milk kept aside. This milk became curd overnight and was eaten the next day. Curd was eaten by us with the rice, and as dessert with sugar or jaggery. Most northerners, being wholly vegetarian or vegetarian many days of the week, depended on curd, buttermilk and milk for a complete and nutritious meal. The cow was treated with much respect and affection. They were celebrated and made much of on the day after the *Pongal*. Many a time I saw the cow belonging to aunt Kamalam led away from the stall by an unfamiliar young man. I was told that the cow was taken to be sired by a stud bull of repute that was in an adjacent village. New blood was always sought for to improve the cattle stock. The owner of the bull was paid handsomely. My other aunt Nirmalam reared goats and their kids. Goats' milk was much in demand by the villagers who had allergic problems especially asthma, which my grandmother had too. Drinking goats' milk reduced greatly the recurrence of these allergies. So aunt Nirmalam had good sales for the goats' milk.

Most of the outdoor work would end by ten in the morning. The washerman living at the end of the compound would have washed our clothes and hung them on clothes lines. The women would have gone to their smoky kitchens to cook the lunch and everything seemed quiet except the cawing of the ubiquitous crows and the barking of the mongrel dogs, the pets of the household. They barked for no apparent reason.

My grandfather would occasionally be summoned by an urgent ringing of the bell of a cycle. The Hindu priest had arrived. He had put one of his legs down, but had not got off his cycle. He, as usual, was in his white *verti* with the shawl thrown over his bare chest. A cotton thread traversed his chest from the left shoulder, a symbol of the priestly caste. His forehead and upper arms had traces of holy ash and sandalwood. By caste he was probably next to God! This was one of the very few instances when grandfather would get up promptly from his chair and walk to the gate to meet the priest. The Brahmin hardly came in or sat down and never took any refreshment.

The visit was to discuss matters that pertained to the village temple, as grandfather was one of the patrons of it. The exchange of words between them was always courteous. The laity managed the temple and the priest looked after all the religious ceremonies. The relationship was beneficial to both. There were a few small temples in the village. The Kannagi or Pattini temple, one of six in the north, was in our village.

The most prestigious temple was the Sivan temple, further towards the coast. It was also known as Rudra temple, but what made it more beautiful were the surroundings. There was the casuarina beach on one side, scrubland on the other. In between there were large green trees, vegetable plots, palmyras and a solitary coconut tree all surrounding this temple. The temple was embellished with two *gopurams*, the intrictely carved tall towers, at the entrance. Siva was depicted as a *Lingam*, the phallus installed within the inner sanctum. Festival time was in December coinciding with the festival of the South Indian Chidambaram temple festival. In fact, it was called the Southern Chidambaram. The whole scenery then was a mass of people.

The temple, built in the sixteenth century, was razed to the ground by the Dutch in 1648 when they sailed the coast to capture Fort Cays of the Portuguese. It was rebuilt in 1848. To me it was a great adventure to accompany grandfather to the evening *pooja* on Friday. When conversion to Christianity took place in our family, I was given strict instructions to stay outside the temple, and not eat any food offered at the *pooja*. I would obey the first rule and stand at the entrance and stare at the ceremonies. Before entering the temple grandfather broke a coconut at the entrance of it. He said that it was a symbolic gesture of breaking one's body and spirit which meant in fact one's ego, before God. To me it seemed that the ceremonies and rituals with many libations took hours. The second rule was harder to keep and I did not refuse to eat the hot gram lentils, the sweet milk rice nor the banana while we walked back home. It was tastier because it was forbidden and was eaten away from the temple.

Friday service was long as the *pooja* was special. Ceremonies started with the blowing of conch shells and the beating of drums. It was explained that a lot of the ceremony involved the rituals offered to a king, and God was a king. The icon was bathed ceremoniously with milk, curd, sandalwood, coconut water and then water. Holy ash was then poured over it and it was wrapped in colourful cloth, gold being the prominent colour. The icon was garlanded, and incense in a brass censer was held aloft and circumambulated. The flag, the sceptre, the fanning whisks and various other ceremonial items were held or waved before the icon. A lamp which looked like an upright exquisite gold chandelier with a myriad lighted wicks was held. The lighted wick lamps of various shapes and sizes were circumambulated and the wrist of the priest gave the circumambulation various patterns and directions. Movement was always clockwise. Finally the priest held and circumambulated a single lamp lighted with camphor. The devotees would shout their salutation, '*Arohara*,' and that would be the end of the *pooja*.

Grandfather would receive the holy ash, milk and food prepared by the priests. I would be impatient by now, as the most wonderful part of the trip was to rush down to the casuarina beach which had groves of casuarina trees. Probably the seedlings came up by chance or they may have been planted to break the harsh howling wind and water of the monsoon. The casuarina trees made a wonderful green backdrop and relieved the harsh brown ground, but they were not comfortable to brush against.

The beach was broad and beautiful. By evening the seawater was cold. We as children stood or waded into the sea and got our legs and invariably our clothes wet. Sea bathing was rare; except by the fisher folk who waded in and out of the boats, swimming was a rarity in these islands. Dusk fell quickly. Sunset over the islands and lagoons in Jaffna was something one could hardly erase from one's memory. The sun went down as a big ball of fire. The descent was rapid and it was chased by the disappearing colours of the rainbow which went down much more slowly. The colour indigo was the last to go. It was something different when the sunsets were close to the beginning of the rainy weather. The beauty of the setting sun vied with silver streaks and splashes of the colours of a prism. The silver streaks lingered long after the sun had set and suddenly disappeared with the fast falling dusk. The moon would come up over the sea. An upward glance at the northern sky would show it filled with more than its share of stars. The twilight and dusk would make pretty silhouettes of the tall palmyra trees. The moonlight would make them look like tall black giants, but the coconut tree's shadow was so sharp and beautiful as if an artist had sat under it and painted, with a sharp stylus dipped in Indian ink, the palm and its leaves on the ground.

The stars seemed to be in millions. As a young girl I would hope that one would get pushed out to the ground by sheer overcrowding of the stars. The sky with its stars was a constant feature in the north till clouds covered it during the monsoon. Twilight and dusk gave a beauty to the usually bleak open coastal places of the north.

Grandfather would occasionally take a few of us to the temple in neighboring Vaddukoddai. The anticipation of arrival a little further away even made the trip by boat more pleasant. We were hurried along the way so as to be on time for the last *pooja* of the day. The walk back to the sea and the boat was the most pleasant walk in the north. The road was dead straight, bordered on both sides by lush green waving paddy interrupted by a few tulip and flamboyant trees. The late evening breeze was gentle and came at you, it seemed, from all sides. The sun was sinking. The walk was enervating with plenty of time to gaze at the empty spaces. Flocks of swallows went overhead and parakeets screeched as they found some ripening paddy.

Dusk would seem to fall suddenly in that open space. The sound of a high-pitched, frequently tolled bell of the village temple would travel across the paddy fields and across the road to the farther paddy fields and homesteads. The temple bell was a contrast to the familiar church bell to us. The latter was low pitched, sombre and tolled slowly. The temple bell had an urgency, calling its people to worship at the end of that Friday. The walk became lovelier with the stars above and, if we were lucky, the moon above too. We reached the boat and were taken safely by the boatman with his oars and lanterns across the inlet. We stepped onto that sandy shore with much banter, chatter and fatigue.

The Jam Fruit Tree
(From *The Jam Fruit Tree*)
Carl Muller

This piece is a funny, ribald account of the lower echelons of the Burgher community who worked in the railways and junior levels of the civil service. Muller was one the first Sri Lankan novelists to use a distinctively Sri Lankan English, capturing in these pages the dialect used by many Sri Lankans. The book was also ground-breaking in its frank depiction of sexuality.

The sky was as blue as an Eskimo's nose on the morning that Sonnaboy cycled sedately to work. A large man with big fists, grey eyes set wide in a broad, brown face, a largish nose that swept down from between bushy eyebrows to just short of a rather petulant mouth and a chin that kept saying 'to hell with you' in a language all its own, Sonnaboy was pushing thirty-five and, in his home in suburban Dehiwela and in the Ceylon Government Railway Running Shed in Dematagoda, was a force to reckon with.

Cecilprins von Bloss had a principle he firmly abided by. Keep the wife in the family way. Women, he maintained, stay out of mischief when they are 'carrying'. Siring a string of children was, to the old reprobate, child's play. In those fine old days a meal of rice and curry, a cup of tea and a cigarette cost a mere nine cents—and the best samba rice with beef, two vegetables, *sambal* (a relish made of ground coconut, chillies, lime, salt, chopped onions, tomato and peppercorns, eaten with meals), a pappadam and *mallung* (chopped leaves basted with grated coconut and seasoning) at that—and an assistant postmaster's job was 'public service' with all manner of perks and pensionable to boot. All a husband could wish for was to come home from office, drink great quantities of tea, consider his fat wife who sprawled on the lounger fingering her rosary and check the time. Cecilprins was a creature of habit. Leave the General Post Office at four, take the 4.18 train to Dehiwela, reach home at five. Sometimes Maudiegirl put a bun on his plate with his tea. After a bath at the well, he'd carry his sagging rattan chair to the porch where he would sit, watch the road and waggle a hand at passers-by. Neighbours would pop heads over walls to say 'how' and 'do you know what?' and Cecilprins would say he knew and nod and slap at his ankles as the early mosquitoes swizzed around.

Boteju Lane, Dehiwela, had a fair wedge of assorted citizenry. Old Simmons who hated dogs, and the Bennett woman with one big filaria leg, and the Fernandos who moved away one night after the Rodrigo boy fucked their daughter. Cecilprins enjoyed his porch evenings. He got, he knew, respect. He was an assistant postmaster and always wore high, white, starched collars and a cravat as large as a table napkin. And such a man, too. Thirteen children. Must be the Dutch blood in him. Or was it German? One couldn't be specific.

When the mosquitoes became too demanding, Cecilprins would go indoors and take the little key he kept on the altar where an old Palm Sunday coconut-frond cross lay propped between two sputtering oil lamps and a frayed St. Anthony's scapular. Over the little altar was a quite spectacular picture of the Sacred Heart of Jesus, all scarlet and butter-yellow with a heart that was crowned with tongues of flame—thirteen points of flame, Cecilprins noted one day and remarked on and the whole family counted and solemnly agreed that Papa was right and thirteen had to mean something. Maudiegirl clutched at her rosary and called on the

Blessed Virgin to witness. 'See, will you, how Jesus is telling to me. Thirteen fires in His heart like thirteen fires in my stomach, no? Thirteen children I give and everyone of you make me suffer.'

Cecilprins would take the key from the altar, open his special cupboard, pour himself four fingers of whisky, top that with water and say 'Cheers' and take a deep swig. Maudiegirl would watch and sniff. 'Small sip is good for my rheumatics, no?' and a carefully measured tot is dispensed, which the old lady would dispatch in a twinkling.

Dinner was a humdrum affair, usually. The children would straggle in at odd times. Terry was in Singapore. He had gone into rubber, and the broker-house he worked for had sent him to their Malayan office. He wrote long letters about tiger shooting and his bungalow and Malay servants with their red caps and the enormous snakes he encountered. Sonnaboy would snort and smack a fist into a palm and stalk off to the well. He liked coming home before dark. Stripped to his jocks he would make quite a hullaballoo drawing and dashing water on himself while the servant-girl next door would creep up to peer through the thatch. Sonnaboy would take out his cock and waggle it at her. He was proud of his penis. It was, he knew, bigger and stood stiffer than Dunnyboy's or Totoboy's. He made an elaborate show of soaping it as the servant girl crept closer to watch, and he thought of Elaine and how they would be married soon. Thin girl, Elaine, not much flesh on her thighs, boyishly undeveloped, small breasts, tight little bum. Yes, Elaine was just right. Like a boy. And Sonnaboy liked boys.

Elsie, his sister, would come to the well. '*Chee!* What you are doing! Wait, I'll tell Mama.' But she would go to the store-room where the rice and flour was kept and rub and rub until her bloomers were wet between her legs and would then emerge panting and run to the bedroom to say a feverish Hail Mary.

Yes, a nice, ordinary family. Terry and Dunnyboy, Leah and Elsie, Totoboy and Anna, Viva and Patty, Ruthie and Vinto, Fritzy and Marla and Sonnaboy who was the youngest and quite the strongest in a clutch of eight strong sons. Three died, however, before reaching their teens. Patty and Vinto succumbed to pneumonia and Fritzy fell off the neighbour's roof where he had perched to steal guavas. Of all the family, Dunnyboy was near inconsolable at their passing. He was the eldest and the strangest. Routed from school in disgrace, he never found work. Strong as an ox, too, and not a man to tangle with, with a twelve-year-old mind in his strapping, adult body. Viva was lean, whip-strong and calculating. Totoboy a gregarious, sunny fellow with pianist's fingers and a great talker.

The girls were all big-buttocked and round-thighed, each promising to be fat and fifty like their mother. The fat clung to their bottoms even as teenagers and they bustled invitingly as they walked and Dunnyboy would squeeze them gently over their knees and rub against their behinds and couldn't stop the trembling in his fingers. The small Boteju Lane house had two and a half rooms, actually, and the boys would lump in one and the girls in another and there were no doors to shut between any of them—not even when Cecilprins would cover Maudiegirl at eleven each night and she would wheeze complainingly as he jerked over her and the girls would listen and shiver deliciously and Sonnaboy would crawl softly on hands and knees to peer into the darkness and discover what being married was all about.

'They're doing, no?' Marla would hiss when he crawled past their mats.

Sonnaboy would nod and Leah would sigh softly and go to the chamberpot to raise her nightdress and squat and do pippy. It was Dunnyboy who would want to play papa with them and crawl over to meddle with them and rub his cock against their legs. But that was the night and everything was all right at daybreak when they rose, stacked their pillows, rolled up their mats and emptied the chamberpot in the lavatory and dressed for Mass. St. Mary's Church was a few blocks away. They would check their Missals and the Saint's day and mark the epistle and gospel with holy pictures. The girls wore veils and the boys snapped loops of elastic under their stocking-hose to keep them in place below the knee. And so, each morning, Cecilprins von Bloss and his family would go to church and Sonnaboy would go to the vestry to put on a red cassock and white surplice and serve at the altar. Father Romiel would beam at them and wish them a blessed morning and they would say hullo to old Mr Capper and Mrs Vanderputt and the Rozairos with their three straw-haired daughters.

'Come go,' Maudiegirl would urge, 'told, no, the *hopper* boy to come by seven.' And sure enough the *hopper* boy would come with his basket and Maudiegirl would count a quantity of *hoppers* (a type of thin griddle cake made of flour and fermented coconut water) for breakfast and tip the packet of *sambol* into a tin plate and note the account in a little book. The boy would whistle and show yellow teeth and pick at a sore on his hand. And it was another day. Cecilprins to the G.P.O.; Totoboy to the liquor merchant's where he counted stock and wrote all manner of squiggles in ledgers; Leah to a florist's where she arranged posies and bouquets and smiled at vinegary customers; Anna to a pharmacy where she spent long hours cooing with a Sinhalese gentleman who was something in the radio station, a Buddhist, and who rode a Raleigh bicycle. He was a fastidious little person, scrawny and a regular fusspot. He was the only one Anna knew who wore bicycle clips at the bottom of his trousers. All the others, she said, including Sonnaboy, just shoved the bottom of their trousers into their socks. Sonnaboy would grin. Mostly, he wore short trousers to work anyway. Viva was a salesman. He would wait at the top of the lane for the company van and make a great show of checking stocks of milkfood before setting off each morning. And Sonnaboy would wear a grimy cap, khaki shirt and shorts and climb on his bicycle take the long road to Dematagoda. He said he was the only labourer in the family. A cleaner in the railway. A grease monkey. For eight hours a day he cleaned and greased huge steam locomotives, tenders, the couplings of carriages, frothy wads of cotton waste tucked in his pockets, gunk on his overalls, tarry oil on his neck and elbows, coal dust in his hair and grime under every fingernail. He carried nine cents for lunch and cigarettes and a snapshot of Elaine in his wallet. He was doing okay. Seventy-nine cents a day was a good 1930s salary for a man. Because the British nabobs favoured the 'educated' Burghers, he knew that someday he would become a locomotive apprentice and actually ride the rails. One day he would be an engine driver but in the meantime he would marry Elaine and spend all his off-time in bed with her.

Oh, all in all a robust, brawny, bawdy family, praising the Lord, church-going, singing their Aves with the same gusto as they would eat, drink and fornicate.

Today, in this year of grace, one thousand nine hundred and ninety-one, none of them is alive. They are all, doubtless in some great, cloudy boudoir in the sky. But let me hark back to that blue morning when Sonnaboy pedalled to work. Life held few complications for him. He had his nine cents, his picture of Elaine, he had pumped air into his tyres and the Galle Road had few cars and charabancs to bother him with their exploding exhausts and chug-a-chug engines.

Rickshawmen scudded along, carrying ladies with gaudy parasols. He free-wheeled past the Holy Family Convent at Bambalapitiya and saw, as he claimed, a vision. Actually a roly-poly schoolgirl, fresh, round-cheeked, with a white pith hat on her head of dark hair. Dark eyes looked impudently into his and she turned into a lane leading to the sea. Sonnaboy was entranced. And glad to realise that true femininity could arouse him. He had always liked boys, to touch them, stroke them, feel them grow hard under his fingers. This was what had drawn him to Elaine. Her thin page-boy hair and figure were more male than female. Braking, he watched the girl walk down the lane, enter a house. He followed, noted nameboard and number. Through the curtains fifteen-year-old Beryl saw him turn around at the gate. Such a big, husky man. Her heart fluttered and she ran to the kitchen where Florrie da Brea saw her daughter's flaming face and immediately grabbed an ear. 'What are you up to?' she demanded.

'*Aiyo*, nothing, *anney*. Let go, Mummee, it's hurting.'

Florrie was not satisfied. She had had her share of shame and her children were a trial ever since Clarence had died. She sighed, pushed her youngest away and poured out a cup of tea. 'You want tea?'

Beryl was feeling her ear. 'You hurt it,' she complained.

'Good. Don't think I don't know you, miss. You're up to something. Can tell by just looking. So what you are up to now?'

'Nothing, *anney*. Fine thing, no? Just coming from school and getting scolded. Can I cut some bread?'

'You leave the bread, will you. If eating now won't have enough for dinner. Here, drink your tea and go and change. Are your knickers dirty? You know very well can't give those things to the dhoby woman. If dirty put in the tub to wash.'

'*Chee*, as if I will wear dirty knickers. You must see Elva's. They're filthy,' Beryl giggled and nearly choked on her tea.

'Never mind Elva,' said Florrie severely, 'You mind how you talk about your elders, miss.'

'But it's true, Mama.'

Florrie cuffed her daughter almost absent-mindedly. It had been hard since Clarence died, God rest his soul. What was to be done?

Sonnaboy returned home, bathed, got into his best clothes and cycled back to Nimal Lane, Bambalapitiya, to number 19, and rapped at the gate. There were no frills about his calling. He was thirty-five years old, a government servant and on the list for consideration as an apprentice driver. Florrie was taken by the grey eyes and the candid manner of his calling. She shooed her daughters indoors and invited him to sit. Sonnaboy was not there to mince words. He wished to marry Beryl. Was that her name? A nice name. So he was twenty years her senior. His parents? Everything was laid on the table for Florrie's dissection.

'But you don't know my daughter even.'

Sonnaboy nodded. 'Can I see her?'

Florrie said no. She was a schoolgirl. A good girl. An innocent girl. She must study. She was still a child. Her little *patiya* (Sinhala for 'tiny tot' or smallest child). 'Sin, no, to marry a girl this age. What she know about anything?'

Beryl, listening behind the inner door, frowned. Elva pinched her, almost made her squeal. 'What she know,' Elva hissed, 'I'll tell Mama how you go to that Lauries Lane house after school. Taking money from that man there. What are you doing with him?'

Beryl tossed her head. All that old man did was sit her on his lap and feel her legs. She regretted ever having told Elva about it. They listened together as Sonnaboy offered to bring his parents. Tomorrow?

Florrie was flustered. If only Clarence were here to deal with this huge fellow and his big hands. Such a big, bulgy man. But a railway man. That's a good job. Pension, too, and later maybe government quarters to live in. But he's thirty-five. That's not good. May die soon and leave my Beryl a widow with children. 'Must ask Saint Anthony,' she muttered as she watched Sonnaboy pedal away.

The girls came out. 'Mama, who is that?'

'You mind your business, will you. Nobody can come and even fart in this house without you asking why. See, child, if have a candle in the whatnot.'

Elva nudged Beryl. 'Mama is going to pray for you.'

Florrie took the candle crossly. 'That fellow coming here sweet as you please and saying never mind the school, he wants to marry Beryl. Cheek, no? I have told you girls a thousand times don't encourage every loafer on the road. Otherwise how he know this place to come like this? See, will you, how nicely he walked in. As sweet as you please. Must be knowing your father is dead. Here, light this. I must ask Saint Anthony to help me.'

Eric de Mello worked in the General Post Office too, and was a mite lower in rank to Cecilprins who had his own desk and keys to drawers he could lock and, glory be, his own row of pigeon holes where he would stuff odds and ends. Each pigeon hole had been carefully labelled 'Standing orders', 'Memoranda', 'PMG's

Circulars', 'Queries', etc., and Eric marvelled at this edifice of efficiency.

Eric shared a counter with a Tamil clerk named Naiswamy and a freckled Burgher lad named Raux who was easier called Rooks and who whistled tonelessly all day. Eric lived in Dehiwela too—in Station Lane—and was always on the platform to greet Cecilprins. He, being younger, would always swing aboard first and secure a window seat, back to the engine, for Cecilprins, which was his first humble duty for the day. You see, Eric had his eye on Elsie and cultivated the father quite atrociously. It did not strike him that, as a couple, he and Elsie would cut quite a ludicrous figure. He, thin as a pipecleaner, slightly stooped with an air of permanent defeat; she, a healthy, strapping woman with calves and upper arms bigger than his thigh. He loved her to distraction. He needed someone to domineer him, even beat him, as his mother still did, yet, to tend to him, for Eric could never tend to himself. His was a world full of stumblings and bumblings, and odd socks and shirts buttoned wrong and leaving umbrellas in buses and sitting on his spectacles. Yet, he had his own little vice: the Ceylon Turf Club, and although he sometimes forgot and carried the race paper home and was soundly pummelled by his mother for venturing on this road to eternal damnation, he was mad on horse-racing. A sad, timid soul, he would resort to stealing from his own pay packet to put a fifty cents each way on horses who always insisted on raising their tails and refusing to finish.

'Canteen!' mother Aggie would bellow, 'What's this canteen nonsense? I give lunch packet and ten cents every day, no? And you have train season-ticket, no? So what for you going to canteen and eating and drinking God knows what? And four rupees cut from your pay. Four rupees! Can buy eggs and meat and pay the baker and get kerosene oil, no? with that money. You are waster like your father. Don't talk! God in heaven, what is this son you give me. I feed him and darn his shirts and only yesterday I cut cardboard with my own two hands to put in his shoes. And I think today he bring his pay home to his old mama who is slaving and grinding away with no rest from morning to night and four rupees gone for canteen. Canteen!'

Eric would cower near the sofa with its ghastly purple flower pattern and say, 'I'm sorry, Mama,' and Aggie would charge him like an enraged buffalo and twist a fat forearm around his neck and drag him to the centre of the hall, pummelling his head with her fist and breathing like an overworked bellows. Eric would yelp and struggle feebly, then stand still and inhale his mother's body smell as she whacked him, then pushed him into a chair and tucked in her hairpins.

'Think that I do this for your own good,' she would puff. 'Responsible you can be if you want. When I die and go what you will do, I don't know.'

Eric didn't know either. But Mama had whacked him and that was balm to his soul. Mama loved him.

It took a long time for Eric to summon the courage to tell Cecilprins of his intentions. The latter was impressed. Runty little fellow, to be sure, but steady, obliging, respectful and good son-in-law material. Could be kept in order, too. So Eric was invited home and he came with a tin of Bluebird toffees and made eyes at Elsie who glared back fiercely and scattered toffee wrappers in the veranda. Close up to his goddess, Eric was positively inflamed. Such a bosom. He could bury his head in that while she beat him and she was welcome to beat him every hour if she wished.

Mother Aggie was pleased. She was always impressed by the von Blosses who had produced such strong girls, each built like a pack-bull. When she learned of her son's intentions she swatted him affectionately and taking out a large bunch of keys, opened the kitchen safe and cut him a large wedge of love cake. 'From Christmas I save this cake,' she breathed, 'to give you one day you make your poor mama happy. So today you take a piece. You marry that girl. I will say a rosary for you.'

Eric, overwhelmed, cried: 'Mama.'

'My sugar ball,' Aggie cried—and that was perhaps the only maternal endearment Eric ever received. Aggie passed away that night with a sneer on her lips and Eric found a pillowcase full of money the old lady had stashed away and had a grand funeral with a band and two Tamil women he paid fifty cents each, to wail at the cemetery and beat their foreheads in the dust.

Cecilprins had had his reservations about Aggie. Now that she was safely interred his last doubts were dispelled. His Elsie would be mistress of a nice home in Station Lane. Eric would have to wait a decent interval, of course, but that couldn't be helped. 'I think six months is enough,' he told Maudiegirl.

'*Chickay*, that's not enough,' said Maudiegirl, heaving herself upright in her lounger. 'Poor mother in the sand and no time even to say twelve masses. Must wait one year, no?'

'You're mad, woman? When he coming here every day. Now not even talking in the house. Putting chairs under jam fruit tree and who knows what he's telling to her? Putting ideas in her head, must be. Everybody going on the road can see also. Tell, will you, to be like normal.'

Sonnaboy regarded his sister's boyfriend with contempt. '*Soththiya*, no? Bugger can't even stand straight.'

'You don't worry, will you,' Maudiegirl would frown. 'He does better job than you, no? Have brains in his head.'

Cecilprins was assured by Father Romiel that there was no harm in an early wedding. 'I'm sure the poor soul would like an early wedding.'

'But what will people think, don't know.'

'Think of the poor soul,' the priest murmured.

Cecilprins bridled. 'What poor soul? My Elsie is all right. I'm giving her almirah and the old sewing-machine. A Pfaff. Only needs oiling. And some pots and pans and some money also. She will be all right.'

'No, no, I'm meaning Mrs de Mello. Surely she is now in heaven, waiting to see her son get married.'

'Oh.'

'Yes. So when shall we fix the day.'

'As you like, Father. Maybe two–three months.' Poor soul. Hah! Must tell that to Maudiegirl.

Elsie was delighted. 'So now we can get married,' she told Eric and seizing his hand thrust it between her legs. She deplored Eric's lack of spirit. She expected him to be more forthcoming. Like Dunnyboy, for example, whose nightly predations were clockwork regular. When Eric rose to go, he held the 'Morning Leader' strategically to hide the bulge in his trousers. He felt, at last, a man.

George de Mello was Eric's cousin, and when he heard of the latter's marriage plans he called to check out the lay of the land. George was a crafty piece of work, a perfect crow of a man. Hooked nose, sunken cheeks and sly eyes, he was a cold fish. From the firm of Bosanquet and Skrine, general importers, he moved to Delmege Forsythe, shippers, where the pickings were infinitely better. The shipping firm took him in as a tally clerk, and he found the port and shipside job one of vast potential. He scorned bus and train. The old Ebert Silva buses were a nightmare to travel in anyway. The hard wooden seats hurt his back and his long, spindly legs were always in the way. So he had his own rickshaw man to carry him in state to work each day and bowl him back. It was a long trot to the most enthusiastic of rickshaw-wallahs, but George's arrivals and departures in so regal a fashion impressed his fellow-workers no end. Yet, he remained a small, mean man and not above stealing or cadging what he could, given the opportunities galore on board cargo ships and merchant packets.

Thus would he bring home boxes of Cadbury's Roses one day and tins of Black Magic another. He made it a point to cadge a bottle of whisky or Martell's Three Stars from ships' captains and swiped what he could from pursers' cabins. He found that he could tally cargo consignments so well that there were always a couple of tins of this or packets of that, which belonged to nobody and were, naturally, his. His dedication pleased his bosses no end. When he came to see his cousin Eric, he was senior tally master and the port of Colombo sang his praises in fifty different sharps and flats.

'You know,' he told Eric, 'high time I also got married, no?'

Eric nodded like a puppet. He had always admired George. Even when they were children he always bowled and George always batted. Eric never had the courage to ask to bat. Today, however, he felt almost equal to his beady-eyed cousin. He was one step ahead, wasn't he? He was going to marry. George was not.

The thought irked George. 'What do you know about getting married, men? You know what to do?'

Eric's lips trembled. He thought about how warm his hand felt between Elsie's legs. 'Of course I know,' he croaked, 'What you think I don't know? Foo, I know all about that.' Then he elaborated: 'My Elsie also know. And she wants to do even now. But better to wait, no, until the wedding.'

George was not impressed. 'You're a bloody fool, men.'

Eric was used to being called so. He didn't mind. Together they went to Boteju Lane and George was introduced and Leah came in after work and George was all eyes for this florist's assistant. His conversation with Cecilprins was forcefully loud; lots of swagger about the docks and the harbour workers he controlled and the ships' captains he knew and how the firm of Delmege Forsythe would surely fold up tomorrow if he walked out on it. All this, naturally, for Leah's benefit, who listened and sighed and brought him a cup of tea and said she had never been to the port or seen a ship close up.

George was in his element. 'I can arrange,' he said, 'You can come on board with me. I have permits for visitors, no? Anything in the port I can do and anywhere I can go. I'll tell when big ship comes and we can go.'

Maudiegirl hauled Leah indoors and propelled her to the back veranda. 'I'll port you. You're mad or what? All coolies there and those ships fellows big cads. Go and wash the grinding stone and clean the fireplace. Listening to all this nonsense. You know what happened to Nellie, no? Went to visit ship and how many fellows got round her. What you girls thinking of, I don't know.'

Cecilprins expelled noisily when George left. 'Pukka fellow, no?' he told Maudiegirl. 'One to talk. Two hours boasting, boasting. And damn cheek, no? Telling will take Leah to big ship. And in front of me! Not even asking. Just telling. Because he is Eric's relation I keep quiet. Tchah! Feel like chasing both from here. What for he bring that fellow I don't know. He coming to see Elsie, all right. What for he bringing his family people also?'

But the next evening George turned up with a box of chocolates and a Swan fountain-pen for Cecilprins. Eric and Elsie, under the jam fruit tree, were surprised to see him walk in and George just nodded at them and proceeded to soften up Cecilprins and Maudiegirl. 'Just passing. I was going to Mount Lavinia to see a friend. So I was passing your lane and I had this and said those people so nice and take me in their home and give me tea. Here, this is for the ladies. From Switzerland. See, have on the box, Swiss Chocolates. And this is for you. Brand new, in box and all. Only got yesterday in shipment. Very good pen, I think.'

So he was invited to sit and half an hour later Cecilprins said, 'Your friend must be waiting, no?'

'What?'

'In Mount Lavinia. You were going to see, no?'

'Ah yes. But never mind. Can go another day. You have nice jam fruit tree. Must be very old.'

Cecilprins melted visibly. 'When we came here, birds must have dropped seeds from the wall. When it started growing owner said cut it. Said the roots will go under the house and break the floor. Told the bugger to clear off. I pay rent, no? What I grow is not his business. When the children start coming it is so high and see today the size. Now forty years. Whole garden it shading now. Always I telling, that tree like this family. Always flowers, always cherries.

Enough for everybody. All the children eating and boys in the lane climbing the wall and eating.'

Nobody then considered the philosophy behind those words. But in truth, the jam fruit tree was so symbolic. The ever-bearing tree. And never-dying, too. Like the stout Burgher women of the age: fruitful, tough, always in bloom, earthy. Like the men too. Hard-working, hard-drinking, as lusty as life itself. Such a tree: always sprouting, reaching out, spreading over the leaf-strewn earth with its umbrella branches. It was the jam fruit tree that first gave the young ones an awareness of each other. Totoboy would climb and Anna would stand below and look up his short trousers and sing out: '*Chee*, I can see.'

'See what?'

'Your birdie. It's hanging like a big worm.'

'You wait till I come down, will you.'

'I'll tell Mama.'

'So go and tell. Good for you to look, no? You also come up and show yours.'

'But I haven't birdie like you.'

'So never mind. You climb, will you.'

And between the branches, hidden in the masses of foliage they explored and wondered at the difference and the wind sang ribald songs and all was right with the world.

George never knew, but it was his chance remark about the jam fruit tree that made him more acceptable. Old Cecilprins thawed enough to even offer him a 'small sip' and was even more gratified when this was politely refused. 'Only on Sunday I take,' George said grandly. 'Put a tot before lunch. Weekdays, when working I don't touch. When having big job with all these ships must be always clear. Those dock workers big rogues. Take your trousers even, if not looking. Some job, this is.'

He came again and again. And he dispensed pilfered ships stores lavishly. Tinned mackerel, a bottle of Booths, spools of

Coats thread, whatever he laid his hands on in the port. But all his swagger could not give him the gall to broach the subject of Leah whom he took to seeing at the florist's and giving her little packets of caramel and tins of Schweitzer's cocoatina.

It was on the day that he brought a bottle of Tarragona and a twelve-pack of twenty underproof Irish whisky (and only the good Lord knows how he got it out of the port) that the Boteju Lane house became positively merry and Maudiegirl kept complaining of recurring rheumatics. Leah, emboldened, sat next to George and said she was tickled by the way the hair grew out of his ears. With the old Irish to break down fences, even Elsie hustled Eric to the bathroom where she raised her skirts, perched on the edge of the cement sink and told him to put it in. Poor Eric, scared out of his wits, fled, and Elsie sulked, said she had a headache and went to the bedroom to cry a little. Sonnaboy walked in and was annoyed. 'What the hell is all this? Look at Totoboy. Drunk and mouth open. Whole damn house in a mess, no?' But he swallowed a tumbler of neat whisky and went in to wash and change. George was happy. All he now had to do, he thought, was to corner the old man and pop the question. But, poor idiot that he was, he decided on another course of action. Had he cornered Cecilprins that day he would have gained ready consent. But George had to do it his way. He would go home and write a formal letter. That, he thought, would impress the old boy no end.

When the letter arrived two days later, Cecilprins and Maudiegirl went into a huddle. They were feeling pretty low about the revels of the day before yesterday. Dunnyboy said how he saw George squeezing Leah's breasts and Totoboy had slept in his chair all evening and did not go to work the next day. Maudiegirl slapped Leah who shouted: 'Fine thing, no. Take all his presents but bad for him to touch me.'

This plunged them into a new awareness of the situation. 'Tchah, damn shame, no? Damn shame for us,' said Cecilprins. 'Now see, writing, and saying want to marry Leah. He and his port. Can come to make us drunk but can't come to discuss like gentleman. Writing letter. All this Eric's fault. Bringing him here in the first place. I suppose now he waiting for me to reply and say here my Leah, take and go.'

Anna, ever the practical soul, said: 'Tell Sonnaboy. Catch and give him good pasting.'

Maudiegirl shuddered. 'You're mad, *anney*. He go to police and tell how he gave us things and damn shame for us, no? Write and tell not to come again. Tell that Leah already promised.'

'Or tell Eric to tell him not to come,' said Elsie.

'And where, pray, is Eric? Two days now he not coming. What you do to him?

Elsie blushed. 'Nothing, *anney*. All your fault. Drinking and drinking. Now he not even coming.'

'So good,' said Cecilprins fiercely. 'Fine son-in-law he be. If put two drinks he running home. If going to be like this better you don't marry.'

'Chut,' said Maudiegirl, 'All your fault, no? Taking his whisky and whole night snoring and smelling like tavern. Tomorrow you tell Eric in office that Elsie very upset. Will come running. And better you write to this George, no? Tell not to come again. Tell will return his whisky. Have some put-away money in the tin on the almirah. Can buy from Cargills and give Eric to give to George. What to do? When have girls always this trouble. From all over coming like as if have bitch in heat.'

So a letter was written and George, ripping open the envelope eagerly, couldn't believe what he read. He was furious, and when George was furious he threw caution to the winds. This, he determined, was injustice of the rankest. What wrong had he done? Those girls were just waiting for someone to get under their skirts. Hah! Old fools with their rosaries and starched collars and all high and mighty. I'll postmaster him. Then, with incredible venom, he actually made a list. At the top he wrote, one bottle Tarragona invalids wine and the twelve-pack of Irish. Then, licking his pencil, he added the following:

1 packet Jordan almonds
3 tins Schweitzer's cocoatina
2 packets milk paste chocolates
1 tin Yeastman's baking powder
1 box Fry's chocolates
1 tin East India coffee
1 packet Harvest's egg powder
2 boxes Congou tea
3 tins Dorset butter
1 ball Cheshire cheese
2 bottles Mason's beef tea
1 tin Isinglass golden syrup
1 packet pudding powder
1 Swan fountain-pen with filler
1 bottle calf's foot jelly
1 tin Abernethy biscuits
6 tins Paysandu ox tongue
1 tin Julienne soup
1 packet Osborne biscuits
1 bottle Bengal Club pickle
2 cakes Rimmel toilet soap
1 flask Hennessy brandy
1 tin Rowntree's cocoa

He scanned the list and furrowed his brows at it. 'So much I give and not a word to thank,' he gritted, 'useless buggers, I'll show who I am. Think they can take and take and then kick my backside, no.' He went to his cousin Jembo with a martyred air and related how shabbily he had been treated. He produced his list and Cecilprins' letter. Jembo's eyebrows shot skyward. 'Damn fool, no? to give like this. Damn good for you. When I asking for bottle for my birthday, you remember? What did you say? Ah, now you're coming running. But good for you to give these people all these things. Why you go to give all this? Once in a way you give girl some toffees enough, no?'

Jembo was a bull of a man. Built like a wardrobe. Nobody messed with him because he was so big, so nobody knew what an arrant coward he was. Crafty George saw distinct advantage in confronting the von Blosses in Jembo's company. One look at Jembo and they will take cover. They reached Boteju Lane rather late that evening and while Jembo stood under the jam fruit tree, crossed his arms over his chest and made menacing faces, George paraded the veranda, flourishing the offending letter and brandishing his famous list. 'So what I do!' he thundered. 'All because of Leah, no? Because I loving her I bring you things out of my goodness. All from my hard-earned, no? How you know how I sweat to buy these things I bring to show I am kind person only thinking of you. Not like other people who only give the girl, I give for everybody. And for that I get slap in the face. Nice way to treat people, no? Pudding powder!'

Cecilprins, growing whiter, tried to calm him down. 'We only think you must not get serious on Leah,' he stammered.

'Beef tea!' George yelled.

'We not mean insult, child . . .' Maudiegirl began.

'Egg powder!' George roared.

'You give all back, right,' Jembo growled from the garden.

George was hitting second wind. He tore Cecilprins letter into shreds and flung the bits all over the veranda. 'That's the way I take your insult,' he hooted. Maudiegirl clutched her heart. The van Dort family were perched on the side wall lapping up the show. Then there was a bang at the gate and Sonnaboy strode in. He didn't have to be filled in with past history. Neighbours on the wall, a strange ape in the garden and George in the veranda shouting his head off.

He never did like George. One big hand closed around the back of George's neck in a grip of iron and the noisy little cockerel was hauled off the veranda and down the steps. Something like a sledge struck him, numbing the entire left side of his face. Jembo uncrossed his arms, dropped his lower jaw and only stayed long enough to give a high squeak of alarm. Then he was through the gate and legging it for the Galle Road like a champion sprinter. George, he decided, could take the thrashing for them both. And George did. He was propped against the jam fruit tree and methodically pulped. George did not know it at the time but he was in the hands of a true craftsman. And Sonnaboy excelled in his craft. Then it was time for everyone to jump on his back and cling to him and somehow drag him off before murder was done, but not before he had scooped up the thinly-screaming George and hurled him through the gate where he lay for all the world like a rag doll after an injudicious encounter with a steamroller.

Leah, whose screams were positively operatic in quality and pitch, pushed past everybody to put her head on George's breast and declare that she would kill herself, so there. The neighbours applauded vigorously. This was better than the Bioscope. Sonnaboy strode to the gate. 'Can he walk?'

George moaned.

'Good. You still want to marry my sister?'

'Grooooh.' A lot of Leah's hair seemed to be in his mouth.

'Good. And you try any more nonsense after you marry her and I will come and hammer you every time. Did you hear?'

'Ooooooh.'

Maudiegirl kept gasping as though she had swallowed a lobster. '*Aiyo*, mother of mercy, take him inside, child, put some embrocation. Blood coming also. Where that other fellow? Who that other fellow. Didn't even tell his name, no?'

So George was dragged in with scant ceremony and Leah fomented his face and Maudiegirl brought cottonwool and flavine and George moaned that he couldn't stand erect and Leah said I know, I know, you lie back, will you, have big bruise on your ribs also. 'Where else it paining,' and she made a great show of tending on her poor martyr and seized the chance to take a close look at this man she was going to marry. Cecilprins came in with an enormous pair of green striped pajamas and a banian, 'Here, you change and give your clothes to wash. Trouser knee also torn. Can darn, no?'

So Leah washed and darned and brought him beef tea—his beef tea—and asked him where it hurt. 'There,' he said and she would feel the spot and venture lower down and say, 'Here also?' and he would nod and her hands would slip to his hips and 'Here also?' and soon she was squeezing his cock and exclaiming at its size and that it would do very nicely, thank you.

The Walauwa

Wimal Dissanayake

The ugly remnant
of a broken
sin-heavy dream;
a ruin
from the blackest this black past
this *walauwa*

I who walked by here then,
bent in two,
today I don't even remove
the shawl off my shoulders.
I enter
through the toothless gate.

An enormous snorting beast
gasping his last;
this *walauwa.*

I push back the stink of mildew
and peer inside,

Translated by Ranjini Obeyesekere

Open the crippled door
and look.
I climb the groaning stairs;
on the faded majesty
cobwebs bloom.

The sounds of victory that resounded then,
the lion might and majesty,
who knows, as a joke, just to trick us,
it may be hidden away;
I search
there is nothing to be found anywhere.

They fought foolishly
times vast rough waves;
they have been swept away,
without even a marker.

From the dead grass a dry wind stutters,
creeps close to my ear and mutters,
I strain to catch what it says.

The Hamilton Case

(From *The Hamilton Case*)

Michelle de Kretser

A Wise Child

A name is the first story that attaches itself to a life. Consider mine: Stanley Alban Marriott Obeysekere. It tells of geography, history, love and uncertainty. I was born on an island suspended midway on the golden trade route between East and West—a useful bauble, fingered and pocketed by the Portuguese, Dutch and British in turn. In 1902, when I was born, Sir Alban Marriott was Governor and he agreed to be my godfather. How could he refuse? He had been in thrall to my mother ever since she sent him the skin of a leopard she had shot, along with a note. *I shall call on you between five and six this evening. The skin is for the small blue reception room, which is ideally suited to fornication and whatnot.* Her name was Maud and she was a great beauty. Also a first-rate shot. In Scotland she had stalked deer with the Prince of Wales; his performance, she reported, was mediocre. He presented her with a brooch fashioned from an eagle's talon mounted on silver and onyx. Mater dismissed it as *monumentally obvious* and palmed it off to her stewardess in lieu of a tip on her voyage home.

My father insisted on calling me Stanley, although my mother hated the name. I have often pondered the significance of Pater's uncharacteristic resolve. His father, too, was a Stanley, so he might simply have been affirming family tradition. On the other hand, might his assertion of my paternal provenance betray some anxiety about it? My mother had a certain reputation. It was alleged that she once swam in a jungle pool wearing only her bloomers, even though there were gentlemen and snakes present. Half of Colombo society followed the lead of Lady Marriott, who was stout and afflicted with shingles, in cutting her dead. Mater said Stanley was fit only for a peon, so it was just as well my initials spelt Sam. These days there is no one left to remember that I was ever called anything else.

Stanley Alban Marriott Obeysekere: between the names that define me as my father's child falls the shadow of an Englishman who didn't serve a second term as Governor. Shortly after his death eight years ago a package from a firm of London solicitors found its way to my desk. It contained a small murky oil painting of a large and largely unclad female gathering flowers and berries against a backdrop of broken marble columns in a woodland glade. The artist—quite unknown to the works of reference I have consulted—signed himself Tom Baltran. The executor's letter accompanying the painting explained that the Baltrans and the Marriotts were cousins. Moreover, it continued, the Hon. Thomas was descended on the distaff side from the first Duke of St Albans, Charles II's illegitimate son by Nell Gwynne. The artist's hefty nymph was held, *in family lore*, to represent the orange-seller, but this was purely speculative. *Sir Alban*, wrote his solicitor, *was most anxious for this painting, the gem of his small collection, to pass to you. He retained the warmest memories of his years in Ceylon, and often referred to happy times spent in the company of your mother.*

An ambiguous legacy, wouldn't you say? I keep the painting in a cabinet, along with Sir Alban's other gift, a silver egg cup presented on the occasion of my christening. Now and then I set these objects before me and study them. An egg, a mistress, a bastard son: their message seems unequivocal. But the testimony of signs is unreliable. Within minutes I have reasoned that an egg cup is a wholly conventional gift on the part of a godparent, and that the Hon. Thomas's daub points only to the ill-judged sentimentality of a nonagenarian. The argument prevails for a brief interval; then doubt creeps in again. These sessions always end the same way: I cross to my mirror where reassurance waits in the solid evidence of my flesh.

If you wish to ascertain a man's lineage, read his face not his birth certificate. My skin is as dark as my father's, our branch of the Obeysekeres being famously black. Like Pater, I am of average height and inclined to portliness in age. We share a high forehead, thick, springing hair, a curved nose and assertive ears. We are not handsome men. But we have *presence.* Whereas Sir Alban, as he appears in my parents' photograph album, is tall and hollow-chested, with pointed features and an entirely unconvincing moustache. He clasps his left wrist in his right hand, holding himself together.

By now it will be apparent that my pen is not constrained by decorum. I have always set great store by the truth, a virtue not usually prized in my profession. But it was my ability to see accurately and to speak the truth, without concern for convention or fear of reprisal, that made my name in a different sense. The very notoriety of the Hamilton Case has seen it shrouded in the fog of rumour, conjecture and misinformation that passes for analysis in the drawing rooms of this country. In these pages I intend to set down the facts of the matter at last.

A Remembrance of Things Past

My grandfather, Sir Stanley Obeysekere, was a *mudaliyar*, an office that placed a man at the pinnacle of our island's social system. A *mudaliyar* was a leader of men, with considerable influence in his ancestral district. By tradition he was a gifted soldier and a skilled diplomat, abilities he placed at the service of his sovereign. With the advent of the Europeans, however, the role of the *mudaliyar* evolved. The Kandyan kingdom remained unconquered in the hills until 1815, but as the Portuguese, Dutch and finally the British occupied larger and larger areas of the maritime provinces, it was for their administrative talents, above all, that my ancestors came to be valued by the colonial powers. Their education, the respect they commanded among their countrymen and their knowledge of the island's customs meant they were ideally suited to assist in the colonial administration: as record-keepers, as intermediaries and interpreters, as presidents of the courts that dealt with native disputes concerning land, contracts and debts.

The Europeans rewarded loyalty with land: whole villages were given in gift to the *mudaliyars*, vast tracts of jungle, tax-free estates. Pater's inheritance included landholdings throughout the southern provinces, four properties in Colombo, six or seven outstation bungalows, a cottage in the hills, a tea plantation and a plumbago mine; as well as Lokugama, our country seat, where my childhood unravelled in splendid isolation.

I have no doubt that my ancestors were vigorous men. One of my lasting regrets is that I never knew my grandfather, who was by all accounts a wise and able administrator. I have by me a copy of the confidential memorandum from Government House recommending his knighthood. It notes that my grandfather possessed *a most complete and accurate knowledge of the practice and procedure of the Island and* describes him as *a man of the highest character, honourable, high principled and unswervingly loyal.*

Alas, Sir Stanley met with disaster at the age of thirty-four. He was boating on the lake in Kandy one afternoon when he noticed that a party of English girls, who had ventured out without a boatman in the spirited way of the young, had got into difficulty. Before his horrified eyes, one of the girls, who had unwisely risen to her feet, was pitched overboard. Ten years earlier my grandfather had swum the Hellespont, *cheered on by a smelly band of very villainous Greeks*, as he recorded in his diary. Now he dived at once into the lake and reached the young lady's side in a few swift strokes.

All would have been well had it not been for the hysterical reaction of Miss Daisy Dawson, one of the ladies left shrieking in the boat. Afterwards her father, the Government Agent for the Jaffna Province, offered in extenuation the terror and confusion his daughter felt at the prospect of capsizing (none of the ladies could swim) and her extreme distress at seeing her friend, a sweet girl on the threshold of womanhood, being manhandled by a native. In her understandable terror, confusion and distress, Miss Dawson brought her oar crashing down on my grandfather's skull. He drowned, of course.

Miss Dawson's party, including the sweet girl in the water, was rescued by two Scottish engineers, whose presence on the lake was taken as proof that my grandfather had acted courageously but precipitately. Two white men would not have sat by and watched an English girl drown. Sir Stanley would have done better to attract the engineers' attention with manly shouts. The sentiment in billiard rooms and newspaper editorials was that the Ceylonese, even the ablest among them, were prone to exaggeration.

Pater was a boy of nine when his father drowned. Some said Sir Stanley had been murdered; it came down to one's point of view. His death served as a pretext for a half-hearted attempt to stir up anti-British sentiment, which floundered at once since the Obeysekere clan failed to support it. In fact my Great-Uncle Willy wrote a strongly worded letter to the *Times of Ceylon* regretting his brother's impetuousness, and absolving Miss Dawson, *a mere inexperienced girl*, of all blame.

It so happened that Willy was involved in litigation at the time. He was the subject of a lawsuit brought by a man called Perera, who was contesting Willy's title to some twenty acres of forested land near Chilaw. This fellow Perera claimed that the land had belonged to his family for generations, although he could produce no certifiable title of ownership. He alleged that Willy had acquired a spurious title to the property and then sent a band of thugs to seize it by force.

Such allegations—indeed such practices—were common enough in those days, when everyone who could afford to do so was mad to get his hands on land that could be used for cash crops. One might argue that the land-grab had been set off by the government, whose Waste Land Ordinance had declared that all lands not permanently cultivated or in certifiable ownership were the property of the Crown. In this way the British acquired acres of primeval forest that were sold for plantations. The local élite followed suit, clearing land for coffee and tea and rubber and coconut with so much zeal that the government was eventually forced to consider measures for preserving the jungle and slowing down sales of uncultivated land.

Willy and Perera had hired teams of lawyers who had been fighting it out in our tortoise-like courts for years. In fact the case had dragged on for so long that Willy had grown quite rand of his adversary, whom he referred to affectionately as The Blasted P. He regaled his relatives with details about this character: his hair-oil, the sturdy umbrella that accompanied him everywhere, his habit of picking his teeth with a long fingernail, his numerous offspring ('I counted at least fifteen. Huge, hairy hulks. And as for his sons . . . !'). When he learnt that The Blasted P's eldest daughter was to be married, Willy sent her a handsome canteen of cutlery. It was returned the next day. Willy slapped his forehead. 'Of course! The Blasted P scorns cutlery. Should have sent the girl a set of fingerbowls.'

Whenever the clan gathered at Lokugama, Pater and his cousins would entertain the adults by acting out imaginary episodes from the life of The Blasted P, who had quickly passed into family myth. The Blasted P at Buck House: much hilarity from the spectators as our hero presses betel on the Crown Prince, slurps his tea from a saucer, ogles the behind of a lady-in-waiting, asks a footman when the arrack will be served, all under the unamused eye of Victoria (my Aunt Sybil, much padded with cushions, who at the age of twelve bore an unnerving resemblance to that redoubtable monarch).

Willy once took The Blasted P aside and made him a sporting offer: settle the matter once and for all like gentlemen, weapon of his choice, circumvent the bally lawyers. But The Blasted P was a devout Buddhist. 'Lectured me on the taking of life and whatnot. Blighter's bleeding me to death in the courts but that's different, it seems.'

With the shift in government policy on the sale of forested land, the matter was no longer farcical. Willy's lawyers expressed pessimism about the final ruling, expected in a few weeks. Then my grandfather died and Willy wrote his letter. The court found in his favour. His jungle acres were cleared for coconuts and in time returned considerable profits. The Blasted P faded from view, although Willy always sent him a card at Christmas. Yet he died a disappointed man, poor Willy, because the OBE he yearned for never materialised. The English have long memories, you see. Their great talent lies in the reconciliation of justice and compromise. A formidable race. I miss them to this day.

Ritzy

Would Pater have turned out differently if Sir Stanley's accident hadn't deprived him, at a tender age, of a father's loving sternness? Speculation of that kind is irresistible and pointless. For myself, I believe that sons are born to disappoint their fathers. In that respect, every man fulfils his destiny.

My father was an indulgent, insouciant man. There was something spongy about him, like a fish that has lain too long out of water. This was perhaps the consequence of his moment in history. With the development of the colonial Civil Service, the *mudaliyars'* power had eroded, and a preoccupation with status had taken its place. Senior chaps like Pater had little to do but advise the British on the doings and the opinions of the Ceylonese. In this way, they came to wield enormous influence in the twice-yearly distribution of imperial honours among their countrymen. Pater travelled at the centre of a retinue eager to laugh at his witticisms and compliment him on his judgement. In private, lists of the coveted honours were drawn up on the backs of dance-cards. Resentment at being passed over would be elaborated into an extravagant narrative of insult and vengeance as obsessively detailed as the petit point over which generations of ladies wore out their eyes in drawing rooms.

Pater loved parties, champagne, horses. His generosity was legendary. If he had particularly enjoyed himself at a house party, his hostess might receive three bottles of priceless Tokay Essence or a comb that had last belonged to a Chinese empress. Sentimental songs made him weep. Once, learning of a critically ailing child on the estate at Lokugama, he despatched a carriage to Colombo for his own specialist. The round trip of two hundred miles took the best part of a day, and the child died hours before Sir Humphrey arrived; but that was not the point.

At Lokugama, petitioners thronged at the gate whenever Pater was in residence. In his hearing true friends desisted from admiring this painting, that bibelot, because 'Take it! I bought it for you! Take it!' he would urge and if they remained adamant in their refusal, he had it sent around to them the next day, anyway.

Like all admirable qualities, this liberality was hard on those in its vicinity. I learnt to keep prized possessions hidden away after Pater spotted my beloved lead soldiers on the verandah, scooped up the Duke of Wellington and pressed him into the grubby hands of our cookwoman's grandson. I flew at the brat and kicked his ringwormed shins, for which I earned myself a thrashing. That night I cried myself to sleep. Not for the sake of my backside—my father's strokes were so light and glancing that in his hands a cane was an instrument of love—but for the injustice I had suffered.

It was Pater's iconic largesse that had first brought him to my mother's attention. Mater, her cousin Iris, and Iris's parents were taking tea at the Savoy on the girls' first visit to London, when Great-Uncle Bertie adjusted his monocle: 'Isn't that young Obeysekere over there by the window? But who on earth is that frightful fellow with him?'

The frightful fellow turned out to be an out-of-work coachman who had stopped my father in the Strand and asked for money, saying he was hungry. Pater invited him to tea. Dumbstruck waiters fetched apricot jam, lemon curd, cheese tartlets, asparagus rolls, shortbread fingers, coffee éclairs, tongue sandwiches, ginger biscuits, coconut meringues, shrimp paste, a raspberry sponge, a chocolate blancmange, plum cake, seed cake and a trembling mandarin orange jelly. After all, Pater was known to tip royally. The coachman rose splendidly to the occasion, filling his stomach and his pockets at the same time. Mater swore she saw him snaffle the sugar tongs, wedged between two currant buns.

Dowager ladies began sniffing and asking in ringing tones for the manager. All oblivious, Pater smoked his pipe and chatted away. When Maud's party approached, he was saying, 'You must promise me, as a man of honour, never again to soil your lips with China. Ceylon tea! The flavour, you know, is incomparable. If you could see those hillsides on an April morning!' There and then, Mater decided to marry him.

Beware of what you fall in love with. I have often observed that we are attracted to those characteristics that we ourselves do not possess; so it is not surprising that they quickly lose their fascination. My mother, a shrewd, pragmatic woman, was charmed by this informal, open-handed stranger. Within days she was calling him Ritzy: a nickname that revealed her disdain for detail (she had met him, as you will recall, at the Savoy) as well as her craving for glamour. But as love's feast was succeeded by familiarity's reckoning, she would realise she had married a man who liked nothing better than giving things away.

Society is intolerant of this impulse—only think where it might lead—and so it was fortunate, from my father's point of view, that a ready-made, socially sanctioned outlet was at hand for his weakness. The horses came from Ireland and Arabia, from Cape Town and Calcutta, beautiful, smooth-muscled beasts, nervous as harpstrings. In the hills during the Season, in Colombo all year round, with a gardenia in his buttonhole and his lucky moonstone set in embossed silver on his little finger, Pater proceeded to unburden himself of my inheritance. From time to time he couldn't help winning. On such occasions he was visibly downcast.

My parents rowed fearfully. Or rather Pater dodged about the room, while my mother hurled abuse and whatever she could reach at his maddening smile: cushions, fruit, fruitstands, first editions of Tennyson, eighteenth-century candlesticks, a set of ivory figurines, a silver salver, a game of dominoes, a maidenhair fern. She plucked a canary from its cage and launched it on a stream of curses. It flew into a mirror and died. Mater seized the yellow corpse and dropped it into her teacup, then flung the lot at my father's head.

She was a great smasher, my mother. Crystal was her speciality. My father took pains to ensure that she always had a supply of costly glassware to hand. Did she never realise he was making her his accomplice in his grand scheme of beggaring us? Vases, decanters, a wine-red Venetian swan and five little cygnets: they shivered apart and Mater's yellow eyes glistened. Her lizard tongue slid over her lips. Once, peeping awestruck from behind an armchair while she raged and smashed a Baccarat jug and a dozen ruinously expensive waterglasses, I saw her grow still. She strode over to Pater, thrust him back onto the ottoman and straddled him. I thought she was going to murder him, slit his throat with an icy splinter. Squeezing my knees together, I rocked for joy. She would be mine, all mine! Imagine my disappointment when she moaned and he laughed, and next thing they were sitting side by side, the best of friends.

But what I remember most about my parents is that they weren't there.

Lokugama

I remember the coming of the monsoons, that intoxicating sensation of rules disobeyed as the earth darkened and the wind grew huge and swung around to a different quadrant. I remember the grassy inner courtyard, where I lay on my back through slow afternoons and waited for a dishevelled cloud to move across the sky.

Beyond the servants' quarters, on the far side of the wall that marked the rear boundary of the compound, loomed the jungle. Green birds flew in and out of it. One day I stacked bricks at the foot of the wall and heaved myself level with the parapet overhead. There I gazed into the face of a cobra, who was coiled in a patch of sunlight. I did not repeat the experiment.

My earliest companion was my smooth grey pony, Moonshine. Every morning and evening I would ride him to the trunk road and back, bracketing each day with his comforting presence. There were dogs, too, five or six Great Danes reeking of Lifebuoy soap sprawled about the place like trophies. Pater was fond of the breed; perhaps they reminded him of horses. He used to feed them toast spread with Gentleman's Relish. They never lived very long: those the snakes didn't get, the ticks finished off.

Forty years earlier, when a fire had destroyed part of the house, my grandfather himself had drawn up the plans for its reconstruction. The resulting admixture of styles and periods bore eloquent testimony to the triumph of zeal over talent. The courtyards typical of our ancient homesteads were now imprisoned between verandahs tiled in the tiny mustard-and-rust hexagons of any Civil Service bungalow. Satinwood doors, three inches thick, that had withstood Dutch bullets, opened onto lavatories. A corridor turned an angle and collided with a bricked-up doorway. An ancient fresco on the gateposts, restored by an artist who had toiled on these scenes from the life of the Buddha for three years, jarred with the marble nymphs and shepherd-boys Sir Stanley had shipped out from Genoa to lurk about the compound. Fortunately Miss Dawson and her oar intervened at this juncture and my grandfather's vision of battlements was never translated into stone.

I had been bored in every cranny of the vast, ill-assorted house he had created. The table in the dining room could seat thirty-two; morose with boredom, I once lay under its ebony expanse throughout a nine-course luncheon, rousing myself now and then to inspect the ankles of a cabinet minister's daughter. Boredom inspired me to gouge our family tree into a calamander sideboard and take a single huge bite from every biscuit and cake in the pantry. Spiteful with tedium, I tortured frogs and birds in oleander thickets, only to weary of their suffering no sooner than it had begun.

At last, desperate for distraction, I would make a tour of all the cabinets in the house, studying the fabulous flotsam of Empire: scarlet-lacquered boxes, ivory-stemmed opium pipes, pewter card trays, an ostrich egg mounted on a filigree stand, even a jade-green tiki from New Zealand. Scattered through this priceless collection was a democratic assortment of leather camels from Aden and seashell ashtrays from Brighton. No distinction was made between the relative worth of these articles. A Georgian tankard might hold a gaudy paper fan emblazoned with cherry-blossom in Birmingham, or a seventeenth-century Persian wall tile painted with ruby pomegranates. All served equally to link our old house, dozing in the jungle, with the great electric world of merchants and machinery. I was the centre that drew and held them all—or so I imagined, and would grow light-headed with pride. Years later in London, as I strolled through the perfumed abundance of Mr Selfridge's emporium, I was visited by the same delightful sensation. Such profusion, such variety! A cornucopia of disparate items, lace-trimmed handkerchiefs and rattan parrot cages, collected *en bloc* from every outpost of the globe. My gaze alone lent meaning to its surreal topography, rescuing it from chaos.

If I close my eyes I can still conjure the liniment smell of the medicine chest that stood in Mater's bedroom at Lokugama. It was painted white and locked with a small brass key. My mental taxonomy pairs this faintly sinister cupboard with an angled cabinet that occupied a corner of Pater's study. Objects that had been in our family for generations were heaped on its shelves in disarray. Ornamental daggers dulled by time, palm-leaf scrolls bearing royal signatures, statuettes of the Buddha, tooled betel boxes, gold-inlaid areca nut cutters, perforated chank shells, a jumble of tortoiseshell and silver hair combs: they all gave off a disagreeable odour of dust and neglect.

We had at least a dozen indoor servants and a regiment of gardeners and grooms. I remember the commotion when a servant-girl threw herself down the kitchen well; for a week, all the household water had to be drawn from the estate wells and brought to the big house in a cart, a welcome bump in the monotonous graph of our routine.

From time to time, out of nowhere, the kitchen courtyard would be full of squawking and feathers. An orchestra from the nearest town would show up in a bullock cart. At least, their instruments arrived in the cart; the musicians trudged along beside it. Tuning up was invariably accompanied by complaints about bunions. Later my parents would arrive from Colombo, sweeping in with presents and anywhere from three to thirty friends. I would rush to Mater and grasp her about the knees. Sometimes, not knowing how else to express my longing, I sank my teeth into the folds of her skirt and worried the material. She patted my head. Her tea-brown hands were diamond-shaped and scented with Russian tobacco. A cat's-eye bracelet winked at her wrist.

Pater always bought champagne by the twelve dozen. The parties lasted until dawn. After everyone had gone away again, I used to line up the empty bottles along the verandah and shoot them with my air-rifle. That's what comes to mind when I think of my childhood: a boy in short trousers and long socks, the listless, bright, empty afternoon, birds flying up from leaves at the first explosion.

Lessons

Once a week, with a servant in attendance, our buggy cart carried me into the nearest town, several miles distant, for my elocution class. The cart was drawn by a black ox with silver bells around its neck. A few years ago, as a pert little BOAC stewardess strapped me into my seat on a flight to England, I thought of that ox, with its lustrous eyes and hay breath. From buggies to aeroplanes in the span of a man's life. Is there a phenomenon more emblematic of our century's accelerating trajectory?

My teacher, Miss Vanderstraaten, seemed wholly ancient to me, so she was probably about forty. She lived with her mother in a dark house devoid of oxygen set within the blackened walls of the Dutch fort. Her academy was run from an antimacassared back parlour, where the starched children of local notables were delivered to her to be drilled in enunciation. Its furnishings included an occasional table crowded with photographs in heavy frames, and a row of monogrammed Delft plates on a shelf.

Miss Vanderstraaten was the first Dutch Burgher I knew. The European purity of her race was her great pride, and she guarded it with the zeal that brands all lost causes. One day I arrived a little early for my lesson, and so encountered a Mrs de Jong and her beefy daughter, Phyllis, in the hall. Phyllis and I eyed each other with mutual distaste, while her mother, one of those women who sticks, exchanged a protracted farewell with Miss Vanderstraaten.

As soon as the door closed behind the de Jongs, my teacher's sugared tones altered. 'The cheek of that woman,' she hissed. 'Black as the ace of spades and always passing herself off as one of us. As if everyone doesn't know she was one of the railway Rosarios before she married.' My mystification must have been apparent, because she added impatiently, 'A Portuguese Burgher. A lot of *very common* Sinhalese took Portuguese names when they converted.'

'Pater says there's not a Ceylonese without mongrel blood in his veins,' I replied, gratified that I could keep up my end of the conversation. 'He says we've all got at least one skeleton in the family closet—a Tamil, a Moor, a Swiss mercenary, someone we'd rather keep quiet about.'

'That might well be true of *your* people,' said Miss Vanderstraaten, enunciating with great clarity. Her eyes flicked over me from head to toe. 'Although you look *extremely Sinhalese* to me.'

Whenever I tripped up in my recitations, Miss Vanderstraaten's wooden ferule thudded down on my knuckles. Mosquitoes congregated in the dim space under the table where I swung my legs. 'How now brown cow,' I intoned until the itching grew wild and I had to break off to tear at my shins, while the ruler crashed about my shoulders for fidgeting.

Miss Vanderstraaten often left the room in the middle of a lesson. I assumed this was for reasons to do with her bed-ridden mother, whose voice quavered down the stairs from time to time. Now I am not so sure. My teacher's habitual odour of lavender water and camphor was subtly different when she returned. In Oxford I was once at a party where a bottle of gin slipped from a girl's fingers. The sweetish whiff of those fumes transported me instantly across the years. I found myself once again in that cramped parlour, I could see the swing of Miss Vanderstraaten's coral beads, feel the nubbly texture of her plum-coloured tablecloth beneath my elbows as I leant over my book of exercises.

One day when my teacher had gone to the solace of her flask, I crossed the room to study her photographs. I picked up a studio portrait of a raven-haired goddess on the arm of a stout European gentleman at least twenty years her senior, posed against a painted backdrop of snowy mountain peaks. Peering at the photograph, I had just realised with a jolt that the beauty was my teacher—the mole fastened like a tick under her left eye was unmistakable—when the ruler caught me hard across my arm. Miss Vanderstraaten snatched the photograph from me and clasped it to her pintucked bosom. She brought her face down so close that I could see the grains of powder caught in the downy hair at the corners of her upper lip: 'Don't you ever, *ever* touch my belongings with your *black hands.*'

Behind Miss Vanderstraaten's house lay a harbour that had seen the fleets of Phoenician merchants; beyond it, the Indian Ocean rolled without interruption to the southern ice. But that spacious blue view was invisible from the parlour, where the blind was always pulled down behind elaborate lace curtains.

My formal education in those years was dispensed by a series of tutors, Englishmen whom the years have blurred into a single pinkish young man with an archetypal chin. The product of a minor public school, he instructs me in Ancient Civilisations (which is to say Egyptian, Greek and Roman) and is tormented by prickly heat. We study Geography with the aid of a globe supported by ormolu caryatids. In Arithmetic he allows that fractions are dashed confusing. He hears out my Latin declensions slapping at mosquitoes; he scratches his bites, which grow red and inflamed. He takes tea on the verandah, staring out at the vegetation that crawls about the house looking for a way in; the milk has turned, again. If he's a good sort, he plays the piano and teaches me a bawdy song; we belt out the chorus together. Once a month he goes into town, where he tries to work up an interest in the magistrate's sister, a lady with buck teeth who conducts séances. After a while he packs up the blank notebooks he intended to fill with piquant detail for his *Travels in the East.* A card at Christmas informs us that he has settled into his post of assistant housemaster at his old school. A wistful postscript adds that in England tea simply doesn't taste the same.

But the most enduring lesson of my childhood was provided, against all expectation, by my father. It happened when I was eight years old. Discipline on the estate at Lokugama was strict, although by no means harsh. As was usual in those days, village cattle that strayed onto the estate were shot. Our overseer, who prided himself on his loyalty to our family—and who no doubt relished the power and prestige that came with his post—always flogged any villager caught stealing coconuts. Yet conditions on our estate were far more lenient than on many others, where it was not unknown for landowners to keep labourers in stocks overnight to prevent them deserting during the coconut-picking season.

One morning, not long after daybreak, we heard a commotion in the compound. It happened that Pater was down from Colombo, seeing to the sale of a few acres to pay off a creditor who was proving a bore. He went out onto the verandah, still in his lounging slippers and foulard dressing-gown. There he found our overseer, two watchmen propelling a snivelling youth and, at a respectful distance, a small group of labourers.

The overseer, who was in some distress, told his story haltingly. For some weeks now, coconut thieves had been operating on the estate. Traps had been set, extra watchmen hired. The overseer questioned villagers for miles around and had one or two known troublemakers thrashed for good measure. Still the thefts had continued. Thereupon the overseer announced that he was docking every labourer a tenth of each day's pay until the thieves were caught. This was grossly unfair; but it produced a startling result.

A few of the men, goaded by the loss of income, decided to institute their own watch, an initiative they discussed with no one. On the third night, two dark hours before dawn, they managed to lay hands on one of the thieves. To their amazement he turned out to be the overseer's youngest son, a fifteen-year-old boy who confessed to working in cahoots with some ne'er-do-wells from the town. Being privy to his father's security measures he had passed the information to his accomplices, and thus they had evaded detection. But that night the thieves had been startled by the unexpected presence of the labourers; the thugs from the town had got away, but the boy had panicked and been taken captive.

Seeing Pater, the boy flung himself to the ground and kissed his slippers, pleading for clemency. But it was no use. During the telling of the story, the number of onlookers had swelled until the entire working population of the estate had gathered in our driveway. Needless to say, the overseer and his family were not greatly loved. All the house servants came out onto the verandah. The gardeners and other outdoor workers clustered on the lawn. The watchmen removed the boy's shirt. His hands were tied, and the ends of the rope fastened around the trunk of a convenient flamboyante tree. The overseer himself, tears streaming down his face, handed the lash to my father.

I am certain Pater was as gentle as he could be, under the circumstances. Nevertheless, by the sixth and final stroke, the boy's back was streaked with blood. He was a screamer: he had been at it since the rope first rose in the air. I had an excellent view from the top of the steps. I remember standing very straight and still, and being careful to keep my face from betraying my emotion. For truth to tell, I was in the grip of a queer exaltation. What I was witnessing was the grand and terrible spectacle of justice.

At breakfast, Pater said as much. He had heaped his plate from the dishes on the sideboard. Now he sat staring at his rashers, tomatoes and green chilli omelette. 'Without fear or favour,' he said, at last. Then he left the room, neglecting to close the door. The sound of vomiting reached me from the hall lavatory.

The whole episode left me much to ponder. Like all children I had believed fairness to be synonymous with justice. *It's not fair!*—so runs the eternal cry of childhood. Was it fair that the overseer's son was thrashed while the men who had led him astray went unpunished? I now realised that it was a childish question. It was essential to the harmonious functioning of our little community that the boy paid publicly for his crime in spite of his privileged standing on the estate. Pater had taught me, by his example, that while we might dread what justice requires of us, our fear cannot be allowed to interfere with the benefit to society.

Colonial Cameo

Regi Siriwardena

My father used to make me read aloud
in the evenings from Macaulay or Abbot's Napoleon (he was short,
and Napoleon, his hero; I, his hope for the future.)
My mother, born in a village, had never been taught

that superior tongue. When I was six, we were moving
house; she called at school to take me away.
She spoke to the teacher in Sinhala. I sensed the shock
of the class, hearing the servants' language; in dismay

followed her out, as she said, 'Gihing ennang.'
I was glad it was my last day there. But then the bell
pealed; a gang of boys rushed out, sniggering,
and shouted in chorus, 'Gihing vareng!' as my farewell.

My mother pretended not to hear the insult.
The snobbish little bastards! But how can I blame
them? That day I was deeply ashamed of my mother.
Now, whenever I remember, I am ashamed of my shame.

Gihing ennang: literally, 'I'll go and come', is a customary polite salutation in Sinhala on leaving.

Gihing vareng: literally, 'Go and come', has the impolite imperative used in giving orders to those considered social inferiors.

Stones of Akuratiye Walauva

Lakdasa Wikkramasinha

Recollections of my grandmother
Of a lineage, silted in the mind,
Deranged to the bone—
Desolation of time grown old.
Now out of reach of scrabbling veins
There is that fever of the brain, lucidity
And flight. She recalls
Verses from that departure
And verses chanted at the marriage of the sister
Verses wrongly made—to bring her
Death at eighteen
And the spoiling of chains and rubies
In the carried trove
Before asylum could be reached; always
It was flight
From sudden unsettlement, from poison,
From that ancient house which lost its hours
And the spirit living by the deciduous river. Days
Were weighed with sovereigns proffered to the coming
Of the evil time. Where are the fields and the groves now
Lying by the skeletal village road

Where the axles of those coaches are for ever sunk now
And the straw and the bony steeds. Now

There is only the fallow smell of obliterated fields.
And the twenty-one windows of the house
That looked inwards into poetry, into the courtyard
And the grain, drying in the sun, is perhaps
The last memory
Witnessed, before emptiness pervades
Forgotten time.

Let's Chat in the Moonlight

N.K. Ragunathan

The Right Honorable Sivapragasam had just returned home after addressing a temperance movement meeting that evening. He had appeared before the thousands gathered there and eloquently held forth in chaste Tamil about the evils of liquor, called for its total prohibition, and explained the ways of achieving this objective. He did not fail to weave in references to Gandhism in his oration.

It was about eight p.m. Not only was he hungry, he also felt tired. The flavours of his dinner still tickling his taste buds, he picked up the paper *One People* and came out to the verandah. Relaxing in the armchair in the corner, he began to read the paper under a dazzlingly bright light overhead.

Hardly had he finished a paragraph than he heard people conversing outside the gate. He turned towards them.

There were ten or twelve of them, poor workers by their looks. One of them hesitantly approached him. The others stayed where they were. Sivapragasam rose, took two steps forward and looked intently at the approaching man.

'Oh, is it you, Kantha, what's the news?' he asked.

'We came to see you . . . it's the ban on liquor,' was the diffident reply.

Translated by A.J. Canagaratna

'Oh, is that so? Yes, let's talk about it,' said Sivapragasam.

'Some others have come too. Let me call them,' said Kantha, turning towards the gate to beckon to the others to come in.

Sivapragasam was flustered, but only for a moment. Raising his eyebrows, scratching his head, he came to a snap decision.

'Kantha, don't call them. These are things that no outsider, not even the wife or children should know. These are dangerous times. Who knows what snake is lurking in which anthill? Look. It's a fine moonlit night. That heap of sand too is as white as milk. Come, let's go there and chat,' he said.

Without waiting for a reply, he stepped down from the verandah and began to walk. Kantha followed.

Then, summoning those who stood at the entrance, they moved a short distance away, sat down in a convenient spot and began talking. The visitors were all from depressed castes. Toddy tapping was their livelihood. 'Ban liquor' was the slogan resounding throughout the village. What was to be their fate then?

They too had listened to Sivapragasam's eloquence at the meeting. That was why they had come to discuss with him this subject that hit them in their very bellies.

'We, too, support prohibition. We know that liquor is a great menace. This livelihood doesn't give us much pleasure. The villagers curse us. Even after bribing the excise men we have to hide ourselves whenever they are sighted. Is that all? Every second we risk our lives, when we are aloft the trees that touch the sky . . . think of our state. A very precarious livelihood indeed. However . . .' said one of the young men present.

'Why do you hesitate? Tell us, Thamby,' urged Sivapragasam.

'We need another livelihood.'

Sivapragasam smiled. 'What's so difficult about that? Surely in this wide world, there is no dearth of jobs.'

'Yes, there are many. But are they for us?'

'Why?'

'If we open a tea shop, who will come to drink tea? If we open a grocery store, what's the guarantee they'll come to buy provisions from us? They are not prepared to give us a job even in a hardware store. They think our touch will pollute the hardware items. Let's not go any further. Are you prepared to employ me as a servant in your house? In such a situation . . .' said the young man and looked at Sivapragasam's face. Sivapragasam smiled and said, 'Don't say that, Thamby. That's entirely different. Are these the only openings? You can take to some industry or other.'

The youth was about to retort when a middle-aged man who had kept silent upto now stopped him and said angrily, 'Yes, all these are entirely different matters to you. What do you care? You will say so many things; look at me. I am getting to be fifty years old now, by the time I become skilled in a job, it'll be time enough for Yama to throw his noose round my neck. When I'm learning the new job, will I be paid at all? Till then my wife and children will have to starve. Isn't that your scheme?'

Sivapragasam sensed he was in a tight corner, but trying to brazen it out, he lamely said, 'Don't get angry. Write and put forward your demands to the government. Instead of tapping toddy, tap sweet toddy. Ask the Minister of Industries to put up a sugar factory for you. I'm sure he'll pay heed.'

A new insurgent voice made itself heard now.

'We don't want any of these. Whether alcohol is beneficial or harmful, our caste has begun to make some progress. That doesn't please you at all. That's why you want prohibition. Abolish liquor, snatch our livelihood in the name of Mahatma Gandhi. We will starve to death. Mahatma Gandhi said Untouchability should be abolished, didn't he? If we perish, then Untouchability will end, won't it? You hit two mangoes with one stone. At the same time, let gin and brandy be sold in pharmacies as medicine.'

'No, no, this is a wrong-headed argument. You shouldn't think like that at all.'

'What else are we to think? Using Gandhi's name, you have set out to abolish liquor. Shouldn't you abolish Untouchability first?' the voice retorted.

Sivapragasam was petrified. He hadn't foreseen this outburst. Those who had come got up to leave.

'We'll get going. Ponder well and do the right thing. Liquor should be banned, no doubt. At the same time we should be able to lead a happy life. Act on this basis, and we too will join you in your campaign,' they said as they left.

It didn't take them long to fathom why Sivapragasam had said, when they arrived, 'It's a fine moonlit night outside. Let's chat in the moonlight.'

The Perfection of Giving

Chitra Fernando

In my family, everyone regarded my father's elder sister as a very good and generous woman. I thought so too; in those days I had great respect for the opinions of my elders. Father said, 'Now try to be like Big Auntie, Mahinda. She's an example to us all.' Mother said, 'Big Auntie has more *shradda* than all of us.' Big Auntie never killed anything, not even a mosquito. And once I saw her saving some ants that had fallen into a basin of water; even the most insignificant creature benefited from Big Auntie's attentions. Big Auntie never stole; she had a large house and garden, a lot of jewellery and a small coconut property in Matara. She had everything she wanted. She never lied. She often said she never did, and of course, we all believed her. Big Auntie's conduct was always irreproachable. She was a broad woman, a bit on the short side and very dark; her nose and lips were thick, her skin coarse. She had a large mole on the tip of her nose and another with a hair in it on her chin. At the back of her head was a very small knot of hair. Unless they were her relations Big Auntie kept all men at a safe distance; and they kept her at an equally safe distance. She had never married. As for drinking or smoking—even the thought of her doing either of these things made me want to laugh.

Once Small Auntie caught Siripala and me sharing a cigarette in the back garden and the first thing she said was, 'How disappointed

Big Auntie will be, Mahinda. You two boys are only fifteen, but you're already doing all these bad things!' Then she told Father about it. Father said, 'I will not have smoking, I will not have drinking in this house.' And then he told Big Auntie about it. Big Auntie looked at me in silence. She said, 'Mahinda, there's no need for me to tell you anything. Why should I say anything? Your own actions, your karma will deal with you. Smoke as much as you like. When you get lung cancer, you'll know all about it. This gratification of the senses brings only disease, death and *samsara*. Don't say I didn't warn you!'

Small Auntie, who was listening, nodded vigorously and said, 'I hope you've taken all this in, Mahinda. No need to look the other way! We're advising you for your own good.'

I often wished they were less concerned with my own good but I could say nothing. So I continued to look the other way.

Small Auntie was also unmarried and so had no household of her own. But though she was always singing Big Auntie's praises, she had a strange preference for living in our house. At the time of the cigarette-smoking incident, she was always talking about yet another instance of Big Auntie's generosity and compassion. Big Auntie's good deeds were uncountable so everyone was quite certain that at the very least she could be sure of a place in the Tusitha heaven. But this instance of Big Auntie's generosity was not an alms-giving; it was not a special pooja; it was not donating a loudspeaker to the temple for the relay of the daily sermon so that all the Payagala townsfolk could not but benefit from the loudness of Big Auntie's piety. This was a meritorious deed which was much better. Big Auntie was going to adopt a little girl from Matara! Not, of course, as a daughter. No one expected even Big Auntie to go to such lengths. It was unthinkable that a toddy tapper's child could be Big Auntie's daughter and, therefore, our relative. Big Auntie had too much consideration, too much common sense for that. She was a very practical woman. Kusuma was to come to her house as a servant.

Mala, my young sister, and I were at Big Auntie's house the morning she arrived. Kusuma, her father said, was twelve, but she looked about nine. She was small and skinny and her huge dark eyes half-filled her little face. Lice crawled in her curly black hair. There was a sore on her knee. In the village she had lived in a hut, one of eight children, half-starved, beaten and bullied. In Big Auntie's spacious house there was the comfort of good food, good clothes and a suitable wage deposited in a post office savings account. As Mother said, what more could any sane servant expect! It was, we all felt, the perfect sum total of a servant's happiness.

Father said: 'That girl must have done a lot of merit in her past lives. Just imagine! After living like an animal in that hut to come to a house like Big Sister's!'

'Must be like heaven to her!' was Mother's contribution.

'She's not bad looking, and with all the good food she'll be eating she'll soon fill out. I hope she's not going to be greedy and steal. That must be firmly stopped, right from the start.' Small Auntie did her best to see that everyone observed the Second Precept.

'Don't worry. Big Sister knows how to deal with stealing. She gives her servants so much! For them to misbehave is just raw wickedness, nothing else. As she always says so rightly, "No one can escape the karmic law,"' Father said firmly.

A week later, Big Auntie came to our house with Kusuma. Already we noticed an improvement in her appearance. Her hair was clean and lice-free. When she'd arrived she had been wearing a badly sewn shabby frock. Now she wore a close-fitting white cotton blouse and a pretty-flowered red-and-white cloth. Everyone complimented Big Auntie on the good work. She looked very satisfied.

'I know how to treat my servants. That's why they never leave my house. Salpi has been with me for fifteen years now.' This was perfectly true. Big Auntie did treat her servants well. They enjoyed a fair bit of comfort in her house. The full effect of Big Auntie's generosity to Kusuma appeared in about three months' time. In that time she seemed to have grown taller, fairer and certainly much fuller. Big Auntie often said there was nothing wrong with her appetite. 'She eats as much as Salpi, and doesn't she love sweets!'

Small Auntie said, 'Now don't spoil her. I hope she won't steal. Have you caught her at it ever?'

'No. She's a bit greedy but I give her plenty to eat. So she really has no need to steal.'

'If she steals, will you beat her, Big Auntie?' asked Mala with interest.

'No, Mala. I don't beat anyone. You know that. I'll know what to do. I believe in the karmic law—it's my constant guide.'

I was sometimes puzzled by Big Auntie's way of talking about 'the karmic law.' Of course we all knew about karma. I remembered very well what the monk in the temple used to say: everyone had to take the consequences of his actions in one way or another. If you wanted too many things your desires would make you linger in *samsara;* you would be a prisoner of your desires. That's what the monk said. But I wasn't sure that I understood. Because Big Auntie, who was so wise, seemed to want a lot in return for whatever she did. But in those days I didn't bother too much about such things. I had so many more important things to think about like how to dodge *Pali* classes, or ways and means of smoking without being caught and lectured to.

Big Auntie was pleased with Kusuma. She was intelligent and learnt quickly. She soon learnt to be neat and clean. She was very helpful in the house. She dusted the furniture—all of Big Auntie's carved ebony chairs and couches in the sitting-room. She cleaned all the brass trays, lamps and vases. She was very good at fetching and carrying. Big Auntie wondered whether she should teach Kusuma to read and write. She thought about it a bit. Then she told us that to teach Kusuma how to crochet would be far more useful. Lace table-mats were in great demand and fetched a very good price. Big Auntie was a very practical woman.

After Kusuma's arrival, Mala began to visit Big Auntie almost every day. Kusuma knew very little. So Mala began to feel very wise, though she knew very little herself. I was, of course, the really wise one among the younger lot. In those days, we all thought ourselves very wise. But everyone acknowledged Big Auntie to be the wisest. This was her own opinion as well—naturally.

It seemed to me that Mala liked showing off a bit. She would sit with Kusuma on the veranda steps and tell her all about the wonders of the world. Had Kusuma ever been to Colombo? No. Then she wouldn't ever have been in a lift, would she? No. Had she ever been on an escalator? No. Kusuma's ignorance was so satisfying to Mala! Had she ever been to the zoo? No. What was a zoo? Mala was in her element. She told Kusuma all about the zoo: the tigers, the lions, the bears, the giraffes, the kangaroos, the zebras, the red-backed baboons, the elephants. Kusuma had seen an elephant! Oh! Mala was quite disappointed. Where had Kusuma seen an elephant? In a religious procession. That wasn't so bad. The zoo elephants didn't do anything so ordinary. They balanced on little stools or skipped round the arena, and then all the people laughed and clapped. Kusuma longed to go to Colombo to see all those marvels. She asked Mala a thousand and one questions. Mala brought her picture books. Kusuma had never held a book in her hands before. She turned over the pages carefully. Mala lent her the books for a few days. She couldn't read, of course, but she loved looking at the pictures. Then Big Auntie ordered Mala to take the books away. Kusuma looked at the pictures too often. That very afternoon she was looking at pictures when she should have been polishing the brass. Of course, Big Auntie didn't mind Mala talking to Kusuma. But she must not spoil her. So Mala took the books away. But Kusuma talked and talked about the animals in the zoo.

'The cat is like the tiger,' said Kusuma. 'It's a little tiger,' she added and cuddled the household cat.

'Yes,' I said, 'the cat is a kind of tiger.' And I told her all about cats and tigers and leopards. She listened to me with her great black eyes wide open. She had a great longing for learning, for knowledge, in those days.

The New Year drew closer. We were going to spend the New Year in Colombo with Fair Auntie and all our cousins. Mala asked, 'Can we take Kusuma too?'

Mother looked surprised. It was such a—such a new idea! She didn't know what to say.

'She's never been to Colombo. She's never been in a lift. She's never been on an escalator. And she's never seen a lion or a tiger or a giraffe, or a zebra or a kangaroo or a . . .' Mala had to stop for breath.

'Big Auntie . . . Big Auntie . . .' began Mother.

'I'll ask her,' said Mala.

I decided Mala was a lot wiser than I had thought her. We went to Big Auntie's the next day. Mala carried a dish in her hand.

'What's that?' I asked.

'Urn . . . nothing,' said Mala.

'Nothing! Let me see, let me see.' I lifted the cover of the dish and saw the mangoes inside. I laughed. I understood all.

'There's nothing to laugh about,' she said a bit huffily.

''Ah, Mala, what's that?' Big Auntie eyed the dish with great interest.

'We had a lot of mangoes at home. And I said you liked mangoes. So Mother sent it.'

Big Auntie smiled. She loved getting presents. Mala said tomorrow she would bring her some mangosteens. Tomorrow Banda would come from Kalutara and he always brought mangosteens at this time of the year. As we were leaving, Mala said, 'We're going to Colombo for the New Year. Can Kusuma come too? Please, please, Big Auntie, please let her come. I always feel so bored at Fair Auntie's. Everyone's bigger than me and they don't play with me. Please, Big Auntie.'

Mala's pleading, almost tearful face—the mangoes of today, the mangosteens of tomorrow! How could Big Auntie refuse? She did not refuse. So it was settled. Kusuma would go to Colombo with us. Mala raced to the back of the house. Kusuma was sweeping the garden.

'You're coming with us to Colombo! You're coming with us!' Mala jumped up and down. She was mad with joy.

Kusuma stood where she was, quite still.

'You're coming to Colombo! To Colombo!'

Kusuma stared. Then all at once she understood. She smiled. A little dimple appeared for a moment. I had never seen that dimple before; I never saw it again. Her teeth were very small like gleaming grains of polished rice. And all the stars in the sky tumbled right into her great black eyes.

We were to go to Colombo the following week. The day before we left, Mala and I went over to Big Auntie's with the two bottles of honey that she had wanted. We were to leave for Colombo by the train the next morning. As we stepped on to the veranda we could hear Big Auntie's angry voice from inside.

'Aren't you thoroughly ashamed, girl? You eat a mountain of rice every day. Yet you steal! Greedy, disgusting, filthy girl! *Chee! Chee!*'

Salpi said something but we couldn't hear her very clearly. Thoroughly curious now, we went into the pantry where all the noise was. The moment Big Auntie saw us she said angrily, 'Kusuma is not going to Colombo. She's not going. Don't I give her enough to eat? Do you know what she's been doing? Quietly eating my oil cakes. They were here in this airtight tin. I caught her stealing—caught her red-handed!'

It was true, Kusuma was clutching a cake in her hand. She stared at the floor.

'Half the cakes have been eaten! She's been stuffing herself these last two–three days. The greedy thing! Mala, you've been spoiling her with all this talk of Colombo—all these lions and zebras. She's getting quite disobedient. No Colombo for her, no new cloth and jacket. I give and give and give and is this my reward? This creature steals my cakes! Now what shall I do?'

'You can make some more, Big Auntie,' said Mala timidly. 'Look, we've brought you some really fine honey.' She held out the bottles eagerly.

Big Auntie ignored the bottles. 'Make some more! Oh! It's easy for you to talk! Will you make them for me? This fine young lady hopes to go to Colombo. And I'm to sweat over a fire making more cakes to replace those she's gobbled up! Oh, no! The karmic law is my constant guide. No Colombo, no zebras and kangaroos for this creature here. She'll stay behind and help to make more cakes!'

Kusuma didn't look up, didn't utter a word. The cake held tight in her clenched fist crumbied and the bits fell on the floor. Mala and I left quietly a few minutes later. We could still hear Big Auntie shouting at Kusuma. Tears of disappointment were streaming down Mala's cheeks; yet Kusuma hadn't shed even a single tear.

We saw her in the garden the next morning as we walked past Big Auntie's house to the railway station. Mala tried to speak to her but she ran inside. Mother said, 'Now, Mala, leave her alone. You'll only make Big Auntie angrier. It was very wrong of her to steal. She has to be punished.'

'Big Auntie's always talking about giving but she's not going to give Kusuma even a New Year present. And Kusuma isn't going to get any cakes, biscuits or sweets! Big Auntie is very mean!'

'Enough, Mala, enough. You talk far too much! Kusuma has stolen. She has to be punished. I agree completely with Big Auntie,' said Father severely. Mala pouted. She was glum all the way to Colombo. But when we arrived at Fair Auntie's, we found that our cousin Leela had come down from Kandy and then Mala forgot all about Kusuma.

After the cake incident, Big Auntie kept Kusuma very busy; she was always cleaning, polishing, sweeping or crocheting. There was little time for play.

In the months that followed I too began to be increasingly busy. At the end of the year, I sat for my first public examination and passed. After that, I went to live with Fair Auntie in Colombo and went to the university there.

I still spent my holidays in Payagala—that small dull town! I remember that last long vacation in my final year at the university very well. Big Auntie was just the same—still full of *shradda,* still busy collecting meritorious acts. But there was now about her an air of relaxation! The air of someone who could rest a bit after a hard life of meritorious toil and labour. Big Auntie knew that she was still a long way from nirvana but she was in no special hurry to get there. She had no objection to remaining in *samsara* for a couple of eons or so, and she was determined to spend those eons as comfortably as possible. She had always been a very practical woman.

A week before my vacation ended we were all invited to a big chanting and alms-giving at her house. Big Auntie's chantings and alms-givings were always a great success. Everyone enjoyed themselves. For at least two days before, the house was full of people, bustle, talk, laughter, the smell of food. There was friendliness and good humour everywhere. This chanting and alms-giving was to be a really grand affair. Twenty-five monks had been invited. Kusuma, who was very artistic, was helping with the decoration of the chanting pavilion. I watched her as she worked. She was at this time about nineteen—tall, slender, light-skinned. Her hair was tied back in a big knot at the nape of her neck. Her face was fuller, rounder but her eyes were as huge as ever. She moved quickly, lightly. And then all at once I realized that Kusuma was a very beautiful woman. So I looked at her often. So did Big Auntie, but for very different reasons. During a chanting and alms-giving there were a lot of young men around. Big Auntie took her responsibilities very seriously. Seeing that everyone behaved in the proper way was the most serious of these responsibilities. Kusuma, in particular, was a special responsibility.

Kusuma wasn't even in the least bit frivolous. Salpi was quite old now, and Kusuma was beginning to have an increasingly important place in Big Auntie's household. She valued that importance very much. She moved gracefully but efficiently from kitchen to veranda, supervising, organizing, advising. One young man in particular was very willing to obey her instructions and orders. He always managed to find work where she was likely to be. If Kusuma was in the kitchen, he was there too, eager to cut, chop, sift or pound. If she was in the sitting-room, now cleared for the chanting pavilion, there he was eager to hammer in nails, paste paper, move tables and chairs. Kusuma spoke to him very briskly, sometimes even severely. There was never the slightest softness in her voice or face. But once I saw her look around as if searching for someone. She looked anxious. Then she spotted him among all the other young men and smiled, a quick, tiny smile. Big Auntie did not see that smile, but I did. I asked Mala who he was. 'Ah, that's Piyadasa. He works in Martin Mudalali's shop.' I looked at him again. He was tall and light-skinned and had a kind face. I liked him.

On the night of the chant, the twenty-five monks arrived in all their yellow-robed splendour, and took their places in the white pavilion. Its walls were made of cutwork paper; its canopy a dazzling white cloth. If the monks, who were seated inside the pavilion, looked up, they would have seen that the canopy had little bunches of young coconut leaves hanging from it at intervals. They had been placed there by Kusuma.

We sat around the pavilion on mats and listened to the monks chanting the sacred texts. I looked around me and noticed Piyadasa seated behind Kusuma. They were right at the back of the room. Big Auntie, who was the chief supporter of the temple and donor of everything, sat by herself on a special little mat right in front. She held her clasped hands high, almost at forehead level. She was the picture of perfect *shradda* and we all admired her greatly.

After the Great Chant, I went off to bed. Big Auntie sat listening to the chanting all night, I was told. This was nothing less than we expected. Yet she was the most energetic of us all the next morning. After the morning meal, the chief monk preached a short sermon. I still remember that sermon very well. It was on *danaparamita,* the perfection of giving. We had heard lots of Buddha's rebirth stories on the perfection of giving before: the story of Vessantara, of Siri Sanghabo, and of course the story of the little self-sacrificing hare whose image God Sakra placed high up in the bright moon for all to see. These stories we all knew. But not the story the chief monk told us that morning; this was new to us.

'Good people,' he began, 'of the ten perfections no one perfection is better than another. All these ten equal perfections reside in the Buddha, brighter than a thousand suns. Bearing this in mind, today I shall discourse on the perfection of giving. The perfection of giving shows itself in one key way: in generosity. Giving of alms is generosity. And those who seek the Supreme Goal must ceaselessly practise such generosity. Our good Payagala Hamine and all you others who have participated in this ceremony have shown your devotion to the Doctrine by your liberality and by your presence here. Yet, hard is the way to Enlightenment. Listen to this:

'Once a *bodisathva* was born a king, Manicuda by name. He was compassionate, generous, a giver and donor of all things. Being so, Manicuda wished to perform the great sacrifice, *nirargada.* Various heretics, Brahmins, mendicants, beggars, princes gathered for the great sacrifice. The *bodisathva,* Manicuda, addressed the assembly: "Sirs, I wish to perform the great sacrifice, *nirargada,* at which no doors are closed, no living being killed. Accept with minds full of sympathy these sacrificial gifts." And gifts were given to all those who came to suit their desires. Then, on the twentieth day, at sunrise, Sakra, the lord of all the gods, wishing to test the *bodisathva,* took the form of a terrible demon and arose suddenly from the great sacrificial fire. He cried out, "Fortunate and compassionate lord, deliver me who suffer severe pain by a quick gift of food."

'"Fear not, fear not, dear one, here is as much food as you desire."

'"It is not this kind of food I eat, great king, but the flesh and blood of the newly killed."

'"The kind of food you eat, dear one, cannot be had without injury to others. I abstain from killing. Therefore, eat my flesh and drink my blood to your content. Today, giving away my flesh and blood, I shall place my foot on the head of Mara. Thus will I delight the whole world that yearns for liberation."

'As the *bodisathva* spoke, the whole earth trembled like a boat in the ocean. Gods, demons and deities, hearing of that wonderful gift, were alike spellbound.

'Taking a knife, the *bodisathva* opened a vein in his brow. The demon drank, quenching his thirst. The *bodisathva* filled with delight, next cut off his flesh and gave it to the demon to eat. And he thought, "My wealth has been fruitful, my flesh, my blood, my life has been fruitful."

'As they read his thoughts, the gods assembled in the air cried aloud with joy. Sakra assumed his own form, saying, "Great king, I am Sakra. What do you wish to gain by this deed, by this most strenuous effort?"

'The *bodisathva* replied, "Kausika, by this gift I do not wish to be a Sakra, a Mara or a Brahma or gain sovereignty over the universe or birth in the heavens. But by this deed may I attain perfect Enlightenment to release the unreleased, to console the unconsoled, to liberate the unliberated. This is my wish."

'This, good people is *danaparamita,* the perfection of giving.'

The monk stopped. The sermon was over. For a moment we were all silent. Then people stirred, joints cracked, and Big Auntie with hands clasped high above her head cried out in a voice trembling with *shradda, 'Sadhu! Sadhu! Sadhu!'* All who were there took up the cry. The monks bowed their heads and gazed steadfastly at their fans. After giving the people his blessing, the chief monk, followed by the others, left.

Big Auntie, her face beaming, came up to Mother and Small Auntie.

'This is the most successful chanting and alms-giving I've ever given—everything went off beautifully! Did you notice how Mrs. Welikala was eyeing the pavilion? It's ten times nicer than hers!'

Small Auntie laughed. 'She asked me who had made it and where we had got all that white paper from. I muttered something, but didn't tell.'

Both aunts laughed gleefully, almost like little girls.

Two days later, when I arrived home after a sea-bath, I found Big Auntie, Small Auntie, Mother and Mala all seated on the veranda talking. It seemed a very serious conversation. Big Auntie looked agitated, angry.

'Kusuma wants to marry Piyadasa!' Mala burst out when she saw me.

'Good idea!' I said approvingly.

Big Auntie stared at me as if I had suddenly turned into a serpent. 'Kusuma, marry Piyadasa?' she exploded.

'What's wrong with that?' I really couldn't see what all the fuss was about.

'That's what I thought too,' said Mala boldly. Mala had just got engaged to our second cousin, Nihal, and felt that everyone should be encouraged to marry as quickly as possible.

We both looked at Big Auntie. In spite of being a final year student at the university, I felt a bit afraid. Big Auntie's chest heaved, her lips trembled, her eyes seemed to shoot sparks of fire.

'The selfishness—the ingratitude of—everybody. After all I've—after all I've done . . .'

Small Auntie said, 'You people—you young people these days don't think of anything serious. Only your own selfish desires matter. Do you ever think of your duty?' She spoke very severely.

'Lust, lust, lust, they're all filled with lust. When I think of what I've done for that girl! She was like a wild animal when she came to me. Covered with sores and lice! I cleaned her, fed her, clothed her, civilized her . . . Piyadasa came to me and said he wanted to marry her . . . said she was willing. I couldn't believe it . . . to do this thing behind my back!'

Big Auntie's chest began to heave again.

I said, 'Now, Big Auntie, don't be angry with me, but they haven't done anything behind your back. Piyadasa came and asked you, didn't he? They haven't run away or anything. As Freud says. . . .'

'Mahinda, what do you know about these things! After you went to that university, your head is stuffed full of useless foreign ideas. Who is this Freud, ah? Who is this Marx you're now always trying to talk about? What do these foreigners know of our ancient Sinhalese culture? I've given Kusuma so much! I've been a mother to her. Is it too much to ask for a little gratitude in return!'

'It's her duty to stay with Auntie. Big Auntie didn't bring her up for nothing!' said Mother.

'But she says Piyadasa and she will live close to Big Auntie. She says she'll continue to work for Big Auntie,' argued Mala.

'I know what those promises are worth!' Big Auntie sounded very sour.

'Will Kusuma have to live with Big Auntie forever then?' asked Mala.

'Why not?' snapped Small Auntie. 'Much better for her to stay with Big Auntie than go off with that Piyadasa and have ten children!'

"I'm not selfish. I'll arrange a marriage for Kusuma to the right person at the right time. But she can't marry Piyadasa.' Big Auntie was very firm about that.

'Arrange a marriage for her! No wonder she's so selfish. You've spoilt her thoroughly, Sister,' said Small Auntie.

"I'm going to ask Martin Mudalali to send Piyadasa away to his brother's shop in Galle. I've done a lot for Martin Mudalali. That man has a lot of respect for me.'

'What if Kusuma runs away?' I asked.

'She'll never do that,' said Mala. 'She's very loyal to Big Auntie.'

'Loyal! Fine loyalty!' snapped Big Auntie.

Kusuma did not run away. She continued to live in Big Auntie's household exactly as before. After a few months, Big Auntie forgot all about the Piyadasa incident. He eventually married a girl in Galle and, as far as we knew, never even visited Payagala again. Kusuma, of course, never married. I never heard Big Auntie talk about arranging a marriage for her again. But she gave over the running of the house entirely to Kusuma. This left her free to study Higher Philosophy. It was Kusuma who arranged for the sale of all garden produce like coconuts and yams. It was Kusuma who bought all the necessities for the household. It was Kusuma who organized all the chanting ceremonies and the alms-givings. She became almost as keen as Big Auntie in the performance of such duties. They seemed to give her an ever-increasing pleasure. She talked a lot about how the accumulation of merit would give a person a better life in the future. She often said that she must have been very wicked in a past life and was determined to be better in this, her present one. Big Auntie was very pleased with her. Small Auntie began to be almost jealous.

I was in Payagala for a few weeks before leaving to study further at London University. 'Mahinda,' said Small Auntie, 'I think Big Auntie gives Kusuma too much to do in the house. That woman is more the mistress of the house than Big Auntie herself. You should listen to her talking! I don't like the way she talks to me! She's turned into a very bossy woman. But Big Auntie listens to everything she says and does everything the way she wants it done. I don't like it.'

It was true that Kusuma occupied a very special place in Big Auntie's household. It was true that she spoke to us all as if she were our equal. There was nothing menial about Kusuma. But I didn't see why she should be menial. And I told Small Auntie so.

'You understand nothing, Mahinda, for all your book learning,' said Small Auntie. She sounded a bit annoyed. But since this is what everybody at home had always been telling me for a long time, I took no notice. I just smiled as I now always did, when they talked to me like that.

It was a very long time before I returned home again. Many things had happened during my absence. Big Auntie had a stroke which paralyzed both her legs. She now used a wheelchair. After Small Auntie's death of a heart attack, Mother had sold our house and gone to live with Mala in Kandy. Mala urged me to go and see Big Auntie, who still lived in Payagala. 'Kusuma looks after her very well—Big Auntie is so lucky to have her—but she's very lonely. I haven't been to Payagala for over a year. I'm tied to the house with all these children.'

'Yes, yes, go, Mahinda,' said Mother. 'I went to see her last year when I was in Colombo, but you know how difficult travelling is these days. The trains are jam-packed. And I'm too old to knock about now. Go, Mahinda, she'll be so happy to see you. She's very fond of you.'

Big Auntie's house was still the same. The garden looked flourishing. The coconut trees were loaded with nuts, the mango trees with fruit. The orchids just beside the veranda were all blooming. Big Auntie was in her wheelchair on the veranda. She saw me, tried to speak, but couldn't. Her face quivered. I went up to her and took her hand. She held it tightly. Her hair was completely white, the skin of her neck and arms hung down in loose folds. In the years I'd been away, she had shrunk into an old, old woman.

'I thought I'd never see you again, *putha,*' she said at last. Her voice was all quavery. 'When did you return?'

'About three weeks ago. Payagala is exactly the same.' We talked for a bit. I gave her news of Mother and Mala. She listened. There was a pause. I said, 'So, tell me what you've been doing all these years, Big Auntie.'

She brightened up. She told me she'd bought half an acre of land next to the temple grounds and had built a new preaching hall there. Kusuma had paid for the whitewashing with the money she earned from crocheting table-mats and pillow lace.

'She's a good girl—doesn't spend her money on clothes and powder like some women. Her one aim in life is to do meritorious acts.'

'Because she wants to be born a rich woman in her next life?' I asked, smiling.

'What's wrong with that? We all want to better ourselves, don't we?'

I couldn't argue with that. 'Well, what other good deeds has Kusuma done?' I asked, mainly to soothe Big Auntie, who was now looking troubled again.

She said that two years ago Kusuma had donated a magnificent brass lamp to the temple. Big Auntie had wanted to contribute something towards it but Kusuma had refused very firmly. The merit from this act had to be hers and hers alone; she didn't want to share it with anyone.

'You must be very proud of all the good things Kusuma's been doing. You brought her up, so the credit is all yours.'

'Yes,' she said quietly. She looked down at her hands. I felt something was wrong.

'Aren't you happy with Kusuma, Big Auntie?'

'Yes, yes, I am, Mahinda. Very happy. It's a great joy for me to see how good she is.' There was a pause. 'Kusuma—Kusuma is building a new shrine-room.'

'Kusuma building a shrine-room! Kusuma! But where does she get the money from?' I asked, quite thunderstruck.

'She gets some money from the sale of her table-mats and pillow lace. Then there's the coconut money.'

'But the coconuts belong to you?'

'I asked her to use—to use the money,' said Big Auntie uncomfortably.

We were silent. I looked around. I could see into the sitting-room from where I was. It seemed strangely bare. Something was missing. Suddenly it came to me. Big Auntie's antique ebony furniture!

'What has happened to your ebony furniture?'

Big Auntie looked even more uncomfortable. 'I asked Kusuma to sell it—to sell it for—for the shrine-room.'

'But, Big Auntie, that—that furniture—you loved that furniture! You said you'd never sell it.' In fact, she had always said that the furniture was for me because it had belonged to my grandfather. I wondered whether she remembered. I looked at her. She was twisting her hands nervously. 'Kusuma has been like a daughter to me. She does everything for me.'

'Where is Kusuma?'

'She's at the temple. She goes every day to see how the building is going on. Don't say anything—don't scold her, Mahinda. She's like my daughter. Her one desire in life is to build that shrine-room.'

'But at your expense! Did you really want to sell that furniture?'

Big Auntie began to weep. 'That furniture was my father's. I wanted you to have it.'

I had never seen Big Auntie weep before. Great rivers of tears streamed down her shrunken cheeks. I noticed she wasn't wearing her ruby earrings. I didn't need to ask what had happened to them. I supposed all Big Auntie's jewellery would be gradually sold to pay for the shrine-room and other meritorious acts.

'I don't want the furniture. I live in a tiny two-roomed flat in London, the size of your sitting-room. What could I do with ebony furniture there?'

'I don't want to cling to my possessions. But that ebony furniture was my father's. I didn't want to sell it.'

'Never mind, never mind, Big Auntie. Building a shrine-room is a very good thing, a very meritorious act.' It seemed strange to be talking like that. But I couldn't really console Big Auntie, though she stopped weeping.

It was almost lunch-time when Kusuma returned from the temple. She was not at all pleased to see me. I could see that. She was now a middle-aged woman—broad, strong, determined, hard. Lunch was served almost immediately. I wheeled Big Auntie's chair to the dining-table. Big Auntie had loved good food in the old days. I looked at the rice, the coconut *sambol* and the bit of dried fish on the table. Kusuma stared at me defiantly, as if daring me to criticize.

I was silent. Big Auntie said, 'If only I'd known you were coming, *putha*! I'd somehow have got some seer fish and prawns for you. You used to like them so much!'

'Now I like dried fish better than anything else,' I said, giving her a bright, false smile.

It was a very silent meal. I wondered whether I should tell Mother and Mala about Big Auntie's plight. But what good would it do? It was impossible for Big Auntie to live in Kandy. There was no room for her in Mala's house. And who would look after her? I just could not see Kusuma living in Mala's household.

As Kusuma was clearing away the dishes and plates I said, 'So, Kusuma, I hear you're building a shrine-room. It must be a very expensive business.'

Big Auntie looked at me pleadingly, fearfully.

Kusuma glared at me. 'I have found the money for it. It's a very meritorious deed. No one should interfere with such a good thing.'

'When will it be completed?'

'The building will be complete in about a month's time. But I need more money for the image and the wall-paintings inside. My name will be inscribed outside because I am the donor,' she said smiling, proudly, for the first time. 'Would you like to donate something, Mahinda Mahattaya?' she asked.

I was surprised. Big Auntie looked at me appealingly. I pulled out my purse and gave her fifty rupees. She took it eagerly and put the notes into her purse.

I wheeled Big Auntie back to the veranda. 'Tell me about London, *putha*. Is it a big city? England must be a very advanced country, no? Who cooks for you?'

She laughed when I told her that I cooked for myself.

'Fine meals you must be cooking! No wonder you look so thin. So why don't you get yourself a wife? Then she can cook for you.'

I ignored these suggestions and got up saying I had to leave. Her face changed. '*Arre, putha*, what's the hurry? Stay the night, stay the night.'

I said I couldn't. I had to be in Colombo for a lecture at the university that evening. And I'd promised Mother to be in Kandy the next day.

Big Auntie gave a little sigh. 'When shall I see you again, *putha*? Next time you come, I'll be dead.'

'Don't talk like that! Next time I see you, you'll be on your feet and running this house yourself!' But neither of us believed in that extravagant lie even for a second.

She tried to smile, then said, 'No, I'll die in this wheelchair. It's my karma. But I'm very lucky to have Kusuma—she's like my own daughter. It's my karma,' she repeated.

I said goodbye. She clung to my hand and kissed it. 'Come and see me again before you leave, *putha, Tun sarane Pihitai*!' And she said once again, 'It's my karma.' A commonplace, almost meaningless phrase mouthed by so many. And yet, as I looked back for one last wave, there seemed to be a truth in it—a truth reflected in that heavy, sullen woman standing in the doorway, so like the other feebly waving a loose-skinned hand.

A House Divided

(From *Island of a Thousand Mirrors*)

Nayomi Munaweera

This piece combines the theme of family and ethnic tension and acts as a great primer for those unfamiliar with the roots of ethnic tension and the subsequent civil war in Sri Lanka. It is a sumptuous read, a breathlessly paced narrative that covers about a twenty-year span in a few pages, while never losing sight of its characters, and also bringing Sri Lanka's landscape vividly to life.

It is 1948 and the last British ships slip away from the island of Ceylon, laboring and groaning under the weight of purloined treasure.

Behind the retreating English on the new nation's flag is poised a stylized lion, all curving flank and ornate muscle, a long, cruel sword gripped in its front paw. It is the ancient symbol of the Sinhala who believe that they are descended from the lovemaking between an exiled Indian princess and a large jungle cat. A green stripe represents that small and much-tossed Muslim population. An orange stripe represents the larger Tamil minority.

But in the decades that are coming, race riots and discrimination will render the orange stripe inadequate. It will be replaced by a new flag. On its face, a snarling tiger, all bared fang and bristling whisker. If the idea of militancy is not conveyed strongly enough, dagger clawed paws burst forth while crossed rifles rear over the cat's head.

A rifle-toting tiger. A sword-gripping lion. This is a war that will be waged between related beasts.

Blissfully unaware of the departing English, my seven-year-old father-to-be, Nishan, cavorts on beaches he does not know are pristine. He dives into an ocean unpolluted by the gasoline-powered tourist boats of the future.

In the months before the thunderous monsoon, the ocean tugs at his toes, wraps sinuous limbs about his own and pulls him into its embrace, out until it is deep enough to dive, head first, feet overhead, inverted and submerged. Eyes open against stinging salt, he sees coral like a crowded, crumbling city, busy with variously marked, spotted, dotted, striped, lit, pompous and playful sea creatures. Now and then, he encounters the curious, swiveling eye of a small red octopus emerging from secret passageways. Approached recklessly, the octopus blanches a pure white and with an inky ejaculation, torpedoes away. So he learns to approach slowly, in rhythm with the gently rolling water, until the creature coming to know this stick-limbed biped is lulled enough to allow his quiet presence.

The sun drops fast, blazing momentarily crimson on the horizon. Father and son wander home. At the front door, his mother waits, a lantern in her hand. In her other hand, she grips the shoulder of Nishan's twin sister, Mala, who by dint of her girlhood is not allowed on beach wanderings. Beatrice Muriel ignores her husband. She is angry that they have spent the day with the fisherfolk, listening to fisher songs, picking up fisher habits, coming home covered in beach sand. It is too dark to bathe, she scolds. Cold well water after the sun has set will result in sneezing and a runny nose. 'Running here and there, like a savage. One day I will find you up a coconut tree with the toddy tappers! That's the day I will skin you alive. Wait and see if I don't.'

As she scolds, she pulls the bones out of fried fish with deft fingers, mixes it with red rice and coconut sambol into balls, which she pops into the mouths of her children; a bird feeding its chicks. Her monologue ceases only when the plate is empty.

Afterwards, he goes to sleep on the straw mat next to Mala, sea sand frosting his limbs and gritty in his hair and eyelashes, the dark shapes of his parents on either side of them, their breathing soothing him into sleep.

His mother, Beatrice Muriel, comes from a prominent Southern family peopled with Vincents, Victorias, Annie-Henriettas, Elizabeths and Herberts in tribute to the formerly ruling race. Now, after marriage to the Hikkaduwa ayurvedic doctor, she is the village schoolteacher. In the small classroom, open to the sea breezes, she teaches the children to read, leads them as they chant loudly an English menagerie, 'Q IS FOR QUAIL! R IS FOR ROBIN! S IS FOR ESQUIRREL!' In the sultry afternoons, she teaches them to work numbers so that they will not be cheated when the Colombo buyers come for fish.

For Beatrice Muriel, marriage has not been the pleasant idyll she had been brought up to expect. In an astonishingly short time, the pleasant softness of her body melts away, corroded by relentless sun, salt air and marital dissatisfaction. Overnight she becomes gaunt, her nostrils pinched, her gaze sharp as knives. She develops the schoolteacher's uncanny ability to detect and subdue childish mischief. Nishan must watch his friends being sent to squat at the back of the schoolroom, arms crossed to grasp opposite ears. As they walk home together, these boys say, 'Aiyo, she has two eyes in the back of her head.' And only filial devotion keeps him from replying, 'Machang, you should see her at home.'

Because marital disappointment has bred maternal ambition, Beatrice Muriel dreams of the day her son will enter university and reverse the legacy of a father who is content in day-dreams and beach wanderings. Daily, she squats over the open flame, her sari pulled up between her knees, and cooks. Into the fish curry, she stirs coconut milk and heady perseverance. Into the sambol, she mixes red onion, green chili and expectation. Under her breath she mutters invocations to protect her son from as-vaha, the poisonous darts of envy thrown by the gaze of those with less illustrious sons.

The days of ocean diving, octopus communing, sand-covered sleep become rare. He spends all his time over books that she has gathered. Head bent over the small pool of light that falls from the lantern, he struggles to memorize English poems and mathematical equations, trace winding Sinhala hieroglyphs. His mother sits by him, her fingers quick with needle and thread, she will not go to sleep until he has finished.

While her future husband struggles over his books, northwards in the smoky realms of Colombo, that humid and pulsating capital city, in the private ward of an exclusive nursing home, my mother-to-be, Visaka Sujatha Ranasinghe, is busy getting herself born.

Having accomplished this feat with no more than the usual traumas, she grows up in a large white house, a short distance but a world away from the Wellawatte vegetable market. Separated from the ocean only by the railroad tracks, the house is ruled by Visaka's father, the Judge, who Oxford-returned, insists upon a painful formalism learned in undergraduate days when he was made to feel the unbearable shame of brownness. In tribute to those frigid days, ankles are crossed, accents carefully monitored, pinkie fingers trained to point away from teacups. The family eats puddings and soups, beefsteaks and muttonchops, boiled potatoes, orange and crimson-tinted sandwiches. They take tea at five, with sugar and milk, choose pastries off a multilayered silver tray. In December, there is Christmas cake, fruitcake, cheesecake. The dressmaker comes monthly. Visaka is chauffeured to school in her father's car and picked up at the gate after. On Tuesdays, she has elocution lessons and on Fridays she practices Bach and Beethoven for two hours on the baby grand piano.

Yet the heart of the house is an interior courtyard, built in the days of the Portuguese who liked to keep their women sequestered in these interior gardens, full of spilling foliage, bird call and monkey chatter. Annoyed by this exuberance and lack of order, the Judge sends the gardener to rip and uproot. But days after these attacks, the mutilated branches send forth vines to once again wind into the embrace of the wrought iron balcony. Birds return to once again build nests in the outstretched arms of the trees. The queen of this domain, an enormous trailing jasmine, impervious to pruning, spreads a fragrant carpet of white. When the sea breeze blows, a snowy flurry of flowers sweeps into the house so that Visaka's earliest and most tender memory is the combined scent of jasmine and sea salt.

It is into this pulsing, green space that she escapes after the boiled beef and vegetables. It is here she plays her childhood games, befriended at a distance by the monkeys, the birds, the geckos and squirrels. She says of her variously prim and jungled childhood, 'Like growing up in a garden of Eden in the middle of cold-hearted England.'

A photograph from this time witnesses the whole family suited and saried on the front lawn, Colombo heat perceptible only in the snaking tendrils that cling to the women's cheeks and necks. Our mother is flanked by her two much older sisters, each beautiful in an entirely different way. One, round faced and dark like a plump fig, succulent. The other, tall, slim and elegant, calling to mind something lunar.

Our mother, a sapling next to these hothouse beauties, poses on the edge of an ebony chair. A serious, spectacled schoolgirl in long braids and a stiff ironed uniform, she is caught in a blur as if about to run off. Our formidable grandmother, Sylvia Sunethra, wears a sari in the old Victorian way, all ruffled sleeves, starch and ramrod straight posture, her hand on the girl's shoulder holding her down. Behind them all, our handsome Uncle Ananda, debonair in a three-piece suit. In the chair sits the Judge, who despite his profound baldness looks too young to be the father of these grown children.

The photograph gives no forewarning. There is no cloud evident on the faces of pretty aunties and handsome uncle. Yet it captures the end of my mother's childhood, because if we enter with the certainty of history into the secret, red passageways leading to my grandfather's heart, we see lurking within his tissue-thin arteries, an amoeba-shaped blood clot which will lead him to sit up in bed six months later, clutching at his chest. He will not die of this first stroke, but some years later under the assault of successive ones and in the midst of his house-building obsession.

It is around the time of this photograph that our mother remembers the coming of Alice. Male relatives from the Judge's ancestral village squat on the verandah waiting for the Judge. With them, a woman, face obscured behind her sari pallu. Our mother remembers the outline of a large, fair-skinned face, round as the full moon, long, she-deer eyelashes. And over the left shoulder, stretching the cheap cloth of the sari blouse, an enormous, quivering hump. 'This is Alice Nona,' the men say and meticulously re-trace the capillaries of familial blood that make her 'our people.'

She is unmarried for obvious reasons. She has been living with her aged parents, taking care of them. But in the last year there has been trouble. The men are vague. They will not specify. The Judge thunders, 'What is this nonsense? You have brought a fallen, hunchback woman to my house?'

The men shift on their haunches. One says, 'She can cook and also clean . . . only take her as a servant.'

The woman is silent, her eyes pulled earthward. But there must have been some mute appeal implicit in the twisting of her large knuckled hands because now, Sylvia Sunethra, twelve years younger than her husband, but already becoming the iron-handed matriarch of her later years, says, 'I will take her.'

The Judge is aghast. But there is something in his wife's eye that threatens unknown violence if he does not comply. So as the men breathe sighs of relief, he says only, 'Alright. She can stay and join the staff. But one problem and I will send her packing.'

The men leave, and Alice is installed somewhere between family member and servant. She sleeps on a mat outside Sylvia Sunethra's bedroom. For three months, her face is a study in impassivity, she moves as if in a sleepwalk, and not even the crashing of a dish just behind her causes the slightest of reactions. Finally Sylvia Sunethra, annoyed beyond endurance, says, 'O enough with this too long face all the time. Tell them to bring the child.'

The very next week, a wizened woman arrives at the gate. From within her sari folds, comes a hungry, kittenish mewing and now Alice goes about her day, laughing and with a baby clinging to her breast. At night, mother and infant fall asleep, rolled together outside Sylvia Sunethra's door, and even the Judge, afraid of the venom of his wife's tongue, dares not question the origins of this baby that Sylvia Sunethra has decided to shelter along with its wayward mother.

It is in this way that we who are not yet born acquire Alice, that beloved Quasimodo of our childhoods, and also her son, Kasun.

Under his mother's eagle eye, Nishan develops the aura of nascent success, evident in his newly acquired eyeglasses and paid for by the loss of cricket games, bicycle rides and beach wanderings.

Yet even as she is proud of her son, a pointed thorn pierces the tenderest areas of Beatrice Muriel's heart. Neither her prayers nor the village women's many potions have made the slightest difference. Mala, the boy's twin and shadow, remains stubbornly dark.

A slip of a girl, she is quiet in company, silent in her mother's presence. Next to her, Beatrice Muriel grows in bulk, the solid folds of her sari firmly anchoring each of them, the wispy female child, the dreamy doctor, the scholarly boy, to earth.

Witness, however, a daily transformation. At noon, Beatrice Muriel returns from the schoolroom for lunch and overcome by the heavy afternoon air, withdraws into her bedroom for exactly two hours. In these hours, a different Mala awakens. Assured of Beatrice Muriel's immobility by the snores erupting from the bedroom, she is in the street lightning fast, playing cricket with the boys, making sure that her voice does not join their cries. Someone screams, 'Look out! There behind you! The ball!' and Nishan knows that Mala is bowling. He goes to the window, sees her poised like the Nataraj, arm over knee, a ferocious whirlwind of limbs and the ball goes whizzing past heads.

In these magic hours, Mala climbs high onto forked branches and throws down fruit to the other children too afraid to follow her ascent. She cavorts on the beach. Stands on her hands, her dress inverted, a billowing tent, white shorts and black legs exposed.

When Beatrice Muriel awakes, there are twin furrowed brows, twin pencils working in tandem, four legs swinging under the table where Kalu Balla scratches fleas in his sleep. When the villagers come to complain, 'That daughter of yours has been in our avocado tree. Stealing all the ripest!' Beatrice Muriel points to Mala, innocent and scholarly at the table, and bellows, 'What nonsense! Look at my girl, doing her work. You mad fellows think you can come and insult us. Better you get out of my house before I call Seeni Banda.' And the poor man, knowing Seeni Banda the family retainer and his ancient rifle, scurries off the porch, cursing the uppity nature of high-caste neighbors and their spoilt children.

As they walk to school, Nishan's friends will say, 'Aday Machang. That sister of yours can bowl like a goddamn champion. We should have her on the school team, even Ariyasinghe doesn't have an arm like hers.' And he will feel the stings of pride and resentment at this sister who exists for exactly two hours of each day.

Seeni Banda spends his mornings at the tea shop sucking steaming, sugary milk tea from the saucer. At the Doctor's house, he gives the children lessons in tea shop politics, 'We Sinhala are Aryans and the Tamils are Dravidians. This island is ours, given to us from the Buddha's own hand long, long before they came.'

Mala says, 'But Seeni Banda, our teacher says the Tamils have been here just as long as we have. She says that no one really knows who came first.'

He flaps a loose-fingered hand at her, continues in the mode of the local pundits, 'Tamil buggers, always crying that they are a minority, so small and helpless, but look! Just over our heads, hovering like a huge foot waiting to trample us, south India, full of Tamils. For the Sinhala, there is only this small island. If we let them, they will force us bit by bit into the sea. Swimming for our lives.'

The children listen, their eyes big. They had not realized that the Tamil children they go to school with harbored such insidious and watery intentions.

In the dry season of the year 1958, Nishan is a gawky teenager, black spectacles slipping down the sweat of his nose, the weight of large textbooks curving his spine. The tea shop rumors have turned into the smoky scent of sulfur drifting down from Colombo. Whispers flutter like insects drawn to the lamp light, 'They are killing Tamils in Colombo.' From the opaque darkness, an answer, 'This is a Buddhist country. Such things cannot happen here.'

He is rendered immune to these rumblings by the drama of his own adolescence. Each night, a Beatrice Muriel–faced vulture gnaws at his liver, his failed examination papers clutched in her curved talons. He wakes sodden in a chilling sweat. His exams are up-coming and wrapped up in a fog of equations, memorized test papers and complicated mathematical proofs, he is not consciously aware of the fear on people's faces, the way in which his parents or Seeni Banda greet strangers with a new suspicion, his mother's hoarding of red rice under the kitchen floorboards.

At dawn, he and Mala walk along the silver ocean towards the railway station. It is quiet, until the terminal. Then schoolboys and girls, giddy in this brief interlude between the authority of parents and that of teachers, chatter like mynahs. There is a girl in this crowd that he likes. She is a few inches taller than him so that the other schoolboys tease him mercilessly. But there is invitation in the girl's eyes, a certain glance he is sure she reserves for him that allows him to endure the ribbing and gives him thrills of pleasure when she looks his way.

In the darkened carriage, boys drape indolent arms around each other's shoulders, talk of cricket scores and slide their eyes surreptitiously towards chattering girls. The forward motion of the train rocks them into delicious, early morning languor.

All this is smashed open with an ear-shattering shriek of metal, the train thrown against some hard, resisting object. Boys and girls are flung like bits of paper from an enormous and uncaring hand, bright blood blooming on white uniforms and bare-chested, saronged, machete-armed men enter the carriage, stalk heavy-footed down the aisle. School kids cower, arms over heads. The men breathe words flaming of coconut toddy, 'Tamil devils! Get up! Stand up! Stand up!'

'Look at this one.' A man grasps Radhini, object of Nishan's ardor, by the upper arm, above the elbow. She is jerked upwards like a fish plucked out of water by a cormorant's skewering beak.

A machete tip traces her upper arm where uniform gives way to smooth flesh. Cold metal on skin. A tear trembles on her lash, catching light in that dark interior.

'Tamil? No?'

Shamefaced schoolboys turn their faces. The odor of panicked sweat settles like a cloud. My father cannot avert his eyes, Mala claws his arm. 'Do something,' her fingers beg, but though his heart drums staccato, his feet remain leaden.

'Tamil? No pottu? Trying to get our boys to think you're a Sinhala girl?'

'Maybe we should make a pottu for you, no? In the middle of the forehead. Nice big one. Red I think.'

Swift as a striking cobra, a streak of red across the girl's curved forehead. The sudden and unmistakable smell of urine. The front of her white uniform yellowed, spreading.

From the back of the carriage, a loud voice. It is a teacher of the fourth standard, a tiny fury in a pink sari and thick glasses. 'Leave them alone! They're just school kids.' She pushes past hefty shoulders, wraps her arms around the girl. 'This girl has done nothing. Let her be.'

'She's Tamil. That's enough. They take our land, our jobs. If we let them they will take the whole country.'

Miss Abeyrathna, sari rustling like angel wings, says, 'Look at her! She's a Sinhala girl. Only a little dark. You goondas can't even tell the difference!'

A rustling in the mob. A collective pushing forward and from the back, a single, toddy slurred voice, 'If she's Sinhala, prove it.'

Miss Abeyrathna pushes Radhini's shoulder. 'Girl. Recite something . . . the ithipiso gatha, say it.'

In a shivering, breaking voice Radhini recites the Buddhist verses preaching unattachment, impermanence, the inevitability of death.

For the rest of his life, the cadence of this particular verse will cause my father's bile to rise. It will conjure grasping fingers of guilt that wrap about his throat and make him remember Radhini in that dark compartment, the Tamil-inflected undercurrents of her accent hidden by her years in Buddhist schools, the front of her uniform dripping yellow with fear and shame.

She was saved, he will tell us, by the courage of that teacher. The mob, deterred by her bravery, left then. But there is something that lingers in his eye when he tells this story that makes us know the weight of it upon his heart.

There is, of course, another child in this tale, a Tamil child growing up in the North where grasping fingers of land reach into the frothing ocean. While Radhini recites terrified verses, he is four years old. At the age of four, the course of any life lies uncharted; there are perhaps no fangs in this mouth, no incipient claws in evidence. He is perhaps too young to remember these days of lootings, when houses were surrounded and set aflame with children crying inside them. He is perhaps too young to have this memory, but he claims to remember these things. Most specifically, he remembers an old woman beset by Sinhala youths who beat her with sticks and then laughing as if at a fair or some other amusement, set her alight so that she squawks and screams, her sari flapping like the wings of a great flaming bird. Perhaps he is too young to remember, but these are the images that filter into his dreams. In the decades to come, when he has become The Leader with blood-drenched claws and ripping fangs, a tiger-striped army ready to die at his command, these are the images he will offer when asked why.

Weakened by his first stroke, his ramrod straight walk broken by an insistent limp, the mutton soup dripping disobediently out of the corner of his mouth and onto his starched white shirt front, the Judge dreams of demolishing his meandering mansion. In its place, he wishes to install a simple two-story house.

An army of sarong-clad men is moved in to trample the carefully laid flowerbeds, spit betel like blood on the floors and abandon tools everywhere. In daylight, the ground shakes incessantly and the family must shout to make themselves heard. At night, they are kept awake by the laughter of the men who squat in a circle smoking beedis like buzzing red fireflies and drinking arrack before falling asleep in the room erected for this purpose.

As her husband battles contractors and shrieks at laborers, Sylvia Sunethra negotiates marriages for her children, spreading photographs and astrological charts of Colombo's most eligible sons and daughters on the dining table.

A single dream emerges: to build a house and fill it chock-full of dutiful children, illustrious sons and daughters-in-law, an army of projected grandchildren stretching into the distant future.

Trying to ignore the chaos around her, Visaka does her schoolwork out of dusty textbooks. She works with ears blocked against the drilling and sawing by puffs of cotton wool. Despite these distractions, she is a good student, bringing home distinctions and prizes, managing by intense effort to leave the house immaculately uniformed. Secretly, she wishes to follow in the steps of her brother Ananda and become that most respected and rare of persons, a doctor.

In the midst of these chaotic months, the unfolding of catastrophe. The Judge, lying in bed next to his wife, contorts like a marketplace marionette, utters a sound like a water pipe bursting and gasps his last. The family has no time to mourn because immediately after the funeral, it is revealed that in order to fund his house-building obsession, he has emptied all the accounts, sold all the lands.

Sylvia Sunethra, who as a bride of fifteen left her mother's bed for her husband's, whose sole monetary experience has concerned the payment of servants, must find ways to spin the empty echoing coffers into gold. Overnight, servants are dismissed. Piano lessons, after school tuition, Tuesday elocution classes rendered dim memory. Ebony furniture and previously coveted dowry jewelry are sold on the black market. Only Alice remains.

Searching for ways to stave off her mounting debts, Sylvia Sunethra places an advertisement offering the upstairs of the house for immediate rent. When an extensive family of Tamils, collected under the name of Shivalingam telephone, she is wary. 'Named after Lord Shiva's privates. These Tamils. So shameless. Who can tell what-all-kind-of-nonsense they could get up to. Anyone but them.'

But when the Shivalingam patriarch shows up early the next morning with a fan of rupees, spread beautifully blue-green like a peacock's tail, an offer of three months' rent, she suspends her suspicions.

Soon thereafter, ancient furniture, cooking pots, bags of flour, statues of Ganesh and Shiva, Tamil and English books are borne upstairs and the Shivalingams settle in.

Overnight, the upstairs becomes foreign territory, ruled by different gods and divergent histories, populated by thick braided, Kanjivaram-saried women, earnest bespectacled young men, a gang of kids, one walnut-lined grandmother and the unsmiling patriarch.

This is the beginning of what we will come to call the Upstairs–Downstairs, Linga–Singha wars. When Sylvia Sunethra calls Buddhist monks to the house, their monotone chant is interrupted by the voice of a Tamil film heroine winding seductively down the stairs. When her flowers die, she is convinced that Shivalingam boys hold pissing contests off the balcony. When she finds splashes of red amongst the yellow, she is sure the ancient grandmother shoots betel as expertly as her grandsons shoot urine. Counting her rent money she mutters, 'Bloody Tamil buggers. Hanging their washing from the balconies. Dirty water dripping on our heads. Enough to give a non-stop headache.'

From upstairs too, come complaints. Once a week, the Shivalingam patriarch comes to grumble that his grandchildren cannot study because Sylvia Sunethra's daughter is again playing her Western songs too loudly or that the smoke from Alice's kitchen is rising into his windows.

The two heads of state engage in battle.

'Please, lady, understand that this all-the-time singing of Elvis-the-Pelvis, as he is known, is not suitable music for the ears of my various unmarried daughters and small grandchildren. In our house, it is permitted for the females only to listen to classical music and sometimes the music from Tamil films. Perhaps, it is advisable that you, likewise, restrain your good daughter in her musical tastes.'

To which, Sylvia Sunethra responds, 'Yes, Mr Shivalingam, having only just come to Colombo from the outstation places, you are not yet familiar with modern music. But in my part of the house, we embrace change and progress.'

'Yes, but perhaps you will be kind enough to keep this "progress" limited to your own part of the house.'

'Maybe that can happen if we downstairs are also no longer bothered by that army of small ones running up and down the stairs.'

Twenty minutes later they exchange polite farewells, retire to their respective empires muttering icy sedition under their breaths.

Daily, Visaka on her walk home from school is followed by various schoolboys on bicycles who disperse when she reaches her gate. On the bus, there are always haggard, languorous-eyed young men attempting to drop notes promising eternal devotion into her lap. So far, none of these attentions have caused the slightest ripple in her slumbering biology. But now, the youngest Shivalingam boy, a few years older than her, nineteen or so, she guesses, loiters at the front gate at the exact time she arrives home. Most days she is unable to lift her eyes to his, but when she does, he is looking at her so intently that she must rush past, hurry into her room, throw herself on the bed and wait until her heart has stopped thudding.

Because, after all, how is it possible that she feels this recognition? As if she knows him! So that despite his foreignness in so many ways, the oil shining in his hair, the scents of unfamiliar foods on his clothes, he feels intimate in a way that shocks her.

His name is Ravan. She learns this when his sisters call him for tea or his brothers for cricket in the lane. She writes this name in minuscule letters in her exercise books, then scribbles over it in dark ballpoint, tears out the pages, teaches herself not to repeat it, for fear of muttering it in her sleep. 'Ravan,' she thinks, 'the name of the Lankan King in The Ramayana, brilliant strategist and warrior, abductor of Sita.' She imagines being carried away by the Demon King, taken to his palace and seduced by a thousand courtesies. She smiles into the darkness, while inches away, Sylvia Sunethra turns uneasily and utters small, wounded noises in her sleep.

It buds with infinite slowness. A romance of glances and tiny signs doled out over months. The slide of a glance as they cross paths and that night she lies in her humid bed, wondering where he sleeps in the rooms above her, pictures his blossoming lips. What would it mean to press a fingertip against them? Would they spring back? Would he bite with those perfectly white, slightly wolfish teeth?

She learns the routines of his day, the hour at which he leaves the house, pushing his bicycle, schoolbooks in a satchel. She watches for his return, wet furrows under his arms, dark against the white shirt. The sound of his bicycle in the lane gives her vertigo. She listens breathless to the creak of the steps until he is swallowed by the unknown spaces overhead.

She starts to find presents on the windowsill of the room she shares with Sylvia Sunethra. A sprig of fuchsia-bright bougainvillea left amidst the flurry of white jasmine, a curving pink seashell. She runs her finger along the rim of it, holds it to her ear to hear sea roar and mermaid call.

One day, as she passes the dark outside staircase, he is waiting. A whirlwind of limbs, like getting caught in a cyclone, being pulled and pressed against his hard, slim body. Madness, desire, his lips so close and then a sound and he is gone. She wonders if this has actually happened and knows it did by the pressure of his fingers still alive on her skin.

The next time he is gentler, pulling her against his chest, where she shelters, wondering at the density of him, the solidity of his sinew and muscle. She inhales the unfamiliar surface of his skin, flavored with spices she does not know the names of. His lips by her ear, whisper her name, Tamil-inflected, so that it sounds foreign to her, the name of an Indian Princess in a fairy tale. The sound of it makes her bold, makes her want to wrap her arms around him, cradle his face against her throat, but even as she decides to do this, there is the slightest sound, Alice in the corridors, and he has pulled away like the tide receding into that other alien world.

One day at the gate, he says, 'Come with me,' takes her by the hand and half drags her along the wall of the house. He whispers, 'I have to show you something. A secret.' A delighted edge to his voice and she lets him take her, like Sita being abducted by the Demon King, trepidation and exhilaration beating in equal measure along her throat. At the very back of the house, he pushes away jasmine and reveals a step leading down. He enters first, holds out his hand for her and then she has stepped into a small, perfectly square room, the floor made of dirt, blue walls revealed by the tiny oil lamp he has placed on the floor, the thick fragrance of flowers. His voice next to her ear, 'It must be from when they were building. A place for the workers to rest. I don't think anyone knows it is there.'

For months, there are kisses by her ears, the corners of her mouth. They whisper in English, their only common language. Haltingly, stumblingly, learning the unfamiliar contours of each other's lives. He tells of the land his family has left, far up in the North, a place of dry soil and palmyra trees, lagoons that reflect the hard blue bowl of the sky. He wants to go to the university he says, study, become a doctor maybe. It makes her remember her own dreams. Maybe they could be doctors together he says when she tells him that she too has wanted this. A dim outline of a shared future reveals itself while the ghosts of their ancestors, her newly dead father, others, similarly unseen, quake in rage.

It is in this small, square, blue room that she learns the intimacy of another's heartbeat. The almost unbearably tender way in which his perfectly rounded shoulder falls into the hollow of her palm, like a ball into its socket. It is here, she learns the contours of her own body, its boundaries and spreading pleasures.

She learns how easy it is to deceive those who do not expect deception. Learns that Sylvia Sunethra, unable to imagine the possibility of her daughter trembling in the arms of the upstairs Tamil boy, perceives threats only from the men on the street, the male cousins at parties, the usual avenues by which deception may be enacted.

Over the months, they become ruthless, disappearing often into their jasmine-shrouded den. Held within the blue walls, they can hear the diverse workings of the house. The faraway-sounding calls of their various families, his brothers and sisters, Sylvia Sunethra and Alice. It is like being submerged underwater, lying on the ocean bed listening to the voices of a different world.

He takes away the necklace of her teeth marks on his shoulder blade like a prize won in battle. A bruise blooms on her inner arm, and she almost flaunts it, spinning an elaborate story concerning a cricket ball when asked to explain. The deception easy to spot, if anyone were looking closely. But no one is, and there is in her, this demon that wants love to be acknowledged, wants to claim the slim, handsome boy as her own despite the punishments that such claiming would entail.

It has been six months since they first found the room. While upstairs Sylvia Sunethra works hard to manipulate the marriage market in favor of her youngest daughter, Ravan holds her head in his hands, the thumbs pulling very slightly at the corners of her eyes, staring into first one, then the other. She tries to pull away, his gaze has become so intense, so demanding and she doesn't know what he is asking for. He says in a rush, 'Let's get married. I have an aunt who married a Sinhalese. There'll be an uproar for some time and then they'll forget.' She stares at him with those enormous and uncomprehending eyes as she realizes what he is asking for, the whole of her life, the weight of her entire life. This is what he wants. Then she is shaking her head violently. Pulling herself out of his hands. Pushing past his reaching arms. Such madness he speaks. As if the differences between them could be blown away like dusty cobwebs. As if Sylvia Sunethra could survive the idea of one of her daughters wedded to a Tamil. She runs from him, bursting out of the room, both hands held out to push past heavy jasmine, but not before she has seen the thing that is smashing open in his eyes.

He will not speak to her. He ignores everything, her frantic, whispered pleas at the gate, the notes left in their various hiding places, her hours of waiting in their small, square love nest. Icy claws squeeze her heart, jab needle deep into the muscle of it. Such pain. When she takes to her bed, Sylvia Sunethra hovers, but she mutters, 'cramps . . . monthly visitor.' Then her mother leaves and she gasps huge, silent, shuddering sobs into her pillow.

Heartbreak, like an illness. The heavy limbs, the aching head, the pain across her chest, akin to nothing so much as childhood malaria. Only Alice seems to know the truth, comes to stroke her head, pull long fingers through her hair, mutter, 'It is alright. It had to happen. This is the best thing.' And she realizes that Alice has always known, since the beginning, that nothing in the house escapes the woman's cat's eyes. She realizes that perhaps Alice too has experienced this sickness, been bereft of love and heartsick sometime in the past, that they are united by the knowledge of loss. She buries her head in Alice's lap, inhales the scents of garlic, cumin gathered there, cries her eyes out. When she falls asleep, it is in exhaustion, like losing a wrestling match or drowning.

Three months of slow despair and then the upstairs servant girl comes dancing into the kitchen. There will be sweets and music! The youngest son of the house is getting married! The old man has chosen him a bride from a northern village and now after months of stubborn, inexplicable protest he has agreed! She hears this and has to clasp her hands tight between her clenched thighs to arrest their uncontrollable shuddering.

At the gate, his gaze slides over her. He strides away into his again-unknown life and a hatred throbs along the passageways of her body, a ferocious, furious blush. She hates him and also the bride being prepared for him. At night she dreams of her rival's face, round and innocent. She rakes claws along the girl's skin, tears across belly and breasts, bites into flesh like dining on fruit. Hate throbs on her tongue, courses through each tiny vein of her body. She thinks that if hate glowed, they would all see her entire circulatory system, exposed like the veins of a leaf, surging with green envy, bright yellow rancor.

'Ravan,' she thinks, '. . . the name of a Demon.'

She grows careless with her heart, and worse, her reputation. She climbs upstairs, ignoring various Shivalingams who stare open mouthed. She stands at the door knocking, and when the servant comes, she says, 'Tell Ravan, I'm here to see him.' The woman scurries away, her eyes enormous and then he comes, buttoning his shirt. He has been awakened from his afternoon rest. She stares at the disappearing triangle of his narrow chest, that space she has placed her hands so many times, her fingers against the fluttering of a pulse in his throat.

His voice is steady, he says, 'Miss Rajasinghe, right? What is it? What can we do for you?'

She, breathless, 'You were right . . . we could . . . like your aunt and . . . Be together. After some time they'll forget, they'll leave us alone . . .' Her arm extended, describing a wide circle to indicate who would forget, the whole world, everyone except him and her. This is what she wishes for now, only them alone together, as they had been.

Fingers close tight around her elbow, the end of a sari thrown over her as if she had wandered up here naked. She is borne away in an iron grip, Alice come to rescue her, but not before she has heard him say something in Tamil. Not before she has heard the resulting giggles and the rising waves of laughter.

In the Hikkaduwa house, the whole family watches Beatrice Muriel slowly scan the newspaper lists hoping desperately to find her son's name amongst those who have passed the national examinations. When she lays the newspaper on the table, pushes tired fingers against her eyes like she does when she has a migraine and it is clear that his name is not amongst the chosen, Nishan feels himself drop into a deep pit of shame and guilt. He makes his way to the door, hoping to slip quietly and calmly to the well and thereby drown himself, when Mala calls, 'But look, there is a R.W. Rajasinghe on the Arts list. Could they have put you in the wrong column, aiya?' And then he is shaking and laughing and jumping about and so are his mother, the Doctor and Mala, because he has done it. He has changed all their lives. He has changed the course of their history.

He has won himself a university seat. He will be one of the fifty engineers trained that year.

At university, Nishan hangs suspended between exhilaration and anxiety. He lives in crowded, disheveled rooms full of books, clothes, trays of tea and snacks bought from vendors. Young men walk about the campus with their arms draped around each other's shoulders, their easy teasing and virile comradeship foreign to him. He worries about the stain of village in his speech, about his ill-fitting clothes and cheap new shoes. When the ragging starts, strapping seniors break into the dorms and exact all manner of humiliations. He is deposited on his bed each morning, aching in every soft place of his anatomy. On other nights, long examinations take over his dreams so that he awakens from a few hours of sleep, further exhausted.

But, Peradeniya is also the site of newfound freedoms. The campus spreads around him like the verdant pleasure garden of an ancient king. He is enraptured by the enormous trees that lift branches like cathedral roofs overhead, shoot roots like polished ballroom floors underfoot. In the hot afternoons he leaves the crowded rooms to study under the protection of these spreading giants. Escape from Beatrice Muriel's domain and the sensation of hours that are solely his, to fill as he wishes, are pleasures he had not anticipated.

At a birthday party in a large white house by the ocean, Nishan meets the seventeen-year-old who will be his wife. Around him, men swirl whisky and politics. 'God only knows what is happening in the North. Those Tamil buggers talking rot, oppression, separate country and what not. Should just send the whole lot back to India. That's what I say.'

Nishan juggles whisky glass in one hand, cake plate in another. It is one of those rare occasions when he has been dragged away from his books by the uncle in whose Colombo house he is spending the university holidays. This uncle now steps forth to play his momentous though short-lived role in our story. 'This,' he booms, 'is the youngest daughter of the house.' Nishan looks, and observes the most delicate of features. The uncle continues, 'Lucky boy who gets this one. She is studying now. Wants to be a lady-doctor.'

Witness Nishan. The sudden sweat that has broken out on his brow. He sees big eyes, sharp chin, fragile collarbones. He can only smile and nod, attempting to keep whisky and cake steady.

In Hikkaduwa, Beatrice Muriel fumes and storms.

Her son! An engineer! How to just give him up to the first girl who takes his fancy? Some Colombo girl of reduced circumstance no less! How is it to be borne?

But histrionics make no difference. For once, the young man has made up his own mind.

On a September afternoon when the skies are liquid silver, Visaka comes home to find her mother in the front garden doing a sort of whirling dance, sari flying, fat arms shaking. She calls, 'Come, come quickly!' Draws Visaka under the wing of her sari, into the house and away from curious eyes. 'Look, Duwa.' She lays down an opened letter, the concentric circles of an astrological chart. 'See who has sent a proposal for you. An engineer! From a far branch of the family. If we catch this one, all our troubles are finished.' Sylvia Sunethra is smiling so broadly that Visaka can only arrange her features in a similar way.

The news flies. 'The eldest son of the Hikkaduwa Rajasinghes! A qualified engineer even!' Female relations gather at the Wellawatte house to offer congratulations. They drink tea, nibble Marie biscuits and pinch Visaka's cheeks. They pat Sylvia Sunethra on the shoulder. 'You have done so well for her. And all by yourself even. No father to help spread the word or negotiate the dowry. She's such a lucky girl.' They scrutinize the girl, trying to ferret out the qualities that draw engineers to young, available daughters. Is it in the tilt of the chin? The delicate forehead? This girl looks like any other schoolgirl, painfully thin in her white uniform, heavy braids hanging on either side of her face. Her eyes are perhaps bigger than usual, her face a little more feline. But by what alchemy has Sylvia Sunethra produced such an illustrious boy for this perfectly ordinary-looking girl?

While relatives conjecture and theorize, Sylvia Sunethra sets the wedding machinery in motion. Astrologers confer with stars. Caterers are engaged. Small girls are measured for lama sari.

On her wedding day, Visaka is awoken before dawn. She is bathed and dressed, her limbs are oiled, her lips and eyelids painted by careful hands. And all the while she is convinced of impossibility. She is not being dressed in yards and yards of white, this veil-like sea mist is not descending over her head. These relatives are not gathered to wish her well, they are not placing her gently in a car adorned in jasmine. None of this is really happening, she tells herself over and over.

At the hotel, crowds of people. She is thankful now for the frothy protection of the veil, hiding her from their eyes, a filmy membrane between her and the real world in which Kandyan dancers twirl and flip and drummers pound her arrival. Her, the bride! This too is not happening. Then Alice is at her elbow, whispering, 'Be careful. He is here.' She looks and sees a crowd of Shivalingams. Yes, they have come too, honoring Sylvia Sunethra's invitation. And there he is, Ravan, next to his wife who wears a leaf-green sari. She must look away. Force herself not to look at that side of the room because she knows that if his eyes meet hers, she will sag under the weight of this sari, this blouse, skin-tight and constraining her breath.

On the poruwa, she is barely aware of the young man beside her. When she bends and unbends, worshiping at the feet of a long line of elders, he too bends and unbends so that it seems he is her double, her shadow, something without substance. It is only when their pinkie fingers are tied together, the water flowing over their hands that she is suddenly aware that he is real, an actual man standing next to her, touching her.

She lets this man (her new husband! she thinks without comprehension) take her hand, lead her off the poruwa to a settee bedecked in pure white araliya, the fragrance from the flowers so intoxicating that her head spins. She sits, she smiles over the heads of the people who come to wish them. She offers first one and then the other cheek to lipsticked aunties who leave their mark on her skin, offers her hand to be grasped over and over by hearty uncles. There are so many people, some she has never seen before, some she hasn't seen since the Judge's death. There are her new in-laws and their various people speaking to her as if from far away, their tones suspiciously reminiscent of some fishing village. She smiles, she nods and is glad that this is all that is asked of her.

She sees him coming towards her. Ravan, as she has not seen him before. Confident, self-contained, not the boy she knew. She knows he has come to claim her. Knows he will lay his strong hand on her skin, those fingers will encircle her wrist, erasing the touch of all these others, she knows he will say to all these strangers, 'She is mine. I'm taking her away now.' She is rising from her seat. His eyes are vacant except for a sort of seething hatred. She watches his familiar lips move while he says, 'Congratulations. All the best to you.' He shakes her husband's hand. The green-saried wife kisses her quickly on each cheek and then they have moved away, into the crowd. Visaka sits down carefully. The edges of things move back into themselves. There is no more uncertainty in this world for her.

They honeymoon in the misty tea country where dark women in bright saris pulled over their heads bend over bushes, fingers twisting about the very top leaves like quick, busy insects. On cool hotel-room mornings she wakes to find him bringing her tea. They spend days in the hushed lunchrooms of various hotels or wandering lush botanical gardens. At night there are awkward gropings. It isn't until the fourth night that she allows him to push hard into her. A completely new sensation, her flesh wrapped around this man. It is painful, frightening, the way his breath becomes tense, taut until finally he shudders into her. She had not thought it would be like this. Had never suspected that this was the ultimate goal in all those long embraces in her hidden love-den.

When afterwards, her husband looks carefully at the sheet to find the splotch of blood that indicates her honor, she turns her head away. In the morning before they leave she strips it from the bed, folds it up carefully and puts it in their bag so that he can present it to his mother. She knows that at the homecoming in two weeks it will be discreetly displayed in the proper way so that all the family will know that he has married a good girl, an unspoilt girl. Now she turns her head, settles it into the crook of her elbow, in her heart, twin shards of gratitude and resentment.

They come together like misaligned planets and yet there must have been passion because after merely a year of wedded life, while people are still asking the usual questions about married life, the bride is starting to swell gently in the right areas. Sylvia Sunethra is delighted. The young engineer outwardly chagrined, but secretly proud. Visaka, herself, astonished at the rapidity with which her body transforms from that of an angular schoolgirl into the softness of maternity.

Upstairs, the wife of Ravan Shivalingam is also pregnant. The two women's bellies grow as if they had been inseminated at precisely the same moment. When Visaka sees her rival, swaying on the arm of her husband, her ire swells and surges so that I, nestled and suspended in the seas within her, grimace and twist my stubs of fingers into minuscule fists.

In more peaceful moments, I must have desired specificities because daily she longs for only one thing, that strangest of fruits, the spiky red rambutan. Every morning Alice returns from the Wellawatte market, her shopping basket full of every kind of delicacy. In the kitchen, she sweats over pots of lentils, fish curries, vegetable curries. Anything to tempt Visaka's appetite, but she, my soon mother-to-be, is only interested in one flavor. She eats rambutan by the heap, splitting the bitter shells between her front teeth, feasting on the gelatinous white flesh until broken shells lie like shattered sea anemones at her feet.

And perhaps it is this glut of the scarlet fruit that brings on my birth because one afternoon, two weeks before she is due, Visaka sucking on a rambutan, feels me twist and turn and begin my headlong journey to light. Her screams summon the household. Nishan has taken the car to work, so Sylvia Sunethra must ask Mr Shivalingam if he will drive. In the ensuing commotion, the other pregnant woman too, perhaps in sympathy with Visaka's shouts, goes into labor. The two are driven to the hospital, pain making them forget enmity so that they grip each other's hands white and scream in unison.

Shiva and I are born on adjacent beds in a large white room while the nurses stroke the thighs of our writhing, crying mothers. We enter the world on waves of our mothers' iron-flavored blood. First, I, secretive and shy. I did not cry, they say, until he too had arrived. Purple faced, I had to be slapped into breathing. And then immediately after me, Shiva, as if he had been waiting for me to test the terrain. But when he does arrive, our crying fills the room, makes our tired and torn mothers laugh. Our fathers come rushing to claim us. They hold us awkwardly along the length of their hands, rest our slightly furred heads in their palms and look at us with shock while our mothers, to whom motherhood comes easily, giggle at their uncertainty.

Later we lie like replete kittens on our mothers' bellies and are taken separately to be blessed by the appropriate gods. Shiva to the temple of his namesake, where the pusari smears turmeric across his scrunched forehead. I, to the Kelaniya temple, where the shaven-headed monk ties a white thread around my tiniest of wrists. It is here that my mother, still undecided about what to call me, looks carefully at the murals depicting the Buddha's life and pronounces with so much certainty that she cannot be contradicted, 'Yasodhara.'

Among the Hills

N.S.M. Ramaiah

This story looks at the life of Indian Tamil tea estate workers who were brought over in the nineteenth century as indentured labour from India. They are some of the poorest people in Sri Lanka, an entire family often living in a one-room dwelling, a string of these rooms euphemistically called a 'line'.

Ranjitham walked on wearily. Her face looked flushed in the rising heat. Sweat beaded her forehead, and a few wet strands of hair had escaped the cloth she had tied around her head. Beyond her the tea leaves were being weighed. She was not fully aware that she too had already been there and returned. Her thoughts were fixed on the events of the previous day.

Even now her body seemed to burn as she thought of it. For one year she had awaited this event. She had woven so many dreams in her imagination, and now the very foundation seemed shattered. This was not the first occasion that Ranji's father had said no to those who came with a marriage proposal. On those earlier occasions Ranji was not surprised. In fact, she had sighed with relief. She had felt that the god to whom she prayed had

---

Translated by Chelva Kanaganayakam

steeled her father's heart to ensure her survival. Now that same god had cheated her.

Between her and Muthiah there had been 'something' for about a year. As a result she had resolved never to risk her neck for any man but him. Yesterday it was Muthiah's people who had come asking for a bride and returned empty-handed. As she wondered what she would do next, a thought, a memory, still fresh in her mind, bloomed and spread its fragrance.

It was almost noon.

The gravelled road sprinkled over with sand made the air intolerably hot. Ranji was walking rapidly as if to seek shelter in her own shadow. She held a tiffin carrier in each hand, and on her shoulders were slung two bags from which peeped a number of thermos flasks like kangaroos. If the tea-picking took place on a hill far away from the lines, then someone had to go and bring lunch for the kanganies. Today it was her turn.

In the distance Muthiah was seated in the shadow of a casuarina tree sharpening a knife on a log the size of a pestle. The knife, sharpened on granules of fine sand, gleamed like silver. The bushes were being pruned on that hill. The other workers had finished their work and gone. There was no one else around at the time—not even a bird. The whole mountain had taken on the appearance of a closely shaven grey head. In his half-finished section, some unpruned tea bushes still stood with their heads high, like a single row of seedlings in a bare field.

'Whoever did that is bone lazy,' thought Ranji to herself.

Muthiah heard the approaching steps and glanced up at Ranji. She was a bit surprised to see that it was indeed Muthiah's section. She knew that he was considered an expert in pruning.

He wiped the beads of sweat from his forehead with his forefinger. A thin stream rolled down. He flicked it off with his thumb a couple of times and said, 'Look, you . . .'

Rani was aghast. He was her brother Kandan's friend all right. In fact, he had come home on a few occasions to meet Kandan. She passed him, took a few steps, then paused, half turned, and asked, 'What?' The anxiety that lurked in her eyes, like that of a bewildered cat, made him laugh.

'Can you give me a little tea if you have some in there?'

The gentleness of his tone reassured her.

'Really?' she asked with mock scorn. 'As if you've been working so hard! Not even half the job is done yet.' As she said this she burst out laughing.

'What did you say? Not even half . . .?'

Neither of them bothered to complete the sentence. Ranji started to walk away.

'Do you know whose portion of work that is?' asked Muthiah, the tone of his voice a shade higher. 'Your brother's . . . it's his.'

Ranji slowed down, stopped, and then turned around to look at him. His head was bent, and he seemed to be testing the sharpness of the knife.

'This is what happens when you try to do good in this world,' he muttered and started whetting his knife.

She felt ashamed. Here was a man asking for a little tea to quench his thirst, and she had attacked him like an enraged buffalo. She bit her lips in embarrassment, lowered the tiffin carrier and then pulled out a flask—her own blue flask. Her whole body seemed to tingle as she gently asked, 'Do you want some?'

Muthiah lifted his head. For a second there was no one to be seen. He let his eyes roam and then stopped. A single eye was looking at him from behind a tree. Muthiah smiled mischievously. That single eye too disappeared behind the tree. With his hands on his knees, he stood up. As he moved towards her she came out of hiding, picked up the flask, placed it a few feet away from her and then retreated. He lifted the flask, opened the lid, and drank at a gulp. In a moment he wrinkled his face.

'Ah, there's no sugar!'

Ranji bit her lower lip to suppress her laugh and then took out a small packet of sugar from her waist. As she opened the packet and took a pinch of sugar he wiped his hand on his waist cloth and stretched it out. A tiny mound of sugar appeared on his palm. He looked at it and said, 'Is this how you drink it? We add sugar to the tea.'

She tried to look severe. 'You are big people. You can do it that way. Can all of us afford to do the same?' Before she could finish, she turned her eyes away bashfully. Her toe scraped the sand, causing a tiny depression.

He licked the sugar, crunched it between his teeth and drank some more tea. A few drops fell on his chin and took a winding path down to his Adam's apple.

As he returned the half-finished flask, she said, 'Give that to my brother.' She then adjusted the flasks and picked up the tiffin carriers.

'Wait a minute,' he said.

Muthiah went back to the spot where he had been seated. He chose the low-hanging branch of the murunga tree, hung the flask, then sat down under a tea bush and spread out his head cloth. Directly under the bush in the shade lay heaped about three pounds of leaves. These he made into a bundle and gave to Ranji. As he put the bundle down in front of her and opened it, her face, eyes, and lips widened in joy and amazement.

'So much!' she said to herself.

'Take it,' he said. 'I didn't feel like pruning with the leaves still on, so I kept on picking. I suppose if I wanted to, I could have collected a lot more. Will you take it with the cloth?'

'No.'

Her waist bag lay folded above her knees. She dropped all the leaves into the bag. A few glances at him expressed all her gratitude.

The relationship which began thus was now in the balance. As she walked, at a distance, Muthiah's sister Valli lowered her basket to the ground and waited for her to come up. This would be their first encounter following yesterday's incident, and Valli had heaps of things to talk about. She had not been unaware of the 'affair.' Yesterday's incident had shocked her.

As Ranji came up to Valli, she looked up for a moment, then lowered her eyes and continued walking. Valli kept pace with her. For a while there was a meaningful silence. Valli felt her head would burst if she didn't talk, so she touched Ranji's hand and asked, 'What happened?'

Ranji gave a lifeless laugh. They chose a shady spot and sat down. Valli opened a flask, wiped the cup with the end of her sari, poured some tea and held it out to her. Ranji took it.

'Why did your father say that?'

Ranji gazed at the cup and remained silent.

'You are already twenty-five. Is that not enough? How much longer are you going to wait?'

Ranji's eyes grew wet and a flood of tears rolled down her cheeks. She wiped her eyes with the cloth on her head.

'Your father is crazy about money,' said Valli with finality. 'If he lets you get married then he will lose your salary of eighty or ninety rupees, won't he?'

For a few moments the surge of emotion prevented further words.

'My brother is awfully upset,' said Valli.

'Did he say anything?' Ranji's voice trembled.

'No, nothing.' Valli, who had been gazing absently at a tea bush now turned and said gently, 'He didn't even eat last night.' Her voice shook, and Ranji breathed a deep sigh. 'I'll tell you something; will you listen?' asked Valli.

Ranji looked up.

'Why don't you simply come home with me?'

Ranji's eyes narrowed.

'Why not? There's no point trusting your father. Even after five years you will still be like this. You come home, and we will look after you like gold.'

Ranji felt there was some truth in what Valli said. She looked sharply at Valli for a moment and then lowered her eyes. A thousand thoughts, like the broken fragments of dried mud, came crowding into her head. Should she go?

What was wrong in doing that? In any case, was there an alternative? The face of Muthiah, disappointed, unable to eat, floated into her mind. A blind desire to go with Valli took possession of her.

Valli placed a hand on Ranji's shoulder and said, 'Why do you delay? Are you waiting for an auspicious hour?'

Ranji finally came to a decision—she would go. She did not know if it was morally right. She did not know if it was legally right. But she felt she had to do it. She had fought a tremendous battle within herself, and now she longed for comfort. If she was to continue the drudgery of her past life, she might as well soak herself in kerosene and set herself on fire. After all, even her passion was burning her up.

That evening, as she held Valli's hand and stepped into their house, it was like going to the bridal bed to meet her husband. Her heart beat fast. She had been in this house a number of times. But now it was different. They hung their baskets on a nail on the wall of the verandah and stepped into the house.

It was somewhat dark inside the old line house. The house consisted of a verandah with a seat outside and one room. There was only one entrance. There was just one window in the room, with bars across, like in a jail.

Valli's mother was totally engrossed in the cooking. She had draped on a sari without a blouse, revealing half her back and half her stomach. She sensed that someone had come in and turned. For a moment she was amazed to see Ranji. But as Valli went up to her, knelt down, and explained, her face lit up, and she smiled. She came to Ranji, stroked her cheeks and pressed her fingers on the dot of paste on her forehead.

Valli cracked her knuckles. She was thoroughly elated. She dragged Ranji around to the garden and the water pipe. By the time they had a wash and returned, Valli's mother was ready with the tea. Even as Ranji drank, she was reminded that at this time her tea at home would be going cold and collecting dust in the white jug. A small child, one of Valli's brothers, appeared. He was naked and stood staring at Ranji with two fingers in his mouth. Ranji drew him to her, held him close, combed back his hair, and said, 'It's not nice to run around like that. Be a good child. Go put some clothes on, will you?' The boy bolted, and all three of them laughed.

Ranji remembered that she too had a brother like this one. She had fed him. He insisted on sleeping by her side. Her heart melted at the thought of him. 'How long can a girl stay in her parental home?' she thought to herself.

It was now over half an hour since she had come. Muthiah had not yet returned. She wondered how he would react upon seeing her. What she imagined was certainly comforting. However, a part of her heart had grown dark and from within the gloom came four or five crying voices. The memory of her brothers and sisters, who were her responsibility, obsessed her. Her family was large. From the earnings of three, nine of them had to survive. It had been a struggle in the past. How would it be for them now?

Her mother was totally incapable of looking after the children. If their mischief became intolerable, she would merely slap her head a couple of times and scream, 'Don't kill me, you devils!' and start weeping. Weakened by repeated childbirths, she too was like a child to Ranji. As she thought of her now, the idea of shifting her burden on to another brought a pang of conscience. Her mother, who would enroll for work only on those rare days when she felt well, would now be forced to work every day. It was difficult and painful to think of her dark, emaciated mother going daily to work.

Outside, the twilight dimmed, and darkness set in. Leaving Ranji alone, Valli went in and brought two lanterns, polished the chimneys, then poured some kerosene and lit them. Valli's mother had finished her cooking and gone to visit her neighbor. For a long time Ranji sat still and then quietly stood up and came close to

Valli. Her eyes were moist, and her lips trembled. She said gently, 'Valli.' Even that word sounded like a sob. She wiped her nose with the edge of her sari.

As Valli looked up, it was obvious to her that Ranji had been crying for some time.

'What is it?' she asked.

'I'm going home.'

'What?'

Ranji wiped her face and nose once more. Valli stood up, shook Ranji's shoulders, and asked, 'What has come over you?'

Ranji calmly went to the clothes line, pulled off her cloth and sack, and returned to the verandah. Valli, who had been following her, held her hand and said, 'Ranji, where are you going? Come inside.'

Ranji's eyes were now red with crying. 'No, Valli, let me go home.' She slipped out of Valli's hold. 'It's not right, my coming like this. Do you think the earnings of my father and brother are enough for my family?' Even as she said this she felt the tears welling up within her. 'I can't bear to leave the little ones alone.' She broke down and sobbed. Valli hardly knew what to say.

The basket was taken off the nail. Ranji put the cloth sack into it, placed the rope over her head and stepped out. She did not speak to or even look at Valli, who stood absolutely still, too stunned even to call her mother.

Ranji merged with the darkness and began to run.

Guava Green and Mango Ripe: Field Trip Memories

Ameena Hussein

My eyes have already started to glaze over, and the paddy fields that surround us begin to blur into a shimmer of green. I hear her voice boring into my head, and reluctantly I turn away from the sheer beauty of my surroundings to listen to her tale of horror. We are perched on a bund under a solitary kumbuk tree. She spread out a sarong for us and invited us silently to sit with her. Scratched and bruised in our attempts to creep through vicious barbed wire that asserted ownership through demarcated acres of cultivated paddy, branded with mud that we clumsily misnegotiated, we gratefully sank down on her makeshift shelter. She was a young woman, no older than Dheeshana, and yet her face was strained and reluctant, and her chronicle of misery escaped a betel-stained mouth. We felt awkward, and realised, despite our rubber slippers and ordinary Anuradhapura-bought dresses, that we came from different worlds. Ours was one of power and self-confidence and belief in ourselves. Hers was one of dependency and tradition and futility. Her face is listless and impassive to the words that spill out of her. I start to glaze over once again, and realise before too long that the interview is lost. I hand over the token Lakspray packet, which she clutches to her chest silently, and stumble my way back to the van. The barbed wire catches a loop on my dress and yanks a small tear.

Back in the safety of our vehicle, seated in the front seat, I can't join the incessant chatter of the others much younger than I am, and I allow myself the luxury of being the team leader to masquerade my turmoil under the guise of planning strategy.

Bumping our way back in the non-AC van our budget has allowed for, through reddish-brown paths that never seem to end, I take a deep breath and wish the troubling thoughts out of the window; and then suddenly a peacock shoots across the path and flees in terror towards the open fields. It hops clumsily onto a low tree branch and screeches a plaintive complaint at the intrusion into his world. We chirp with excitement, and then hear Premalatha's voice softly advising us to look out for more peacocks as this is the time we are most likely to see them. And we do see another soon after. Framed by a thicket of Gandapaana, the peacock slowly circled with its tail fanned out. It shimmered and danced a slow ballet. And while the setting sun cast a golden glow over this narcissistic expression of Nature, I wondered at the futile exercise I was engaged in.

The five women stand outside the house, waiting for us. We troop in and the obligatory series of introductions take place. Premalatha loves her new importance and always speaks to me in English in front of the others. 'Ameena!' she says, 'Look! Look! They are wait for us. I do good. Ha?'

'Hondai, Premalatha,' I reply, determined to match her bad English with equally bad Sinhala on my part. It's a sore point for me, the fact that I can't speak Sinhala properly. I laugh and smile with others when they poke gentle fun at me, and realise that there exists a suppressed fury for this handicap on my part. I have tried repeatedly to overcome this failing, and even though I find myself word-perfect in my mind, am unable to express even the simplest of commands when called upon to verbalise. Is it some subconscious rebellion? I wonder, and soon push that thought away to rationalise it under having a language handicap.

We try to negotiate a sense of space in an environment where privacy is abnormal. Each of us requests a woman to accompany us, and with authority we place our chairs, demarcating a boundary of space where we conduct our interviews in full view, and yet not within hearing distance. The other two stand under some teak trees and chat in low voices with Premalatha. We are besieged with pleas to eradicate the thriving kassippu trade in the village, and horrified, we lay down the terms of our inadequacy. I'm sorry . . . Our hands our tied . . . We can only hope . . . It is dreadful, I know . . . Hopefully this research will have a positive influence on the laws . . .

'Premalatha!' I wail at her. 'What did you tell these women?'

'No, Ameena! It not me. It is Prabha. She the one who tell them all wrong.'

Futile to protest, I think with a sigh. Convenient to blame it all on poor Prabha who is not there to defend herself. Short fat dark-skinned Prabha who is not as sharp as Premalatha. She seems to be bullied by the older woman who pushes her younger unmarried colleague around.

With the next bunch of women we move cautiously. 'What have they been told, Premalatha?' we inquisition her sternly.

She realises her game is up and quickly wants to disperse the crowd. 'No. Not right. These women. Not right. Prabha has told mistake again. Yanna. Yanna. Epa kiyanawa.' The women are confused and mutter their discontent. They scowl at us, and we cringe within the van. We want to leave the vicinity as soon as possible, but Premalatha, sensing our discomfort, wickedly prolongs her chat with the organiser of the group of women. 'Ameena! Goodbye say!' she gaily instructs me. 'Api gihin ennang. Sthoothi.' I bid them farewell and ignore Premalatha's scowl, smugly smiling to myself, unseen by those behind me.

The afternoon heat saps the energy out of us. We haven't eaten lunch, and I can feel ourselves sinking into the apathy of temporary starvation. A small packet of Marie biscuits disappears into our stomachs with alarming alacrity. The remaining bottle of water is grudgingly passed around, and conversation has sunk to monosyllabic grunts. We are heading to another village ten miles away. We pass occasional homes, mud huts with small windows, sometimes decorated with little bits of fretwork placed over the windows. The huts look cool and dark and shadowy. Rivulets of sweat run down my back and my face has a layer of perspiration that gives it a startling sheen. We are beginning to be uncaring, and I worry about continuing with the interviews in the next village. Fragments of past conversations with the village women float into my head. The same story is played out over and over again, village after village. Drink, violence, helplessness, passive acceptance. Their lives are undeniably hard without having to take the violence into account. Is it fair? I question God. On top of it all you give them this. What did they do to deserve this kind of life? Is it karma? Is it fate? Those are the easy explanations. These are the bromides that are supposed to lull a divine casualty into stoic acceptance.

Suddenly my wanderings of consciousness are arrested. A jackal, then another, darts across the path and forces the van to stop. We stare motionless after them as they gambol carelessly along the field. Then a mongoose, handfuls of kalu kavuda, parrots, green against the blue sky, swoop alongside giving wicked shrieks of delight; acres of water, cranes, white-breasted waterhens, sandpipers, storks, and gulls. A karamal kirala shrieks, 'did he do it, did he do it,' taunting a black kite that circles above patiently with angled wings. A multitude of life that revives us and makes us sit up in our seats, taking vigil by the windows, sticking our heads out of them, breathing dust and heat and aridity and for a brief moment reveling in it. We are soothed. It takes very little in these times and this land for us to clutch at the infinitesimal things that will invest us with hope in times of despair. Stories of hopelessness that surround us. An interpretation of politics that reinforces despair. They are all smoothed away by the sheer beauty of the landscape. The red earth that lies together with smooth grey water. The flash of a white crane's wing that silently and yet powerfully powers the movement onwards and forward. A symbol of hope. Of things to come. For now we can only believe.

The village is deserted. No one ventures out in the heat, and Premalatha's call for Bisomenike goes unheeded. We are upset. No interviews, all this time taken in travelling. What do we do? I sit at the foot of a banyan tree, cradled by its thick and sturdy roots. The village has built a shrine for the elephant god Ganesh, and in a twist of humour painted it a bright fuschia. There is nothing else for us to do but wait. Life here in the villages is an eternity of waiting. The sheer distance between villages and towns, the lack of access to anything, enforces a sense of passivity. I begin to comprehend the expression of nothingness in their eyes as they relate stories of burning, beating, rape, and sexual perversions. I begin to discover the reason for the small giggle that accompanies descriptions of insults, enforced conjugal rights and the enumerating of violent encounters. My limitations are brought home to me. I understand that I understand nothing.

My eye wanders towards the unfamiliar teak trees with their huge green leaves that look as if they have wasted away in parts to reveal a delicate web of brown lines beneath. The wind rustles by and soothes me down like a cool drink. The sound of the leaves against it, a low reassuring comfort. But it doesn't last. I am worried and I begin to pace. Go for a walk, I am urged by my younger colleagues. They worry about me. They think me too anxious about the research. Sometimes at night, when they sleep, I lie awake and listen to their regular breathing. I muse at the way Dheeshana sleeps with her legs bent upwards and Tharanga needs a mosquito net that transforms her bed into a romantic hideaway. We talk for hours, seated cross-legged on our respective beds. I am much older than they are, and I am startled at how little the world of women has changed. Now they hold me by my shoulders and gently nudge me away from them towards the path. 'Don't worry,' they say optimistically, 'they will come.' And so I am urged on my way. There is no choice. You either walk east or west. I choose west, and trudge along the red path in my cracked and warped rubber slippers, churning up a minute cloud of dust. Then in turning a corner I am delightfully surprised by a vast weva that lay hidden like a gem in a miner's earth-stained palm. The sheer peacefulness of the scene, the surprise of it, makes one begin to look with critical eyes for flaws. There are none. Even the odd white rock at the end of the weva, which mythically is supposed to be the resting-place of an albino crocodile, doesn't seem odd after all. There are clumps of lilies and lotuses in full bloom, and the sun bounces off the water like spun gold. Herons and egrets congregate on the far side as if in council, and a lone water buffalo sinks to its nose in contentment, its trunk asunder with the sun's warmth and the water's cool.

As I am returning, excited, to bring the others to this place of tranquillity, I see an army of women marching towards the van. They are determined and purposeful, but as they get closer, I see that my much wished for army has diminished to a group of six. And yet I am elated, and in my head hurriedly racking up the number of interviews I would have by nightfall. I hate this side of me, but at the end of the day numbers are the only things that funders understand. Bloody funders, I think, for having made me almost Silas Marner–like with regard to my interviewees. I find myself counting over and over how many we have done, how many more to go, despising myself and yet continuing to keep a strict and stringent record of numbers. I conduct my interview under the spinach flower bush. The small pink flowers with little yellow stamens are sweet, and incongruously placed with the thick rubbery leaves. Reminds me, I idly ruminate while getting ready to talk to the woman, of a big fat clumsy man on top of a delicate fine-boned woman.

The woman has come with her seven-year-old daughter, and I feel uncomfortable to talk about the world of violence in front of innocence. But it is not so: the daughter too has been assaulted by the father, and so the mother dismisses my inquiries about not conducting the interview in front of the child. 'They know everything. They are old enough to know everything,' she asserts firmly. And I think to myself: what age is young in this world of theirs? After the interview the woman gives the packet of Lakspray to her daughter, who smiles at me and clutches it to her chest, and all of a sudden I feel so tired. I look at Tharanga and Dheeshana who are also finishing their interviews, and I know they feel the same way too. My thoughts are uneasy. What are we doing here? I wonder. Will it ever make a difference? This intrusion into their lives, which they grasp, seeing it as the only straw of help offered in a long long time. Despite our insistence that we can't help them here and now. That we hope to change the laws to ensure that they are protected, but that it may take years and years to change. They brush our cautioning aside and disgorge their story. There is much weeping, and much hopelessness, but they are grateful that someone, anyone, bothered to come out to them and hear their stories. They are grateful that we thought them important enough. They have given us so much, I think, and what have we given them back? I then remember Soma looking at Dheeshana after the interview as she stood up to go, saying 'Thank you, Nangi! Thank you for listening to me and treating me like a human being.'

We ride silently in the van and wish Premalatha would shut up. But she notices nothing and chatters on and on about this and that. Her gums have receded badly, and I am hypnotised by her teeth with long exposed roots that click like Madame Defarge's knitting needles every time she speaks. Every day she points out her abandoned house that the jungle is slowly taking back. Vines and shrubs are its only occupants during the day, and sometimes at night elephants come to survey the prodigal land. Even while they lived there elephants came, and she remembered how her husband would throw burning rags at them to drive them away. Then her husband left her, and soon after she couldn't cope with the house alone. Now she lives with her aged mother and nieces and nephews. One day she took us to visit her mother who never appeared. She insisted we sit and gave us delicious fresh squeezed lime juice and, while we drank, we desperately wished not to get hepatitis. She showed off pictures of her nephews in the army. One dead and one in the special task force, a splendid specimen of masculinity. His sulky wife ambled about and scowled at us. She carried her year-old baby on her hip and stood at the doorstep with a faraway look in her eyes. I wondered if she wished her husband back from the killing fields. To sleep at her side every night. To play with their child every day. To hold and touch and see. But it was not so. The state had him. He was pampered and bribed, and in the photographs he strutted and flexed and held guns that were as big as I was. The house was a shrine to death and killing. After that, we made every excuse not to visit there again, and instead we would wave cheerfully from the van and plead fatigue. The sulky wife began to get used to us after some days, and deigned to give a half-wave in return to our cheery ones. Then one day she brought out some limes for us to take and smiled, and I saw that she was very pretty.

In town, Tharanga and I saunter into a hopper kadé for dinner. We are greeted by a crowd of unsmiling faces who stare and stare at us, but by now I have grown a thick skin and can withstand the harshest of attitudes. I hoist my satchel onto my shoulder firmly, and we stare back at the crowded kadé. It is late, and the other kadés are beginning to shut down. Dinner is our only square meal, and so we are loath to leave and go looking for another place. The kadé owner is nonplussed, and does not even attempt to ask us to sit together with the men at a table. We continue standing there, wondering what to do. We whisper our alternatives to each other. Then two police officers occupying a table stand up, and even though they haven't finished their dinner, they hold their plates up and walk away, all the while motioning us to sit down at their tables. We are utterly grateful and insist they sit with us. The ice is broken, and soon the whole kadé chats informally with us. Who are we? What are we doing? Where are we from? When we get back to our guesthouse, we regale Dheeshana with stories from dinner, and she laughs while hiding her stomach pain from us. We exaggerate the quality of food and say that it was rubbish, and try to conceal the fact that we had delicious hoppers plopped onto our tables straight from the fire. We ate them with katta sambol, fiery red-hot chilli ground into a paste, and with chicken curry gravy. We talk instead of being taken to the kitchen to wash our fingers and having to hold our breaths and not look elsewhere but firmly in front, in case we catch sight of scenes that might make us run away from there. We don't speak to her of eating bananas wrapped in hoppers smeared with sugar that melts due to the heat. We tell her instead of drinking flat Sprite through straws that look suspicious and may have been retrieved from under the next table.

Dheeshana has been eating kimbula buns all day. She seems to think they are invested with miraculous healing powers for stomach aches. When she is threatened by both Tharanga and myself with guest house arrest the next day, she promises to have some soup for dinner. The watery soup that promised to be cream of chicken arrives, and we force her to eat it while distracting her from the taste by talking about the unexpected wildlife encountered during the day. Inevitably the conversation turns to the research. It has been a particularly rough day, and the anger that burst out from within us and the fact that it was turned towards us surprises me. What right do we have to talk to these women? Who the hell are we to think that we can make a difference? Look at the lives they lead. Look at the suffering they go through. And then look at us! We come sauntering here, thinking that we fit in, thinking that we are doing this great big thing, and in reality have we made a difference? True! The report will be published. True! We will have some high-powered meetings where English-speaking women will deconstruct the fates and futures of their village sisters while sipping tea and eating cake. Lots of money will be spent, and what is the guarantee that things will change? We are exhausted with all this conscience-pricking and fall flat onto our beds. We don't speak any more and soon fall asleep with the lights on. At 3 a.m. before switching off the lights, I survey their sleep-calmed faces and envy such idealism. Such passion. Have I burnt out? I think. Am I now an almost middle-aged disillusioned woman? To tell you the truth, I don't know any more.

Shall we? Tharanga's eyes asked me as we stood there and surveyed the abandoned fruit stall. Like us, the cadjan shack looked incongruous, stuck there in the middle of nowhere. We surveyed the fruit, and our mouths began to water at the selection. Perfectly ripe plantains, mangoes, watermelons, guavas, papaw tinged with orange, Nas Naarang, pineapples, woodapples, and a whole lot more. A little girl materialised suddenly, and quite spontaneously held out two fruits, saying in English, 'Guava green! Mango ripe!' We laughed, and she laughed with us. The ice was broken, and we bought a whole basketload of fruit that was to be our lunch for that day. Later, with watermelon juice dribbling down our chins, crouched under a nameless tree soaking up the shade, amidst the noon heat, we looked at each other and said in pseudo-English accents, 'Pass me the guava green and mango ripe, will you, old chap?' and for a brief moment, without a care in the world, we sank our teeth into the delicious fruit and thought ourselves happy.

April, 1971

Ashley Halpe

I do not know
the thin reek of blood, the stench
of seared flesh, the
cracked irreducible bone; I know
only the thinner reek of pity,
the harsh edge of self-contempt,
the ashy guilt of being too old,
salaried, safe, and comfortable.
I would know their reasons,
the rigour of their hot hate, their
terrifying faith. But
they have said everything
in dying, a communication
beyond all our speech.

I sit through night hours
trying wonted work, compelled
into blank inattentions
by these images
young bodies tangled in monsoon scrub
or rotting in river shallows, awaiting

the kind impartial fish,
and those not dead—
numb, splotched faces, souls
ravaged by all their miseries and defeats.

The poet was Proctor at the University of Peradeniya, which was the site of some of the worst killings during the first JVP insurrection.

Court Inquiry of a Revolutionary

Parakrama Kodituwakku

I (School Report)
Doubts all teachings.
Questions continuously.
Thinks heretically.
Disregards rules.
Works as he chooses.
Conduct Unsatisfactory.

II (Priest's Report)
Disbelief verily signifieth a sinful mind.
The horoscope too is inauspicious.
Choleric humors have been incited.
Is ignorant of the doctrine of the gods.
I take refuge in the Buddha; he should do likewise.

III (Court Report)
In the name of truth and nothing but the truth,
has attempted to break the law;
has disturbed the peace.
Should be sentenced to a whipping.
Re-educated into a good citizen.

Translated by Ranjini Obeyesekere

IV (Doctor's Report)

Psychiatric treatment recommended.
Phobia, mania, paranoia, hysteria,
Neurotic, psychotic,
Abnormal—Criminal,
Behavior deviant.
Brain surgery recommended.
Demonic fantasies to be controlled.
Prior to bedtime, administer
Several tablets of phenobarbitone.

V (Statement of the Accused)

Do not turn me into a snail
My feelers chopped off.
Do not make me a coward
By preaching of gods
Do not turn me into a buffalo
Burdened with false views
Do not make me 'a good boy'
With hands and mouth gagged.

Allow me to question like Socrates
Doubt like Descartes
Crash through like a gushing river
Cut clean as a knife
Let me rise erect
Like a penis.

The Hour When the Moon Weeps

Liyanage Amarakeerthi

This story is set during and after the second JVP insurrection of 1987–89, which was put down with much greater brutality than the first uprising. By the time the JVP was destroyed, an estimated 40,000 people had been killed, a generation of young men and women decimated.

Soft moonlight and artificial electric lights fall on the stunted, fruit laden mango tree as well as on the overgrown, multi-coloured croton bushes in the garden. John Aiya who was gazing through the garage window at the lawn could easily distinguish between the two kinds of light. What a difference between the scorching electric light and the pleasant, soothing moonlight! The moonlight filtering through the dark green leaves of the jak tree, which are spread out between the other branches in the garden, turning the jak leaves a lurid red, is as cool as a tear; and as sad.

John Aiya felt that it must now be past midnight. The lights in the bungalow have been switched off. Only the bulbs on the outside wall glow in the dark. John Aiya is not sleepy.

Translated by Kumari Goonesekere

He cannot see where the moon is. Gazing at the moon is unnecessary. Surely the moon must be sad, he thought. This is not a night in which one could rejoice with the moon, he mused.

John Aiya has not forgotten the nights he spent in prison when he kept company with the moon as with a woman. The pitch of moonlight that came into the cell through the tiny window ten feet above it, made a square of light on the opposite wall. The iron bars of the window were sketched on the wall by cutting this square of moonlight into narrow strips.

The three men in the cell gazed at the moonlight as if they were gazing at a young sweetheart belonging to them all. But when the moon waned, that patch of light traveled slowly up the wall and disappeared from sight. This moonlight mistress never descended the wall so she could be touched.

The three men were all murderers. Of them all, John Aiya was serving the longest sentence of fifteen years. During this time, all of them looked forward to moonlit nights. Sometimes they climbed on each other's shoulders, leaned against the wall, grasped the thick iron bars, and took it in turns to stare at the moon-filled sky. When John Aiya's turn arrived, invariably the other two had to shout at him 'Get down, get down!'

How quintessential had been that moon to their life in jail! Now when he sees the moonlight streaming over house and garden, it is a desolation that fills John Aiya's heart.

John Aiya arrived in Mr. Hassan's bungalow with a subtle plan in mind. Though a few months had passed since, he had not been able to execute it. But he would, of necessity, get his revenge. Every night he sits on his bed and brings to mind the great purpose of his arrival at the bungalow. He is afraid that even without his conscious knowledge, this purpose will weaken and slip from his grasp. He feels his resolve weakening as he ages, day by day. He cannot let this happen. In any case, he is a murderer . . .

Exactly a week since John Aiya returned home after being released from prison, his wife died. Nevertheless, the villagers informed him that she had started deteriorating a year ago. At the time, his wife visited him in jail and told him what had happened to their elder son. She cried as the jailer's rough words burst forth.

Tears flowed from John Aiya's eyes for the first time that day. When he was sentenced his elder son was just seven years old. On his release, he had expected to see two strapping lads.

'Have you had no news since they were taken away?'

'They came in the middle of the night and took the boys away—that was the last we saw of them—only the gods above know what has happened—they burnt eight children at the Appaladeniya junction. There . . .'

'There . . .?'

'There . . .,' she sobbed. The rest of her words escaped in a garbled whisper accompanied by a gesture of despair.

'They say our son was there.'

John Aiya's prison sentence was cut short to fourteen years, and he returned home immediately after.

Of the granite boulder that loomed like a gigantic tusker when he entered prison, only a fragment remains. The huge, granite mountain on which he stood and chipped as a young stone mason is now missing. He could see the exposed rib cage of a man hammering at an iron drilling pin in the cavernous stone pit, with its mouth open to the burning sun.

The garden had not been swept in quite a while. The compound was littered with jak and mango leaves, and pieces of paper. Someone had removed the metal covering of the hut containing the clay lamp where his wife used to light lamps to the gods every evening. The yellow berries of the ginithilla vine that had grown rank and luxurious, twining around the post of the hut, were now visible.

The sound of moaning came haltingly from the inside room of the house. He entered swiftly. The dim light prevented him from seeing anything clearly. A faint smell of urine and faeces enveloped him.

'Dingiri Menika!'

He could see her particularly well, perhaps because her eyes were shining so brightly through the surrounding gloom. It was certain that she was suffering from paralysis. He didn't ask any questions. He just sat down on the ground beside her and gazed at her like an immovable statue. John Aiya knew that he had never been able to look at her with such love, even when he had been a very young man.

Dingiri Menika's tears flowed copiously, but nothing she said was audible. He understood, however, that there was much she wanted to tell him, hidden within her breast.

'Father of my sons . . .'

John Aiya wiped the tears with the back of his hand. They were silent for a long while more.

'I have been on this mat for three months now.'

He has nothing to say.

'I would have died by now if my meals had not been sent from my brother's house . . .'

That evening, John Aiya had many visitors from the village. They stared in amazement at him who looked young and attractive at fifty years or more. He saw that they honored and respected him in their own way.

The villagers informed him that his younger son had also been abducted by the police after having been thrown on the ground and beaten at the Welpillawa junction. It was also rumoured that he was now in a rehabilitation camp. At that time, John Aiya had believed that this son, who was very bright and keen on his studies from childhood, would never have to become a stone mason in the future. He had mentioned to his wife at that time, that he should take his son back to his hometown, Moratuwa, and enroll him in a Colombo school after the child had passed his grade five examination.

John Aiya couldn't comprehend any of it. Dingiri Menika's brother, Somadasa, mentioned to him that his elder son had possessed a rifle and the younger, some subversive posters.

Somadasa had become a middle-aged stone mason with an exposed rib cage.

John Aiya believes now that he had been a bad example to his children after he had killed the one-time village thug Ukkuwa in a bomb blast. He hadn't been at home to supervise the bringing up of his two sons. Ukkuwa became his enemy after he had arrived from Moratuwa and entered into a 'Binna' marriage with Dingiri Menika, a village beauty. Ukkuwa who had boasted that 'village grass is for village cattle' had spread a rumour that he would bed Dingiri Menika for at least one night, even, with 'Johna' around, and that if he didn't accomplish this, his name would not be Ukkuwa.

One day when Dingiri Menika was alone at home, Ukkuwa broke in and attempted to seduce her. Dingiri Menika fled in search of John Aiya who was in the quarry. He picked up his drilling pin and rushed home, but Ukkuwa had disappeared. A few days afterwards the two finest birds from Dingiri Menika's chicken coop disappeared. Ukkuwa had said at the Welpillawa junction that he had not stolen the chickens but 'brought them by force.'

John Aiya did not volunteer to take to the streets and threaten Ukkuwa with such statements as 'I'll show that bastard what Moratuwa people are capable of.' Instead, he traveled to Moratuwa one day and brought home some red arsenic from 'Bomb Dugia.' John Aiya had with him some gunpowder, sulphur and potash.

On a certain day on the bund of the Midella tank, a bomb wrapped by John Aiya blasted on Ukkuwa's breast. It came to light in the village that the cunning art of fine-wrapping a bomb between two tiny stones was well known to John Aiya.

Before John Aiya could accustom himself to village life after returning from jail, his wife died. Thereafter, the life he led became more confined than the one he had led in prison. When he left his hometown Moratuwa and arrived in Kuliyapitiya, he had at least his wife and two sons to call his own. Now he had nobody.

He saw the moonlight gradually disappearing as he watched the garden through the garage window. It was moonset. The moon was not covered by a cloud.

When they climbed each other's shoulders and looked out through the prison window, the stars scattered in the night sky were clearly visible. John Aiya remembers those stars that had been his friends, relations and companions during those fourteen years he spent in jail. But today, he is reluctant to look at the sky.

He closed the window. He conjured revenge into his mind until sleep overtook him. A man who has been in prison once, would not want to go there again. But now, he has nothing to lose by going to jail. He has already lost everything.

John Aiya's next target became Mr. Hassan because of village gossip. It was difficult to find a single villager who had a good word for him. According to these villagers, Hassan had murdered many young men in cold blood. It had caused the nickname 'Mahasona,' the demon of the graveyard, to be applied to him by the villagers, after the bloodthirsty devil of folklore. John Aiya used to grind his teeth with rage in those days, repeating 'Mahasona! Good, Mahasona!'

When John Aiya returned from prison, two years had elapsed since his elder son and several other youths had vanished. The turmoil in the country, news of which had also reached the prison, had subsided. Here and there on either side of the road running from Kuliyapitiya to Digalla were patches of singed ground and metal tyre rings. John Aiya believes that his son would have been killed and burnt at one of these spots. A father of a schoolgirl mentioned to John Aiya that Mahasona had entered a school premise when the students were engaged in a demonstration and attacked them with a hose, and that his daughter had bled from her nose and mouth.

John Aiya couldn't imagine why those villagers brought their tales of woe to him—horror stories of how their children were beaten, incarcerated and killed. Perhaps there was a vague feeling amongst them that John Aiya had the power and resources to do something about it. He thought that perhaps these complaints were brought to him because a solution was expected.

John Aiya resolved to find some gunpowder, red arsenic and potash again.

After a time, he heard that Mr. Hassan had bought a twenty-five acre coconut property in Nattandiya and had begun constructing a twenty-four roomed mansion there. He mooched around and discovered that Mr. Hassan or 'Mahasona' had also been promoted as an Assistant Superintendent of Police. Very soon he also learned that the contractor who was in charge of building the house was a workman from Pallapitiya. John Aiya was clever enough to meet the contractor twice and secure for himself a job as a labourer on the building site. Construction proceeded pell mell, and the house was finished in three months. During this period the ASP visited the construction site only a couple of times.

Anger blossomed in John Aiya on seeing the ASP with his huge body, the strap across his massive barrel-liked trunk, the pistol at his waist and his compressed, unsmiling lips. When he spoke, the sound echoed as though someone were shouting in a high-pitched voice with his mouth on an empty clay pitcher. Customarily, a workman is courteously addressed as 'baasunnehe' instead of merely 'baas.' The ASP always called a worker 'baas.' When he shouted 'baas' it was as though a brick were being flung into a barrel of water where the workers were mixing mortar.

When the bungalow was completed and the opening ceremony celebrated, the whole twenty-five acres blazed with electric lights. A band arrived from Negombo. The workmen were also treated to whole legs of chicken and innumerable bottles of sealed arrack. Many army and police friends of Mr. Hassan came to the party. They downed arrack, devoured loads of meat and sang themselves hoarse till morning. Ladies made up to look like heavenly damsels danced, sang and sipped their beer.

Only John Aiya retained his senses. He spent the night regretting that he had let slip the opportunity of preparing the necessary materials to finish off Mr. Hassan. It seemed to him as if the singing, dancing lords and ladies were making merry at his son's funeral. And yet it would be difficult to kill Mr. Hassan tonight. A few police officers and a dozen or so village security wardens stood guarding the bungalow with shouldered rifles, gulping a drink or two and chewing legs of chicken intermittently.

It was late morning when the workers dragged themselves up, vomiting all the time. John Aiya who had not even consumed a quarter bottle of arrack and who had kept watch till dawn, created a good impression on Mr. Hassan.

'Loku Unnehe!'

'Sir!'

'I will need someone to do small small jobs around the bungalow and act as a watcher as well—would you care for the job?'

Mr. Hassan approached John Aiya directly.

John Aiya's tasks included feeding the chickens in the shed behind the house, collecting eggs, killing and plucking a fowl at least thrice a week, and making a trip down to Kuliyapitiya or Chilaw and picking up whatever Mrs. Hassan asked him to buy. Although he has lost the safety of his own home, he now feels that he has become a cornerstone of Mr. Hassan's. When he hoists Mr. Hassan's mischievous little boy onto the rickshaw and trundles it all over the lawn, he becomes afraid of the little boy's endearing ways lodging in his heart; so much so as to overshadow his own motives and purposes. And then he chides himself mercilessly.

He who lay confined within four massive, towering walls, had returned home expecting to find the familial companionship of wife and sons that he had missed for fourteen years; expecting to experience the tenderness of life. He had always imagined that though the fourteen years had been stale and profitless, this lack would be filled up when his teenage son cried 'father' on his return home.

A man who has been imprisoned in one room for a long period of time, cannot feel himself aging. It is only a father who beholds his own sons growing up, who feels himself growing older—becoming an aged man. It is only when a sable beard appears on the face of his sons, that a father realizes that his own beard is greying. When a traveller traverses a vast, barren desert, he does not realize the distance he has travelled. In like fashion, John Aiya feels he cannot remember or comprehend the past events in his life.

He must fling that bomb and kill Mr. Hassan. And yet he also feels his resolve weakening gradually.

What about Mrs. Helen whose head was full of aspirations for Mr. Hassan's adorable little son? And Mr. Hassan himself who drops by suddenly in his white car in the middle of work to look up his son? Observing all this, John Aiya feels his purposefulness melting away.

'I came here to kill Mahasona . . . to kill . . . to kill . . . kill . . . kill . . . kill.'

During these few months, the hope of dwelling content within Mr. Hassan's mansion attempts to wrestle its way into John Aiya's mind. And yet every night when he shuts the window and stretches himself on his donkey bed, the last thought that invades his mind as he drops off to sleep is always connected to Mr. Hassan's killing.

One morning he went to the chicken coop, retrieved and inspected a parcel of gunpowder wrapped in polythene and buried under the sawdust. Afraid the gunpowder may become damp, he hid it under a fresh lot of dry sawdust. The strips of cloth needed to wrap the bomb had already been collected. However the decision not to wrap the bomb was taken because of the fear of moisture interfering with its function.

Usually when Mr. Hassan, accompanied by his entourage, returns home and enters the house, his security forces leave. The day after, he bathes in the bathroom inside his house, gets into the car that drives up to the porch after he finishes breakfast, and goes to work. It is difficult to target Mr. Hassan during this time. John

Aiya tried to avoid pushing Mr. Hassan's kid around in the rickshaw. He decided not to let the little one's mischievous, childlike ways weaken his purpose.

John Aiya tried to spend the major part of his time confined to the garage or else in walking up and down the garden. Sometimes the cook, Maggie Akka, pushes the rickshaw containing the child and approaches the garage.

'Malli! If you are free, could you push young master around a little . . .'

'Aney Akka, take him away and go. . . .'

'This is a fine how do you do! What has happened to you? What's wrong with the man who couldn't spend a moment without Chooti Bebi?'

John Aiya realized that the words that had escaped his lips were unseemly.

'No, I was just going down to the bottom of the garden. Here . . . give him to me.'

John Aiya emerges from the garage and pushes the rickshaw in circles around the lawn. The child laughs and swings his dangling legs.

One evening, two police officers who alighted from the ASP's car, supported Mr. Hassan under the arms and conducted him into the house.

John Aiya came rushing up to investigate. Mr. Hassan's right leg was swathed in a bandage. John Aiya beheld it swollen up like a drum. The pain in his leg was etched on Mr. Hassan's face. John Aiya realized that Mr. Hassan was vulnerable in the face of pain though he was built like a huge, royal elephant.

One of the officers who escorted Mr. Hassan to his room left, leaving the other behind. Stepping across the garden, John Aiya walked up to the constable who was striding up and down the lawn.

'Officer, what has happened to our master's leg?'

'A small accident.'

'Is he very bad?'

'Not too bad.'

That evening Mrs. Helen called John Aiya in.

'John Uncle! Here . . . the master is calling you.'

At this time John Aiya was inside the chicken shed inspecting the materials for his bomb. It will now be possible to murder Mr. Hassan in bed before he recovers.

'Uncle . . . can you massage my leg with this ointment? My wife can't do it firmly enough.'

Mr. Hassan's voice had a pleading note in it.

The leg without the bandage had swelled up like a filaria-infected limb. John Aiya massaged it with some kind of special balm. Though Mr. Hassan is displeased with a gentle massage, he moans aloud when the leg is rubbed too firmly.

'I feel very comfortable, Uncle.'

'What has happened to this leg, sir?'

'A small accident.'

When John Aiya came out after massaging Mr. Hassan's leg until the latter had fallen into a deep sleep, the police constable was standing near the door.

'The master's leg is swollen very badly. I was wondering whether we should seek local treatment.'

'Now that is a good idea Loku Unnehe. But we don't know whether the ASP will consider it seriously . . .'

'I know a bit of local treatment myself . . . but I can't do anything without knowing exactly what happened to Mr. Hassan's leg.'

'Nothing serious has happened to the leg . . . he has just knocked it on a table. He kicked one of those filthy worms, who was pasting posters. That son-of-a-bitch bent down. Mr. Hassan's leg went straight through and struck the table.'

Without crying 'Serves him right!' John Aiya murmured with an effort, 'Appatahudu, what then?'

'What else can happen? He gave it to the fucker properly. Now that rotten bastard is vomiting blood . . .'

The constable blew out his chest. He flung a supercilious glance at John Aiya as if to indicate that it was he who had beaten the accused until he vomited blood. For a moment John Aiya's entire being was sucked out to form a vacuum. Then it filled up again with resolutions concerning his goal. He felt as if he had caught Mr. Hassan red-handed, thrashing his own son.

This was the best opportunity to do away with Mr. Hassan.

An hour after, Mr. Hassan woke up and asked his wife to call John Aiya in again. John Aiya applied some more ointment on the leg and massaged it. Heavy massaging caused Mr. Hassan to shut his eyes with relief. When John Aiya loosened his grip, Mr Hassan would open his eyes and look at him. He kept gazing at John Aiya who moved his hand rhythmically down his master's leg. A pleasant sensation was being induced into Mr. Hassan's mind as well as into his leg.

Mr. Hassan saw in his mind's eye how he used to crush insurgent villages in combat vehicles during the time he had been a police inspector. In those days he imagined all the half-starved, unsophisticated villagers to be his bitter enemies. That was the reason he would rush in and abduct unknown youths the instant a petition reached his desk.

That night Mr. Hassan dreamed that his leg had festered beyond redemption and that it had had to be amputated. He awoke with a start. Young men who had been assaulted with that leg till they bled and bled, were all carrying red flags and marching in rows towards him.

If my leg has to be amputated, those rascally dogs will put up posters about it! The Police Thug's Leg has Been Amputated . . . Chandi Hassan Becomes Nandi Hassan . . . the scum know how to manipulate words . . . The ASP Sacrifices a Leg to Keep a Murderous Regime in Power . . . these will be their slogans . . .'

Defeatist, negative thoughts began to haunt Mr. Hassan. He had never in his life imagined that something like this could happen to his limb. He asked his wife to summon John Aiya to his bedside again. John Aiya was wrapping the bomb on his coir rope bed. He had decided to kill Mr. Hassan that night. Although he heard the sound of Mrs. Helen calling him, he paid no attention whatsoever.

'Loku Unnehe, there, sir is calling you,' the police constable came to the garage window and said.

John Aiya covered the parcel of explosives with his covering sheet and proceeded towards the bungalow with the constable. He was certain the constable had been unaware of what he had been doing.

'Helen! Prepare a room in the house immediately for Uncle. You didn't even mention that it was not proper for him to live in the garage.'

Mr. Hassan's voice had a note of endearment. John Aiya fought with his conscience to prevent the comradeship inherent in those words entering his mind.

'Uncle, hereafter you must not behave like an outsider . . . consider yourself one of the family.'

Mr. Hassan remembered his father. After his mother's death, he, Mr. Hassan, went in search of his brother who lived in Australia. He realized the lack of an elder, such as John Aiya, in his own family. He also realized that he had missed the opportunity of looking after his own father. Mr. Hassan who was gazing at John Aiya massaging his leg, felt as though he had re-discovered a near and dear relation who would be sufficient for a lifetime.

'Uncle, you cannot live like this all by yourself . . . you realize now, don't you, the foolishness of not having married again? I shall look after all your needs . . . you attend to this garden and farm and live here happily. . . .'

John Aiya did not expect such pleasant words or such a mellow tone to issue from within Mr. Hassan's massive, robust body. He had never heard more than one or two such kind and compassionate words during his entire lifetime. He had longed to hear such words uttered by his sons on returning home from prison. In jail he needed to be convinced that there were those who loved him and who were his very own.

'What are you thinking about, Uncle?. . . . I really meant what I said.'

'Putha.'

The word burst from John Aiya's mouth. He didn't know whether it was uttered because he recollected his sons or whether it referred to Mr. Hassan. The concept that he was now an old man was etched in his mind by Mr. Hassan's conversation. He could feel his eyes becoming moist. The Sinhala word 'putha (son)' was an unfamiliar one to Mr. Hassan as well. From his childhood his own father used to address him as 'sonna.' The soft, delicate quality wrapped around the word 'putha' was felt by Mr. Hassan too.

Nevertheless, even while Mr. Hassan was looking on, John Aiya's face changed and assumed a rough aspect.

'This garage is quite enough for me, sir,' he declared in an emotionless tone.

Thoughts of his elder and younger sons and of his wife who lay abandoned and later died in his hut, began to emerge. His life's purpose after they had passed away, surged up in his mind as well.

He must kill Mr. Hassan tonight.

'Uncle! There, I have prepared a room for you. Please, Uncle, don't refuse. You have to stay here, O.K.? When the master calls it will be easier for you to come in also, no . . .'

John Aiya wonders whether there is not, in Mrs. Helen's words, the urging and coaxing of a daughter.

'For me of course it doesn't really matter where I stay, madam, . . . as soon as Mr. Hassan calls I will come . . .'

He perceives the fear of defeat in the war being waged for his goal.

The next morning, Mr. Hassan survived to request his wife to call in John Aiya. The latter could not be found anywhere near the four boundaries of the bungalow. Nobody ever saw him around anymore.

The Rag

(From *The Ginirälla Conspiracy*)

Nihal de Silva

I have chosen to put this piece last because it is a toxic portrait of class rage turned inward and outwards. It also captures the harsh university initiation new students undergo, an initiation that still continues to this day. The JVP appears in the story, thinly disguised as the JSP, and has now entered into electoral politics as it did after the second insurrection.

My first day at Jaypura University!

I had been warned that the rag would be severe and had tried to prepare myself for it. There is no way to avoid being ragged; it is something to be endured and then forgotten; one more torturous obstacle to overcome on the way to my goal.

I had convinced myself that, having faced so many tragedies and setbacks in the past, I could survive one more test. How was I to know it would be like this? At this moment I only want to run away but lack the courage to do even that.

I had prayed for mental strength to meet this challenge. I had hoped too that my native place and my parents' poverty would endear me to the seniors. I am from the South and I had heard that this would count as a point in my favour. I am poor too;

even these 'champions of the downtrodden' would not believe how poor I am.

But no one seems to care.

The physical proximity of the seniors terrifies me. I had not expected so much anger and aggression from them. They seem to really hate us and I can't understand why. We are just like them, only one year younger. Where is the crime in that? They seem intent on bruising our bodies just as they crush our spirits. I hate it when they press so close to me as I stand on the bench. I can smell their stale breath and feel the spray of spittle on my hands as they jostle each other just inches away from me. It makes me feel ill.

I can't bear it.

'My name is . . .' a treacherous tongue chooses this most terrifying moment to rebel against me. Panic stricken, my mind begins to scream:

Say it, say anything! Just don't get noted or you'll be singled out later.

I am standing on a bench before a crowd of seniors, all of them shouting obscenities. The tables and chairs in the canteen have been pushed aside to make room for the introduction ceremony. The freshers are huddled together in a corner behind me, afraid to speak to each other, all waiting fearfully for their turn. I feel perspiration bead my forehead as I strain to speak. My hands, clasped tightly before me as if in prayer, begin to shake.

I feel my vocal chords straining with effort but the words will not come.

'*Nama kiyapang, bälli,*' a bearded fellow holding a foot rule yells above the general hubbub. '*Umbata katak nädda?*'

State your name, bitch. Don't you have a mouth?

'My name is Sujatha Mallika. I'm from a village called Angunuwewa. My father is a farm labourer and my mother is a housewife. I am an only child.'

The questions and jeers rain in from all around.

'So after one look at you, your father gave up having any more children?'

'Why did you come here? Why didn't you go to Dubai as a domestic servant?'

'Why don't you work in the city as a prostitute?'

How can I answer these questions? I feel my eyes beginning to smart and bite my lip to control myself.

The bearded senior raises his hand and the noise subsides. He asks:

'In which courses have you enrolled?'

'Arts. Department of Sociology and Mass Communications.'

'What school did you attend?'

'Maha Vidyalaya, Tanamalwila.'

'Are your parents sending money to support you?' the bearded fellow demands.

'No. They have no money to send. I hope to get a Mahapola Scholarship.'

'What will you do if you don't get Mahapola or a bursary?' a heavily built girl asks from the rear.

'I will have to give up and go home,' I say bravely, knowing that I have scored a point. I sense that they have lost interest in me . . . for the moment.

'*Umba bähäpang. Eelanga satha geneng*,' the beard yells.

Get down, you. Bring in the next creature.

One by one trembling newcomers are made to climb on the bench and introduce themselves. Those who are better dressed than the others, or have studied in a school in Colombo, are herded to one side. The others are sent to my corner.

The safe corner for the 'have-nots'!

A boy with a severe limp is next. As he comes up to the bench one of the seniors calls out:

'*Moo nondiyek ney? Madamakata dānna thibunā.*'

Isn't this fellow a cripple? He should have been put in a home.

The boy tries to climb on the bench but is unable to do so. When he places his crippled leg on the bench, it doesn't have the strength to lift him up. When he tries to lift his good leg, the weaker right leg buckles under his weight and he has to grab the bench to stop from falling.

'Nägapang, bälligey puthā. Nätthang umbey anith andath kadanavā.'

Climb up, you son of a bitch. Or we'll break your other leg.

The boy finally sits on the bench, folds his left leg under his body and tries to push himself up with the strength of his arms. The seniors jostle each other to get a better view of the spectacle, laughing and jeering as they watch.

'Okā minihekkda, panuwekda? Balapanko badāgana häti.'

Is this creature a man or a worm? Look how he crawls.

The bench wobbles dangerously as the boy straightens himself; he is upright at last. I see that his face is covered with perspiration and his spectacles have misted up. Despite all this he seems calm and unafraid, ignoring the taunts of the seniors crowding around the bench.

'Ado nondiya, kiyapang umbay thorathuru,' the bearded fellow calls out.

Cripple, tell us about yourself.

'My name is Mithra Dias. I studied at Royal College in Colombo. My father works in a bank. I have been admitted to the Faculty of Management Studies & Commerce.'

The perfect victim!

Mithra Dias is neatly dressed, he has been to a good school in Colombo and his father is a bank official.

In addition to all these negatives, he has a serious physical disability.

I am relieved that the seniors have found a victim to amuse themselves with. It means that, for a little while at least, they will leave me alone. Just the same, I can't help feeling a twinge of pity for the wretched fellow on the bench.

I have seen the effect weakness seems to have on bullies. When Pincha's white cow gave birth to a calf that couldn't walk properly, the village dogs sensed its weakness immediately. Although there were many other calves, a pack of dogs harried the disabled one, day after day. In the end, despite all the efforts of its brave mother to drive them off, the dogs tore the little animal to pieces.

I can't bear to watch another spectacle like that. I look down and try to shut my ears.

It had been drilled into my mind at an early age that my only chance of escape from poverty is through education. The long hours of study by the light of a bottle lamp, the endless weary miles on foot along a forest road for tuition classes, and the pleas to other children for textbooks they no longer needed had finally won for me good results at the A level examinations. Looking back, it seems as if those were the easy tasks. It was the prospect of being ragged, of being physically in thrall to unknown men and women that had terrified me. I had wanted to give up university, and very nearly did.

The crippled boy is still being interrogated. The bearded leader has his foot on the bench. He jerks his foot from time to time, making the bench wobble. The poor fellow has to flap his arms desperately to save himself from crashing to the ground.

The seniors think this is very funny.

'Is your father also a cripple? Is this a family disease?' one fellow asks amidst general laughter.

'No,' the boy answers calmly, 'I had polio when I was a child.'

A group of seniors tell those of us standing in the 'have-not' corner to follow them. The 'have' group, standing in the other corner, are told to stay back for further questioning . . . and insult.

They make us stand in formation, as we did at school assembly. Nalini, a girl I had met at the registration desk that morning, is next to me. She is a Buddhist but has studied at a Christian convent in

Galle. She has lied to the seniors about her school and has got away with it for the moment.

A dark-skinned girl with protruding teeth gives us our instructions.

As from now, all seniors are to be addressed as *jesta uththamayo* . . . august seniors. There is to be a very strict dress code, but when the dark girl goes on to describe it, I want to cry. As a form of harassment they want all the girls to dress . . . exactly as I am dressed already.

Everyone is to wear a *gamey gowma*, the village gown, a loose single-piece dress made of printed cotton material that comes down to the ankles. Rubber slippers are the only permitted footwear, no shoes or sandals. Jewellery is not permitted and hair is to be worn in two plaits, held in place by ordinary rubber bands.

I squirm with shame as some of the others look at me and smile knowingly. My white frock with little pink flowers nearly brushes the ground and I am proud of my new Bata slippers. As for jewellery, I have never owned any.

The boys are also given their instructions. Shirts to be worn outside the trousers and no belts are allowed. Rubber slippers, of course, and hair cropped short.

The midday meal is served in the main canteen.

I am feeling ill after standing to attention in the sun, listening to the 'august seniors' lecture us on how we are to conduct ourselves during the rag. I am thirsty, hungry and terrified that I will faint!

We quench our thirst at the tap meant for washing our fingers. We are then instructed to pick up a plate each and form a queue. We move slowly past a crew of kitchen staff serving rice and curries directly from cauldrons placed on a counter.

Some lecturers have come into the canteen and happen to stand close to us. I want to kneel on the floor and worship them because their appearance compels the seniors to move off. It is as if a foul odour has been blown away by a sudden breeze.

I see the crippled boy Mithra in the queue. He seems distressed and his clothes, crisp and white when I had seen him earlier, are now stained and crumpled.

The seniors manage to pass a message to us from the far side of the canteen. No fresher is to eat beef or fish, only vegetables and rice.

Some of the others, including Nalini who is seated next to me, are incensed. How can they survive on cabbage curry and mallung? They grumble to each other knowing the seniors can't overhear them. I don't mind, though, for we never ate beef at home, and fish was a rare luxury.

The lecturers leave after they finish their meal, and the seniors surround us once again. But the afternoon, although extremely strenuous, is easier on the mind. Some of us are taken to the courtyard and trained in performing a perahära.

All temples of any size and significance conduct a perahära, especially when religious relics are to be carried from one place of worship to another. These processions include drummers, dancers, acrobats, stilt walkers and elephants. The boys are given the tougher parts; the stouter ones are made to lumber along as elephants.

I am selected as a dancer and, after the first awkward minutes, play my part with just enough competence to avoid being singled out.

Another group of seniors descend on the courtyard. There is a lot of shouting; threats are hurled at the group conducting the rag. The raggers respond with counter threats and, for a while, it looks as though they will assault each other.

One of the elephants just behind me mutters:

'*Ung kelagaththoth apita hondai.*'

Good for us if they hammer each other.

The raggers remaining in the courtyard are clearly outnumbered because the bearded leader has taken the other group of freshers elsewhere. They mutter threats at the newcomers and walk off towards the canteen.

The new group of seniors tell us to remain where we are. One of them brings a stool; another man climbs on it and prepares to address us. He is dressed in neatly pressed clothes and shiny brown shoes, very different from the sandals and rubber slippers worn by the raggers.

He addresses us in Sinhala.

'My name is Harith Jayakody. I belong to the Independent Student Federation. We are opposed to the ragging of freshers. The raggers belong to the Socialist Students Union. The SSU undertake the rag to frighten you and to force you to join them. They are aligned to the JSP and are powerful today because the JSP has many members of Parliament.

'We are smaller in numbers but we will protect you whenever we can. Don't be afraid of them. Stay together and survive the rag; then come and join our union.'

The boy jumps down from his stool and comes towards us. He stops to talk to one or two freshers. He is so tall that I can see him over the heads of the other boys as he moves closer.

'He's handsome, isn't he?' Nalini whispers. 'I feel like joining his union right now.'

'Be quiet, he will hear you,' I whisper back, for he is quite near to us now. 'We must be careful till the rag is over.'

Suddenly he is towering over us. It frightens me.

'What is your name?'

'Sujatha Mallika.'

'Department?'

'Mass communications.'

'I will try to protect you,' he says confidently. 'Join our union when this is over.'

I don't answer.

How can I answer when he is standing so close to me?

He stares at me for a moment, waiting for some response; he then frowns and moves on.

'He's interested in you,' Nalini breathes. 'Why didn't you answer him? I think he was upset.'

'I don't want anybody to be interested in me,' I say harshly. 'I just want to be left alone.'

A boy yells:

'Let's get out before the other devils come back.'

He uses the term *perethayo*—unclean spirits, which in my opinion is just right.

We collect our files and run, the girls towards the halls of residence within the campus, the boys to theirs outside.

Nalini and I have been assigned to Alwis Hall, located at the rear of the campus, behind the Science Faculty. The three-storied building with a steel gate across its dingy entrance still seems luxurious when compared with my house. But its clay-lined floor is spotless and our tiny house always smells clean and fresh. What would I not give to be back for just one hour?

I had noticed a strange smell in the hall when we entered it that morning to leave our bags, a smell of mustiness and also of latrines. I had found it suffocating and wondered how I could possibly put up with it. It is better now that someone has opened all the windows and aired the rooms but still . . .

The freshers have been assigned a long dormitory on the first floor. Steel bunk beds are arranged in rows, ten on either side of the room. Tiny lockers have been placed in the space between each set of beds. Common toilets and showers to serve the forty freshers can be accessed through a door at the far end of the dormitory. Nalini tells me that senior girls, four to a room, are housed on the second floor. The hall canteen, providing us with breakfast and dinner, is on the ground floor.

The matron, Mrs. Prelis, is an unsmiling woman whose thick-lensed spectacles seem to flash as she moves her head from side to side. She informs us of the house rules. No men are allowed in the hall, meals will not be kept for those who are late and the hall gates will be locked at 7.30 p.m. each evening.

I look at Nalini and catch her eye. From her amused glance, the first for that terrible day, I know we share the same thought. This place is a wonderful refuge: why not spend the next three months inside the hall? We could leave only when the rag is over!

Nalini is afraid of heights so I volunteer to take the upper bunk. We are both desperate to use the toilet but when I get there I am puzzled by the porcelain seat and cistern.

How does one use these things?

Nalini notices my confusion and endears herself to me by not shaming me in public. Without a word she pulls the seat down and then works the handle of the flush. Having done this she calmly goes into the next cubicle and leaves me.

Without seniors around to harass her, Nalini turns out to be a chatty character with a nice, if slightly wicked, sense of humour.

Someone screams.

I wake up confused and disoriented. I have no idea where I am. Female voices wail and call out from all sides of the dormitory but I can't make out what they are saying.

The lights are switched on. I see some girls run out of the room and they are laughing. There is water all over the floor and dripping off the beds.

Those wretched seniors have thrown bucketfuls of water over us.

Nalini sits on the edge of her bed. She has covered her face with her hands but from her heaving shoulders I know she is crying. I jump down and nearly fall when my feet slide from beneath me. Nalini is soaked, her cotton nightdress clings wetly to her body. I sit down beside her and jump up again when I realize that her bed is dripping with water.

I tell Nalini she can sleep with me in the upper bunk. I hate it. I hate having someone so physically close to me but I have no choice, for she has nowhere to go. I turn away and squeeze myself against the railings at the edge of the narrow bunk. I can hear her sobbing from time to time.

I have learned a new word today—bucketing. Why did these seniors inflict such misery on innocents like us? How can they possibly consider bucketing good fun? Hadn't they been freshers themselves? What transforms them into devils after just one year?

Nalini settles down after a while and, from her breathing, I know she is asleep. I toss and turn but sleep doesn't come.

I have never slept on a mattress before. This is quite a thin one, and is spread on a board. Just the same it seems to envelop me in its softness. I feel as if I might sink into it and be suffocated. In my home, I have always slept on a mat spread on the tamped clay floor.

I long for the familiar surroundings of Angunuwewa, especially at night. The sound of wind lifting the woven cädjan of the roof, of night birds calling by the wäwa, the rare trumpeting of an elephant on the far side of the water.

There are nearly seventy students in my class. Nalini is reading for a degree in Sociology and Anthropology while I have selected Sociology and Mass Communication. We leave the hall together soon after breakfast and manage to reach the faculty without running into the seniors.

We have two lectures today, each of them two hours long.

'Why only two lectures?' Nalini grumbles. 'We struggle so much to get here and now they won't even teach us.'

'The seniors will catch us when we go for lunch,' I tell her, knowing very well why she is unhappy.

'Jesta uththamayo!' she says with a grin, 'I'll give them "august senior" once this rag is over.'

She has recovered her good humour. By the time we have spread her mattress to dry in the sun, she is making plans to foil the inevitable attack that will take place tonight.

I don't make friends easily, preferring to keep everyone at a safe distance. But with the seniors surrounding us like wolves, I need at least one person I can rely on. Fate must have brought Nalini and me together in the queue at the registration desk.

She is a happy person, full of mischief and fun to be with. I sense that she wants to be my friend . . . at least for now. After the rag, who knows? She might find me too dull.

They are waiting for us outside the canteen.

'Umbala eeyey pänala giyaney? Ada balamu beraganivida kiyala.'

You ran away yesterday, didn't you? Let's see if they will rescue you today!

The raggers are out in force. Some of the seniors carry sticks and bed poles to use as weapons. Nalini catches my eye with a resigned shrug. There will be no rescue today.

They split us up, twenty to each group. Nalini and I are separated but I find the crippled boy Mithra in my group. We are taken to a corner of the quadrangle and made to stand in three rows.

We are each given a rag name. Our given names are not to be used till the rag comes to an end.

Mine is 'Milkmaid'. Mithra is predictably named 'Nondiya', meaning cripple, while another boy, a bulky chap with round, staring eyes, is called 'Avathare', meaning apparition.

They ask those who can speak English to raise their hands. Mithra raises his hand without hesitation and, after that, two others follow.

They make Mithra and the other two move to the side of the group and kneel. I see Mithra's face twist in pain as he lowers himself on to the uneven ground. His jaw clenches as he struggles to balance his weight on his one good knee.

They start questioning us individually but, from what I overhear, their questions are strange and meaningless, calling for equally meaningless answers. I wonder about it for a while, knowing it to be some test, but find no answer till a girl standing next to me says: *'Gihin ennadada?'*

Literally this means 'shall I go and return?' but is a common term in Sinhala meaning, 'may I take leave of you?'

But I say *'Gihin ennan'*.

I understand at last.

Rural southerners speak a slightly different dialect.

For 'is it true?' we ask *'äththei?'* instead of *'äththada?'*

For 'shall I do it?' we ask *'karranei?'* instead of *'karranada?'*

The seniors have not believed the accounts we gave of ourselves. They are trying to segregate us by dialect.

The questions take forever.

I am hungry and my throat is parched. We have been standing in the sun for nearly an hour when they finish with the last of our group, a girl they had named 'Kanduli'. Mithra's face is drawn in pain and he puts his hands on the ground from time to time to take the weight off his bad knee. One of the seniors would spot it and yell at him to straighten up.

I expect them to release us so we could have some food, but it is not to be. The seniors divide us into two groups. Those who fail the dialect test are put with Mithra and the other two English speakers, and ordered to stand in the sun. The rest of us are allowed to stand in the shade of a tree.

The bearded leader comes up and there is a discussion with the other seniors. He turns and addresses us.

'My name is Kumudu Prasanna. I am one of the elected leaders of the SSU. Many of you will wonder why we conduct this rag, why we subject you to this punishment. I want to explain the reasons so that you will understand the importance of it, the need for it. One day you will realize that this is not about you and me, it is about nothing less than saving our motherland from the rot and corruption that are destroying it.

'I know that you believe you should be left alone to do your studies and collect your degrees. You think that you will then find good jobs and earn big salaries, that all your problems will be solved.

'But you are wrong!

'None of you will get jobs. You will have to go back like beaten dogs to your villages and explain to your parents that all their suffering was in vain. Is that what you want to do?

'Do you know why you will never get a job? Because a corrupt system reserves all the jobs for people from the cities, for the children of people who are already rich! There is nothing there for you. Nothing!

'All the money your parents spend, all the effort you put into your studies and all your suffering will be utterly useless unless we are able to change this rotten system.

'That is why the rag is so important for it has three objects.

'The first is to make everyone equal. Some of you are accustomed to privilege. The rag will teach you that those privileges only earn you suffering.

'The second object is to teach all of you discipline. You know nothing yet about the corrupt system that works to help the rich and oppress the poor. You must learn to follow wise leaders who will show you the correct path.

'Finally we want to teach you the truth. We are starting on a great struggle to cut out the cancer of corruption from our society. When you realize the great wrongs that have been done to your forefathers, and to you, you will rise up with us to put this right. Don't think we are alone. Students from all over the country, thousands and thousands of them, are being prepared for this great task.

'Listen carefully to your leaders and join hands with us. Our moment is coming and it will be soon.' Kumudu drops his voice to a whisper and continues. 'A word of advice to all of you, don't even dream of opposing our cause . . . for the punishment given to traitors will be terrible.'

Kumudu speaks with great intensity. He gestures with his clenched fist from time to time and stares intently at each of us in turn, as if daring us to contradict him.

Kumudu stalks off to address the next group of freshers. Although it is now too late for lunch, I hope they will allow us to rest and have a cup of tea.

Again it is not to be. Perahära practice is resumed and I am given a stick and an old paint can to use as a drum.

'Hoi Nondiya, umba adha aliyek weyang,' one senior yells.

Hey cripple, you will be an elephant today.

The elephants are to lead the procession. The unfortunates selected to play elephants have to crawl on all fours over the stony ground and then, when the perahära comes to a halt every ten yards, raise one hand like the elephant's trunk and pretend to trumpet.

I see that the crippled boy is already suffering, having knelt, and then stood, in the sun for so long. Crawling with his bad leg will be hard enough but to lift one arm, while keeping his balance, will be impossible.

But they force him to do it, laughing when he falls on his face. They keep us at it, going round and round the quadrangle till I fear I will faint from weakness and exhaustion.

I hear a thud behind me. Turning, I see a girl dancer sprawled on the ground. I drop the tin can and rush to help her. When we turn her over we see that she is unconscious.

It is the timid girl the seniors had named Kanduli. She has a cut on her lip and her face is bruised. A boy runs off to fetch some water. I expect the seniors to object but find that they have quietly moved away and left us alone.

We rush to a garden tap to wash our faces and drink water. Then, before the wretched seniors can return and get hold of us again, we help Kanduli to her feet and hurry to the hostel.

Once we are safely in the dormitory, all the girls are furious . . . and brave.

'Those sadists . . .'

'We should complain to the Dean.'

'He's useless. We should go to the police . . .'

'Did you see what they did to that Nondiya? His hands were bleeding.'

'How can we survive without food? I'm dying of hunger.'

I am too tired and depressed to speak. I crawl into the upper bunk and fall on my face. This rag won't end in a few days; it will go on for months and months. It will go on till the seniors get bored with it.

When will that be?

Is it true, what that union leader Kumudu told us? Are there no jobs for poor people like us? Are the jobs all reserved for wealthy urban folk?

If that is true, then my careful life plan is a mirage; all the hard work I did will be wasted, all my fine hopes will be dashed.

The seniors make us balance files on our heads when we move from class to class. They also make us reverse the slippers on our feet.

On the other hand, the lectures are becoming interesting. Apart from notes, we are given plenty of reference reading to do and these books are in English. It is evident that we will not be able to prepare the tutorials without many hours in the library. There are groans from the students.

Even Nalini, sitting next to me, makes a face.

They are waiting for us at the canteen.

They allow us to serve ourselves, just vegetables and rice again, but they will not allow us to eat. They separate us into two lots as before. Those of us who come from remote villages are referred to contemptuously as dirty, 'kunu' freshers. Those who come from the cities or appear to be wealthy are now called 'alayo', whatever that means. They keep us waiting and wondering till the bearded Kumudu Prasanna comes in, followed by his close supporters.

He stands on a table to harangue us:

'Kunu freshers, today we will teach you how to be united. How to live like brothers and sisters,' he says, turning his head to stare at each of us in turn. 'You might not like what you have to do, but one day you will thank us for it.'

As Kumudu is speaking, seniors come into the canteen with sheaves of banana leaves. They spread out, tossing a single cut piece into the centre of each table. Another group of seniors come up, one to each table, and stand by looking expectantly at Kumudu. I notice that the boy at our table is a thin fellow in a very ragged pair of brown trousers and a shirt with long sleeves rolled to his elbows.

When Kumudu raises his hand, the boy takes Nalini's plate and turns it over on the banana leaf.

Nalini is outraged:

'Aney.'

The senior turns on her furiously.

'What did you say, bitch?'

Terrified, Nalini just shakes her head. Brown trousers stares at her for a while and then speaks to the rest of us.

'Turn your plates over on the banana leaf,' he orders.

This can't be true. The banana leaf has been brought as it was cut from the tree. It is unwashed and covered with a layer of dust.

'Turn your plates over,' the fellow yells angrily. 'Anyone who doesn't do as I say will get no food and will spend the afternoon under the table.'

Slowly and reluctantly we tip our plates over, trying to keep each plateful separate from the next person's, for there are six of us at the table. It isn't any use because the senior takes a short stick from his belt and mixes all the food together, as though he is blending cow dung with clay to apply on the floor of a house.

Kumudu is still standing on his table at the other end of the canteen.

'Now that the food has been mixed together,' he says, 'we want all of you to eat from the same banana leaf. We are all one family, so you must show your solidarity by eating from one dish. We want you to learn this lesson. You must also learn to trust your leadership when we say this is for your own good and future development.

'As you know, alayo have been given special lessons in discipline. So far they have obeyed the leaders so, . . . as a reward, we will be serving a special mallung only for them.

'Part of your training is to appreciate the food you have been given. Many people in our country are starving. There must be no waste. Everyone of you must finish all the food, every grain, on the banana leaf.'

I know that Nalini is looking at me but I keep my eyes lowered. Even speaking to each other will only attract the attention of one of the seniors. But when I try to separate a small portion of rice to one end of the leaf, brown trousers notices and uses his stick to mix it up again.

Two seniors come out of the kitchen carrying an aluminium pan; another comes with a long spoon. He starts serving a portion of the green vegetable on to the middle of the banana leaf on each table. But they only serve the 'alayo'. I watch them go past our table and serve the next one where Mithra is seated.

They tell us to start eating. The rice is full of grit from the unwashed banana leaf but we dare not stop. I try to take my food from the top of the pile but that only delays the inevitable.

A girl sitting at the next table screams:

'Mällumata Kärapottho däla.'

They've put cockroaches in the mallung.

There are shouts of horror from all over the room. The seniors crowd round tables assigned to the 'alayos'. They are all laughing and shouting.

'Kärpalla kärapothu mällung. Umbala duppatunta denney owa nedha? Däng kāpalla!'

Eat the cockroach mallung. Isn't this what you give the poor? Now you eat it!

The thought of crushed cockroaches mixed in the food makes me ill. I can feel my stomach churning dangerously. Although they have not served us that mallung, I know I will throw up if I eat another morsel.

And I feel ashamed.

I should feel sorry for the alayo but all I feel is relief that it is they who are being subjected to this treatment, and not us.

Despite the shouting and threats, the alayo at the next table refuse to eat. A fair girl seated next to Mithra, and facing us, is clearly unable to cope with the horror. Her eyes are wide, the whites showing all round; her hands are gripping the edge of the table and the tendons of her neck are standing out, taut with tension.

A senior reaches over her shoulder, mixes some rice and mällung with his fingers and tries to force the handful into her mouth.

She throws up on his hand and on the table, vomit spewing across the banana leaf like dung bursting out of a sick cow. The senior, a short fellow with a scraggly beard, howls in disgust and wipes his hand on her hair. Tears pour down the girl's face; her eyes have a look of madness. I have seen eyes like that before, when Kusuma's daughter was possessed by a demon. The girl puts her head down and rests it on the edge of the table.

More seniors gather round the table. One fellow takes a stick and mixes the food with the girl's vomit.

'Dhäng bathata hodith thiyanawā,' he yells gleefully. *'Kāpalla!'*

Now there is gravy for the rice. Eat!

The alayo sit still with their eyes lowered. They don't obey the seniors but they don't defy them either. They wait.

Some of the seniors laugh.

The senior with vomit on his hand must think they are laughing at him because he gets very agitated. He screams at the alayo to obey him but still no one moves, stunned into stillness by the horror of it.

'Umba, Nondiya,' he shouts, *'kāpang.'*

Cripple, you eat it.

When Mithra ignores the order the senior catches him by the scruff of his neck and forces his head onto the table. With his free hand the senior pulls the banana leaf closer and then . . . pushes Mithra's face into the foul mixture.

Jesta uththamayo are not august seniors, they are animals!

All the other seniors gather round that table to watch; some of them are cheering. Even the fellow assigned to our table has gone over. Nalini touches my arm. We look at the others and, without a single word being spoken, leave the table and sneak out of the canteen.

No one notices us leave.

On the way to our morning lecture we meet the crippled boy, Mithra, coming out of the Management Science Faculty.

Nali, ever the forward one, speaks to him while I hang back feeling awkward.

'You must be Mithra. I am Nalini and my shy friend is Sujatha,' she says as she drags me forward.

I'm not really shy. A little, maybe! It's just that I don't feel comfortable near strange men.

But Mithra doesn't have a threatening face and his eyes, behind the spectacles, have an expression that surprises me. After the incident in the canteen the previous day, I thought he would be crushed; I expected to see fear. Instead his eyes have a touch of . . . gentle amusement.

How is this possible? How can you be amused when you are a cripple and everyone is picking on you?

'Hullo. Yes I am Mithra. I saw you both at the next table yesterday,' he says with a small smile. 'I wonder what treat they're preparing for our lunch today.'

'Something awful, I'm sure,' Nalini says, suddenly depressed.

'My guess is they'll give us earthworms,' Mithra calls over his shoulder as he limps away. 'Worms are very nourishing.'

The Mahapola funds have come at last. It isn't a day too soon as my money is nearly finished. Nali and I join the others rushing down to the bank soon after the morning lecture. I go to the canteen for lunch, relieved of at least one of my many worries.

The 'boga set' is there in force today.

Kumudu and the SSU refer to the Independent Students Federation (ISF) by this name because they are thought to flaunt their wealth. The ISF refer to the SSU as 'Jeppo' because they are aligned to the Janapriya Samajawadhi Peramuna (JSP), the leading leftist political party.

Harith Jayakody is there, moving between the tables and talking to the freshers. Nali and I fill our plates and move quietly to one of the vacant tables near the door of the canteen.

Some seniors from the 'boga set' come over and speak to us kindly, asking how we are coping with the rag, telling us not to be afraid. Nali answers their questions and they soon move away to speak with some others.

Harith comes over to our table. He speaks directly to me.

'You are Sujatha, aren't you?' he asks, smiling easily. 'Which is your hostel?'

'Alwis Hall,' I answer shortly, wishing he would go away.

'Where are you from?' he persists. 'What school did you attend?'

'My village is called Angunuwewa.' My eyes are on my plate. I am trying hard not to look at him. 'My school was Tanamalwila Maha Vidyalaya.'

'You know, you don't have to be afraid of me,' leaning over, he says softly. 'I will not harm you.'

I have to look at him then.

'I am not afraid of you,' I say angrily. 'I just wanted to . . .'

Kumudu is standing at the entrance with some of his members. He is staring in my direction and his bearded face seems to bristle with anger. Harith glances around casually and, seeing Kumudu standing there, strolls off.

More and more SSU members come in; Harith and his friends drift away through a door at the far end of the canteen.

We are told to report to the upper playground for further training in 'political awareness'.

The SSU have arranged a platform and a public address system. We are told to gather round; Nali and I stand at the back in the shade of a giant mara tree. Kumudu is the trainer.

'How many of you know that there are over forty thousand unemployed graduates in the country?' he asks. 'Raise your hands.'

A few brave hands go up.

'It is quite true. Believe it,' Kumudu goes on. 'Why do you think they are unemployed? Is it because they are fools? Because they are unable to hold down a job?'

He looks at the faces of those in front, not really expecting an answer.

'No, of course not! These graduates are as good as any of the others; better even. They can do the job . . . but they are NEVER selected. To understand the reason for this, you must go back in history, to colonial times.

'When the British occupied our land they gave jobs to the minorities. There were also some Sinhalese families who supported the invader. These traitors were rewarded with vast tracts of land and with prominent jobs.

'The favoured ones learned English so they could lick the invader's boot. Once their positions were secure, their children were educated in the English medium in the best schools in the cities. They spoke this foreign language in their homes in preference to their mother tongue. Meanwhile, the children of patriots could only educate themselves in Sinhala in poor rural schools.

'Everyone expected the system to change after independence. Everyone expected change after the Sinhala Only act. But did it? Many of you may, in your ignorance, think that it has. There are forty thousand graduates out there who learned the truth when it was too late. They came to university full of hope; confident that they would find a good job as soon as they graduated. Now they know that all the sacrifices their parents made, all their own efforts, were in vain.

'So why is it they can't get jobs? Because rural folk can't speak English like the city folk . . . just that! They tell us to study English for six months and then compete with those who have spoken the language since childhood. How can we?

'They never give the jobs to us; those jobs are reserved for the children of the privileged.'

Kumudu is now grasping the microphone with both hands. His bearded face is covered in perspiration; his eyes widen as he turns his face from side to side to glare at the freshers standing in a semicircle before him. His voice has risen and now thunders at us across the playground.

'Do you fools understand what I'm telling you? You think you know everything but you know . . . nothing! Do you realize that your hopes and plans for the future are all illusions? Can you see that unless we can change this rotten, corrupt system we are all doomed?

'Those in power will do anything to keep things as they are. They want to keep all the benefits for themselves and they want to keep us in eternal poverty. They control the government and the armed forces. And they have the wealth.

'We have nothing but our numbers. If we are divided they will surely crush us.' Kumudu pauses for a long moment and seems to gather himself. His voice rises to a scream.

'But if we are united, if we are fearless, we will triumph. If you trust us, your leaders, we can and will change this unjust system. Nothing and no one can stop us.'

He pauses again and his voice drops to a whisper, harsh and threatening:

'We have chosen you to join us in this noble struggle. A cause that will help you, as it will help all poor young people who want to better their lives. Those who refuse to join us automatically support our enemies, for the rich rely on the apathy of the poor. So remember! Those traitors who refuse to join us will be crushed without mercy.'

The meeting is over.

The freshers begin moving away in small groups. Nali and I follow them, hoping our instructions are over for the day.

A tall boy with long hair parted in the middle comes to the microphone and says harshly:

'Indapalla.'

Wait.

'Api athara vesiyek innawā. Eki mehe ävith thiyenney minihekwa hoyanna. Api ekita honda pādamak ugannana oney.'

We have a prostitute in our midst. She has come here with one intention: to get hold of a man. We must teach her a good lesson.

I don't like this at all. I stand still, unable to breathe.

'Sujatha Mallika, meheta vareng.'

Sujatha Mallika, come forward.

I pray for the earth to open and swallow me. Many freshers are laughing. Someone nudges me from behind; the crowd moves apart to make room for me. I walk forward like a clockwork toy with no control over my hands and feet.

This can't be happening. What did I ever do to deserve this?

I am standing before the platform. Through brimming eyes I see Kumudu and the other leaders standing there. The boy with the microphone speaks again.

'Sujatha Mallika, this is not the place to look for a husband. We shall teach you a lesson today to make sure you remember that.'

I stand there trembling, speechless at the injustice of it.

What awful punishment have they planned?

Two senior girls come forward and stand before me. One of them has a closed saucepan in her hand. They are both grinning in anticipation.

One of them walks round, twisting my arms behind me, holding them tight. The other girl uncovers the pan. I see that the pan is filled with cold cooking oil, acrid and black from repeated use.

They pour it slowly on my head making sure it dribbles through my hair and then onto my face and body. I can't open my eyes. My mouth and nose are clogged. I know I will die now. I wish I would die now.

I hear them laughing as they go away.

My eyelids are gummed shut, eyeballs on fire.

Don't let me go blind. Oh please, don't let me lose my sight.

Nali saves me.

I learn later that she had stood there in public and removed her underskirt. I feel her hand on my shoulder, soft material wiping my face.

Nali cleans my nose and mouth and I am able, at last, to breathe freely. She holds me tight till I stop shaking and then, with the help of some others, guides me to the hostel. They have to carry me part of the way.

The stink of rancid oil is being gradually replaced by the sharp fragrance of Lifebuoy soap. I manage to open my eyes.

The sunlight streaming through the window is like fire, searing my brain. The pain recedes after a minute but every object in the shower room is blurred.

I scream in terror then, sure that my sight is lost. I am a beggar already, but to be blind as well? Then with water cascading on my face from the outside, and my tears welling up inside, the film of oil gradually slips away and my sight returns. I sit on the floor under the shower and cry.

Tears of relief!

I go to the mirror fitted at the end of the shower stall. My hair is plastered to my skull and across my face. My eyes are inflamed; blood vessels spreading like tiny red worms.

I stare at my face, filled with despair. I know very well what has brought this about.

Will it never end?

A hubbub of excited voices wakes me.

I roll over and see several girls running into the dormitory. Nali comes hurrying in; she is breathing rapidly and looks upset.

'They are fighting,' she gasps. 'They are hitting each other with iron rods and chairs. It's . . . it's awful.'

'What are you talking about? What's happening?'

'Where were you? Didn't you come to the canteen for lunch?'

'No, I didn't feel like eating.'

She looks at me for a moment.

'We served ourselves but they wouldn't let us eat. We had to remain standing while Kumudu and a girl called Renuka made speeches about the importance of discipline; that we had to trust the leadership and rubbish like that.

'Then they told us to let the plates remain on the table, remain standing and only use our left hand to feed ourselves.'

'Nali, you're a lefthander,' I point out. 'You would have been all right.'

Nali allows herself a quick grin.

'Yes. I'm the only one who was able to eat anything,' she said. 'But before even I was able to finish . . . the ISF fellows charged into the canteen from all sides.'

That would have been the right wing student body, Harith Jayakody's group.

What do I care if the unions fight each other?

I think that, on the whole, it is good for us. I turn back to Nali who has got her breath back and is probably thinking the same thing.

'So what happened next?'

'The ISF came well prepared. They must have brought outsiders also because there were people with them that we had never seen on campus. They had clubs and chains in their hands. The Jeppo had no weapons so they grabbed the chairs and started fighting. They were hitting each other and running between the tables. Anyone who fell down got whacked.

'It was horrible.

'We left everything and tried to escape but the doors were

blocked. We ran near the serving counter to get out that way but the staff had closed the kitchen door. We were stuck there, forced to watch.'

Nali's eyes grow bigger as she recreates the scene in her mind. We are seated on her bed now; the other girls have gathered in small groups, discussing the violence in shocked whispers.

'I think they had targeted the Jeppo leaders. Two men cornered Kumudu and beat him with clubs. I wasn't one bit sorry when I saw him fall down. Very good for him!

'Then the Police came in two big trucks. Everyone started to run away, they even jumped through the windows. Some of our boys broke down the kitchen door and we escaped through that.'

Lectures go on as usual the next day; a few of us visit the library afterwards. Some senior students poring over books give us unfriendly looks but don't accost us. We go nervously to the canteen for lunch.

To our intense relief there are no activists from either union to be seen. The freshers hold their plates out joyfully for a serving of the insipid fish curry. For me, as a vegetarian, the meal is no different, but being able to have it without harassment elevates it to a feast.

We keep looking nervously at the door, expecting the Jeppo to come charging in, but nothing happens. The room gradually becomes noisier as we gain confidence and start talking freely.

Mithra limps over to our table.

'Nalini, Sujatha, how are you keeping?'

'Never mind us,' Nali replies. 'How are you?'

'Ahh, nothing that a bit of sticking plaster won't cure,' he says airily; the eyes behind the lenses seem to sparkle. 'And you Sujatha? Are you all right now?'

'Yes. Yes I'm all right,' I say quickly, wishing he would go away. If the Jeppo come back suddenly and catch him speaking with me they'll really make him suffer.

'Your eyes are still a bit red,' he says easily. 'You should get some drops for them.'

'No. I'm all right,' I answer. 'Really.'

'Well don't let them frighten you,' he goes on quietly. 'There is a limit to what they can do . . . and you can take that.'

I look at him with some surprise. We had, all of us, been sorry for him, not only for his disability but seeing him as a perennial victim. The girls had wondered how long it would take them to break his spirit; make him give up and go home. And here he is, advising me about courage!

'That scoundrel Kumudu seems to have it in for you,' Nali says. 'Why does he go out of his way to torment you?'

'He was also at Royal,' Mithra answers quietly, 'two years ahead of me.'

'What? That rascal was a Royalist?'

'Mm.'

'I don't understand,' Nali goes on with a puzzled frown. 'Then why does he . . .'

'He was a grade five scholarship student transferred to Royal from some remote village school,' Mithra explains. 'I think he was one of those who were unable to cope with the . . . change.'

'What do you mean?'

'His classmates mocked him, you know, called him names like "gamaya" and "godaya",' Mithra says. 'It never stopped . . . even in the senior years. He was never . . . accepted. I think Kumudu took it very hard.'

'So he wants his revenge on all Royalists?'

'I think he wants his revenge on the world.'

Mithra nods pleasantly and limps away; his whole body sways with each stride as he bends to support his wasted knee.

The raggers have been quiet for nearly two weeks. Occasionally a few of them would corner some of the freshers and give them a difficult time but these incidents only took place on a small scale. Nali has heard that many of the leaders, including that awful

Kumudu, are still recovering from their injuries and have not returned to the campus. To my intense relief, I manage to escape the attentions of the remaining seniors.

The Jeppo are back. We are leaving the lecture theatre on the first floor when we hear slogans being shouted near the main gate. From the safe vantage of an upstairs window we see the leaders of the SSU being escorted into the campus by a large crowd of supporters.

Kumudu, a part of his head shaved and covered with a dressing, is in the lead. The supporters are making a deafening racket, mostly denouncing the ISF. We watch as the procession goes towards the union office where a small stage has been erected. Kumudu and a few others mount the stage and address the crowd.

The rag starts again and, after the respite we had enjoyed, is even harder to bear. We are forced once again to wear our slippers on the wrong feet and carry files on our heads whenever we walk about. Mealtimes become a period of torture.

They select a number of freshers and begin training them for a musical program. By a rare stroke of luck, Nali and I are not picked for that.

The *Bōttuwa* group came in today.

Of those selected to enter Jaypura University each year, some students decline the offer and follow courses of study elsewhere. Those who are next in the various merit lists are then given a chance to fill these vacancies. They come to the campus some weeks later and are referred to as the *Bōttuwa* group, those who have arrived like 'boat-people'.

There are thirty-two such newcomers and the Jeppo fall upon them like jackals. They might have become bored with us because, while the rag remains in force, there is a slackening of interest in harassing us. The new ones get a double dose of it and suffer greatly.

Kalinga is coming to the campus!

The Socialist Students Union (SSU) strenuously denies affiliation to any national political party. However everyone knows that they are part of the Students United Front (SUF) that, in turn, is a part of the Janapriya Samajawadhi Peramuna (JSP). Which is why Harith and his union call them Jeppo. We do too, only very quietly.

One fresher tells me that Kalinga is the leader of the SUF and controls powerful unions in all the universities. It is rumoured that Kalinga is already a member of the politburo of the JSP.

The SSU become so heavily involved in preparations to receive him that the intensity of the rag diminishes.

'I hope one of their big shots come every week,' Nali says cheerfully. 'Then they'll be too busy to harass us.'

'I wonder what he's like,' another girl says. 'Must be a bearded ruffian like that Kumudu!'

'I hear he's very powerful. He can close down any campus if he wants to,' a boy tells us knowingly. 'My brother at Kelaniya Campus has heard him speak. He was very impressed; says Kalinga will be a national leader one day.'

'What will he talk about?' Nali asks derisively. 'Bringing the revolution? All these fellows are extremists when they are students, then they get jobs and settle down to exploiting the poor; just like everyone else.'

'My brother tells me Kalinga is different,' the boy, whose name is Sujith, replies. 'He really believes in him, my brother. He told me that you only need to listen to him once and you'll also be a follower. My brother is thinking of giving up studies and going in for politics full-time.'

'Is your brother mad?' Nali asks and then goes on recklessly. 'Tell him these fellows are tricksters. They will lead everyone to ruin. They don't care about the poor . . . they only want power. They . . .'

'Nalini, don't talk like that,' Sujith says urgently. 'It's very dangerous and anyway I hear that Kalinga really is different . . .'

'I don't believe it.'

'Don't believe me. Just listen to him when he comes, then you'll see.'

'We'll have no choice, I suppose,' Nali observes ruefully. 'They'll force us to listen to the fellow.'

He looks like any other student.

Kumudu and his committee members escort Kalinga towards the stage. An excited buzz rises from the gathering as the visitor mounts the steps and turns to face the crowd. He raises his hands to acknowledge the cheer that slowly swells to a roar of welcome. I look at him closely as he stands a few feet away from me.

A little older than the average student perhaps, above average height, slightly stooped and thin to the point of emaciation. His hair is parted neatly at the centre and falls down to his ears, giving him a studious appearance. He is simply dressed in dark trousers and a white shirt with long sleeves unbuttoned at the wrist. Leather sandals.

As freshers we are forced to the front of the audience, directly below the stage. The meeting has been arranged in the upper playground and a really large crowd has turned up to listen to the man. I see Mithra standing close by. He catches my eye and, ignoring my warning frown, pulls a sour face. I look away quickly, terrified that one of the seniors will notice.

Some of the others on stage address us briefly and then Kumudu rises to speak.

'Fellow students, we are very fortunate today for we have an opportunity to listen to one of the great leaders of our time. Today he is the convener of the Students United Front. I can confidently predict that he will soon be a leader at national level.

'I have worked closely with him for many years so I can sincerely tell you; this man can show us the way. He has studied the injustices inflicted on our people. He knows the sufferings of our educated, unemployed youth. He knows why these sorrows never go away, why we must always be poor so that the corrupt may prosper. He has a plan. He has a solution.

'Listen to him; believe him; follow him. Together we can destroy this evil system of government that keeps us in eternal slavery.'

Kumudu stops and gathers himself.

'I ask all of you to welcome Kalinga Lokuge.'

The applause is long and loud. Kalinga stands grasping the microphone for some time, staring expressionlessly at the crowd. The clapping rises to a crescendo and then ceases abruptly when Kalinga raises his hand.

He allows the silence to stretch, making us quiver in anticipation. Even Nali gets carried away enough to squeeze my hand. When I think he is never going to speak, he does.

He has a slightly hoarse voice, as if there is something obstructing his throat. He speaks slowly, in clear colloquial Sinhala, emphasizing each word as his eyes move over us at the front of the crowd.

'The future of this country must belong to educated, rural youth. It must belong to you. You have been robbed of this birthright . . . and you don't even know it. In your innocence you believe that you will find a place in the sun if you work hard and graduate from university. That is an illusion.

'There are forty thousand unemployed graduates who have returned to their villages in shame and despair. Do you think they are less clever than you? Less qualified than you will be?'

Kalinga stops as if he is waiting for an answer from us. Angry eyes drill holes in our heads.

'No, of course not! So why are there no jobs for them? . . . The answer is that those with wealth and power, the corrupt people in the cities, want it that way. They want the jobs and the positions for their own kind. There is nothing left for people like you.

'Do you know how these city dwellers got their wealth and their power?'

Kalinga pauses again.

'I will tell you. When the British imperialists conquered our land, Sinhalese patriots were in rebellion. So the invader gave all the jobs to minorities. The minorities would do anything to keep the invader in power, for their jobs depended on it. Then there were Sinhalese traitors. They were rewarded with lands and positions. They were given licenses to make and sell arrack. Both groups prospered while Sinhalese patriots sank into poverty.

'If that was all, we could say that it happened in past times . . . let us forget about it and get on with our lives. But that is not the whole story.'

Kalinga raises his head and with it, his voice.

'No. Bribes from the invader and rewards for treason gave these people position and wealth. Then they were able, not only to acquire more wealth, but also to educate their children in the best schools and to send them abroad for higher studies. So, generation after generation, these families moved to the cities and accumulated more and more wealth and political power. The rural patriots were left in misery, ignorance and degradation.

'They now tell us to compete on an equal footing with the privileged class. We are supposed to go to the city, dress in western style and above all speak English like Englishmen. Can you compete with those who have learned these things from infancy?

'More importantly, . . . *should you?*

'A few of you will be called for interviews, but that is only for show. When the interview is over they will laugh at you; call you the not-pot fellows. Did you know that?

'Once in a way, they will allow one person to succeed. They will put that person on a platform and say: 'See. You can become one of us if you learn our ways and are loyal to us. Then you can enjoy the fruits of wealth and power.'

'That is only for show, like a lottery winner. For every winner there are thousands of losers.'

Kalinga pauses and lets his eyes wander over the faces in the crowd. He has our attention all right.

There is a deathly silence.

'Our leaders tell us that things are changing. They tell us to be patient. That soon we will be able to claim our rightful place in the sun.

'Do you know what they are planning? They want to teach English in rural schools. They will set up libraries with English books. They will teach our children to sing English songs and to perform the ballet. Then they will say: "Ahh, now you are like us. Come to the city, there are jobs for you."

'Do you believe it? Do you think people with wealth and power want to share it with you? Rubbish! This is just another sham to keep us quiet for another generation. Even if they are sincere, you must ask yourself this. Why should we, Sinhalese people who are heirs to this land, have to learn western *thuppahi* ways to get a job?'

Kalinga bows his head over the microphone. He is holding the stand with both hands and his fingers are corded from the intensity of his grip. I feel the tension grow around me as we wait breathlessly for him to continue.

He raises his head and looks at us. I feel his eyes boring into me, as though he has a special message for me alone.

'The corrupt system will never allow real change. It is foolish for us to expect the elite in the cities to voluntarily give up their wealth and power. Why should they, when their prosperity depends on oppressing the poor?'

Kalinga raises his voice. It thunders at us through the speakers.

'No. We will NOT be fooled any longer. We will not wait any more. We will topple this oppressive system and take control of our destiny. We will cleanse the cities of their corruption. Banish, for all time, the evil western culture with its pornography, gambling, prostitution with its alcohol and drugs.

'Only when we crush the cities, only when we right the historic injustices inflicted on us by the imperialists, will our people . . . that means you . . . gain their rightful place.'

Someone starts clapping. Soon the whole crowd takes it up and wave after wave of deafening applause shakes the air. Some of the boys are shouting and whistling. Even my sceptical Nali is clapping. Only Mithra, standing close by, holds his hands firmly gripped behind his back.

The idiot!

'It will not be easy. Don't ever think it will be. The city folk have wealth, they run the government and they control the police and the army. They will not give up everything just because we ask for justice. The oppressors will act with extreme violence to crush any threat to their position.

'So what force will rise up to challenge the system? The old left tried to get the workers in the cities to rise up. They failed because the workers were already corrupted. They had jobs that they wanted to protect. They yearned for the material things that Western culture dangled before them.

'What about the farmers? What about the people from your village, your parents? Do you think they will be able to unite to topple this system? . . . No, of course not. They have been oppressed for too long. They are sunk in apathy; they think poverty is their proper station.

'Who then can carry out this patriotic duty and save our motherland?'

Kalinga pauses again with his eyes closed. When he opens his eyes and starts speaking, his voice is a hoarse whisper. He points his finger at us dramatically.

'You!

'Only you can save the motherland from the clutches of this city filth. You are educated. You have the numbers and you are united on campuses and schools around the country. All you need is leadership and training.

'We will give you both. We have a vision. Trust us and be patient.'

Kalinga stops abruptly and stalks off the stage. Kumudu and the others rise quickly and follow him.

In a moment he is gone.

I get a full bucket of stinking canteen waste on my head . . . and I'm delighted.

The seniors have, over a period of days, used some discarded tar barrels to collect wastewater from the canteen. The food residues have fermented into a foul, oily mess with yellow froth covering the top.

It stinks.

We are told to line up, two abreast, and take our turn. I am next to a fellow named Previn from the Management Faculty. Nali is just behind me, poking me with her finger to hurry me on.

The senior stirs the barrel with a stick to make sure that my bucket has its proper share of muck from the bottom. I close my eyes and hold my breath. I feel the putrid mess dribble through my hair and then on to my face and body, and I don't care. My heart is singing.

They have done everything they could to break my spirit but I have stood up and taken it. This is the final torture and now the rag is over. Sujatha Mallika has survived.

Nothing will stop me now!

No State, No Dog

The theme of this section is displacement from home and alienation. The initial pieces look at internal displacement, within Sri Lanka, and feelings of alienation because of ethnicity. The pieces in the middle, starting with Michael Ondaatje's 'The Cat's Table', are focused on the migrant experience, and the last few stories and poem deal with the subject of return to Sri Lanka—the challenges and often the impossibility of return.

Inheritance

Jean Arasanayagam

I often wonder what he wore, that Coopman or
boekhouder in that steaming climate?
He never went back to that dykeland
that country I knew only as well
as a Breughel painting or one by Vermeer.

Am I the only page of an unwritten diary
he has left behind and not in his own language either,
even his Bible, he must have had one,
where is it? Strange that I search for his behest
more than anyone else's, the behest of this inheritance;
not a guilder did he leave behind nor any territory
only that vault in the Galle kirk and from the casque
of his body, this vintaged blood.

The poet is descended from the Dutch colonizers who ruled Sri Lanka between 1640 and 1796.

No State, No Dog

C.V. Velupillai

This story addresses the repatriation of six hundred thousand Indian Tamil estate workers back to India in the 1960s. They were descendants of workers sent from south India to Sri Lanka in the nineteenth and early twentieth centuries to labour in coffee, tea and rubber plantations, and they were important contributors to the economy. Many of them had no family or connections in India.

The day ended all too soon for Muthiah. It was his last day in the sifting-room in the factory. To go away from here and never return, it was something impossible, inconceivable. Fifteen years of his young life had been counted away by the turn of the wheels. The handles on the side door to the sifting-room had been worn out by the constant touch of his hands. He came to the sifter when he was only fifteen. Since then the factory had been his world and the work there his life.

It was only three months ago, just before he went on his pilgrimage to Madurai, that the whole atmosphere had begun to jar on his nerves. The ceaseless rumbling of the wheels and the sifter with its dull monotony depressed him. It spoke to him of more sweat and long hours. That was one of the reasons he had gone. But today there was a strange rhythm in the movement. It was bound up with his pulse beats. As the men and women went out one by one, Muthiah lingered behind to have a last look.

The sifting-room, so drab and bare, suddenly came to life. The smell of dust and fresh tea, the silent wheels on the shaft, potent with power, seemed to be struggling in his breast to be released into motion. Fifteen years of his life had been made up of the rat-tat-tat of the sifter and the rumbling of the wheels.

'Tomorrow,' he thought, 'tomorrow, somebody else will take my place. And the bustle in the sitting-room will go on as if nothing different had happened. Everything will be in its place; only I will not be here. How strange is the order of life. After all, nobody is irreplaceable.'

With deep regret, as if he had left behind a part of his being, Muthiah came out of the factory onto the open road. Yes, the open road without a morrow, without a future. He joined the crowd of men and women who were going home after their day's work. Unconsciously, he felt that he had lost caste with them. That old familiar scene was a desert to him now.

Many an old scene flitted across his mind. He thought of the first day he went to Colombo to get his travel papers. He remembered the inquiry desk at the Immigration office.

And that heavily built man with a bull neck, with a menacing glint in his eyes. He thought of him as a wild creature caught in a net would. He thought of the second day he went to this officer to renew his Temporary Work Permit. The officer growled at him. The other mortals who had come there shrank before his glance. Muthiah handed over his papers and waited.

'Your TWP cannot be renewed,' grunted Bull Neck. 'You will have to clear out.'

'Sir,' faltered Muthiah, 'I only went on a pilgrimage to Madurai. I was born and bred on an estate here.'

'Yes,' sneered Bull Neck, 'so every beggar is now a Ceylonese, eh? You go back to India when you like, and then you think you belong here. If you have nothing to do, go home and do it.'

'Go home and do it,' Muthiah thought over what had happened, as he had done so often. 'What a nasty way of speaking. Why are these officers so inhuman? Even the Citizenship Officer was nasty to me. He had the vulgarity to ask me whether my mother was married to my father.'

The scene shifted. He recalled his mother, her loving, tender face; those dark liquid eyes and her sad smile. A sharp pain shot through his heart and spread all over his limbs. How vividly he remembered the day of her death. How he had cried till his eyes ran dry. Even as she laboured to breathe her last, she spoke to him in the usual way.

'Muthiah, son, do not think of me sadly. I shall always be with you.' After a pause, she added, 'Look after yourself and our little Sooty. Your father brought her into this house. She has been part of our family.'

In those days Sooty had been a full-blooded little thing. Tiny sparks shimmered in the sunlight on the coat that clung so close to her supple body. The way she used to draw her ears back and wag her tail, moving the front of her trunk from side to side, was a sight he could never forget. Since his mother's death Sooty had been even closer to him. Yes, she was his mother's parting gift, the little shred left behind from their torn ties.

Now that Muthiah had to leave his home, his uncle and aunt, and above all his dog, he was dazed; his inside was like a demolished hut. He had decided to give Sooty away to the factory watchman because his aunt did not really like her. When Muthiah hinted that Raman wanted the dog, his aunt did not make the slightest sign of protest.

That was the thing he could not bear.

When he reached home, everything was ready for his journey. His uncle had come home. His aunt had collected all his belongings in a cloth bag and kept it in a corner of his little room. Muthiah never spoke much anyway. And that day he was tongue-tied.

'Muthiah,' said his uncle, 'I know it is very, very hard for us and for you. We left our village during your grandfather's time. We have no ties there now. There may be some distant relation still left, but who knows? Have faith in God. God is the only protection for the destitute. Don't forget to take your papers.'

'Yes, uncle. Yes, uncle,' said Muthiah, many times, as if those two words contained all that he wanted to say.

When the time for parting came, Muthiah collected his bag and gathered Sooty in his arms and took his leave in silence. As he walked across the field to the factory watchman's house, his forced departure was the talk of the workers in their line rooms. They thought of it as if he were being led to the slaughter house.

Sooty kept close to Muthiah. From time to time she pushed her nose into his face. She did not know that this was their last journey together. He wondered why dogs were not required to get citizenship papers. Perhaps they too should have some kind of paper. Otherwise their lives would be in danger. He hoped that such a tragedy would not befall Sooty.

Muthiah saw Raman waiting for him. There was little time for talk.

'I shall lock her up in the little room,' said Raman, pointing to a small room behind the kitchen. 'She will get used to me in due course. Don't worry. I shall look after her.'

'Yes, I know,' said Muthiah, moving towards the door. Sooty clung to him. He left her on the ground and called her into the small room. She crouched. He coaxed. She refused to move and looked pitifully at him as if she was about to be beaten. He lifted her, put her in the little room and pushed her in, and snapped the door shut.

The little creature scratched desperately at the door, whimpering. Without a word, without looking back, Muthiah hurried along the road to the railway station. Raman walked with him, hurrying to keep up. The evening was growing into night. Sooty's moaning came to him from the distance and faded away like the cry of a child in the night. Muthiah felt as if it came from the grave of his mother. Yes, a handful of dust calling to him from under the tea bushes.

At the railway station there was the usual clamour and activity. Muthiah went to the booking-office window and got his ticket to Trichy Junction. It was issued as though people travelled so far away, across the sea to India, all the time.

The last bell.

'Get in, Muthiah. Don't worry,' said Raman.

Muthiah passed through the gate. The train had pulled in by then. There was a disorderly crowd of men and women sobbing and crying. There was no one to cry for Muthiah. He got into a compartment and sat in a corner beside a young woman. He was too confused to notice anything. The train shrieked and rumbled out. Raman stood leaning against the gate, his hand on his chin. Muthiah looked out and saw him. The train gathered speed and rumbled on with a flat incessant rhythm. It tortured him, this rumbling of wheels! Yes, his very life had been passed on wheels. For the last time he peeped out and saw the light in the factory. The light in the factory, the wailing of women at the railway station, and the cry of Sooty; they hammered on his brain. Suddenly Bull Neck of the Immigration office grinned at him from the depths of the night.

'I told him the truth when I said that I went on a pilgrimage; and today is an even longer, more difficult one,' he thought.

The train sped on. He looked out again and saw the stars blink. Before this he had never bothered to look at stars. Tonight he did not know why he looked at them. The moaning of Sooty seemed to come from the stars and echo in him. The young woman had come close to him with the warmth of her body. He looked at her. A moment of distraction. The train sped on. The rumbling of wheels; the sifting room!

Next morning Sooty arrived at the old house, wet and mud-stained. Muthiah's aunt shouted out.

'Look at that wretched thing. She had run away.'

Sooty ran up to Muthiah's aunt and put her paws on her, only to be shouted at again.

'Get out, you ungrateful beast!'

Sooty went onto the verandah and looked for her usual corner. It was occupied by the fowl cage.

'Get out, you slut!' came the harsh voice of her old enemy. The dog sat by the cage with outstretched paws. She was waiting for Muthiah. But he did not come out of the house. She could not understand why.

The morning advanced. The people from the factory and the field came for their noonday meal. Sooty sat in the compound looking at the road. Muthiah's uncle came. She ran up to him, smelt his feet and wagged her tail. He stood there strangely moved. The dog whined and looked at his face.

The day wore away. It grew dark. Sooty sat in the compound looking at the road.

The Whirlwind

(From *The Whirlwind*)

Ayathurai Santhan

In 1987, the Indian Peace Keeping Force (IPKF) was invited to Sri Lanka by the government, with support from the LTTE. Their role was to bring about peace by helping disarm the militants and set up an Interim Administrative Council. Within a short time, however, differences between the militants and the IPKF led to an all-out war, with dire consequences for the local population. Operation Pawan, described in the story, was a battle for control over Jaffna and the northern cities that the IPKF won. The IPKF became so unpopular that the government finally united with the Tigers to oust them from the country in 1990. The Indians suffered a high number of casualties, but also stood accused of civilian massacres, disappearances and rape.

'Is this going to be a refugee or a detention camp, Sivan?' The tall, gray-haired person asked in a nonchalant voice, as he walked with measured steps. There was an air of a refinement about him, so typical of a middle-class Jaffna man. He was in traditional dress, a *verty* and a full-sleeved collar-less shirt, a folded shawl draped round his neck, all white, befitting that retired head master of the local Tamil high school. The eyes, which appeared bigger behind the glasses, stared at his much younger and stouter companion walking by his side.

'Of course the second,' replied Sivan curtly. 'Why doubt Thevar *maamaa*?'

The sneer turned his dark but pleasant, clean shaven face set with piercing eyes, to embittered. Sivan had thick curly hair and he had a brownish leather bag hanging from his right shoulder.

Thevar, Thevarajan, liked the way this smart young neighbor addressed him as 'uncle', though they were not related. A gentle smile appeared on his lips under the white moustache as he said, 'anyhow, a lecturer like you should be better dressed than this . . .,' the voice sounded reproving. 'And a decent appearance would surely impress them, wouldn't it?'

Sivan looked at his white sarong and the brown shirt carelessly worn and his lips parted in a silent smile.

'You really believe it, *maamaa*?' he asked. 'I don't think our dress would in any way change their opinion about us.'

'What makes you think so?' Thevar turned towards him.

'Do you think that they're yet to form any opinion about us?' He continued gravely, 'in their eyes, we are all culprits, people to be punished, for harboring their enemies! It is just because of that impression they're now herding us in here.'

Thevar did not say anything.

They were walking towards the long cemented concrete steps leading to a two-storied building roofed with dark brown tiles, in front. The house appeared dark and deserted. A big frangipani tree with its leafless branches like giant fingers, was brushing the high eaves.

Both stopped short. The whole place seemed strange, with an extraordinary eeriness in that vast compound surrounding the house. Even the entire vicinity remained frighteningly silent.

'None of those soldiers seem to be here?' Thevar's voice was soft.

'It looks so.'

Maroon colored dragon flies flitted about here and there. The sky was cloudless and grayish blue, a color particular to evenings of November, the only month with considerably heavy rainfall in Jaffna. The earth was clean, having been washed by the previous night's rain and the trails left by the water were still undisturbed and untrodden.

'Be careful, the stair is steep.' Sivan turned back towards his wife, who was closely following him, carrying their baby daughter in her right arm and a small blue plastic basket stacked with some bottles and a flask in the other. He went closer and gently touched the chubby cheeks of the child who was fast asleep. He smiled at his wife, as if to show that he was not dispirited by all that was happening around them. And indeed he felt a kind of invigorating feeling within him when he saw Suba reflecting the smile. With a prominent red *pottu* marked on her forehead, the lean, brown skinned woman looked reassuring and beautiful as ever. She was in a casual pink sari, something she managed to drape amid all that excitement and hurry.

'*Amma* must be tired,' Sivan thought of his mother as he looked at the frail old lady being led by his younger brother Ravi. Both of them were behind Suba.

Ravi, despite having the same facial features as his brother, appeared much taller and slimmer. He was leading their mother by holding her shriveled, bony arm in his.

He too was in a casual indoor dress, a blue striped sarong and a light yellow colored shirt. There was a small leather suitcase in his hand. Sivan went up to his mother as she was about to climb up the steps, raising her white sari above her ankles.

'I can climb by myself,' she objected.

'It's alright, let's help you. There are so many steps,' Ravi replied without loosening his grip.

Slowly they climbed up the stairs.

Though Sivan had passed by this house often, this was the second time he happened to be inside. This house was a landmark in their village. The bungalow must be more than forty years old and was built a few years before he was born, his father had once told him. It belonged to an affluent trader, Kanthar, who ran a popular textile business in the city of Jaffna. Sivan first visited this house with his parents when he was a small boy to attend the wedding of Kanthar's only daughter, Kamala. It was a grand function. Spacious *panthals* were erected to accommodate the guests. The wedding was followed by a grand feast and the guests were entertained by lively musical programs provided by well known *melam* troupes. Even on that day there was a big crowd, like the one following him now. But that was a happy and cheerful crowd!

Sivan felt heavy in his heart and turned round to look at the people coming behind. He saw some of the villagers still waiting outside the broad wrought iron gates hesitating to enter or not.

'Why are they waiting there?' Sivan asked Thevar, his voice full of concern.

'Haven't they heard what those soldiers had said? We have to stay here tonight.'

And his voice changed as he continued, as if murmuring, 'this'll be our home for God only knows how long . . .'

'These people must know that this is not a matter of their choice,' Thevar stopped for a moment, and then turned round saying, 'after all they've been told to bring what they need with them!'

He then hurried down towards the gate, without paying heed to his wife shrieking, 'where are you running back?' The fat old lady looked much fatter in her thick coffee colored sweater, a woolen scarf and house coat. She had gold framed spectacles.

'Uncle is not going anywhere *maami*, he'll be back now,' Suba pacified her.

They removed their sandals outside on the verandah and walked in timidly, feeling the chill of the green cemented floor decorated with neat diamond shaped patterns.

'It's sticky,' said Ravi.

'Don't you know that nobody uses this house at present except that caretaker Mani?' his mother reminded him.

The elevated verandah was not so wide, but very long. A lot of heavily framed pictures and some old family photographs were hanging in a neat row high above along the white washed walls on the three sides.

'Let's go in,' said Sivan and slowly walked ahead.

They went into the *koodam*, a square hall with a high ceiling. A musty smell pervaded the place.

'It's very dark here,' Suba said.

'All the windows are shut. Shall I open them?'

'No, let's wait for that Mani to come.'

Sivan ran his eyes over the place to choose a small area which would suit his family. He went to a corner away from the windows.

'Is this alright?' He asked Suba in a low voice. She nodded in agreement, but her face was not as bright as it was a couple of minutes ago. He wiped the floor with a piece of old newspaper he had pulled out from his bag and carefully arranged all their belongings there. Sivan then turned towards Thevar's wife.

'Is this place okay for you, *maami?*' He pointed to the place next to theirs.

'What's there to choose, *thambi?*' The panting lady replied with a sigh and quickly fanning the floor with a piece of cloth she pulled out from her shoulder bag, sat down immediately.

'True, we've to be satisfied with what we get at times like these,' agreed Sivan's mother and sat down beside Thevar's wife, leaning against the wall.

'You, too, better relax,' Sivan told Suba taking out a bed sheet and spreading it carefully on the floor for the child. The baby was still asleep on her mother's shoulder, her tiny thumb in her mouth. Sivan then turned towards his brother.

'You stay with them, Ravi. Don't go anywhere. I'll be back in a moment.'

'Okay,' said Ravi.

When Sivan came out to the verandah, people had already started coming in, though reluctantly. Most of them were still clutching the white flags in their hands as they were asked to do by those who had driven them there. The faces were dark and desperate. He went up to them. 'Just find a convenient place and occupy it. Keep your things there and relax,' Sivan told them in a soothing voice.

'This is our fate, *raasaa*. Leaving our comfortable homes and crouching in corners like this for no fault of ours and with our hearts filled with terror and uncertainty,' fumed the squint eyed Navam. He was a successful farmer who had acres of land at Poonery, just across the Jaffna lagoon, a place famous for its fertile paddy fields.

'No one seems to worry about our plight, even the One above,' he moaned. His tall wife and three teenaged children, two boys and a girl, were behind him, their faces fear stricken.

'You must've heard about what happened in places like Kokuvil and Jaffna town during the last couple of weeks and now it seems our turn,' remarked Navam.

'Look here, Navam, don't talk like that.'

Thevar went up to him and cautioned him in a soft but firm voice. 'Don't make others get scared. Why not be hopeful and optimistic? Leave everything to the Almighty.'

Naagu, a dark giant of a man with a slightly balding head, the miller of the village, came towards them excitedly. 'It appears that those soldiers didn't want to come in, *thambi*. They're still at the gate, counting the number of people coming in,' he said in a whisper.

'Don't worry,' Sivan replied calmly, 'let them do it; have to expect that.'

Mani the caretaker suddenly showed up in the middle of the crowd and started addressing them in a low voice. He was noticeably nervous, and the bare body above his waist was very dark and lean. He had a slight stoop.

'You can move in here also,' said Mani, opening the back door of the *koodam* which was ajar all the time and pointing at the place with a gesture of his close-cropped head.

'You'll find the four wings around the inner court and there's another large verandah behind. There's more than enough space for all, for the whole village even!'

'No rooms?' asked someone.

'Sorry, all the rooms are locked and the keys are with the owners in Colombo, as you all know.'

'What about the upstairs?'

'Yes, there are two small verandahs like balconies. You may go up there, if you wish.'

Lanky Logan nodded towards his people, and all of them, his wife, two children, his father and uncle and aunt walked towards the wooden stair case which was at the far corner.

'Shall we come to that place next to yours, Sivan? Is anybody else there?' The familiar voice made Sivan turn around and there was the smiling face of his friend, the Mathematics teacher of the village high school, fondly nick-named 'Pythagoras' by his students.

'Raju! You, too, are welcome. Nobody there, yet,' Sivan patted his friend's shoulder and smiled. 'We are always neighbors, even in a camp like this! Aren't we?'

All the people were in a hurry to secure a few square feet, which they could call their 'own' for the night or till they were allowed to get back to their houses again. Most of them carried a small bundle or a bag each, the only belongings they were able to bring in.

'Hurry up, everybody. It's getting dark and in no time you'll be unable to see each other's face. Don't you know these are the rainy days?' Old Essem, the retired station master, asked them in his husky voice. His pot belly was protruding behind the mauve colored tee shirt. There was a black woolen muffler around his neck hanging like a shawl.

'I saw a couple of people bringing lanterns,' observed Mani.

'Ha,' cut in Essem, stroking his bald head with his palm, 'can you rely on just two lanterns for all these people, and especially when you don't have kerosene anywhere?'

The night was quiet. Except for the brief cry of a child somewhere inside, there was no other noise in the whole house. Some were talking in the dark, in whispers, their agitation reflecting even in those hushed voices. It was not yet half past seven, but everybody had retired already. They were lying on that cold, bare cement floor, next to one another with scarcely any room between them even to turn aside. Narrow spaces, lined with old people or baggage, demarcated the boundaries between families. Virtually all of them, except for the children, were awake, their minds occupied with the same question, 'will they allow us to get back home at least tomorrow?'

'This is what our people called Fate,' Rasamma aunty's voice sounded stoically from somewhere in the dark. 'Leaving all our comfortable homes and coming here and lying down on this cold bare floor like this!'

Somebody else, a woman again, laughed bitterly, 'how many of us are going to catch pneumonia tomorrow, one cannot say.'

'How many of us will be alive tomorrow, you tell me that first?' They all heard Eason now, 'they are going to kill us all here!' Before finishing what he wanted to say he broke into sobs.

He then continued, 'I've read about the concentration camps set up during the time of the Second World War and I surely know that this is going to be one like that.'

All those who heard him remained silent without knowing whether to pity him or themselves.

Thevar got up at once and consoled him.

'Hush, *thambi* Eason, nothing like that will happen. Don't be frightened like a child.' The old man, flashing his dimmed torch went up to Eason who was still weeping and being comforted by his old parents. The yellow circle of light revealed the face of a well built youngster, the sharp features of which he seemed to have lost long ago. Thevar caressed his head, 'don't worry Eason. We all are here, aren't we? They'll definitely allow us to get back to our homes tomorrow, alright?'

Eason looked up, wiping his face, 'are you telling the truth?'

'Sure,' promised Thevar.

'He has been brought to this state by all our "saviors",' Thevar heaved a big sigh as he returned, 'and what a nice young man he was, helpful to all.'

'The worst thing was that he had to undergo the ordeal not once but twice or thrice; each militia suspecting the poor innocent chap for reasons best known to them only and penalizing him!' Essem remarked.

'How charming and energetic he was when we were in the lower forms,' Sivan thought of Eason. 'I've still not forgotten that friendship. Tomorrow I must speak to him and reassure him,' he decided.

Silence reigned again.

A single hurricane lamp lit by Mani hung on a thin rod from the roof of the western wing, flickering. The pale yellow light seemed unable to ooze out of the chimney covered by soot.

Sivan and Thevar were seated on the cold white sand in the middle of the big inner court yard, each lost in his own thoughts. The star lit sky was clear, without a trace of any cloud and the air was still. Behind the tiled roof were the dark silhouettes of the tall areca nut trees standing by the well, in the backyard. A sudden screech of a *sudalai kuruvi* pierced that eerie silence and reverberated across the sky as it darted across, and gradually vanished in the distance.

'Thoo, thoo,' Sivan heard old Valli *Aachi* spitting, from a dark corner somewhere in an attempt to ward off any possible curse imparted on the already cursed people below by the bird's cry, and mumbling, 'a bad omen . . . O, God.'

As if distracted by these, Sivan turned towards Thevar.

'Could any of us have ever thought that a thing like this would happen to us, *maamaa*?'

'This is like what our proverb says, *Vaeliyae payirai maeyuthaam*—the fence itself grazing the field,' Thevar scoffed. 'The same people, whom we looked up to bring us peace and protection, are doing this to us!'

'Have you both finished your dinner?' Essem appeared from the dark. He was holding something small in his hand which appeared to be a small piece of paper.

'What dinner at a time like this? Had just two balls of plain rice! My wife was able to bring at least that much in that hurry,' said Thevar.

'What about you?' Essem turned towards Sivan.

'Finished,' Sivan said briefly, thinking of his child. The little girl had to forego her usual string hoppers and milk tonight. Suba had forcibly fed her with a piece of rusk soaked in water with sugar and she herself nibbled another piece. Only their mother was able to have her dinner as usual, a single plantain and plain water . . .!

Are these sufferings only for tonight? Sivan felt that heaviness in his chest again.

Suddenly he thought of that small calf at home which was staked away from its mother in the morning for the afternoon milking. He got up.

'What's the matter?' The other two asked, in unison.

'I'll be back in a minute,' he walked towards the *koodam*, to the place where his family was.

It was a fairly difficult task to walk in that semidarkness without trampling on anybody's limbs.

As soon he returned, Thevar and Essem asked again. 'What happened?'

'Thank God, Ravi had remembered to untie the calf,' he said. They understood. 'I've no cattle at home. That's a relief at times like these,' said Thevar.

'See? Everybody was in a hurry! And everybody had to leave everything and rush here helter-skelter,' complained Essem.

'First they said that their big man wanted to see us all at once. And it was that big man who gave us an hour's respite to collect our things before shepherding us here. They could've given us some more time, breathing space at least.'

'That must be their way of doing things and cannot be helped.'

'You know, I heard that they've code named this operation of theirs as *Pawan,* which means "wind" in their language. But this is not going to be an ordinary wind, but a whirlwind, a real whirlwind which has come to destroy us, our lives, land and everything!' Essem laughed in a voice full of bitterness. The others were still quiet.

An owl was hooting somewhere in the backyard.

'I can't understand why they asked us not to close the front door of this house for the night,' Essem began after some time, lowering his voice.

'I too wonder about it,' Thevar replied in a grave tone. And then he asked, 'why not both of us go and sleep in the front verandah?'

'Why not,' Essem agreed, 'surely we're not going to have even a wink of sleep tonight, so it's better to keep vigil, at least.'

'There's no one else there, is there?'

'No. But, if we go, some other men too will join us.'

'Let's do that,' agreed Essem.

The people who were gazing in the dark without sleep started gathering around them one by one.

'Do you know what happened to our Sellar *pariyariar*?' Navam started talking.

'He told me that his wife was then cooking their noon meals and the couple had to leave the half boiled rice with the pot and run here on an empty stomach!'

'Where's he?' asked someone.

'He's in the rear verandah,' replied Navam and continued. 'Luckily, my wife was able to bring whatever was left in our home and we were able to share something with Sellar and his wife now.'

'In my case, as I was about to recline in the easy chair after my lunch and was about to light a cigar,' Essem began relating his story. 'I heard somebody hammering at the gate . . . But didn't know who it really was and almost shouted at them. Then, thank God, I was lucky enough to recognize those foreign voices immediately and went running to the gate.'

Essem paused for a moment, took out what he had in his hand and started stretching and smoothening it. A piece of tobacco leaf! He went on with his story.

'When I opened the gate, there were four of these strange looking men with guns, trying to tell me something. They knew neither Tamil nor English and in fact it took a couple of minutes for me to comprehend that they were summoning all of us to the school at once! Just imagine! Can you ask them why? Or can you explain your problems or difficulties? What I was able to get was only an excuse for a couple of minutes to get things ready!' Essem then started rolling a cigar, pulling apart the tobacco carefully along the edges.

'That was the story everywhere,' said Raju. 'My father was taking a bath and had no time even to wash the soap he had applied on and had to wipe it off! They were in such haste.' Sivan noticed Ravi seated besides him.

'Some people were so upset that they had forgotten to secure their houses! It was so terrible,' Naagu remarked. 'Anyway, if you compare, our army would've been a hundred times better!'

'*Your* army?' somebody asked from somewhere, baffled.

'Yes, the Sri Lankan army. At least we would've been able to speak to them in one of our languages,' said Naagu who had worked in a rice mill in Pollonaruwa when he was young and could speak Sinhala well. 'And further,' he continued, 'they're all like us. Here, the mere sight of most of these people itself is enough to make us scared!'

The same person cackled from the dark, 'Yes, it's always better to forget and forgive!' The others were silent.

The pungent smell of cigar slowly filled the air.

'But, let's come back to our problem. All these troubles are only for tonight, right?' asked Vellai with optimism. Vellai earned this nickname meaning 'fair' because of his fair complexion, and most of the people in the village had forgotten his real name now. Vellai then continued, 'most probably they'll allow us to get back tomorrow.' It looked as if he was consoling himself rather than others.

'I doubt it very much,' observed Sivan slowly, in a matter of fact tone.

'Why? Why do you say so?' Vellai's anxiety was reflected in his voice.

'Haven't you noticed what their big man said at the school when we gathered in front of him?' Sivan looked at Vellai.

'What did he say?'

'We'll allow you to go back once we finish our search operation,' he said. Do you think that it is possible for them to finish that within a day? Or more exactly, how can they do that within a night, that means tonight?'

The others were speechless, realizing the gravity of that argument.

'Don't imagine things. Don't start worrying too much. Grumbling or complaining is not going to take us anywhere. We have no one to worry about us, neither leaders nor governments, to care for us except the Almighty himself. Haven't you heard our people say that God is the refuge of the helpless?'

Thevar went on as if delivering a sermon. 'Just think of what had happened during the whole of last month, when these Peace Keeping Forces were trying to capture the other areas of Jaffna. They were firing shells every day and every night, weren't they? How did we feel at that time, when the shells hissed past just above our heads and exploded nearby? How did we put up with that and how did we survive them? Who gave us the power to endure all those? Who helped us then? Leave everything to that unseen power and wait till they allow us go home.'

'In that case,' Essem spoke again, breaking the silence after a while, 'how are we going to deal with our needs here? We've got to think of a way to sort out these problems.' There was a shade of panic in his voice.

'We all came with the idea of staying for a single night at the most, didn't we?' wondered Jegan, a building contractor turned broker. He was originally from a far away Northern coastal village of the peninsula and he and his family were badly affected and their belongings lost during the military operation early that year. They settled in this village, started their life anew and were now integrated fully with the local community.

'Even a single night's stay away from home is terrible, and that too, during the rainy days like these!' Jegan's wife, a chronic asthma patient, complained as if crying.

They heard a child whining and it was followed at once by the voice of its soothing mother. But the moaning did not stop.

'Why, daughter, why then is your child crying?' Thevar asked from where he was, even without knowing who that young woman was.

'Nothing, *aiya* . . .' came out a hoarse male voice.

'Is that your wife and child, Arumai?' Thevar identified the voice. 'Weren't you able to find time to bring anything for the child to eat tonight?'

There was silence for a minute and then it was broken by soft voices from several places in the dark.

'Arumai, why not give this rice?'

'We've some extra *rotti* and banana . . .'

'Would the child be willing to have some plain tea, may be a bit cold?'

'Come on Arumai, get up,' Thevar told him and then turning behind he called gently.

'Raju, go and fetch something for the child. Arumai may find it embarrassing to take from somebody.'

Raju got up and went.

'If what you say is going to happen,' Essem started again in a pensive tone and asked Sivan, 'what are we going to do?'

'What are we to do?' repeated Sivan, dejectedly. 'We've to do whatever they order us to do. That's all!'

'What do you think they have in mind? What are they going to do with us?'

'They say that they're going to do a combing up operation. That means a house to house search in the village while we are being detained here. And . . .'

'And, what else?'

'The chances are they might screen us, right here, at this place!' Sivan then turned towards his brother.

'Ravi, you've your identity card and other documents safely, haven't you?' His voice was full of anxiety.

He could see Ravi nodding, even in that faint light. 'Yes *annai.*'

'But, don't worry too much,' Thevar consoled others. 'What can they do with us? We're innocent civilians, involved in nothing objectionable. We are all occupied, either with our studies or our work.'

'Fate is playing against us,' observed Essem in a grave tone. The others listened quietly as if agreeing with what he said and Essem continued. 'That great lady Indira died unexpectedly and if you don't call that our bad luck, then what is it? Even that good soul who was interested in our well being, the Chief Minister of Tamil Nadu, MGR is in his sick bed at present. If not, things would've been definitely different.'

Sivan thought how the whole of Jaffna had mourned the death of Indira Gandhi, the then Prime Minister of India, for two days, everybody grieving as if that lady had belonged to their own family. All the roads were deserted and shops and offices closed and there were only black flags and funeral decorations everywhere. The entire peninsula would've never seen such bereavement before.

'After all,' said Raju in a convincing voice as if to assure others, 'these forces have come here not to fight the Tamils or the Sinhalese! What do you say?'

No one spoke and Raju went on. 'We're all aware of the deteriorating situation which started in seventy-seven and worsened in eighty-three and ultimately reached the climax with the outbreak of this civil war. Over the last five years we have had more than enough troubles because of the actions of the various parties concerned. And now these people have come on the scene with an assurance of bringing us peace and a political solution.'

'That's what they say,' said some one, following a silence. 'But, you can't trust these Northern chaps, the most unreliable lot!'

'What shall we do then, *thambi?*' Thevar asked Sivan.

'Better to be prepared. If they tell us to stay here for a couple of days, then we've to ask for permission tomorrow morning to go home to bring provisions,' replied Sivan.

'And also the valuables we left there,' Navam pointed.

'Don't mention anything about the valuables to them,' cautioned Raju's father, a person who had lost his well-paid job due to the closure of the KKS cement factory following the disturbed state of affairs.

'So, bringing things from home is priority number one and number two is to make arrangements here for an orderly way of life for all these people, even if the stay happens to last longer.'

'Water, cooking, bathing, washing, toilet . . .!' Essem counted on his fingers.

'*Chalo!*' said the one who looked like the leader of that small group of soldiers waiting outside. He must be from the North, knowing neither Tamil nor English and was fair and tall with a sharp moustache pointing upwards. Sivan understood the meaning of what he said because of his limited vocabulary of Hindi. 'Let's go.' The *Jawan* took two strides ahead and stopped. He then looked back at both the men whom he was supposed to escort. Thevar and Sivan gazed at each other and gestured mutually, to go in front. And both very well knew that the gesture made by the other was not due to fear but respect. After a moment's hesitation, Thevar, appreciating the respect given to his age, strode in front and stood by the side of the soldier. Sivan went and stood behind him and turned towards the house. The high verandah was full of people. He saw his family standing in front of the others.

Though Suba was trying to make the child wave to its father, her face was covered by an obvious gloom. The faces of his mother, and Ravi, too, seemed to accuse Sivan for his stupidity in jumping forward to go and make arrangements for provisions. 'You, too, should've kept quiet like others,' they seemed to say. He thought that he was able to hear them wishing him well in silence and praying for his safe return. He smiled at them courageously as if suggesting everything would be alright and there was nothing to worry about.

It was a bright morning. The sun could not penetrate through the leafy-fronds of the palmyrah grove behind Ratnam Master's house. A peculiar silence prevailed everywhere, even beyond that house; even in the entire surrounding. This has never been the way in this village. What curse has befallen us mused Thevar.

'*Chalo!*' repeated the soldier and started walking in front with his chest pushed forward.

Thevar followed and Sivan, with a quick nod towards the verandah as if bidding farewell, stepped behind. Outside the gate, four other men, who had been waiting there, joined them. Two in front and two behind and thus formed an array. Ahead of them was Ratnam Master's house. It was full of *jawans* bustling around! They had made a well fortified sentry box in front with cement concrete blocks which they must have obtained by breaking some wall, somewhere nearby.

Seeing these two civilians, their heads popped up above the parapet wall and they stood staring at them. The one on sentry duty uttered something loud and the others laughed. The blended smell of ghee and groundnut oil hung in the air. They walked past the men, looking ahead. They had to walk slowly. The one going in front did not seem to be in a hurry. Sivan had an urge to turn around and have a look at Kanthar's house. But he gave up that idea fearing the soldiers might misinterpret his action.

Thevar walked in front of Sivan, at an arm's length. As he walked, a measured screech came from his black leather slippers. Thevar was in his usual dress, the white shawl neatly wrapped around his neck merging neatly with his dense gray hair at the back. Usually he had holy ash and sandalwood paste on his forehead, but Sivan remembered seeing only the holy ash this morning, the sandalwood paste was missing. His appearance was as usual, even on a day like this! Sivan looked at himself—he had the same sarong, with the tail of his shirt hanging out, and the pair of brown rubber slippers. His usual 'off-day' wear, the ones he had worn after his noon bath the previous day. 'It's alright, I can change into freshly washed clothes once I return after attending to this provisions matter,' he thought. But, it was doubtful if he would be able to have a bath before afternoon when looking at that large crowd in the camp! Let's see to that after returning. The important thing is to make arrangements for three or four days' supply, at the least. How to allow those in the camp go hungry? Let alone the grown up people but what about the children? Nobody would consider our request seriously unless some people from the camp went and talked to them, the officer had said this morning. He was a helpful sort of person. Captain B.C.D. Singh was his name. He must be in charge of the camp at Ratnam Master's house. A young man with a pair of spectacles and a fully shaven face, he looked more like an academic than a military man.

The whole area remained quiet, dominated by an unusual weirdness which he had never experienced in his village. There were small puddles of flood water here and there and they had to dodge them. The previous night's rain had washed the sand along the road side clean and it glistened in the bright morning sun. Their long shadows cast onto their left glided along the terrain. They walked, unable to enjoy the fresh and cold air. Where are they taking us? Where is the local Red Cross office? B.C.D. Singh had assured them that the officers would attend to the matter without delay. It would be fine, if they could finish it soon and let us return early. That temporary office of the Red Cross must be somewhere close to the *Amman* temple, at the far end of the village main road.

That's correct. The man going in front was turning left. They, too, followed . . .

What is this? Sivan was shocked to see what was in front. The fences on both sides of the road remained burnt and the parapet walls razed . . . Even the door boards of Kathiresu's grocery shop were missing . . . What on earth had happened? A heavy deathly silence reigned over the place. It was disturbed by the cawing of a lonely crow from somewhere in the neighborhood. Then it, too, fell silent. The entire scene was disgusting! Sivan looked at Thevar. Certainly, he too must have been affected by this dreadful sight. Thevar's careful movements reflected that he, too, was upset. Couldn't they talk to each other? The soldiers, like robots, walked in front and behind. Why are they taking us like this, handling us like prisoners? Why such fuss and precaution for two civilians, thought Sivan.

The soldier in front walked cautiously with his gun pointed. His steps were watchful, his eyes scanning the surroundings! The pair of *jawans* who followed him, too, did the same. Though he couldn't turn round and have a look, Sivan presumed the pair escorting them from behind did the same. Where are they taking us in this way? Have we been deceived and trapped into this foolishly, mused Sivan. Suddenly he saw the burnt out remnants of something scattered between the patch of dense grass and the line of a small mound, which was once a fence . . . The tread of the soldiers' heavy boots on the road . . . That was the only sound they could hear now. A scary bleakness prevailed all over. 'Is this our village? Certainly this is not a dream,' wondered Sivan. They went on walking.

Atop the portico of banker Ponniah's house, there was a sentry post. The concrete blocks from the parapet walls that stood in front must have gone into its construction. A gun barrel projected out through a watch hole in that sentinel's house . . .

The fences of overseer Thurai's compound had been torn apart, the backyard clearly visible from where they were. In his car shed was the burnt-out shell of Thurai's old *Morris Minor* . . .

Where could the people have gone from this area, maybe to the *Amman* temple? Has this part of the village, too, been taken up by the soldiers, like ours? Or, were those people wise enough to have gone elsewhere before this search operation, like Ratnam Master?

That same smell of ghee and groundnut oil again! It was getting stronger. They must be somewhere close by! There were two more sentry posts behind the green boundary walls of Gunam's compound, with guns jutting out from both. Beyond those there were another two! All built out of concrete blocks taken from Packia Akka's and Jothi's parapet walls! The corrugated GI sheets from the lean-to roof of Paddu's bicycle repair shop were also missing. They must be the ones atop those sentry posts! The whole place was ravaged, like the outcome after a fierce storm. Or who knows, the storm is yet to ravage? The man who led the column turned to the right. It was the private car-track, leading to Health Inspector Param's house. They followed.

What is this? There were so many men, crowded together like a swarm of caterpillars! Sivan could not trust his eyes. He shuddered. This, surely, is not a dream! Why did they bring us here? How could one expect to find the Red Cross office at a setting like this? How could this place remain so quiet with so many men? One would never believe that this blind lane could house such a crowd. Soldiers were found everywhere, either sitting or squatting, in neat rows along both sides of the track, silently smoking *beedi*. And the strong smell of it was trying to overcome the aroma of ghee. Sivan felt his stomach turn. Would anyone have ever dreamt of such a thing happening? Ever dreamt that our village would be occupied by such a massive number of these elite soldiers, the Gurkhas? And what was the need for all these?

The column made its way between the two rows of men seated on the ground. Sivan heard a few grunts from here and there, some whisperings, an unexpected whistle . . .! All the faces remained alike, and wooden. The two tried to walk past without looking at them. Suddenly one of the seated soldiers raised his head and shouted at them angrily. It sounded something like 'LTTE'!

Sivan felt like laughing but controlled himself as he knew the possible consequences.

The file went straight to Param's house and as they entered through the gate and turned, the large compound came into view. It was full of tall coconut palms above and dense grass covering the ground. There was no one there. But, a little further away, in front, was the spacious portico, busy like a beehive. They walked further and when they approached a coconut tree, the *jawan* who had brought them there gestured for them to stop. And he went to report. So, this is their place, camp or quarters or whatever one might call it. The same portico where Param used to park his old motorcycle was their command post now! A patch on the floor darkened with the stain of engine oil could be seen from where they stood.

The portico was about thirty feet away and they could clearly see all that was going on there. In the middle was a man seated on a sofa. He must be an officer and looked like a Gurkha. Just away from him was a table with wireless sets on it. Three men around the table were issuing orders one after another. Orders sent out to various places perhaps! A tall man was standing behind the wireless operators, slightly bent, his hands clutching the back of a chair, giving instructions. He was not a Gurkha. He was very tall and fair, his head and the youthful face completely shaven and was dressed in a full black uniform.

The *jawan* who brought them here went and stood in front of the seated officer and saluted and reported. He returned, immediately, taking his orders. Sivan and Thevar looked at him coming towards them. As soon as he came closer, he commanded.

'*Aav!*' This was the second word that came out of his mouth after '*Chalo!*' which he uttered while they were about to leave Kanthar's house! Both the civilians followed him, their hearts thumping heavily.

The officer, not tall, was seated with his legs crossed. He was staring at them. His beret was on his lap and the streaks of grey hair on his head were prominent. He must have been about fifty. It was only after coming close to him they found that there were no other chairs.

The officer remained silent, continued staring at them, piercingly.

'Good Morning!' greeted Thevar. The seated man frowned.

'Wait there!' he replied harshly pointing to a pillar, and then called. 'Vikram Singh!'

Vikram Singh, the one who brought them here, stepped forward, and standing at attention he listened to the officer's instructions. Then he saluted smartly and returned.

When he left the place, his four men also followed him.

Sivan was shocked. Food or no food we should not have come here at all! The men who are going away are B.C.D. Singh's men. They've brought us here and are leaving now. Is it possible for us to return on our own? Would any man here take us back? At a time like this, we can't go alone even though it's only half a mile. By the way things are going it is doubtful if we would ever return! Sivan wiped his face with the back of his hand. Whether genuine or not, B.C.D. Singh had at least a pleasant smile on his face. But there's no trace of such a thing on the face of this officer seated in front. He looked fierce, as though he would devour them . . . Their hearts thumped.

A soldier came out of the house. There was a silver tray in his hand. It was full of small white pieces . . . Thinly sliced coconut kernel! He held the tray forward and the officer took a handful and at once started munching. Then the *jawan* took the tray to the shaven headed person. Sivan now noticed that the man's head was not fully shaven but there was a small, finger thick tuft of hair, tied into a knot. It looked so thin, like the tail of a rat and reminded Sivan of some of the characters he has seen in *Ambulimama*, the popular children's magazine when he was a school boy. The *Ambulimama* man took a white towel with his left hand and wiped his face and with the other he took a handful of pieces of coconut kernel. The soldier then left the tray on a stool in front and went in. The two officers continued munching the pieces of the kernel without paying any heed to Thevar and Sivan who were standing in front of them. Sivan felt annoyed . . . These officers did not even have the good manners to offer them seats . . .

Sivan wanted to have a look at Thevar's face. Thevar was standing by his side, their shoulders touching. But, how could he turn? The name tag tied on to the Gurkha's breast was clear now and Sivan was able to make out the name . . . a Major! Patha.

Pathaa, or Paathaa, he wasn't sure of the pronunciation.

The other was a Captain. Vanpar. Vaanpar, or Vanpaar?

'You . . .,' the Major seated in the chair with crossed legs pointed at Sivan, '. . . come, here.'

Sivan was affronted at the officer's rude manner. Does this alien know who I am? No one had ever treated me in this fashion. Sivan felt a mute anger. He went two steps forward.

'Can you speak English?'

It was my speaking English that made B.C.D. Singh send me here! Sivan now regretted revealing his ability to speak that language.

'A little . . .,' he said.

'You should answer me honestly . . . Don't try to come up with lies and deceive me . . .'

Is this military man trying to frighten me by looking that way? Sivan wondered. A fine way to solve the food problem!

'Are you a member of the LTTE?' came the first question.

'No.'

'Don't tell me a lie. You must know what will happen . . . ?'

'No, I am a state sector employee, a teacher . . . A family man,' replied Sivan defiantly.

'As a teacher, you must tell me the truth. Where are the LTTE? Who are the LTTE members here?'

'There's nobody here . . .'

'You're a young person. Surely you must have had contacts with them . . .'

'I've nothing to do with them.'

'Shut up!' shouted the Major, jumping up from the chair, his facial muscles quivering.

He frowned at Sivan, without batting an eyelid.

'Don't try to teach me,' roared the Major, his facial muscles still trembling.

Without knowing what to say, Sivan stood there silent.

'Alright,' the Major started again, 'this place is considered to be the stronghold of the LTTE. You are a person from this area and yet you deny any knowledge of them. You want me to believe that?' The officer shouted and raised his hand as if to hit Sivan.

'That could have been . . . but I don't know anything.'

'How can that be . . . ?' ridiculed the Major aggressively. 'Are you trying to make a fool of me?'

'Let me speak, sir . . .' said Sivan, determined to face the consequences.

'Now, you all are here. But we don't know how many of you are here. Who is an officer? Who is a *Jawan*? Where did you come from? Where do you plan to go next? We do not know anything. As far as we are concerned, you were here, that's all. This is what we would be able to tell anyone who questions us once you leave . . . !'

Sivan got alarmed, had he said too much?

Patha's gaze continued to scrutinize him. The small eyes under the arched brows narrowed further into slits and tried to bore through him. . . . Is he trying to test my will? Unfolding his arms crossed over his chest, Sivan wiped his face. After a momentary silence, Patha spoke. 'Look here! I could now ask you to turn and run away from here . . . But I would see how far you could run!' said the Major.

It took a couple of seconds for Sivan to understand the meaning of what the Major said! He couldn't have said 'I'll shoot you,' better than this. Sivan was alarmed. What's this man really up to? Is Thevar behind?

The Captain was busy with the wireless sets, handling two conversations simultaneously, his eyes roving . . .

'Get back,' hollered the Major.

'What's he going to do?' Sivan wondered. 'Is he really going to shoot me? Oh, God . . .' He stood immobile, petrified.

'Go and stand there!' shouted the officer again and then turning to Thevar, called out to him. 'You come here!'

Sivan could not believe his luck. Has his life been spared by the Major for the time being? He stepped back, automatically. Thevar, stepped forward, adjusting his shawl.

'Now, you can tell us,' shouted the Major.

'What do you expect me to tell you, sir?'

The tone and Thevar's mastery of the English language must have amazed the officer.

'The truth, tell the truth!'

'We've a great respect for your country. Some even consider it their mother land . . .'

The Major didn't allow him to finish. 'Stop with that trick!' he shouted. 'We've enemies within our country, too!'

Sivan was affronted at the rough manner in which the Major treated Thevar, leaving that old gentleman to stand in front, without even having the courtesy to offer him a seat! How could this foreigner understand the old man's education, wealth and standing in society? How can they treat us this way and for what reason?

'So, you don't know anyone?'

'No sir!'

'Get back,' shrieked the Major.

'Excuse me . . .' said Thevar, 'you've misunderstood us, I think. Your Captain B.C.D. Singh visited our camp this morning and informed us that the villagers will not be allowed to return to their homes till you give permission and till then, we have to make arrangements for food for all the people. That's why . . .'

'Shut up,' interrupted the Major at the top of his voice, his face red with anger and shining in perspiration.

'Both of you,' he pointed, 'go and stay by that wall.'

Facing the wall? Sivan once again felt the churning in his stomach, his whole body perspiring.

The ground beside the wall was covered with green grass soft as a cushion. Param's flower plants also looked luxuriant due to the recent rains. What a wonder, there were the seedlings of the rare *sarakkontrai* in front of him! The plant with those swathing, beautiful golden yellow flowers would attract anybody. The seedlings he had been looking for all these days were within reach now! Call it a paradox?

Thevar stood beside him. They looked at each other. The old gentleman's face was full of perspiration. He removed the glasses and wiped his face with the shawl. Both wanted to speak to each other, but they were afraid to do so. 'They'll do anything to us . . .' Sivan turned and had a look at the portico. If we speak in a muffled voice they may not be able to hear. The Major was not there. The Captain was still busy with his wireless sets, surrounded by five or six of his men . . . They heard sounds of washing of big metallic cooking pans and pots coming from the rear of the house. Maybe the meals were being prepared.

The men in the access lane must still be there. The smell of *beedi* lingered in the air. However, nothing could be seen from where they were. Both were tired. Not hungry, but thirsty. They hadn't had a drop of water since early morning.

'It won't take much time, you could finish your matter and

return in ten minutes,' B.C.D. Singh had assured them. What a cheat! Anger, fear, grief and distress tormented them.

'Shall we sit down?' Sivan asked, looking at Thevar. 'Wouldn't they object?'

'Let's see.' Sivan scoured the grass with his foot and sat down. And at once he felt a sense of relief. Thevar, spreading his shawl on the grass, sat down next to him. Is anybody looking at us? No, no one seemed to care about them . . . Pulling up a stalk of grass, Sivan began nibbling it absent mindedly. What's going to happen?

The sound of something crashing suddenly, made them turn. The fence on the western side was collapsing and an advancing monster of a lorry was pushing it down with its engine roaring on top gear. The life stakes gave way one by one and that whole fence lined with strong stalks of palmyrah fronds yielded slowly, almost unwillingly, except for a stout *vathanarayani* tree which remained a challenge to the advancing lorry.

A soldier came running with an axe and started felling it down.

Beyond the fallen fence was the next compound which, too, was full of coconut palms. It belonged to Murugesu, the pharmacist, now working in a government hospital somewhere close to Kandy. There were some internally displaced people like Jegan and family who had been occupying that house for the last couple of years. What would have happened to them?

Beyond Murugesu's compound was the Mathavady road. The lorry must have come here bulldozing its way from there. Aware that heavy vehicles could not pass along the narrow lanes, the soldiers had found a way out by demolishing the fences and other obstructions that blocked their path. The giant of a vehicle zigzagged its way between the coconut trees and advanced with groans and growls. The peculiar smell of the fuel fumes engulfed the whole place.

The way things are going, it seems these people have no intention in leaving the place in a hurry . . . Suddenly Sivan remembered what Ganesan had told him at that time these troops poured in. The roar of low flying planes landing at Palaly Airport one after the other seemed unending that day and Ganesan remarked, 'Sivan, I don't think they really have any idea of leaving quickly, look at the way they are teeming down! I have read about such large scale air lifts that took place during the Second World War.'

'Yes, instead of all these they should have pressed for a genuine dialogue between the rebels and the government here. That may have been more sensible and successful than sending in troops,' agreed Sivan.

'Using military force will never bring peace, anywhere in the world. Even if it does it will be short lived.'

The men were now mending that newly made short cut. . . . Sivan would have never guessed that Mathavady road was so near. Beyond the road was the vast palmyrah grove which stretched up to the play ground of the primary school and further, the paddy fields where the Indian helicopters had landed like a dream, a few months ago, in July 87, sowing seeds of hope and anticipation in the minds of the tens of thousands of people who were affected by the prolonging war.

Sivan was extremely thirsty. But where could he get water? On that side of the fence, in Murugesu's compound was a well with its tall well-sweep. And the bucket is still in place. A well in every compound full to the brim, and yet not a drop to drink! He felt so exhausted and wanted to lie down on the bed of cool grass. Won't their people in the camp be awaiting their return? They would've started worrying about them anyway. 'We were brought here and delayed on purpose with the intention of making us yield! But, what could we tell them about when we ourselves don't know any damned thing?'

The lorry parked under the mango tree was imprinted with the model's name *Shakthiman*. Its body camouflaged with paint was covered with dust, despite the recent rains. But the wheels were caked with mud.

The driver, a dark guy, was all alone and busy attending to the vehicle. He stopped his work for a while, and called somebody. When the other person showed himself up, the driver spoke to him in a loud voice telling something '*paani*', '*paani*'. The other, without any reply, walked back towards the house. The driver, wiping his face, saw the two men seated by the wall. Sivan realized that the driver was looking at them but avoided facing him.

The day proved much warmer as the sun rose higher. Sivan looked at his watch. It was two hours since they had left their camp.

The one whom the driver had spoken to returned with a large silver jug, *sombu*. Could that be a *sombu* from Param's kitchen mused Sivan. The man who brought it handed it over to the driver. The sight of the driver gulping down the water aggravated Sivan's thirst.

Thevar too must be feeling thirsty. He stretched out his legs and cracked his knuckles. 'Shall we get up?'

'Yes.' Sivan stood up.

Nobody noticed them. The driver, having finished drinking, wiped his mouth with the back of his hand and handed over the *sombu* to the one waiting in front. Sivan noticed through the corner of his eyes that the driver was again looking at them. Was he coming towards them?

The driver stopped and called out to the other man again. The soldier returned. The driver took the *sombu* back from him, came up to Thevar and Sivan and stretched the vessel out to them.

'Would you like to have some water?' He asked in Tamil.

After a moment's hesitation, Thevar took the *sombu* offered to him.

'Thanks. Are you a Tamil?'

'You'd better drink this first . . .'

'Why have they detained us?' A trace of annoyance was obvious in Sivan's voice.

'What happened?'

Sivan related the story.

'They'll soon allow you to go. They're just making enquiries. Drink it,' he said and then switched to English. 'No problem!'

'You're the only person who has considered us . . . and given us water . . .'

'Whatever it is, we are one people, aren't we?'

'What's your name?' asked Thevar.

'Gopalan.'

Thevar handed the *sombu* over to Sivan. Sivan drank the water slowly, relishing each mouthful, allowing it to wet his parched throat, cooling the chest. He felt refreshed.

'I'm a Malayalee . . . I've to take your leave now, *saar* . . .'

The driver, receiving the *sombu* from Sivan, walked hurriedly towards the lorry.

Sivan and Thevar looked at each other wondering what had come over the driver for him to leave them in such haste. Had anyone seen him speaking to us? Was he afraid of anything? What had made him withdraw from admitting that he was a Tamil? It all puzzled them.

'Come, let's sit down!'

They sat down once again. The cushion-like grass gave off a pleasant smell. How long should we continue to wait here? What on earth is going to happen? Both felt exhausted.

The group in the front lane must still be there. And the same five or six men were still busy in the portico in front. How many of them could be there altogether, inside and outside the house? Except that Gopalan, nobody had paid any attention to them. Where was he now? Where are those men who had mended the fence?

A gust of wind, blended with the smell of *beedi*, ghee, dust and diesel fumes wafted past them. Coconut fronds swayed in the wind like waves. Patches of shadows in front changed patterns rapidly. It was unusually warm for a day in the rainy season. All of a sudden Sivan felt the terror, the gravity of the situation.

What are they going to do with us? Are they really going to shoot us as that chap threatened, or detain us here? . . . He felt the shiver running along his spine . . . If so what will happen to my family, my people . . . ? He turned towards Thevar.

Having finished softly reciting the prayer hymn *Kantharsashdi Kavasam*, Thevar began to recite another, a *Thevaram* beginning '*Naamaarkkum kudiyallom, namanai anchom* . . . Subjects we are to none, nor do we fear *Yama*, the lord of death . . . when we surrender ourselves to those benign feet of Thee. . . .'

It was mid-day. Sivan's digital watch displayed the time—12.02. As he looked at it, the .02 changed into .03. The life beat of the tiny gadget was unaffected by this external turmoil . . .

If not for this present chaos forced on their land, the noon *pooja* bells would've started pealing by now in all the temples of the area.

Sivan tried to pray silently, his eyes closed.

Suddenly they heard the rattling of guns from somewhere. Thevar and Sivan looked at each other, their faces dark with fear and worry. Guns barked and went on non stop. Neither far nor near but certainly somewhere in the east, the direction they have to take to get back to the camp.

'A shoot out . . .' Thevar's soft voice was heavy with fear and anxiety.

What will happen to us? To those back in the camp? The firing continued without respite. The guns rattled from two sides. What would happen next?

Sivan locked his hands round his knees and leaned forward . . . The shadow of his tousled hair fell in front of him.

They heard muted footsteps near the house and turned . . . The row of soldiers was gliding silently like a giant snake. That speed without even the slightest noise made them shiver. The men were fully clad in combat uniforms, their steel helmets camouflaged with twigs, the holsters bulging and guns ready in their hands. Their heavy boots made muffled thuds by pounding the wet ground in quick succession, like a rhythm.

The column was moving towards their direction. The man at the head of the line appeared close to them. Would we have to get up or not? Any movement on our part may result in misunderstanding . . . Besides, Sivan felt frozen. He could not move his limbs . . . Even Thevar remained motionless. Possibly, the soldiers in the advancing file did not care about the duo . . . Turning at the gate they went past. What about the men already waiting in the lane?

The column seemed non stop . . . How many men!

A tall soldier with a broom like moustache was rushing about; the thin long aerial of a wireless set on his back swaying according to his movements. More and more men went past. Some looked at them as they went by. One soldier passing by made some remark. It made no sense to Thevar or Sivan.

About two hundred odd men must have gone by and there were coming still more. Surely, there must have been soldiers in the neighboring house, too. The *Ambulimama* man emerged from the house. He was still in his black uniform, but was now wearing a helmet and carrying a wireless set on his back. Two of his men followed him. He really had an impressive figure, handsome, too. Should have been a hero in Hindi films! No, there is none to beat that B.C.D. Singh if it came to acting, how he persuaded us to come here!

Captain Vanpar looked at them as he passed by and said casually, 'You may go!'

They were perplexed. Did he mean it or was he making fun of them? Are we to take him at his word and go? Suppose we did and then? Sivan thought of the Major's threat. He felt his body sweating. . . . Both looked at each other, baffled.

'Let's go,' said Sivan finally, his eyes looking around. The Captain was not to be seen anywhere now.

'Let's wait for some more time. Let these people go . . . If we leave now, it may cause problems . . .' Thevar advised.

They waited.

The men continued to march by. The column seemed endless. It was very difficult to differentiate one from the other. In complexion, height, features, they all looked alike! Sivan suddenly realized that he was watching the men unintentionally. Better not to look at them, he reproved himself. And when he was about to turn away he thought he saw a man come running towards them from their right . . . Sivan turned and saw a soldier breaking rank and rushing towards them, his gun pointed. What is this? Why hadn't the other soldiers stopped him? What was he shouting at them? And in which language, Hindi, or . . .

Sivan could only make out the last word. 'LTTE!'

When the man jumped at them, his face was just three feet away. A lock of hair out of the helmet was hiding the forehead and his eyes filled with that hatred of a killer . . . The soldier thrust his gun on the chest of Sivan . . .

Sivan closed his eyes.

Later, Thevar confessed that he, too, had closed his eyes at that moment. Sivan and Thevar were then walking towards their camp along the deserted roads. The silence peculiar to noon times was overwhelmed by the scary quietness of the unusual atmosphere.

They came out of Param's gate and saw the column that passed them advancing in the direction opposite to what they had to take.

'That's good,' thought Sivan.

When they were about to turn on their way, they saw Vanpar watching them from the other side of the road. They were stunned and hesitated for a second. The Captain's retinue was behind him and he looked much taller among those men. He yelled at the duo.

'You go straight to your camp and if you happen to come across any of our people, just raise both your hands above your heads and stay where you are without moving.'

He advised when they went up to him, 'but don't try to hide

from the soldiers or run away from them. That'll be a fatal blunder, remember. The full day curfew is still on!'

'Alright sir, thank you.' Both nodded and moved on. 'How could this chap tell such serious things so casually?' Sivan murmured when they were out of ear shot. 'He may be used to such things but it's a matter of life or death to us!'

'Bringing us here deceitfully and leaving us astray on the road during curfew hours!' Thevar said bitterly. 'You know our proverb, *sirupillaikku vilaiyaaddu, sundelikku seevan poachu,* what's fun for the child is death for the mouse!'

They plodded on. Every bend and every turn appeared a death trap. A gun-totting *jawan* could emerge from behind any wall, any lamp post . . .

The sun was above their heads, not very bright but very warm. The air too was stagnant and Sivan felt stuffy. And instantly he felt pangs of hunger and he remembered he hadn't had a morsel for the whole day. He had only plain water Gopalan had given him an hour ago. Today was not a normal day to go home expecting Suba to wait for him with a hearty lunch! That stark realization made him gloomy . . .

What'll be there for them to eat once they return to the camp? A situation he had never experienced in all these forty years of his life. Never mind him, an able bodied person. What about his child, his old mother, his wife and brother? What about all the others expecting the two with the hope that they'll bring provisions? Surely it'd be a disappointment to them. Not only a disappointment but a terrible shock as well!

They kept on walking, slowly, their eyes watching all around. The tarred road appeared like a straight long ribbon stretching into infinity. Sivan thought he saw mirages along the desolate road ahead.

'If we see the chaps in front we can put up our hands above heads. But suppose they see us from somewhere without our noticing them, what'll happen then?' Thevar laughed at such a thought. He was obviously exhausted. What else could one expect from a person in his late sixties after such a trying day, however smart he might be? Covering his head with his white shawl to shield it from the hot sun, Thevar asked again, 'What'll happen to us?'

'Better not think of it,' replied Sivan, 'but somehow or the other, we'll be alright.'

'Yes,' agreed Thevar. 'Our merciful mother, *Amman,* the guardian Goddess of the village, will never let us down!'

They kept on walking.

The Cat's Table

Michael Ondaatje

He wasn't talking. He was looking out the window of the car all the way. The two adults in the front seat spoke quietly under their breath. He could have listened if he wanted to but he didn't. For a while, at the section of the road where the river sometimes flooded, he could hear the spray of water under the wheels. They entered the fort and the car slipped silently past the post-office building and the clock tower. At this hour of the night, there was barely any traffic in Colombo. They drove out along Reclamation Road, past St. Anthony's Church, and he saw the last of the food stalls, each lit with a single bulb. Then they entered a vast open space that was the harbor, with a long string of lights in the distance along the pier. He got out and stood by the warmth of the car.

He was eleven years old that night, green as he could be about the world, when he climbed aboard the first and only ship of his life. It felt as if a city had been added to the coast, more brightly illuminated than any town or village. He went up the gangplank, watching the path of his feet—nothing ahead of him existed—and continued till he was on the other side of the ship, facing the dark harbor and sea. There were the outlines of other ships farther out, beginning to turn on their lights. He stood alone, smelling everything, then returned through the noise and the crowd to the side that faced land. A yellow glow over the city. Already it felt as if there were a wall between him and what took place there. Stewards began handing out food and cordials. He ate several sandwiches, then made his way down to his cabin, undressed, and slipped into the narrow bunk. He'd never slept under a blanket before, save once in Nuwara Eliya. He was wide awake. The cabin was below the level of the waves, so there was no porthole. He found a switch beside the bed, and when he pressed it his head and pillow were suddenly caught in a cone of light.

He did not go back up on deck for a last look, or to wave at the relatives who had brought him to the ship. He could hear singing and he imagined the slow and then eager parting of families taking place in the thrilling night air. I do not know, even now, why he chose this solitude. In films, people tear themselves away from one another weeping, watching their loved ones' disappearing faces until all distinction is lost.

I try to imagine who the boy in the narrow bunk was. Perhaps there was no sense of self in his nervous stillness, as if he were being smuggled away accidentally, with no knowledge of the act, into the future.

It had been arranged that I would travel alone from Ceylon to England, where my mother was living, a twenty-one-day journey. No mention had been made that this might be an unusual experience or even an exciting or dangerous one, so I did not approach it with any joy or fear. I was not forewarned that the ship would have seven levels and hold more than six hundred people, including a captain, nine cooks, engineers, and a veterinarian, or that it would contain a small jail and two chlorinated swimming pools that would actually sail with us across several oceans. The departure date had been marked casually on the calendar by my aunt, who had notified my school that I would be leaving at the end of the term, and it had been explained to me that, after I'd crossed the Arabian Sea and the Red Sea and gone through the Suez Canal into the Mediterranean, I would arrive one morning on a small pier in England and my mother would meet me there. It was not the scale of the journey that was of concern to me but the detail of how my mother could know when, exactly, I would arrive in that other country.

And if she would be there.

I heard a note being slipped under my door. It allotted me to Table 76 for all my meals. I dressed and went out. I was not used to stairs and climbed them warily. There were nine people at Table 76, and that included two other boys roughly my age. One of them was named Ramadhin, and the other was Cassius. The first was quiet, the other looked scornful, and we ignored one another, although I recognized Cassius. We had gone to the same school, where, even though he was a year older than me, I knew much about him. Cassius had been notorious, and was even expelled for a term. I was sure it was going to be a long time before we spoke.

We were situated far from the Captain's Table, at the opposite end of the dining room. 'We seem to be at the Cat's Table,' a woman called Miss Lasqueti said. 'Were in the *least* privileged place.' But what was good about our table was that it seemed to include several interesting adults. We had a botanist, and a tailor who owned a shop up in Kandy. Most exciting, we had a pianist who cheerfully claimed 'to have hit the skids.'

This was Mr. Mazappa. In the evening, he played with the ship's orchestra, and during the afternoons he gave piano lessons. As a result, he had got a discount on his passage. After that first meal, he entertained Ramadhin and Cassius and me with tales of his life. It was in Mr. Mazappa's company, as he regaled us with confusing and often obscene lyrics from songs he knew, that we three came to accept one another. For we were shy and awkward. Not one of us made even a gesture of greeting to the other two until Mr. Mazappa advised us to keep our eyes and ears open, because this voyage would be a great education. Thanks to him, we discovered that we could be curious together.

I found out unexpectedly that a distant cousin of mine, Emily de Saram, was on the boat. Sadly, she had not been assigned to the Cat's Table. Because I had no brothers or sisters, my closest relatives were adults, an assortment of unmarried uncles and slow-moving aunts who were bound together by gossip and status. For many years, Emily, who was older than me and lived almost next door, was my link to their grown-up world. I'd tell her of my adventures and listen to what she thought. She was honest about what she liked and did not like, and I modelled myself on her judgments.

Our childhoods were similar in that our parents were either missing or unreliable. When my parents abandoned their marriage, it was never really explained to me, but it was also not hidden. If anything, their life together was presented as a misstep, not a car crash. So how much the curse of my parents' divorce fell upon me I am not sure. I do not recall the weight of it. A boy goes out the door in the morning and is busy in the evolving map of his world. Emily's home life was, I suspect, worse than mine—her father's business dealings were never assured, and the family lived constantly under the threat of his temper. From the scarce amount she told me, I knew he was a punisher. Even visiting adults never felt safe around him. It was only children, in the house briefly for a birthday party, who enjoyed the unpredictability of his behavior. He'd swing by to tell us something funny and then push us into the swimming pool. Emily was nervous around him, even when he grabbed her in a loving hug and then made her dance with him, her bare feet balanced on his shoes.

Much of the time, he was away at his job, or he simply disappeared. There was no secure template that Emily could rely on, so I suppose she invented herself. She had a free spirit that I loved, even though she took too many risks. She taught me to dance, to hold her waist while her upraised arms swayed, and to leap onto and over the sofa so that it tilted and fell backward with our weight. In the end, Emily's grandmother paid for her to go to a boarding school in southern India, and even when she returned for summer holidays I did not see that much of her, for she'd got a job with Ceylon Telephone.

By the time Emily came on board the *Oronsay*, I had not seen her for two years. It was a shock to catch sight of her leaner, more distinct face, and to be conscious of a grace that I had not noticed before. She as now seventeen years old, and school had, I thought, knocked some of the wildness out of her, though there was still a slight drawl when she spoke which I liked. The fact that she'd grab my shoulder as I was running past her on the promenade deck and make me talk with her gave me some cachet with my two new friends. But most of the time she made it clear that she did not wish to be followed around. She had her own plans for the voyage, a final few weeks of freedom before she arrived in England to complete her schooling.

Larry Daniels was the botanist who ate with us at the Cat's Table. A compact, well-muscled man. He always wore a tie, always had his sleeves rolled up. Born to a burgher family in Kandy, he had spent much of his youth studying forest and plant cultures in Sumatra and Borneo. At first, the only thing we knew about him was that he had an overwhelming crush on Emily, who would barely give him the time of day. Because of this lack of interest, he went out of his way to befriend me. I suppose he had seen me laughing with Emily and her friends by the pool, which was where she could usually be found.

At dinner, I was unprotected from Mr. Daniels's queries about Emily, for my assigned seat was next to his, and I had to talk about her and nothing else. The one piece of information I could honestly give him was that she liked Player's Navy Cut cigarettes. She had been smoking the brand for at least four years. The rest of her likes and dislikes I invented.

'She likes the ice creams at Elephant House,' I said. 'And she often wishes to got to the theatre. To be an actress.' Daniels grasped at the false straw.

'There's a theatrical company on the ship. Perhaps I could introduce her.'

I nodded, as if recommending it, and the next day I saw him speaking to three members of the Jankla Troupe, entertainers on their way to perform their brand of street theatre and acrobatics in Europe, who also gave performances now and then for the passengers on our journey. He introduced himself to say that he had a good friend, a very talented young lady who loved the theatre, and perhaps she could watch them rehearse if he brought her along?

The Jankla Troupe would juggle, sometimes beginning casually at the end of afternoon tea, with their plates and cups, but most of the time they performed formally, in full costume and excessive make-up. Best of all, they would call passengers up onto the makeshift stage in order to disclose private things about them that were sometimes embarrassing. Usually, it was about the location of a lost wallet or a ring or the fact that the passenger was going to Europe to be with his sister, who was ill. All this was revealed at the end of a performance by the Hyderabad Mind, whose face had streaks of purple and whose eyes, rimmed with white paint, looked as if they belonged to a giant. Truly, he could terrify us, strolling into the depths of the crowd to reveal the number of children a person had, or where his wife was born.

Late one afternoon, wandering alone on C Deck, I saw the Hyderabad Mind crouching under a lifeboat, putting on his makeup before a performance. He was holding a small mirror in one hand while the other quickly gashed on stripes of purple paint. He had a slight body, and his painted head appeared too big for his delicate frame. He peered into the mirror, improving himself, unaware of me as he worked in the half-shadow of the lifeboat which hung from the davit. When he stood and stepped into sunlight the colors burst forward, the ghoulish eyes now full of sulfur and perception as he glanced briefly at me, then walked past as if I were nothing. I had witnessed for the first time what took place behind the thin curtain of art, and it gave me some protection the next time I saw him on-stage, decked out in full costume. I felt that I could almost see, or, at least, was now aware of, the skeleton within.

The friendship between the quiet Ramadhin and the exuberant Cassius and myself grew fast, although we kept a great deal from one another. At least I did. What I held in my right hand was never revealed to the left. I had already been trained into cautiousness. In the boarding schools we'd gone to, a fear of punishment had created a skill in lying, and I had learned to withhold small pertinent truths. Punishment, it turns out, never did humble some of us into complete honesty.

The *Oronsay* was a chance for us to escape all order. And I reinvented myself in this seemingly imaginary world, with its adult passengers, who, during the evening celebrations, staggered around in giant animal heads, dancing with women whose skirts were barely there, as the ship's orchestra, including Mr. Mazappa, played on the bandstand in plum-colored uniforms.

What was I in those days? I recall no outside imprint, and therefore no perception of myself. If I had to invent a photograph of myself from childhood, it would be of a barefoot boy in shorts and a cotton shirt running along the mildewed wall that separated our house and garden in Boralesgamuwa from the traffic on the High Level Road, or looking away from the house toward the dusty street.

I found it difficult to be alone on the ship. Most of my day was spent with Ramadhin and Cassius, or sometimes Mr. Mazappa or others from the Cat's Table. To be by myself, I would retreat to my hot cabin in the late afternoon and lie back on my bunk to study the ceiling a foot or two above me, and think backward. Sometimes I turned on the yellow light above my bed and looked at the map of the world I had traced from a book. I had forgotten to put names on it. All I knew was that we were going west and north across it, away from Colombo.

Occasionally, just before dark, I'd find myself on C Deck when there was no one there. I'd walk to the railing, which was the height of my chest, and watch the sea rush alongside the ship. At times, it appeared to rise almost to my level, as if wishing to pluck me away. I did not move, even with a havoc of fear and aloneness in me. It was the same emotion I'd felt when lost in the narrow streets of the Pettah market, or while adjusting to new rules at boarding school. But, no matter how scared I was, I held still, half wanting to pull myself back from the sea, half desiring to leap toward it.

Sleep is a prison for a boy who has friends to meet. We were impatient with the night, up before sunrise surrounded the ship. Lying in my bunk, I would hear Ramadhin's gentle knock on the door, in code; two taps, a long pause, another tap. A pointless code, really—who else could it have been at that hour? If I did not climb down and open the door, I would hear his theatrical cough. And if I still did not respond, I would hear him whisper, 'Mynah,' which had become my nickname. Ramadhin and I would meet Cassius by the stairs, and soon we were strolling barefoot on the first-class deck. First class was an unguarded palace at six in the morning, before the night lights on the deck blinked and turned off. We removed our shirts and dived like needles into the gold-painted first-class pool with barely a splash. Silence was essential as we swam in the newly forming half-light.

Our nighttime explorations were not as successful. We were never quite sure what we were witnessing, and we would fall asleep later with our minds still half grasping the rigging of adult possibility. On our first 'night watch,' we hid in the shadows of the promenade deck, then at random followed a man, just to see where he was going. I recognized him as the Hyderabad Mind, his face unpainted now. Somewhat surprisingly, he led us to Emily, who was leaning against a railing and wearing a white dress that seemed to glow as he came closer. The Hyderabad Mind half hid her from us, and Emily held his fingers cupped within her hands. We could not tell if they were talking or not.

We stepped back, farther into the darkness, and waited. I saw the man move the strap of Emily's dress and bring his face down to her shoulder. Her head was back, looking up at the stars, if there were stars.

Should our journey to England have been noted for any reason in the newspapers of the time, it was because of the presence on the *Oronsay* of the philanthropist Sir Hector de Silva. He was travelling with a retinue that included two doctors, one Ayurvedic, a lawyer, and his wife and daughter, most of whom were stationed in the upper echelons of the ocean liner and were seldom seen by us. No one in his party had accepted the invitation to eat at the Captain's Table. It was assumed that they were above even that. Although the real reason was that Sir Hector, who had ground out his fortune in gems, rubber, and plots of land, was now suffering from a possibly fatal illness and was travelling to Europe to find a doctor who would save him. Not one English specialist had been willing to travel to Colombo to deal with his illness, in spite of being offered considerable remunerations.

At first we did not concern ourselves with Sir Hector's illness. His presence on board was seldom mentioned by those at the Cat's Table. He was famous because of his great wealth, and that held no interest for us. But what did make us curious was our discovery of the background to this faithful journey. It had happened this way. One morning, Hector de Silva had been breakfasting on his balcony with friends. They were joking among themselves in the way that those whose lives are safe and comfortable do, when a Battaramulle, or holy priest, walked past the house. Seeing the monk, Sir Hector offered up a pun, saying, 'Ah, there goes a Muttaraballa.' *Muttara* means 'urinating,' and *balla* means 'dog.' It was a quick-witted but inappropriate remark, especially when addressed to a priest. Overhearing the insult, the monk paused, pointed to Sir Hector, and said, 'I'll send you a Muttaraballa.' After which the monk, reputedly a practitioner of witchcraft, went straight to the temple, where he chanted several mantras, thereby sealing the fate of Sir Hector de Silva.

The next month, Sir Hector was coming down the stairs of his house, his pet terrier at the foot of the steps waiting to greet him. A usual occurrence. But as Sir Hector bent down to pet the dog, the normally affectionate animal leaped for his neck. Sir Hector pulled the dog off him, at which point the animal bit his right hand.

Two servants eventually got hold of the creature and put it in a kennel. Apparently, the terrier had been behaving strangely that morning, racing around the kitchen under the feet of the servants, and had been chased out of the house with a broom, before slipping back, calm and muted, at the last minute, to await its master at the foot of the stairs. Twenty-four hours later, the dog died, having shown symptoms of rabies. But by then the 'Muttaraballa' had already delivered its message.

One by one they came. Every respected doctor who serviced Colombo 7 was brought in for consultation. In the end, Sir Hector decided to take the ship to England. Acquiring wealth, he had also acquired a complete faith in the advancements of Europe, whereas a cure in Colombo seemed to rely on village magic, astrology, and botanical charts in spidery handwriting. He had grown up knowing some local cures, such as urinating on a foot to alleviate the pain of sea-pencil stings. Now he was told that for a mad dog's bite the seeds of the Black Ummattaka or thorn apple should be soaked in cow piss, ground into a paste, and taken internally. Then, twenty-four hours later, he should take a cold bath and drink buttermilk. The provinces were full of these cures. Four out of ten of them worked. That wasn't good enough.

These surreal revelations about the man with a curse on his head thrilled Ramadhin, Cassius, and me. We gathered every fragment of Sir Hector's story and remained hungry for more. We cast our minds back to the night of embarkation in Colombo Harbor and tried to recall, or to imagine, at least, a stretcher, and the body of the millionaire being carried at a slight tilt up the gangplank.

Whether we had seen this or not, the scene was now indelible in our minds. For the first time in our lives, we were interested in the fate of the upper classes, and gradually it became clear to us that Mr. Mazappa and his musical legends, and Mr. Daniels with his plants, who had until then been like gods to us, were only minor characters, there to witness how those with real power progressed or failed in the world.

Our ship continued to move north-west, crossing into higher latitudes, and the passengers could feel the nights becoming cooler. One afternoon the chief engineer ordered that the engines be slowed while the emergency electrical systems were tested, and for a while it seemed as if we had stalled in what was now the Arabian Sea. An eastbound steamer passed us at dusk, all of its lights on, and it was a fantasy among the three of us to now over to it and return to Colombo.

Aden was the first port of call, and during the day prior to our arrival there was a flurry of letter writing. It was a tradition to have one's mail stamped in Aden, where it could be sent back to Ceylon or onward to England. All of us were longing for the sight of land and, as morning broke, we lined up along the bow to watch the ancient city approach, mirage-like, out of the arc of dusty hills. Aden had cisterns built out of volcanic rock, a falcon market, an oasis quarter, an aquarium, a section of town given over to sailmakers, and stores that contained merchandise from every corner of the globe. It would be our last footstep in the East.

The *Oronsay* cut its engines. We were docked not on the quay but in the outer harbor, at Steamer Point. If passengers wished to go ashore, they could be ferried into the city by barges that were already waiting beside our vessel. It was nine in the morning and, without the sea breezes that we had grown accustomed to, the air was heavy and hot.

That morning the Captain had announced the rules about entering the city. Passengers were allowed just six hours of shore leave. Children could go only if accompanied by 'a responsible male adult.' And women were forbidden to go at all. There was the expected outrage at this, especially from Emily and her group of friends by the pool, who wished to disembark and take on the town's citizens with their beauty. We ourselves were mostly concerned with finding an irresponsible male, who could be easily distracted, to chaperone us.

Mr. Daniels, we heard, was eager to visit the old oasis, where, he said, every blade of grass was swollen with water and as thick as our finger. We offered to help him transport any plants he discovered back to the ship, and he agreed. We went with him down the rope ladders into the barge as quickly as we could.

Onshore, we were surrounded instantly by a new language. While Mr. Daniels was busy negotiating a fee with a taxi to transport us to where the great palms were, we slipped away. A carpet salesman gestured to us, offered us tea, and we sat with him for a while, laughing whenever he laughed, nodding when he nodded. There was a small dog that he indicated he wished to give us, but we moved on.

We began to argue about what to see. For some reason, Ramadhin wanted to visit the aquarium. He was sullen about having to see the markets first. In any case, we entered the narrow shops that sold seeds and needles, coffins, maps, and pamphlets. Out on the street, you could have the shape of your head read, your teeth pulled. A barber cut Cassius's hair and poked a narrow, vicious pair of scissors quickly into his nose to clear away the possibility of hair in the nostrils of a twelve-year-old. I was used to the lush chaos of Colombo's Pettah market, the throat-catching smell of sarong cloth being unfolded and cur, and mango-sterns, and rain-soaked paperbacks in a bookstall. Here was a sterner world, with fewer luxuries. There was no overripe fruit in the gutters. There were, in fact, no gutters. It was a dusty landscape, as if water had not been invented. Although Aden was a harbor city, the air held hardly a particle of dampness. The only liquid was the cup of dark tea offered to us by the carpet-maker, along with a delicious almond sweet.

The aquarium was a deserted concrete building beside the sea. Ramadhin led the way through a maze of mostly subterranean tanks that housed about a dozen garden eels from the Red Sea and a few colorless fish that swam in a foot of salt water. Cassius and I climbed to another level, where there were taxidermied species of marine life, lying in dust, alongside whatever technical equipment was being stored—a hose, a small generator, a hand pump, a dustpan and brush. We gave the whole place five minutes, then revisited the stores we had already been in, this time to say goodbye. The barber still had no other customers and he gave me a head massage, pouring unknown oils into my hair, before attacking my scalp.

We reached the wharf before curfew. Out of belated courtesy, we decided to wait for Mr. Daniels on the dock, Ramadhin wrapped up in a djellabah, and Cassius and I hugging ourselves because of the brisk air coming in from the ocean. We realized that we had seen only a small silver of the city. We had missed the reconstructed cisterns and wherever it was that Cain and Abel were buried. Still, it had been a day of intricate listening, of careful watching, all our conversations made up of gestures.

Finally, we saw Mr. Daniels striding along the wharf. He was carrying a cumbersome plant in his arms and was accompanied by two slender men in white suits, each holding a miniature palm. He greeted us cheerfully—obviously he had not been too concerned about our disappearance. The men helping him were silent, and as one of them passed me his small tree he wiped the sweat from his face and winked and smiled, and I saw that it was Emily in a man's clothes. I took the palm and carried it onto the barge for the ten-minute ride to the ship.

Once back on board, the three of us made our way down to Ramadhin's cabin, where he unfolded his djellabah to reveal the carpet salesman's dog hidden inside.

We came on deck an hour later. It was already dark, and the lights on the *Oronsay* were brighter than those on land. The ship still had not moved. In the dining room, there were loud conversations about the day's adventures. Only Ramadhin and Cassius and I kept silent. So excited were we by our smuggling of the dog onto the boat, we knew that if we spoke even one syllable we'd slide uncontrollably into the whole story. We had spent the last chaotic hour trying to bathe the animal in Ramadhin's narrow shower stall, avoiding the swipe of his claws. We had dried the dog in Ramadhin's bedsheet and left him in the cabin while we came up to eat.

While listening to the stories of the others at the Cat's Table, Emily came by and bent down to ask me if I had had a good day. I asked her politely what she had done while we went ashore, and she said that she had 'carried things,' and went off laughing. There was a shudder during dessert as the boat's engines started up, and we all went to the railings to watch our departure, our castle slipping slowly away from the thin horizon of lights, back into the great darkness.

We guarded the dog that night. He was fearful of any sudden movement, until Ramadhin managed to take him into his bunk and fall asleep with his arms around him. When the three of us woke the next morning, we had already entered the Red Sea, and it was during this passage, on our first day steaming north, that something astonishing happened.

It had always been difficult to penetrate the barrier that separated us from the first-class level, which was guarded by two polite but determined stewards. But even they could not stop Ramadhin's dog. He had leaped out of Cassius's arms and bolted from the cabin. We ran up and down the empty hallways looking for him. But within moments the little fellow must have emerged into the sunlight of B Deck and run beside the railings, racing into the lower ballroom, up its gilded staircase, and past the two stewards. They managed to get their hands on him but could not hold on. He had eaten none of the food we had offered him, which we'd smuggled out of the dining room in our trouser pockets, so perhaps he was looking for something to eat.

No one was able to corner him. Passengers caught sight of him for just a blurred moment. He did not seem at all interested in humans. Well-dressed women crouched down, calling out high-pitched greetings, but he charged past them without a pause and into the cherrywood cave of the library, disappearing somewhere beyond that. Who could know what he was after? Or what he was feeling, in that no doubt pounding heart? He was just a hungry dog, or a scared one, on this claustrophobic ship, whose alleyways turned into cul-de-sacs as he ran farther and farther from daylight. Eventually, the creature made his way along a mahogany-panelled and carpeted hallway, where he slipped through a half-opened door into a master suite, just as someone left, carrying a tray. The dog climbed up onto an oversized bed, where the prone Sir Hector de Silva lay, and bit down into his throat.

All night the *Oronsay* was within the protected waters of the Red Sea. At daybreak, we passed the small islands off Jizan, and we could see in the distance the hazy presence of the oasis town of Abha, sunlight glinting off a piece of glass or a white wall. Then the city dissolved under the sun and was gone from our sight.

It was at this hour, shortly after daybreak, that the news of Sir Hector's death raced through the ship, quickly followed by whispers that there would have to be a burial at sea. It turned out, however, that a funeral could not take place in coastal waters, so the body would have to wait for the open spaces of the Mediterranean. Next came the more startling news of how he had died, followed by the story that we had already heard, about the charm put on him by the priest.

Ramadhin reasoned that fate had killed him, not us, by bringing the dog on board. And, as the little creature was never seen again, we came to believe that the smuggled dog had been a phantom.

During lunch, most of the questions had to do with how a dog had boarded the *Oronsay*. And where was it now? Emily came over to our table and demanded to know if we had brought the dog onto the ship, and we responded with an attempted look of horror, which made her laugh. The only person who showed no interest in the opinions around him was Mr. Mazappa, who sat mulling over his oxtail soups. His musical fingers were, for once, motionless on the tablecloth.

I woke the next morning without the usual desire to meet with my friends. I heard Ramadhin's familiar knock, but I did not answer. Instead, I took my time dressing, then went up to the deck alone. On the other side of the ship, passengers with binoculars were attempting to catch a glimpse of the Nile, somewhere deep inland. They were all adults, no one I knew, and I felt without a connection to anything. I went to Emily's cabin.

I was fondest of Emily when we were not with other people. In those moments, I always felt that I learned the most from her. I knocked a couple of times before she opened the door, wrapped in a dressing gown.

'Can I come in?'

'Yes.'

Emily stalked back and slipped under the sheets, discarding her robe, it seemed, in the same movement.

'We're still in the Red Sea.'

'I know.'

'We went past Jedda. I saw it.'

I stayed with her all morning. I told her about the dog, and how we had brought him on board. I was lying beside her on the bed holding one of her unlit cigarettes, pretending to smoke, when she reached over and turned my head toward her.

'Don't,' she said. 'I mean, *don't* tell anyone else about this—what you just told me.'

I said that I wouldn't.

She touched the top of my head in a gesture that said, Let's forget about it. Don't worry.

But I didn't turn away and kept watching her.

'What?' She raised her eyebrow.

'I don't know, I feel strange. Being here. What will happen when I go to England. Will you be with me?'

'You know I won't.'

'But I don't know anyone there.'

'Your mother?'

'I don't know her like I know you.'

'Yes, you do.'

She leaned over and kissed me. 'Now, make me some coffee. There's the cup. You can use hot water from the tap.' I got up and looked around.

'There's no coffee here.'

'Then order some.'

When the steward arrived, I met him at the door and, when he had left, brought the tray over for her. She half sat up, then remembered her robe and reached for it. But what I saw hit me in the heart.

There was a tremor within me, a mixture of thrill and vertigo. Suddenly, there was a wide gulf between Emily's existence and mine, and I would never be able to cross it. It was as if part of the desert in the distance had reached into the ship and touched me. But where had it come from? And was it a pleasure or a sadness, this life inside me? I felt as if I were lacking something essential, like water. I put the tray down and climbed back onto Emily's bed I felt in that moment that I had been alone for years. I had exited too cautiously with my family, as if there had always been shards of glass around us. And now I was going to England, where my mother had been living for three or four years. She had already become a stranger.

That morning, in Emily's cabin, shuttered away from the dazzle of the Red Sea and the desert, I knelt on her bed and shook. She leaned forward and held me, so soft a gesture that I felt barely touched, an envelope of loose air between us. My hot tears rubbed off on her cool upper arm. The small props of necessary defense with which I'd surrounded myself, and which contained and protected me, marking the outline of me, were no longer there.

'What is it?'

'I don't know.'

Perhaps we talked then. I don't remember. My breathing eventually calmed to the pace of hers. I must have fallen asleep for a moment and woke when she reached over her shoulder in a backstroke gesture for the cup of coffee. Soon I heard her quick swallows, my ear against her neck. Her other hand was still gripping mine, convincing of a security that probably did not exist.

After I left Emily's room—and there was to be no repeat of this kind of intimacy—I knew that I would always be linked to her, as if by some underground river or a seam of coal or silver. I had never known the grip of another's hand, or the smell of a body that had just emerged from sleep. I had never wept beside someone who also excited me in a way that I could not fathom.

It was probably a casual, if genuine, kindness that Emily gave me—and saying that takes nothing away from her gesture. 'You should go now,' she said finally, and rose from the bed and walked to the bathroom, shutting the door behind her.

A new rumor percolated that the two-day-old corpse of Hector de Silva would soon be dispatched into the sea. The Captain wished to wait until we reached the Mediterranean, but the all-powerful de Silva widow was now insisting on a quick, private burial. And so, within the space of an hour, everyone had discovered the location and the time of the final ceremony. Stewards roped off the section of the stern where the service would take place, but gawkers soon assembled behind the rope and crowded the metal stairways, and some looked down from the higher decks. A few, less impressed souls regarded the proceedings through the windows of the smoking room. As a result, the body—the first sighting of Hector de Silva for most of us—had to be carried along a very narrow aisle, grudgingly opened by the crowd. It was followed by his widow, his daughter, his doctors (one of them dressed in full village regalia), and the Captain.

I had never been to a funeral, let alone one for which I was partially responsible. I saw Emily a few yards away, and she gave me a cautious look and a slight shake of her head. Everyone from the Cat's Table was there.

We gazed down at the small figures of the entourage surrounding a trestle table, which held a bust of Hector de Silva and some flowers. We were barely able to hear the last rites. The voice of the priest faltered and faded in the shuddering winds that were drifting over the water. When the family approached the body wrapped in its white shroud, we all leaned forward to witness whatever secret was being passed to the dead. Then Hector de Silva slid from the ship and disappeared into the sea.

Migrant Poet

Yasmine Gooneratne

'Then did (this Indian) King cause the Prince named Vijaya, the valiant, to be placed in a ship and sent forth upon the sea. He landed in Lanka, where one of his followers found by a lotus-shaped pond a witch named Kuveni, sitting at the foot of a tree spinning as a woman-hermit might. And she said to him: "Stay! thou art my prey!" Then the man stood there as if fast bound. And there in like manner she served all his companions, one by one. And when they did not return fear came on Vijaya: armed with the five weapons he set out, and when he beheld the beautiful pond, where he saw no footsteps of any man coming forth, but saw the woman-hermit there, he thought: Surely, my men have been seized by this woman.' (Defeating her witch's wiles, and taking Kuveni as his companion) Vijaya rescued his followers, founded the city of Thamba-panni, and ruled there in peace and righteousness thirty-eight years.'

(Adapted from the *Mahavamsa* or *Great Chronicle of Ceylon*, as translated by Wilhelm Geiger)

Behind him a Kingdom sliding to decay
dragging with it lost childhood, sheltered youth
Before him alien shores, an unknown bay,
another Vijaya he ventures south.

A strange bird dreams on a dry bough; marsupials
lift liquid eyes in silence, questioning
a stranger's footfall. Here no leopards snarl—
do beasts turn also from the pain of living?

And is this pleasant landscape, then, to be
the chosen setting for his spirit's death,
the hammering media's brash mythology
to breathe on him immobilising breath?

Somewhere in this enchanted woodland brims
the secret well; and there her golden thread
his lost Muse sits and spins, and as she spins
the fallen blossoms listen for his tread.

False step to east or west, and desert grows
between these two. Look, landward from the sea
light footprints lead, through glades alive with shadows:
Others have passed this way ahead of me.

Perhaps in a lost age another kindled
here, in this glade, from that bird's dip and flight
or from the shape the moon took as it dwindled,
bright myth to lie beside on a cold night

or built a legend he could crawl into
and warm his blood to health and fruitfulness.
Lost myths, tumed rubble now beneath the new
towering chainstore, rammed under the express-

way. I, a wanderer in this land,
turned by necessity to new material
strange to my eyes, uncertain in my hand,
shall I be fortunate enough to call

into forms unimagined in my youth
new life? Create in joy, here, on Death's lip?
Another Vijaya, I venture south
here to reshape my art, refit my ship.

Hole-in-the-Heart
(From *Love Marriage*)

V.V. Ganeshananthan

This piece offers a brief primer on Sri Lanka's ethnic conflict from the 1980s onward, the history woven very skilfully into this story of two generations of immigrants, told from the point of view of a young Sri Lankan–American woman.

In this globe-scattered Sri Lankan family, we speak only of two kinds of marriage. The first is the Arranged Marriage. The second is the Love Marriage. In reality, there is a whole spectrum in between, but most of us spend years running away from the first toward the second.

Among the categories that bleed outside these two carefully delineated boundaries: the Self-Arranged Marriage, the Outside Marriage, the Cousin Marriage, the Village Marriage, the Marriage Abroad. There is the Marriage Without Consent. There is the Marriage Under Pressure. There is even Marrying the Enemy, who, it turns out, is not an Enemy at all.

You cannot go unfettered into a family's history if you are one of them. The nature of certain unions will be hidden from you, rephrased to you, the subject dropped, the music changed. There is Proper Marriage; there is Improper Marriage. This Tamil family speaks of the latter in whispers.

The rule is that all families begin with a marriage. And the other way around.

You don't marry a person, my father says to no one in particular. You marry a family.

The Self-Arranged Marriage: my father has married my mother's family so successfully that he now fits into it as well as—if not better than—he fits into his own. My mother is an Aravindran and, further back than that, a Vairavan, which means that the members of her family—especially her siblings—are nosy, noisy, close, and concerned with domestic comforts. Years after they stopped living where they had always lived, in a small house in the village of Urelu, in the town of Jaffna, they remain connected by telephone lines and carefully written aerograms. They never forget birthdays, favorite curries, or unkindnesses. They were once three but are now two. My father loves my mother's family, and in return for that they draw him in. They have forgotten that when he wanted to marry my mother they circled around her protectively from the far corners of the globe, opposed to her marrying a man they had never even met. They only remember that she has a happy life in a country far safer than the one in which she was born.

And twenty-five years after their wedding, my parents like to give the impression that their marriage was Arranged, because they are both very Proper. But their secret is out: they fell in love. Those who are watching can see how in certain moments they become each other. This has been their way of falling in love: the acquisition of each other's habits, mannerisms, preferences, and witticisms. They have built a wall around their two-ness, and each brick laid in place is a secret that only they share, or perhaps an exception one has made for the other. They have become an example of how you can Have Your Love and Eat It Too. They let everyone think that they took no responsibility for the way they came together. They engaged in all the dances of manners and the ceremonies involved in a Traditional Marriage, which is to say, an Arranged Marriage. This, they say, is not a romance. It begins with an introduction, a handshake, which is not the custom of the East but has become the greeting of the West. The touching of fingers is a strange, luscious intimacy, a preface to the story.

These two, my parents, have not acknowledged their secret—perhaps not even to each other. And they have exchanged rings and vows and hearts without eliciting the frowns that Improper Marriages frequently do.

Murali: It had once been thought that the young doctor who would later become my father would not marry at all. He came from a family in Ariyalai, a village on the outskirts of Jaffna. And his was a family full of doctors, a family full of poor doctors with heart problems. His own murmured persistently; he was told he would not live past forty. *Don't exert yourself too much, young man.* He tempered any enthusiasm for sports, believing strenuous activity would shorten his life, moment by moment. He was last on the cricket field, first out of breath. In a family of five sisters and three brothers that was all too obsessed with Marriages (regardless of category), he decided—rather nobly—not to marry at all: he would only leave a husbandless woman like his mother. His schoolmates, with the canny cruelty of children, called him Hole-in-the-Heart.

Every year from the age of three, when the murmur was first discovered, he had his chest X-rayed so that they could check the size of his Heart. They were afraid that it was too big. This happened sometimes to children with murmurs, the whispers of childhood turning into an adult sickness. An enlarged heart. Later, as a doctor, he would ask for impromptu ultrasounds, echo cardiograms. *Sound out my heart. Please check to make sure it's still there. Do you see it?* He had grown into a scientist. He wanted to know that the blood would continue its flow through his veins, that his pulse would not stop without warning one day, like an alarm clock gone off not at its appointed hour, but years too early. He wanted to see the proof of his own life for himself. He listened to his own heart sometimes when he was alone, unbuttoning his shirt as though it was a gateway into his shallow chest. He slipped in and out of radiology rooms as he pleased, without appointments. Lying on his back, his doctor's coat open, he exposed the Heart that had betrayed him to the eye of radiation. No matter which method he used to see into his own body, he would always leave with an image in hand, his sweaty fingers holding the evidence of his own mortality. Weak-kneed because he was weak-hearted.

Over the years, despite himself, he would imagine his own dying: how on his fortieth birthday he would suddenly look into some mirror and see death on a face that had always looked younger than it really was. He would be eating breakfast, or perhaps walking up the road to post a letter to his mother, and would crumble to his knees, his body collapsing limb by limb, the Heart slowing, and slowing, and slowing. The blood no longer flowing to his brain. The sound of a heart—his Heart—stopping.

He had a dream of being buried in a coffin of red lacquer, with a crowd of mourners wearing hats, singing and carrying pictures of him. In the dream he is passed from person to person like a torch. In this absolute stillness of death, he can sense himself traveling, moved by the hands of strangers. When the crowd of mourners reaches a bridge, the undertakers take the coffin from them and begin to run. The mourners cannot cross the bridge but watch him drift away from them. He is carried away into a distant, foggy death: A vagueness. An ending.

He wakes up. He is sweating. He is cold. As a Hindu, he will not be buried in a coffin. Someday, fire will find his body; a man of his family will hold the torch to the pyre. And then his ashes will find the sea. But as a young man, he cannot get rid of this body. It bears him up and holds him back.

Murali: He was the first in his family to come to the United States. Sri Lankan doctors were well respected in the medical community there, if only because they were Asian. He had secured a position at a hospital in New England, where he would be a resident and complete his training. But it was not so easy to leave Jaffna, where he had grown up. He is not well, his relatives said to his mother, the widow. How can you send him away? His mother, Tharshi, feeling guilty and thinking that she should not let him go, asked him to stay. The young doctor, last on the cricket field and first out of breath, had never before insisted on any desire. But suddenly, like a tide, he was unstoppable. He was going. He was going. His family, like his Heart, murmured in disapproval. He left his family behind. His disapproving Heart went with him.

His mother packed his suitcase with tea leaves, which came loose from their wrapping during the flight. When he went through customs, the agent opened the suitcase and asked him what it was. Tea—just tea that has come out of its package, sir, nothing to trouble you, Murali said. But Murali saw that the agent did not believe him. He felt himself beginning to sweat, and his Heart beginning to patter nervously. The agent called for a dog, and the dog came and smelled the suitcase and barked. Murali took his handkerchief out of his jacket pocket, knowing people were looking at him, this brown man with loose leaves in a suitcase. They had not even taken him to a private room. Embarrassing. The man called for his supervisor, who came and looked at Murali's passport again.

A doctor, eh? the supervisor said encouragingly, and Murali nodded mutely. What is this, doctor? He told you it was tea? The man lifted a handful of leaves to flared nostrils and inhaled. You idiot, you could have smelled it yourself—it *is* tea. Excellent tea, actually. Ceylon tea, probably. Let him through.

And the young doctor landed in America. He walked out into the cold. It was January, and New England, so it was cold. He had not known what that meant until this moment. As he looked out into the light and air of this place he discovered snow. The cold bit into his bones and he ignored it, because the snow was beautiful. But his Heart protested. *So cold here,* it murmured. Please do Shut

Up, Murali told it politely. All his life he had been told his Heart was sick. He had seen his Heart himself; he was tired of its tiredness. What reason, after all, did it have to be tired? To hold him back? Fresh off the boat—so to speak, since it was actually a plane—he walked into the examining room of a heart specialist.

There is something wrong with my Heart, he said to the cardiologist.

Let's have a look, the American doctor said.

Another entrance into an X-ray machine, shirt unbuttoned to expose the Betraying Heart that had for so long offered the young doctor martyrdom. The lights flashed and the Eye of the machine entered his chest. Pumping, screaming, throbbing Heart. He closed his eyes. *So cold here*, the Heart murmured. *What are you doing here? Shut Up*, the young doctor told his body.

They pulled him out of the machine.

The cardiologist waited with him for the film to be developed. They talked in the meantime, kin, as all doctors are.

You're a resident?

Yes.

Where are you from?

A country where it is always warm, he said, and shivered. Outside, it was still snowing. They looked at the film, pressed it against a viewer to read his innards, the maze of veins, the shape of his arteries. A glimpse into Eternity, an X-ray. Breathe in for me, the cardiologist said, pressing a chilly stethoscope to the skinny chest holding the Betraying Heart.

He put the stethoscope down.

There's nothing wrong with you, he said.

Thank you, said the young doctor, who was not yet my father, but edging ever closer.

Vani: He met her, my mother, in New York City—which as always was full to the brim with immigrants—and the Heart said plaintively: *Thump thump thump*. That was not the sound of illness.

Theirs was an auspicious meeting, although no one had troubled to check the alignment of the stars; the young woman was twenty-seven—old for a prospective bride?—but she did not look it. She had a generous face, he said to himself.

He liked her glossy sheaf of dark hair, her sparse brows, her pronounced chin, her full lower lip. She smiled with her mouth closed because she did not like her teeth. He could already see within the structure of her face how she would become thinner, that her bones would give her older face a certain elegance, a chiseled and austere severity. He liked her precision in even the smallest of tasks, like arranging hibiscus in a vase. Her reserve, her inability to say anything truly personal in public. He thought she might be full of secrets and wanted to know them. She never raised her voice, but she did not speak softly. *How are you? That's a beautiful sari. How are the children? I like this rice.* She liked her food steaming and spicy, as he did. She made her own clothes, staying up late into the night, her foot on the pedal of a Singer sewing machine that had belonged to her mother and had crossed the ocean with her. Her hemlines were high, and it suited both the times and her young pale slimness, which reminded him of a flowering tree by his home in Jaffna. He never caught her admitting she was wrong; her words clambered around that impossibility, but so sheepishly that he found it endearing. In a roomful of noisy Sri Lankans he learned to tell the clear bell sound of her bangles apart from the rest.

Suddenly, he was no longer thinking about widows or about repeating his own father's collapse. It was as though an invisible conductor was directing the pulling of strings to draw them together. Whether it was Murali who managed to get introduced to Vani or the other way around, no one else really remembers. And they will never admit which one of them was responsible. And yet, it was this simple: a friend of his noticed that they were staying near each other. Perhaps Murali could give Vani a ride home? Yes, yes, two heads nodded. They left the party they were at too quickly to say all their good-byes. After the door closed behind them the space where they had been was filled with the laughter of friends.

He took her home. She boarded with a family in Brooklyn. During the car ride they were silent. It was a strange and comfortable silence for two people who had waited for so long to be alone. The thrum of the motor was loud because the car was old. When they turned around the corner he pulled over and turned the engine off and there was a quiet as loud as the motor had been. He walked her to her door and she thanked him. She did not ask him in for a cup of coffee; it was not her house. But it was out of his way and both of them knew it. She forgot that she did not like her teeth and bared them at him. Her smile, for once, was not self-conscious. She watched him drive away, waving from the window. It is something Aravindrans always do for each other when they say good-bye.

The Sri Lankan elders of New York City were all too eager to play parents to the couple. She was Proper: smart and polite and a good cook and lovely. Vani had a job, and more important than any of these things, she had grace, which was something that could not be taught. Murali, of course, was their Beloved Parentless Boy; their favorite bachelor-doctor whom they took into their homes and bosoms and tried to smother with welcome and curry. Friends can arrange a Marriage as easily as parents, they said among themselves, delighted. Occasions were arranged; even the very rooms seemed to conspire to make the two end up next to each other. And then one day something was suggested by one of those elders. And somehow the pair of them were *talking* about it. To each other. Directly.

Which was a faux pas. But neither of them minded.

Oceans away, families exploded. True to form, his family's discord faded quickly. But her family almost did not consent: afraid of the

Improper, they questioned his intentions, his failure to observe certain formalities, his ancestry, his habits and character. He heard about what they had said and turned to her, his eyes full of questions.

They may not know these things about you, she said, but I do.

Are you sure? he asked her. The unsaid: they may not forgive you for this.

Positive, she answered. Countries away, Vani's brother, Kumaran, crashed into Murali's brother's house, yelling at the top of his lungs: *Who* is this doctor who wants to marry my *sister*? *Who* is this doctor who is *in love with my sister*?

The nerve of Murali, they thought. In Love? These were not words they were used to saying.

The wedding: It was cheap. Murali, growing closer to becoming my father, built the traditional wedding altar himself; he rented a local hall; he recruited the Sri Lankan elders to help with food and organization. Without the relatives who were scattered across the world, with the friends drawn close in New York City, the Marriage was Arranged.

There is a photograph of Vani looking very young and bashful and Proper in her Wedding-Red sari as he proposes a toast, her happiness veiled, her smile shy, so that no one could see it too clearly. *I never thought I would get married here,* her Heart said to his. *I never thought I could find you here.*

No one heard it, as is decent. Except—

Thump thump thump, replied the doctor's Heart, pleased at its success.

This is not the story they tell us at first. They say they did everything according to tradition, with methods of irreproachable propriety. And her family pretends they always loved him.

There is Proper Marriage; there is Improper Marriage.

Even now, my parents still love each other so much that they would never admit it. But no matter which version of the story you know or how softly you whisper it, Vani and Murali were married and became, at last, my parents. I told you a story about that place, and about their leaving it, but how do I know it? I am not the end of my parents' story, but I am the reason for its telling.

I am Yalini, their daughter. In July of 1983, I was born in the same New England that had welcomed my parents, Vani and Murali, into its arms so long ago. They had waited a long time for me. I came into the world squalling, as children should. As I was born, Murali held Vani's shoulders. I was born with jaundice. My hair was glossy like Vani's and wavy like Murali's. The nurses, gathered around my perspiring mother, said to each other that they had never seen a baby with quite that much hair. I came into a place anxious for my arrival. My parents, who did not know whether they should expect a daughter or a son, had already prepared a room for me. After Vani's water broke, Murali brought her into the hospital and announced that his child's room had already been painted pink. Now the nurse told him he would not have to redo it. It's a girl, the nurse said to Murali, at last my father. I was swaddled in blankets and placed in his arms. I immediately caught hold of his Heart with both tiny fists.

I was born in the early hours of the morning, on a day in late July. And as I entered this new world, my parents' old one was being destroyed.

Black July: More than two decades later, I think that almost every Sri Lankan Tamil knows what it means. I was born, and halfway around the world, Tamil people died, betrayed by their own country, which did nothing to save them.

Murali was in a hospital room with me and with Vani when a younger doctor came to get him.

Sir, there is—something. I think you will want to see it.

Murali moved to turn the television on in the room where we

were sitting, but the other doctor looked at Vani and shook his head subtly: no.

Why don't you come with me, he said. Murali, sensing rising alarm in the other man, left us there and followed him down a long blue hospital hall, to a large waiting room, where the television was already on. My father's colleagues sat around it. They had been waiting for the new father to emerge, to offer him congratulations, to ask about baby weight and names. Now their good wishes died on their lips. No glad handshakes, no questions about the child. Instead they watched my father watching the news.

And there on the screen, my father saw everything he had once believed in, burning. Halfway around the world, in the country he had loved first and best, people were being killed for their Tamilness. The news showed anti-Tamil riots on the streets of Colombo, the capital of Sri Lanka, where members of the Sinhalese majority rioted against thousands of their Tamil countrymen. The news showed Tamil civilians beaten, robbed, and killed, their property seized and ruined. And the Sri Lankan government had done nothing to defend them. My father watched, and saw that he had constructed his life inside laws that were nothing more than a house of cards.

Standing there, Murali thought of his classmates, his friends, his old village neighbors, some of whom were almost certainly in Colombo. Later, he would hear stories of organized mobs stopping vehicles on the streets, looking for Tamils. He would hear that those they had discovered were stabbed or set aflame. Later, he would come to understand that government authorities had handed enraged rioters voter lists, which showed ethnicity, so that they could go door-to-door and hunt down their Tamil neighbors, co-workers, and schoolmates. He would read about the government's failure to declare and enforce curfews. Later, people would debate emigration, asylum, property damage, and casualty numbers. Later, he would mourn, when he learned which of his friends had been among those attacked.

And later, Tamil separatist groups would rise, newly powerful, from the ashes of those riots—their ranks strengthened by the young people whose families had been hurt in 1983 and before. Those young people would have no reason to believe in Sri Lanka, and so they would become militants. Rebels who would fight for a separate nation for Sri Lankan Tamils in the decades to come. Of these, one group would emerge the strongest: the Liberation Tigers of Tamil Eelam. They would blow themselves up to take others with them, targeting symbols and representatives of the state; they would attack civilians and eat cyanide to avoid imprisonment. They would kill other Tamils who did not agree with them—other rebels, politicians, and even civilians. They would fight against a government that shelled, starved, and tortured its own citizens. They would renounce their families and bring children and women into their ranks.

They would be called terrorists. They would enter into a world in which no one was right.

Murali did not know any of that yet. But standing there at that moment, he knew that he had left Sri Lanka totally and absolutely. He would not retire there, or grow old there, or die there. He would go back, perhaps after a long time, for a visit of a month or perhaps two. But he could never live there again. And he had never really believed that before.

He was a father now. Murali looked around the room at the doctors who worked with him and realized how alone he was in this roomful of friends. Their faces were full of sympathy, but they did not understand who he was. They never would.

My parents named me Yalini, after the part of their home that they loved the most. It is a Tamil name, with a Tamil home: a name that means, in part, *Jaffna, Sri Lanka*, the place from which they came. In Sri Lanka children do not leave their parents or resist becoming them. They fall into it easily, gracefully, take their mantles of responsibility without protest. Even those who became rebels have inherited their parents' struggles from the days after Independence, and before 1983.

But I grew up and out of my parents' house. I grew up and went to a university far away from them. At this school my work consumed me, because that was what I wanted. I mired myself in it. I called my parents infrequently, in the snatches of time between work and class, or class and meals, or lying down and sleeping. I grew up, went to school, and went away from my parents. I left their war-torn house in our peaceful country.

There, Away, I became more like them than ever before, because no matter how American I was, I was also the only Sri Lankan. I was alone as my mother had been, stepping onto her first escalator in New York. As alone as my father had been inside the X-ray machine, before meeting my mother.

Everything in this place—so far from the home my parents had constructed for me—felt old and unremarkable. I had made myself unable to be surprised, and so I took no joy in my first independence, as my parents had taken in theirs. I had traveled a great distance, and my eyes were tired and saw nothing fresh. If you had found me there then and asked me what I missed, I could not have given you an answer.

At the university, the other students only made me feel lonelier. I went there in the fall of 2001, and two weeks after I left my parents, terrorists attacked their adopted country, the country in which I had been born, and that I loved. Everything around us fell into disaster, in a place where we had thought that impossible. War had always mattered to me, and now, finally, far too late, it mattered to everyone else too. When I finally went to the airport to go home again on the first holiday, the faces of the security men made me think of my father and his loose tea leaves, the story he had told me of the dog barking at him so many years earlier. Their faces searched mine, or I imagined that they did. I thought of my father as a very young and innocent man and felt a strange cold gladness in being a woman, as though it made me safer, although in fact all it did was make my life more dangerous in different ways.

When I stepped off the plane, I gripped my father's shoulders and kissed him. He seemed smaller to me. I seemed smaller to myself.

School did not make me happy, but that had nothing to do with the school itself and everything to do with me. And of course I went back there. Perhaps I thought that as a Sri Lankan, it was my obligation to re-enter my own misery without naming it. If it had not been for the obvious despair of the world around me, I would have seen my own unhappiness earlier.

In the cold, dim weeks after what happened, the world looked at once more dangerous and more welcoming. The weather seemed cold, although it was not yet winter. The ground was still green, but it became harder and colder, as though readying itself for snow. People who would never have stopped to speak to each other before met each other's eyes squarely with what they thought was honesty. I thought that this was a lie; this was temporary. People did not care about each other like this. I felt certain that people would return to the way they had been before, as though nothing had happened. Students who lived with me gathered to talk about what had happened, but I did not join them, because that would have accomplished nothing. I wanted to be alone. I wanted to read. I went to the library and studied, even when our professors canceled their lectures and classes.

In the library, I liked to read at a particular long, dark table. My father had taught me to treasure libraries. He had done this by repeating the story of his own childhood library, the Jaffna Public Library, which had been burned by thugs in 1981, two years before I was born, as members of the Sri Lankan cabinet looked on and did nothing. I looked around this American university library and noted its fire alarms and fire extinguishers. Security personnel stood at each entrance. This library was well guarded, if not well loved. In Jaffna, many irreplaceable single-copy manuscripts had burned. As a child, I had imagined it many times, in each library I had entered—men in uniforms laughing, with torches and gasoline and guns. How each shelf would fall into and break the one below it, wood blackening and metal melting. How the cover of one book would embrace the one beside it, touching it gently, so gently, with a ring of sparks.

Nothing would burn here. In fact, during these days it was almost empty. Nobody else ever sat there, because the chairs lining the table were uncomfortable. I preferred these chairs because they made it difficult to sleep and easy to focus. Every day, after breakfast, before class, I went to that table in the library. Light came in from a long, low window above it, and the books on the shelves around it stood dusty and undisturbed. No one came there because the books were about histories that had ceased being interesting to anybody. Sometimes, if I was very tired, I laid my head down against the edge of the table to rest. After a few minutes, the sharp edge would wake me up again. If you had asked me what I was studying there, I could not have told you.

One morning, I had laid my head down on the edge of the table to close my eyes for a moment when someone tapped me on the shoulder. A tall, pale boy held a book out to me. His hair, so brown it was almost black, needed to be cut. His finely drawn, open face looked younger than mine.

I found this in the library yesterday, he said. I think it has your name in it. Aren't you Yalini?

I blinked at him. He stood slightly taller than my father, perhaps six feet. He had a firm but generous mouth. I took the book from him without touching his hand. It was a leather journal of the kind found in large bookstores. My father had given it to me for my last birthday. A strap wound around it held it closed. Without thinking, I unwound the strap and flipped through its pages. This revealed nothing because I had never written in it. I had left it in the library without missing it because it had not yet become important to me to write things down.

It's blank, he said.

Thank you, I said. I hadn't realized that I had left something here.

I didn't open it, he said. I saw you get up without it.

He looked at me, and I thought that he was going to leave, but he stood there. I turned back toward the table so that my shoulders were set against him. I had finished talking to him. But he did not leave. He came around to the other side of the table and sat down as though we were going to continue the conversation.

I had never before met a person who had decided to be my friend without waiting for my consent.

He had decided that we were friends. In that long, blank time when everyone treated everyone else with a false equivalence, that meant something to me, and I did not want to argue with the generosity of his persistence. We were friends for three years. Then, in the winter of 2004, I went home to spend the holidays with my parents.

On the day after Christmas, I was walking out the door with my mother when someone called: my mother's sister, Kalyani. My mother turned around to pick up the phone.

Ah, my mother said. All right. We will call back.

She hung up.

What did she say? I asked.

Something about water in Sri Lanka, my mother said. Something bad happening. Let's go.

Something bad was always happening. Later, I thought how tired she must have been, how weary of the updates from the front. For years she had taught herself to avoid them. Or maybe it was just that her sister, in trying to be gentle, had not told her enough to make her understand. None of us had used the word *tsunami* yet. No one understood what it meant.

We walked out the door and into the winter sun.

By the time the car rounded the first corner away from the house, my relatives in Australia had called my relatives in Germany, who called my relatives in France, who called my relatives in England and Canada. They called us again. The phone rang and the house was empty. Watch the news, they said into the recording. The earth had shifted, and in doing so, moved the ocean. Water rolled over Sri Lankan homes, over fields, over trees, over temples, into the sky.

In the days after that, when my phone rang, I did not pick it up. It seemed like that first fall, three years earlier. I did not want to pick up the phone and hear concern that I knew would disappear. My friend called my phone, and I did not answer. He called the house, and when my mother gave me the message, I shook my head: no. I could not stand the idea of that in his voice. I watched the news and saw bodies. We did not know if anyone in our family had died, and then we learned that someone related to me had gone to the temple and drowned there, in a place full of water and gods. I had never met him and felt no right to any grief. I sat tearless before the news. And the news talked about the war, our war, as though it had just begun again. Dear Americans, there has been a war in this place. As though there had been no war for the decades before this. I heard my father say, bitterly, that at least now people would be able to find Sri Lanka on a map.

I have never been one for talking, and I did not want to talk to my friend, because he seemed too far outside this. He seemed too far away from everything I missed. He came from a place full of people who were just learning about war, and I realized then that I had grown up full of it, without realizing it, and that I did not know what to say about it to anyone, even my parents, who were still the people I loved the most. I had been born lucky, outside of war and unable to forget it. We came from different worlds, my friend and I, even though we had both grown up in America, in houses that in my parents' country would be considered rich. There was still a space there. It would have taken bravery to walk across that divide, and at that moment, water in my head, I did not have it. I was sorry for the difference between us and too tired to reach through it. Without waiting for my consent, he had decided that we would be friends; now, without waiting for his consent, I cut him off.

I cut him off and then I did not think of him. I thought of those bodies in the water, and even more, the bodies before them.

A Night in Frankfurt

V.I.S. Jayapalan

A room in the meanest quarter of Frankfurt.
Crammed like the womb of an impregnated sow.
Like Egyptian mummies
swathed in blankets
lie a pack of helpless Jaffnese.

Wandering mongrel
dog-tired, prone in bed,
scavenging for a living
his days crawl.

The mercury in the stem
contracts to below zero.
A cry rings out in the stillness of night.
Sisters wait, fondly—
with expectations and dreams.
He, a mortgaged title deed
trapped in the village VIP's chest
orphaned in his native land.
A refugee in foreign lands

Translated by S. Rajasingam

his youthful life wracked
like storm-stricken Batticaloa.
A something rankles
like a nightmare.
Beside his bedstead
saucepans lie strewn.
Grim reminder of a home
he'll never have.

In his hands, crumpled,
news of a betrayal.
Abandoned,
without home or hearth
a wretch,
he weeps silently
with the snowy evening.

Many Tamil men, fearing conscription by the LTTE, or torture and death by the government forces, fled to Europe as refugees during the war. Their families had to often mortgage their lands and houses to pay unscrupulous agents for these men's passage.

The American Girl

A. Muttulingam

One day she had a boyfriend, the next day she did not. He had gone his way, looking for another girl. To date, this was her third boyfriend. She didn't seem to understand how to attract these boyfriends, leave alone how to hold on to them. She didn't seem to possess that certain something that they were looking for. Either that, or even if she possessed it, she failed to give it away; so much was clear.

She was indeed a beautiful girl, although she neither wore make-up, nor adorned herself particularly. She didn't have time for such things, either. She dressed just like other students, but you couldn't say she spoke like them. She had come to an American university on a scholarship, directly from Jaffna, Sri Lanka, and so her pronunciation lacked a little in nasal sounds. On the other hand, she used several new words which other American students could not comprehend. She said 'sweet' while they said 'candy'; she said 'lift' while they said 'elevator'; she said 'torch' while they said 'flashlight'. All this, though, was only when she first arrived; she corrected herself very swiftly. She didn't deploy her fine intelligence exclusively towards pursuing subjects like chemistry, physics and mathematics.

Translated by Lakshmi Holmström

Men were drawn to her, anyway, like swarms of ants, attracted by her long dark hair and her darting black eyes. But then they turned away with the same haste. Or else they abandoned her and fled to other girls. To this day, she would remember with shocked surprise, the very first question put to her by the very first youth who approached her. 'Why do you always stand with your head bent, as if someone were playing the national anthem?' How was she to answer this? For seventeen years she walked to school and back in that stance, looking down at her feet. She couldn't change that, all of a sudden. But she liked the boy who posed the question. He came to some of the courses which she attended, and so it became his practice to attach himself to her as she walked to her class.

He invited her to attend a basketball match one day. She had no idea about the rules of the game; she only knew that the ball had to land inside the basket. There were many girls wearing short skirts which showed their thighs, and long red socks, who jumped up and down enthusiastically, cheering as they did. Sometimes they clapped their hands even when the ball did not fall in the basket. So she too clapped her hands. On their way back, he bought her an ice-cream. When a tiny bit dripped on to her lower lip, he wiped it away with a finger. On the third day, he invited her to study together with him. She was stunned by the sharpness of his mind. Unlike her, he never learnt anything by rote. He thought things through logically, and could work out the most complicated chemical equations instantaneously. Three days later, he told her his roommate was away, and invited her to stay the night in his room. When she refused, he vanished and was not seen again.

The second boy to come after her was a daring fellow; a bit of a prankster. She knew the atomic structure of Benzene; he did not. That was how their friendship began. One day he appeared suddenly and stood in front of her as she was studying. When his shadow fell on her and she looked up, he gave her swivel chair a spin. It whirled round three times and came to a stop directly in front of him. He said, 'Look, I've drawn the prize! Now you have to come and have coffee with me.' She wanted to laugh; she agreed. As they were drinking their coffee, he asked her, 'Are you a princess in your country?'

'No,' she told him, 'I was actually driven away from there. I have to find a country for myself, hereafter.'

'You are as beautiful as a princess,' he assured her and asked whether he could stay in her room that night. After that, he too disappeared.

All these people wanted something from her. But although she lived in America, she remained a Sri Lankan still. No one here knew that even before she left for America, the people of her village used to call her 'American Girl'. She had even forgotten her own name. Both at home and at school, everyone called her 'American Girl'. Her mother used to say she was even cleverer than her two elder brothers. She had learnt to speak English at the early age of four. She would read all the American comic books that her brothers brought home, and relate the stories to her classmates at school. She'd dream that she had turned into Superman or Archie, and lived in America.

Even as a young child she'd ask her mother, 'Am I an American Girl, really?'

'No,' her mother would reply, 'You are Sri Lankan.'

'Then when can I become an American?'

'You can't.'

'If I go to America will I become an American?'

'No, you'll still remain Sri Lankan.'

'What would happen if I married an American?'

'Then you'd be a Sri Lankan girl married to an American. Whatever you do, you can never turn yourself into an American.'

She was deeply disappointed on hearing this. She was ten years old at the time.

The third person to fall in love with her was a boy of some means. She was, by then, a second year student. He approached her directly as she was coming out of a class and introduced himself. At once, several girls turned to look at her with jealous eyes. He told her he lived in a student hostel and visited his parents in Portland every weekend.

He had a novel way of alighting from his car. Having stopped the car, he'd thrust both legs out at the same time, stand up and then step forward. He never seemed to concern himself with the lessons that went on yesterday or today, nor the lessons that were to come tomorrow. He seemed to think that the entire university was a playing field. He kept following her about everywhere. One day he asked her to close her eyes. He usually did this whenever he brought her a present, so she did as she was told. 'Open your mouth,' he said. She opened her mouth, thinking he was going to give her a piece of chocolate, or some kind of candy. She used to open her mouth in exactly the same way when her mother gave her medicine. Instead, he bent down and kissed her open mouth. She didn't like this one bit.

'It's no great deal,' he said. 'I've kissed your hand. I've kissed your forehead. Your mouth is just two inches lower than your forehead. So let's say this was an error of two inches.' He invited her home to Thanksgiving dinner. The previous year, she had gone to her friend's home. She accepted his invitation, since there would be no one at all in her hostel on Thanksgiving Day and travelled for two hours with him, in his car. This was the longest car journey she had done so far, in America.

His parents were very respectable people. Although his father looked just middle-aged, his mother appeared much older. Her face was criss-crossed with lines like a wooden block at the fishmonger's. Having found out somehow that her son's girlfriend was a Sri Lankan, the old lady had collected a number of newspaper clippings, all to do with recent events in Sri Lanka, which she now handed to her. Her heart was touched by this. At the dinner table, the conversation was all about the war in Sri Lanka. It was then two years since the Indian Army had arrived in her country. She told her hosts how her mother had moved to three different locations during this time, and how she had to keep changing the addresses when she wrote her letters. She did not mention that her two brothers had died during the conflict.

When it was night, before he went upstairs, he pulled out the sofa-bed and told her she was to sleep there. She fell into a deep sleep. At around midnight, a soft hand closed her mouth gently. She opened her eyes to see him standing there. She was terrified. She began to shake all over, and her nightdress was soaked through with sweat. Although she managed to drive him away, she did not sleep a wink for the rest of the night. The next day, she spoke no more than two sentences during the entire two hours they travelled together in the car.

It was at the end of her third year that her university life saw a great change. She had allowed two years to pass by without participating in the annual multicultural event. That year, though, she could not avoid it. She was the only student there from Sri Lanka. She named her contribution 'A Traditional Dance'. She didn't have a single sari with her, nor any other appropriate dance costume. She borrowed some clothes from a Panjabi friend, and got ready, making herself up as best as she could. She had decided to dance to a song she had once performed at school, '*Enna thavam seidanai?*', 'What penances did you do?' She had already recorded the song on to a tape. The curtains slid away as she stood on the platform. Although she was trembling slightly, she explained the song in a couple of lines and proceeded to dance. She didn't expect the enthusiastic applause that followed, the students cheering and clapping.

Just before her performance, a Vietnamese student sang, accompanying himself on a stringed instrument. When she came out, having washed off her makeup, this boy praised her dancing extravagantly. For the sake of conversation, she, in her turn, said his music had been wonderful. He told her that he had learnt to play that sixteen-stringed instrument, usually reserved only for women, from his Vietnamese mother. He said he only played it occasionally, and in memory of her. She was amused by what he wore: a long robe covered in a thousand mirrors, and a round cap on his head. His clothes reflected a thousand tiny images of herself. He was a third year student of English Literature, and said his name was Lan Hing.

The next morning, Lan Hing had somehow managed to seek her out in that university of 27,000 students. 'You never told me your name yesterday,' he said.

'Mathi,' she replied.

He asked her her surname.

In three years, no one had asked what her surname was. She wanted to laugh. She said, 'I have a very long surname. It will take you half a day to learn it off by heart.'

'Really? What does "Mathi" mean in your language?'

She told him it had two meanings: 'intellect' and 'moon'.

'The moon is very sacred to the Vietnamese, it has a special place in all our festivals,' he said. He went on, 'Your dance yesterday was very beautiful. The movements were very similar to the Vietnamese style of dancing.'

'Is that so? Thanks,' she said.

'You included some movements like a baby crawling. Why was that?'

She wasn't sure whether he really wanted to know, or whether he asked it merely to keep the conversation going. All the same, she explained the story contained in the lines 'You tied a child to the stone mortar and made him plead, hand held to his mouth'.

He had grown up in America. When she explained, he said, 'Really?' He added, laughing and displaying his large teeth, 'Truly, that mother was fortunate she wasn't born in America. If any mother here were to tie up a child to a stone mortar, she would be arrested and put in prison.' She couldn't stop laughing at that. He looked at her eyes in surprise, as if seeing them for the first time. Her eyes began to laugh before her mouth started.

It was a matter of surprise to her that even after their third or fourth meeting, he didn't ask to stay the night in her room. This really pleased her. She didn't know why, but it felt very natural to be with him. She didn't have to make any sort of effort when she sat with him, or walked about with him, or talked to him. She didn't have to try in any way to please him. In his presence, somehow, her heart beat differently.

She used to write to her mother every month. Her mother didn't have access to a telephone in the village where she lived. So every two or three months she would go to a nearby town, telephone her daughter and speak to her for three minutes. Her call would arrive precisely at six o'clock. The blue aerogrammes that her mother wrote too arrived regularly. That same month the army had slaughtered many people in their home village of Kokkattisolai. The mother didn't breathe a word about it. When Mathi wrote at the end of that month, she finished with these lines, 'Amma, I was born your daughter, but I've done nothing at all for you. I haven't even bought you a single thing that you wanted. Yesterday I bought myself some shoes for the winter. They cost me forty dollars. Had I sent you the money, it would have seen you through your household expenses for three months. I was the "American Girl" only while I was there. Here I am a mere Sri Lankan. I have made friends with a man who has a strange name. Lan Hing. There is only one such name in the entire telephone directory. He is a good man. I must see you again. Don't die before I do that.'

A phrase that Lan Hing often used was, 'Surprise me!' They would go out to dinner in the evenings. She'd ask him what they should order. 'Surprise me,' he'd say. They'd decide to go to the cinema. 'What movie shall we watch,' she'd ask. 'Surprise me,' he'd say. One day when Lan Hing came looking for her, she was doing some work on her computer and took no notice of him. He watched her for a long time. Her fingers were very narrow and slender. He gazed at them as they played swiftly upon the keyboard. He told her that when they touched the keys, there was still so much space left.

As he said this, he took one of her fingers in his hand and stroked it. Who knows what struck her but she stood up suddenly and kissed his large-toothed mouth.

Another evening after it had rained, she sat in the shade of a birch tree, thinking of her mother. A picture came to her mind of her mother getting ready to teach at her school, shaking out her sari and putting it on, tying up her hair in a knot with a hair-net around it, setting off finally with her umbrella. As she wondered whether it was raining at home too, Lan Hing appeared, his shoes squelching through the wet earth. When he saw a puddle of water, he leapt across it like an ancient warrior and landed in front of her.

'Such a big leap to cross such a small puddle?' asked Mathi. She looked very lovely in a clinging, transparent dress. He bent down to touch her and remarked, 'Today your skin is even softer than your feather-like dress.'

'Is it? Today I'm not going to surprise you. Why don't you surprise me for a change,' she said.

'Do you know what I learnt in English Literature today?'

'I will know if you tell me.'

'The Russian novelist Tolstoy had thirteen children. Did you know that?'

'No, I didn't. Tell me more.'

'The thirteenth child was a boy. Do you know what Tolstoy did when the child was dying? He was learning to ride a bicycle. He was sixty years old at the time.'

'Why are you telling me this?'

'You told me to surprise you, that's why.'

Slowly she began to smile.

'Look, look, your eyes have started to laugh.'

She began to study for a doctorate, while he finished his graduate degree and accepted a teaching post. When he rented a small one-roomed apartment, they decided to live together. She moved in with him, bringing her bed and her desk, and all her other belongings. When they placed her bed next to his, it was considerably lower in height. 'Never forget that a man's place is always higher than a woman's,' he told her.

They had a registered wedding first, after which he put around her neck the *tali* her mother had sent, strung on a chain. 'Aren't there any appropriate Vietnamese rituals?' she asked. So on a full moon night, with the old man in the moon as witness, he bit into a piece of ginger dipped in salt, ate part of it, and she ate the rest. With this, their married life began grandly, blessed by the Moon-man.

From the day they were married, she abandoned the use of a pillow. She became accustomed to sleeping with her head against his upper arm as he lay on his slightly higher bed. Lan Hing looked after all the household jobs as well as holding down a teaching position. He was a splendid husband. But there was no way he could keep the house tidy, however hard he tried. He was continually surprised by her method of studying. Her reference books, notebooks and scraps of paper on which she had scribbled notes lay scattered everywhere, on the bed, in the kitchen, in the bathroom, on her desk. He never ceased to wonder how on earth she managed to study. He would spend a couple of hours cleaning the house and putting everything away tidily, but within minutes she would scatter her things again.

For her Ph.D, she had to spend a long time in the laboratory. Sometimes she worked for twenty hours at a stretch. All the same, she wrote to her mother every month without fail. 'Amma, do you know something? Even when I was an embryo in your womb, I already had embryos in mine. So any baby that is born to me will actually have come directly from you.'

One Saturday afternoon, she didn't go to the laboratory. She had finished her research and was at the point of finishing her thesis. Lan Hing came into the bedroom and stood stock-still. The dirty plates from breakfast had not been removed. She was bent over her notebook and writing something into it, a half-drunk mug of coffee held in her lap. Lan Hing pushed away some books from the bed to make a space, sat down and took her hands. 'You are the finest student in all the world; there is no doubt at all about it. But although we have been married for four years, we still don't have a child. You should think about that, too. Let us consult a doctor.' Silently she gazed up at him. His cheekbones were sticking out distinctly; she had not noticed that before.

The doctor subjected both of them to extensive tests, and came to a conclusion which they had not expected at all. Her husband, who had always said, 'Surprise me, surprise me', got the biggest surprise of his life on the day they learnt the results of the medical examination. The doctor went inside to fetch the results. As the sound of his shoes retreated, their heart-beats grew louder and louder. 'In order to conceive a baby, a man should have a sperm count of at least twenty million per millilitre. His wasn't even half that,' the doctor said. There was no possibility of her becoming pregnant by him.

The two of them, who had thought all these days that it would be pleasant to have a child, were now in a frenzy for a baby, somehow or other. Mathi's mother's letters began to ask, 'Are you pregnant yet?'

He asked, one morning, as she was lying in her bed at his right side as usual, 'Ei, Sri Lankan girl, why did you marry me?'

'A rich girl will marry a rich man, a poor girl seeks a poor man. An educated girl goes for an educated man; those who have nothing marry each other.' Her mouth smiled, but her expression revealed an unbearable grief.

'Look here, I didn't tie you a *tali* like a pen chained down in a post office. If you like, I will leave you. Please marry someone else and have a baby.'

She said nothing, but moved swiftly up to his bed, pulled his arm to herself and lay down, pressing her head against it even harder than usual.

Throughout that day, on every channel on the television, the Clinton–Monica affair was being discussed. The same thing was transmitted on radio. The newspapers lamented, page after page. Nothing caught her attention. At evening time, she sat in her room, gazing out of the window at the street outside. She had submitted her thesis three days earlier, so her mind swung about, like the last garment left forgotten on a washing line. A police van raced past, its siren sounding. She didn't know how she would spend all the hours of the day hereafter. Footsteps sounded suddenly, along the street. Students, boys and girls, were coming from a basketball match, in crowds. One young man walked carrying a girl on his shoulder. Everyone of them looked so joyful. She couldn't make out who had lost and who had won. In the kitchen, Lan Hing was clattering the dishes as he made her a Vietnamese soup. Its aroma wafted all the way across to her. When he came out, bringing a bowl of soup, wrapped in the the loose end of his robe, he found her asleep in the chair.

The next day the two of them discussed the situation and came to a decision. They determined to use their entire savings to investigate the chances of conceiving a baby through IVE. An African colleague from his school offered to be their sperm donor. The doctor had to do many tests and it took six months to prepare her. She had to have twenty-eight injections of hormones and three days after her periods ended, the embryo created in a laboratory was inserted into her. As soon as her pregnancy was confirmed, she wrote a letter to her mother. 'I am pregnant. Soon you will have news of the birth of a grandson or granddaughter. Wait.'

She was beset by many doubts. One day she asked her doctor, 'What exactly will a baby be, if it is born to a Sri Lankan and Vietnamese couple through the sperm donated by an African?' The doctor answered without any hesitation, 'It will be an American.'

In exactly two hundred and eighty days, a beautiful baby was born to her. It was a comfortable childbirth. She took out the paper and pen she had brought in her handbag, all ready, and wrote just one line to her mother. 'I have given birth to an American baby.' She gave it to her husband and asked him to mail it immediately.

That letter, with its stamp in the northeast corner of the envelope, would somehow reach her mother whose address had neither a house number nor a street name. That whole day her mother would walk up and down the entire village, holding up the letter so that its American stamp was clearly visible to everyone.

Twenty days later, exactly at six o'clock, her mother telephoned. It was just as she expected. Her mother would have woken up at five in the morning to make that call. She would have caught the first bus to town, at six o'clock, waited outside the telephone office, entered before anyone else, as soon as the doors opened. It would be seven o'clock there at the time.

The twenty-day-old baby lay on her lap. She heard her mother's voice, 'Daughter, what sex is the baby, you didn't write that?'

'It's a girl, Amma, a baby girl. Amma, can you hear her crying?' She lifted up the baby and held her to the phone.

'Daughter, what have you named her?' She didn't hear her mother's voice, only the sound of her breathing.

'Amma, she's an American girl, through and through. You must see her. Don't die before you do that.'

They both spoke at the same time. Their voices clashed somewhere above the Atlantic Ocean.

It seemed to her that the baby lying on her lap had exactly the same features as her mother. Her hair grew in tight curls all over her small head. When she grew older, she too would tie her hair in a knot like her mother and cover it with a hair-net. She'd go to a basketball match with her friends, wearing a short skirt and clap her hands at the right moments. She would not run away if her boyfriend invited her to stay the night in his room. At a multicultural event, she might dance to the song, 'What penances did you do?' Or she might play a sixteen-stringed instrument. At Thanksgiving Day she would bring home a new boyfriend and introduce him to her parents. She would make sure, well ahead, that his sperm count was not lower than twenty million per millilitre.

That Innocent Smile

Sunil Govinnage

I carried you clutched against my shoulder
Freed you from fighting fierce and cruel
Gave you a refuge in this new country
So you could access the waters of learning

I watched you grow
Overflowing with kindness
A black crow queen among white girls
I watched you grow and my heart was glad

Seeing your glorious head of black hair
The children mocked you with hurtful words
How you wept your heart out when you got home
My own heart melted with concern that day

Your lovely face with golden coloring
How deck it like any white girls?
You who grew up a black crow princess
Now look at the world with a white mind.

Translated by Ranjini Obeyesekere

I brought you with me that fateful day
Freed you from fighting fierce and cruel
Brought you to this land that never ages
Today you war with aged me.

That innocent smile you lavished on me then
Your soft affectionate childish prattle
The sapphire blue of your eyes—all gone
Your words are now rapiers thrust at me.

A House in the Country

Romesh Gunesekera

The nights had always been noisy: frogs, drums, bottles, dogs barking at the moon. Then one evening there was silence. Ray stepped out on to the veranda. There was no wind. He pulled up a cane chair and sat down. The fireflies had disappeared. The trees and bushes in the small garden were still. Only the stars above moved, pulsing in the sky.

These were troubled times in Sri Lanka, people said, but nothing had happened in his neighbourhood. Nothing until this surprising silence. Even that, he thought, may not be new. He was becoming slow at noticing things.

Then a shadow moved. A young man appeared, his white sarong glowing in the moonlight.

He was much younger than Ray. Not as tall, but stronger, smoother skinned. His eyes were bright and hard like marbles. He came and stood by a pillar. A moth flew above him towards a wall light.

'What has happened?' Ray asked, looking around.

Siri scratched his head, gently rocking it. 'Don't know.'

'There's not a sound.' They spoke in slow Sinhala.

Ray liked this extraordinary silence. He liked the way their few words burst out, and then hung in the air before melting. It was the silence of his winter England transplanted. The silence of windows and doors closed against the cold. Lately Colombo had become too noisy. He had never expected such peace would come so close to war.

'The radio?' Ray asked. Siri always had a radio on somewhere in the house droning public service. 'Radio is not on?'

Siri shook his head. 'No batteries.' He bit the edge of his lower lip. 'I forgot to buy new ones. Shall I go now?'

It was late: nearly eleven at night. The little shop at the top of the road would have closed. Ray felt uneasy about Siri going too far. 'No. Go tomorrow. Better than now.' Siri nodded. 'Too quiet. Maybe another curfew?'

But it was not simply the silence of curfew. There seemed to be no sound at all. In the two years Ray had been back in the country there had been many curfews. They had lost their significance. Only the occasional twenty-four-hour curfew had any impact. Even those rarely inconvenienced him; he was often content to stay in his house.

But in recent months there had been a new wall to build, shutters to fix. Each day had been shattered by hammer blows aimed at protecting his future privacy. Ray had taken to escaping to a bar off Galle Road; it made him more than usually melancholic.

'Didn't you go out at all today?' Ray asked.

'These shutters,' Siri pointed inside. 'I wanted to finish the staining . . .'

'Good. They are very good.' The wood had the perfume of a boudoir.

'I was working on that, the last coat. Finished about seven-thirty. And then, when I was listening after my bath, the radio stopped.' He twisted his fingers to show a collapse into chaos. 'I didn't go out then because I thought you would be coming home soon.' His face widened in an eager smile.

Ray looked away. His long shadow danced down the steps. A gecko twitched. Ray had come home late.

Siri shifted his weight and moved away from the wall. He sat on the edge of a step. 'What do you think they'll do, Sir?'

'Who?'

'Government.'

Ray leaned back in his chair with both hands clasped behind his head and stared up at the night sky. He saw only a waning red moon. 'I don't know. What do you think?'

Siri rubbed his thighs. He'd heard people say they should hold elections—the government might even win; but people also said that there probably wouldn't be any elections. They'd try another 'military solution' against the JVP—the People's Liberation Front—like against the Tigers, and get stuck with war.

'Trouble is no one knows.' Siri's mouth turned down at both ends, but his was not a face that could show much distress. 'Nobody really cares, do they? Except for themselves.'

Ray put his hands together, matching fingertips, and half nodded. 'Not many people do.'

Ray had not planned on having any help or company when he first returned to Colombo from England. He'd had a secure job with a building society, a flat in London, a car, and a happy circle of acquaintances. There had also been a woman he'd spend a night or two with from time to time. But they never had much to talk about and quite often he simply thought about going back to Sri Lanka. One summer she went back home to Ulster; she got married.

That year he too decided he would go back home. He resigned from his job, sold his flat and left. The business of moving absorbed his energies, and he had no time to think. He had a house left to him in Colombo and money saved over the years. He hoped he would find out what he wanted once he had freed himself from the constraints of his London life, and once he had retrieved his past.

The first time he saw the house his uncle had left him, his blood turned to sand. It looked like a concrete box shoved into a hole. Nothing of the elegance of his converted London flat, nor the sensuality of the open tropical houses of his Sri Lankan childhood. But then he found Siri.

It was the luck of a moment. Ray was with a friend at a bar. They were drinking beer. His friend asked about the house, and Ray said he had too much to do. He needed builders, renovators. His friend mentioned Sirisena, Siri, who had done their house.

A few days later Siri turned up. Ray liked his quiet competence; the strange innocence in his eyes. He didn't quite know how to develop their working relationship. To him it should have been simply a relationship of employment. The old conventions of Colombo serfdom died years ago, but Siri kept saying 'Sir' and circumscribing their roles. He developed his job from artisan, to supervisor, to cook, night-watchman and, in effect, the servant. Ray felt things had to change incrementally: he acquiesced and played the roles Siri expected. Siri himself was too deep in this world of manners to feel the pull of revolution being preached across the country.

Siri did the carpentry, found the plumbers, the electricians. He moved in and slowly rebuilt the old house around Ray. Walls were replastered, doors rehung, floors tiled. And he kept the house in order.

Although in England Ray had done many of these things himself, here he found he needed Siri. Much of the renovation was straightforward, but from time to time he would see the need for change. He would talk it over with Siri, his fingers designing in the air. The next day Siri would start on the work.

In this way a new veranda was created; rooms divided. The curfews allowed him to examine progress. They provided the snapshots when activity was suspended. The workmen didn't come; it was only Ray and Siri.

It was the first time since childhood that Ray had had a constant companion. He encouraged Siri to talk and wished, in a way, that Siri could turn into his confidant. He wanted to ask, 'Why do you treat me like a . . .' but could never bring himself even to suggest he saw himself as a master. Siri simply showed respect in his antiquated fashion.

Ray's only response was to care. He didn't know how to respect in turn, but he felt a need to protect in a way he had never felt before. He tried to be generous with the pay and reasonable in his demands, but Siri seemed to want to do everything that needed doing and to spend all his time in the house. He hardly ever went back home to his village.

When Ray bought furniture for Siri's room, Siri looked dismayed.

'What's wrong?'

'I don't need all this.' Siri pointed at the cupboard and the new bed, the new pillow and mats.

'Some comfort won't harm.'

'I have nothing to put in the cupboard. The old bed was fine, just as it was.'

Ray said now that Siri had a steady job he might accumulate some possessions.

'What for? My family need things, my mother, my brother. I only need something to do. Some place . . . Sir, this house I am making for you. It will be beautiful. To me that is enough.'

Ray didn't know what to do. He was embarrassed and puzzled. He pulled down his chin and snorted, like a bull backing out of a shed. The early days were confusing. Siri seemed exhilarated by the freedom he had to use any material he desired to turn ideas into reality, even his own ideas. He had never been given such complete responsibility before. Ray didn't understand this. It took time for him to see Siri as himself.

That night, that silent night, back in his room Ray kept thinking about Siri. He felt uncomfortable. He would have liked to have talked some more. To have said something to Siri that would have helped them both understand what was happening. Instead they had sat there swallowing silence.

The next morning Ray woke to the scream of parrots circling the mango tree in the garden. He dressed quietly and stepped into the soft rubber of his shoes. In fifteen minutes he was out of the house.

The road was deserted. He walked to the end and crossed over into the park. He had a route he could follow with his eyes closed, carefully planned and timed to avoid other people.

He liked walking alone, in control of the sound around him: the thud of his feet, the blood in his ears.

The sky that morning was grey. Large, heavy clouds rippled overhead. Crows crowded the flame tree by the main road. Bats hung on the telephone lines.

Usually Ray walked for about twenty minutes. On his way back he would collect a newspaper from the small general store near the temple. Then at home he would savour a pot of tea and read the news. This morning he was looking forward to returning to an almost completed veranda.

Siri would have prepared the tea and disappeared: a tray with a white cloth, a small blue Chinese tea pot filled to the brim and protected by a embroidered tea-cosy, one plain white cup and saucer, a silver jug of boiled milk. A silver spoon. Ray would normally find the tray on a glass table. He had learned to accept this service as a part of life. He no longer resisted it and he never did the same for Siri. He never went that far.

But sometimes, in the evening, he'd offer Siri a drink.

He would find Siri sitting on the steps or stalking about the garden.

'Have a beer?' he'd say.

Siri would nod hesitantly and approach Ray smoothing his sarong. He would take the glass and sip slowly. He never sat down when he had a beer. He would stand while Ray sat. Whether they shared a beer or not, Siri was usually quite happy to talk. He'd tell Ray about life in the village: river bathing, family feuds, someone running amok. In the middle of such a story, Siri would sometimes stop and peer at Ray. 'Why do you look so sad?' he'd ask, and surprise Ray with his directness.

One evening Ray asked, 'Have you built your own house?'

Siri's mouth wrinkled; he slowly shook his head. 'No. Not my own. I have no land.'

'What about the family farm?'

'It's very small. We have one field.'

His father had tried milch cows, but couldn't compete with the local MP's people. They had commanded everything until the JVP moved in. By then the cows had dried up and Siri's father died. His brother stayed to work the one field, but Siri left.

'Could you ever go back to live in the country again? Now, after a city life. After what you've learned.' Ray wanted to know how genuine his own feeling of returning to roots was. He knew it was never possible to go back to exactly the same things, but at the same time he felt the old world never quite passes away. Suddenly the frame shifts and you find yourself back where you started.

'Go back to the country? Village life?' Siri smiled like a little boy thinking about the ripeness of mangoes. 'Yes. Yes, I could go back to a life in the country. Like my brother's. If there was a house like this in the country.'

'Maybe you should start saving some money?'

Siri found this suggestion amusing. 'There's never been the chance.' He clicked his tongue and added, 'Until now.'

The next day Ray went with Siri to the National Savings Bank and got him a savings book. He arranged for a part of Siri's salary to go straight into savings. But even after that Ray felt Siri was still not thinking far enough ahead. He was going to lose out. It troubled him at the time, although his own concern about Siri puzzled him more.

Months later Ray heard that some private land was being sold close to Siri's village. He asked him about it.

'No, Sir, I didn't know.'

Ray took a piece of paper from his pocket and unfolded it. 'Look, this is what it says.' He described the position of the land. It was near the coast.

'Yes,' Siri nodded. He knew the area.

'That land is a good price, I'm told.'

'I don't know, Sir. But there's not much growing there.' He delicately licked his thumb and forefinger, 'You can taste the salt in the air there.'

'No, it is good land. You can grow cinnamon or cardamom. Something like that. I know Mr Wijesena has some land there.'

Siri nodded. 'He has grown some cloves I think. Are you thinking of buying some land also?'

Ray was standing by the door. He took a deep breath. Suddenly he realized he was nervous. Sweat ran down his back. Things were not very clear in his head. He had started talking about the land with the simple intention of planting a seed in Siri's mind: land was sometimes available. He had probably hoped, he now thought as he stood there, that Siri would connect the idea of his savings with the possibility of a piece of land out in the country. But as they talked he realized that it would take Siri years to get a living out of such land. That Siri's life would be, at best, only a life of subsistence. He would sink into the earth, unless something radical could be done.

'I was thinking about a piece of land,' he said, looking down, away from Siri. 'I was thinking about you.'

'Me?'

'Maybe you should take some land.'

'Impossible, Sir. Even with the savings you arranged. Good land in our area is expensive.'

'I know. But if you could, would you like some land? Is it what you want?'

'You know me, Sir. I like to build. I like to grow. With some land there I can do both. And I can do as I please.'

'But when?'

'When my luck comes. When the gods take pity.'

'I can lend you the money,' Ray said quietly. It was not exactly what he wanted to say. The words slipped out like moonlight when the clouds move.

'But then I will be a debtor. I could never pay it back.'

Ray could see that. It could be the rut in the ground one never got out of. But he had a plan working itself out as he spoke.

'I'll buy the land. I'll *give* you a portion. You for your part can plant the trees for us both. Cinnamon or *cadju* or whatever.'

Siri's eyes brightened. There was a slight smile playing around his lips. The smooth boyish cheeks rippled. 'Why, Sir? Why do you want to do this for me?'

Ray could say nothing except that he wanted to.

'You are good, Sir, very good.'

Ray made arrangements to buy the land. He felt better for it. He had followed his instincts. But his instincts had changed. They were not the fine financial instincts that had served him in London: land prices plummeted as the troubles in the country spread. But this did not worry him. Things had to improve, he thought. Meanwhile he was happy to be serving in his turn.

In about ten minutes he reached the top of the hill on the side of the park. His route had already curved so that he was in fact now on his way home. A few minutes' walk along the road would bring him to the shop where he collected his paper.

He noticed the sky was dark and smudged. Crows were flapping about. Down the road he could see the white dome of the temple near his shop. The flowers of the temple trees, frangipani, were out. White blossom. Those were the trees he would like to have on the borders of the land he bought for Siri. But the white of both the dome and the flowers was grubby, as though settled with ash.

Ray thought the sky should have cleared by now. He walked quickly towards the temple. By the wall he stopped to look again at the frangipani. Many of the white flowers had fallen. But in the garden next to the temple a tree with the blood-red variety of the flower stood in rich bloom. Ray was sweating.

Then, around the corner, he came to the shop: the charred

remains of the shop. Bits were still smoking, thin wisps disappearing into the grey sky. A small crowd had gathered.

The vague thoughts in Ray's head evaporated; every muscle in his body was tense, but he felt extraordinarily calm. He stepped forward. 'How did this happen?'

Several people started talking. One man said the police had a statement from the JVP claiming responsibility. The shopkeeper was dead. He had been asleep inside. Kerosene had been used. Ray picked his way through the shattered glass and boiled sweets strewn along the roadside. Practically the whole of the tiny shop had been burned. One or two big blackened timbers still remained at the back, and buckled bits of the corrugated tin from the roof lay like petrified sheets of magma. The old *na* tree that had shaded the shop-front was scorched; the trunk looked as if it had been gouged with a hot knife. Two policemen had cordoned off the place.

Ray waited for a while absorbing the babble around him, watching the smoke rise in small puffs out of the heaps of ash. The veins in his arms were swollen. *A store burns like so many others up and down the country. Only this one's closer to home. Nothing else has changed.* But Ray knew that proximity made a difference. The air was pungent. He wondered whether the dust on his shoes now mixed earth with the ash of the shopkeeper's burnt flesh.

When he got home Siri was at the gate. 'Did you see . . . ?'

Ray nodded and brushed past him.

Siri had heard about the fire from a neighbour. 'Is it very bad?'

'The whole shop has gone. Completely burnt out.'

'Mister Ibrahim?'

'Dead. He was inside.'

Ray went to his usual place. The tea tray wasn't there. A fine layer of dust covered the table. 'Water's boiling, Sir. I'll bring the tea now.'

In a few minutes Siri came with the tea. 'Will you have it here on the veranda?'

'Inside may be better today.'

'You know Sir, they warned him. He was very foolish.'

Ray asked him who had warned the shopkeeper. Why?

'Several times they told him to stop selling those newspapers. Mister Ibrahim didn't listen. Even two days ago he told me that he will not stop selling newspapers just like that. But they said he must stop, or it will be the end for him. I don't know why he continued.'

Who had warned him?

'I don't know, Sir. These thugs who come around.'

Ray raised his eyes. 'Why do you think he didn't stop selling those papers?' he asked. 'He was not a Party man.'

Siri shrugged. 'He was a *mudalali*—a businessman. Making money. You make money by selling what people buy. People wanted his newspapers, so he sold them. That is his work. Was his work.'

Ray wondered whether Siri was right. Was Ibrahim killed by the market? Or was he simply caught in between? He could see the flames leap at Ibrahim's straw mat; within seconds he must have been wrapped in fire. But he must have screamed. How did they not hear it? The shop was not far, and the night had been so silent. The smell of kerosene? Flesh? But then, countries have been in flames before and the world not known.

'Sir, do you think there is any danger here?'

'What do you mean?'

'Will they harm this house?'

'This house means nothing. It has nothing to do with anyone.'

'I hope no harm will come. It is becoming so beautiful.'

Ray and Siri both felt uneasy all day. They avoided each other. Ray spent the morning alone and then went out to a café for lunch. He came back early in the evening and disappeared into his room. He had a shower and lay down on his bed to rest. Clean and cool; naked on the cotton sheet. He felt his body slowly relax. The evening was warm. As day began to turn to night the birds screamed again. Through his window he could see the sun set in an inflamed sky. When he closed his eyes the grey smudges came back. His skin was dry. He looked at the polished wood of his new windows. Siri had done a fine job. He had brought out the wood grain perfectly. Ray wanted to ask Siri to build another house. A house on *their* land out in the country. He thought if he provided the materials Siri could design and build a house with two wings, or even two small houses. One for each of them. If Siri were to marry it would make for a good start. Ray wondered how he'd feel if that happened. He would lose something. The intimacy that had yet to be. But he would feel some satisfaction. He would have made a difference.

Later, when he came out on to the veranda he found Siri sitting on the steps. Siri looked up; his hard black eyes gave nothing to Ray.

'Sir,' Siri said in a low voice, 'I want to go.'

'Where?'

'Away, Sir.' Siri remained sitting on the steps. His face was in shadow.

'What's wrong? What is it?'

'This destruction. I want to go away.' The eyes softened slightly. 'And you, Sir, have seen the world. Tell me where. Where is a good place?'

Ray looked down at Siri. 'What do you mean? You know, shops have been burned many times before. In Matara, in Amparai, here in Colombo it has happened before.'

Siri shook his head.

'It has happened all over the world,' Ray said.

Siri kept shaking his head. 'But it can't always be like this. It can't.' The night air slowly curled around him.

'We have to learn. Somehow. We are no better, but we are no worse.' Ray turned on the wall lights, pushing at the darkness. Then he saw one of the new shutters was broken: several slats were splintered; the wood was raw. Ray felt a pain in his chest. He took a deep breath. 'Never mind. It can be fixed.' He was determined.

Siri stared up at him, then shook his head again as if at a fly. 'Sir . . .' his face slowly crumpled. 'Sir, my brother back home. They've used a lamp-post for him.' Siri shut his eyes.

Ray's throat felt thick, clogged. 'You should have told me,' he said at last tugging at his neck. The body would have been mutilated, then strung up as a beacon; the corpse would swing in the wind for days. 'Why?'

Siri's bare feet dangled over the steps. When he spoke his voice was hardly audible. 'Who can tell, Sir, in this place?'

Ray looked at their shadows cupped in a circle of yellow light on the gravel below the veranda; the light on Siri's arms. He tried to lean forward but couldn't move. He couldn't clear the space between them. Siri's skin was mottled.

'It happened last night,' Siri said.

Ray nodded, 'Maybe you should take a few days off. Find your people,' he heard himself say. 'The veranda can wait . . .' His voice faltered. They were not the words he wanted. Ray saw himself alone again in his house, picking his way through the debris at the back. There were two rooms still to be done; pots of yellow paint in the corner of the bedroom would remain unopened. He found himself thinking that without Siri he would have to make his own morning tea again. Drink alone on his incomplete veranda; wait.

But Siri said nothing. Ray could not tell whether he had heard him. Siri slowly straightened out and stepped down on to the path. He looked at Ray for a moment, then turned and started walking towards the back of the house, towards his room in the servant's quarters. Ray opened his mouth to say something about the new house, the cinnamon garden, but Siri had melted away in the darkness. Ray remained standing on the veranda. He felt he was on fire, but the palms of his hands were wet. Out in the garden fireflies made circles. Frogs croaked. The sky trembled like the skin of a drum.

The Homecoming

Vijita Fernando

Thousands of poor Sri Lankan women go to the Middle East as domestic workers, labouring there under difficult, often abusive, conditions. This story reflects the reality of those women returning with dreams of a prosperous existence at home.

Not a word had been said about the money since she returned. She didn't always think about it, but at night when sleep was impossible, her thoughts kept returning to the money. Every month, for two years, she had sent home nearly three thousand rupees. What had they done with it? No one mentioned the money. Certainly not Siripala, her husband. How could he? Most of the time since she came back he had spent his days in a euphoria of drink. The duty-free stuff she had brought—she laughed a humourless laugh when she thought of it—had not been enough. Now the last drops were being diluted with kasippu.

The nights were hell. The long, thick Arab-style dress did not help much. So comfortable during those chilly nights in that distant land. But here, the long sleeves enveloped her into a prisoner of yards of thick warm cloth. The mud walls of the shanty shut her in. In those dark moments before the dawn, she felt them closing in, closing in, strangling her. The mosquitoes added their bit with their chanting and stinging. The heat stifled her. Added to all this was the drunken snoring of her husband, his nightly tirades at last silenced. Millie eased herself out of the narrow bed, careful not to wake Siripala and drive him into another session of haranguing the whole neighbourhood as had happened night after night since she came back. She stooped at the low door of the shanty and went out into the night. She sat on the half wall—the broken bit—that shut off shanty-land from the affluent neighbourhood and breathed freely.

A quick calculation buzzed round and round in her head. Three thousand rupees for each month of two years, and not word about it. Not one word. How much did all that add up to. A great deal, she knew, though rupees and cents did not seem to mean much these days. Not like when she left two years ago.

Things had changed so. All the years of her life everything had remained the same. But two short years had changed everything. That first morning at home when she stepped out in her long dress—rather self-consciously—no one had given her a second glance. No neighbours came running to her for tales of fairyland. They were friendly. They were inquisitive. But only about what she had brought.

A cassette recorder?

No? Then what?

Oh, only a radio? Why?

Clothes? But you can get anything here now. Yes, even wet-look materials.

She showed them the two thin gold bangles on her arm, bought with such care and contemplation.

Gold, they laughed. Ha, ha, imagine bringing gold and no television!

Yes, they had changed. Money meant nothing to them. Or it meant only liquor, TV, coarse plentiful eating while the cash lasted.

What about MY money, she wondered for the millionth time. What had they done with it? Not eaten and drunk only? There was not even a television set in their house.

Suddenly her thoughts lurched back to a long forgotten moment when she had woken, her body racked with fever. She was only about five years old then, but recalled with a vividness which scared her, the sight of her mother bent at the hearth, digging the soft ash with the handle of a coconut shell ladle. Her digging brought out a rusty powder tin. She shook it into her palm and a few coins fell out. She tucked the coins into her waist, wrapped the feverish child in her outer cloth and rushed to the dispensary . . .

She smiled ruefully. That was a long time ago. Today everyone knew of banks and savings and illegal lending at enormous rates of interest. For a moment her face brightened. Perhaps that was what they had done with her money. In a moment a dark cloud passed across her face. No, they wouldn't . . . not her shiftless husband with his penchant for drink and idleness, nor her greedy sons.

She remembered their beady eyes alive with greed as they rummaged through her boxes the day she came back. Greedy hands had grabbed and pulled. Vicious words had passed between father and sons, between brother and brother. Upali, with his brawny body and his grudge against the world, had pushed the other two aside. Cyril, the oldest, had been just a shade less obvious. His teenaged wife, the baby tucked under her arm, had looked on, with her whining expression, saying nothing. The youngest boy, Nimal, had later bashed Upali's nose, fighting over a T-shirt.

But Pushpa, the thirteen-year-old girl child, had not even looked at the things her mother had brought. Her brothers had flung them aside, the things they did not want, the colourful sarees, the gay dresses, the baubles and trinkets.

At the Jeddah market place they had shone and glittered in the harsh sunlight, the silks shining in the open air stands, the baubles glittering on the shiny tin trays. Looking at them, her eyes alight with wonder that she could pick and buy anything she wished, Millie had ignored the leers, the suggestive glances, the tugging at her dress and shut her eyes to the babel of foreign tongues.

Standing in the middle of that unreal scene her thoughts had suddenly flown to a child woman she had left at home, a slender, tender body with tiny breasts sprouting in a too thin chest, a mass of wild hair which she so loved to tame into a sleek curtain about a doe-eyed piquant face with a petulant mouth.

Daughter, she cried, my girl child, what have I done to leave you with that shiftless father and your brothers who have not a thought in their heads other than money and food and drink when they can steal enough to buy them . . . ?

The tears shut away the market scene around her and she was back in a mud-walled, zinc-roofed shanty in a green and pleasant land, warm, thin hands round her neck, a wild mane of hair snuggling against her breast . . .

That day she did an orgy of buying for the girl. Chains and bracelets, dangling ear drops, sarees, dresses. These she had longed for in her own childhood. Now she wanted desperately to make Pushpa's dreams come true.

Pushpa, little flower child, so true to her name, so like a flower. The piquant face gained charm and beauty in her mind, making up for the thousands of miles she had placed between her and that little scrap of her being she had left behind, in a mud-walled shanty, in a faraway land with her adolescence.

The clothes had lain in the only chair in the shanty from the day she came back. They made a bright splash of colour in that drab room. Pushpa hadn't touched them. The baubles were still in the boxes. Only that morning Upali had rummaged through the boxes again, for the hundredth time, looking for money or something to sell. He had scooped the trinkets in his palm and thrown them at the girl.

Take them, take them and put them on yourself, make yourself look like one of those street women. Take them, you little slut, what are you so proud about . . . ?

With a sudden movement she had collected a handful of them in her hand and flung them at her brother and rushed out of the shanty, her eyes streaming with tears, her sobs choking her.

Leave her alone, you whore, thundered her husband as Millie started to run after the girl.

WHORE?

The word reverberated in the stuffy room, going round and round in a frenzy of shock in her head.

WHORE?

In a moment of release from his drunken stupor, Siripala stood in shock at the word he himself had flung at her. It was not so much the word—common enough in the neighbourhood, used even in affection at times—it was the hate and loathing which accompanied it, the obscene ring to it, the gesture of revulsion with which he had tossed it across the room, and at her very being.

Whore? the sons stood where they were without even shifting their gaze from their drink-sodden father to their mother who stood so straight and still, frozen with shock, her long loose robe touching the ground. Like a queen from some streetside play. Not a murmur disturbed that awful tableau, not even a gust of wind.

How like their father they were, Millie thought with ironic irrelevance. How like him, loathsome as he is, she thought, with not a twinge of conscience for so branding them. Her sons, flesh of her flesh, little infants she had smothered with caresses in some far-off distant time, little boys whose scratches she had sucked and soothed, little mouths she had fed with morsels from her own skimpy plate. . . .

Whore? That was the unspoken word that had hovered in the air since she came home. All those drunken orgies celebrated a whore's homecoming, rich with the spoils of her whoring in some other land.

A whore come home. Let's give her a whore's welcome.

Now she understood her husband's nightly ranting. Sitting on the broken wall he had raved every night till way past midnight. One night some sleepless man had informed the police. They had all hidden when they saw the green jeep coming down the road. That night there had been a little quiet . . . but only for a while.

Whores, the lot of them, he had shouted, come with their money and their fancy clothes. They and their work, housemaids they are called . . . at that point he had laughed a long deep-throated gurgle which ended in a bout of coughing. But that had not stopped him.

An honest carpenter like me, what has he got now, with the whores bringing their ill-gotten wealth from the Arab lands?

These people—he had spat across the road at the affluence of the big houses, the men and women across from shanty-land who spoke in English, drove cars and had children with bicycles and shoes on their feet.

They? What do they know of money, real money? They pay me a measly forty rupees for an honest day's work, for toiling nine, ten hours. They should come to our side of the wall to know what money is like . . . thousands these women earn in those Arab lands . . . they say the Arabs are generous . . . generous with their favours . . . ha, ha!

Millie had tried to coax him in. She had tried to be kind to her husband, poor drunken Siripala and paid no heed to his words. But now she knew what those words had meant. Remembering that night, his frustrated frenzy afterwards, a moment's pity crept into her.

Poor wretch, she said under her breath.

The chill of the distant dawn soothed her flushed body. She walked to the well, a few yards away and drew a pot of water. The cool water was balm to her burning face. A slight stir in the pre-dawn stillness made her turn round. There was Leela, her son's wife, coming towards the well with a bucket of soiled clothes.

She grinned her smug smile at Millie, irritating her unreasonably. Why, she wondered briefly, do I feel no affection for this creature, this newest member of my family? There was not even curiosity about how Cyril had married her, this big-bosomed nondescript girl with the oily hair.

No one had any sleep last night, Leela said in a voice full of promise of more to come.

An unnecessary remark. Millie knew that every word Siripala said would have been heard all over the shanty garden. Those filthy words would have found their way into every nook and crevice, penetrated into every sleeping hovel, obtruded into every sleeper's brain, woken the babies and disturbed the fitful sleep of the sick. She knew it only too well.

Cyril and I wondered whether to come and call Father to our house, she added in self-righteous tones, quite unaware of Millie's unconcern. Father has had a bad time you know . . . two years is a long time you were away. Pushpa doesn't look after him properly. Anyway she is too young to take on her mother's responsibilities. . . .

The whining words were hammering a message into Millie's brain. They made her head whirl. She wanted to vomit. She took a handful of the cool water and drank it to stop the awful retching in her stomach.

True, he had money to spend . . . but a man needs more than money. After all, Father is not an old man, you know . . . she paused pregnantly and took a long time to draw a pot of water and soak the clothes.

Anyway we are lucky to have good neighbours. They were very good to him. You know, Father is a good man though when he drinks he shouts and scolds. Old woman Asilin Achchi and her granddaughter Sumithra—you remember Sumithra, don't you?—they were very kind to Father. Sumithra is such a nice girl. Of course we did what we could. But it was Sumithra who was always in and out of the house, cooking for him.

When he had that fever—I don't know whether Pushpa told you—Sumithra did everything for him. My word, the number of nights she spent in your house when he was not well . . .

But she didn't do all that for nothing. Father was always giving her plenty of money, buying her all sorts of things. You should see now when she goes out, all dressed up with gold chains and all . . . he gave her everything. Only when we asked him for a little something, even when little Ranjit, his own grandson, was ill, he said he had no money . . . and that day itself he had a letter from you with a money order. Anyway, whatever it is, he didn't give us any money, not a cent of what you sent home.

Millie suddenly knew that she did not care at all about the money.

Three thousand rupees a month for twenty-four months. What does that mean in terms of your lifetime's hopes scattered about your feet? All those promises of a piece of land, a better house, a dowry for little Pushpa, a decent life for them all . . . what was the use?

Leela's plaintive voice went on and on, inexorably.

You bitch, you little bitch, shut your smug little mouth and stop your whining. I have had enough of your talk. You have plucked my heart out and thrown it away and now you want to trample on it. I don't care about the money, or Siripala or what the neighbours said or did. I don't care any more, do you hear, not about any of you, not anyone of you goddamned dogs and bitches. . . .

With a sudden lunge she took the girl by the hair and twisted her head back and fixed her eyes with her own burning ones. She shook those tresses once, twice and taking her right hand away, struck her across that whining mouth till the blood spurted and a red film flashed across her eyes.

But of course, she didn't do it, or say anything. She wanted to, dear god, she wanted to. All she did was to walk wearily towards the house, leaving the girl still talking.

She had a sudden recollection of Sumithra at the well, her lithe body draped in a thin cloth streaming with water, her black tresses down her back, drops of water glistening in the sunlight, a symphony of black and white. Suddenly the girl had turned and Millie saw the swelling belly straining against the thin damp cloth.

Sumithra, so it was you who got the money I toiled to earn in a strange land. Can you imagine what I felt when I got off that frightening bird with its brain-bursting noise? I wanted to run away, run somewhere with the sand burning my feet. Can you imagine what it is to find yourself in a strange land, to look upon a landscape where there is no grass as far as the eye can see, no trees to cover the burning blue of the sky, to hear tongues that make no sense, intercept glances that you cannot interpret, where smiles are leers because you are a woman of another colour, in strange clothes, where you sense invitations though their words have no meaning, where obscenities are flung at you because you are at their mercy?

The humiliation had been the worst to bear.

Day and night, day and night, the dark-eyed mistress had flung at her a torrent of words, venomous and cruel. Later she began to understand some of them.

Fakir, she said a hundred times a day. Sri Lankan fakir.

Yes, she was a beggar. On her knees shining their floors, on her knees cleaning their lavatories, on her knees hushing their infants to sleep. Standing at the hearth, a day that sometimes stretched into a million years.

And the fear at night. Trembling like a virgin in that closed-up box-like room, listening to footfalls that pause at your door, keys softly turning in locks . . .

Can you imagine what it is like, Sumithra? And me, a woman nearing forty, my body used to a man from the age of fourteen, a woman who has borne four children?

And the loneliness. Something that I cannot even talk about.

The indignities I went through to earn those thousands. The yearning for a friendly smile, a known tongue, the eagerness to see a face that smiled at you as if you were a human being, not a piece of dirt to be used and made more dirty.

But I kept going, Sumithra, not because, as you might think, of the money. It was not the money that made me strong. But something did. I was able to stand all of it because, Sumithra, I had a dream.

The dream of coming home had been so alive during the two years. One night she opened her box and rummaged under the newspaper at the bottom of the box and took out the polythene bag in which her precious passport and return ticket were carefully kept. She took the two bits of paper and pressing them against her breast lay on the floor in a paroxysm of loneliness.

The long trip was short and swift in her eagerness to get home. The emerald green of her homeland seen from the air brought tears to her eyes. Happy tears spilled over when she saw her family eagerly looking through the crowd to spot her. She felt her husband's affectionate gaze, her daughter's arms round her neck, her sons around her, the coach waiting to take her home.

That was the dream that had kept her alive.

And now, looking round the tiny room, she saw the relics of her real homecoming scattered around her. In the first light of dawn they mocked her, those colourful cardboard cartons and bottles, the spurned gifts about the floor, the drunken naked man on the bed, the sulking girl in the next room. And, enveloping all, the incongruous and nauseating smell of hair lotion the sons had so liberally used.

With sudden resolve Millie flung the things back in her box and tidied them into some sort of order. Then she knelt on the floor and like a thief in the night easing a treasure from a carefully guarded hiding place, she lifted the newspaper at the bottom of the box and took out the polythene cover in which the precious passport and return ticket were carefully kept. She took them out and laying them in her lap, caressed them tenderly.

The House in Jaffna

Isankya Kodithuwakku

When Mr. Nadarajah rode the train each evening from Waterloo Station to his home in Teddington, he almost always had a bright, peaceful look on his face. Most people who saw him probably thought he was a man with a happy family life, who rode the train in anticipation of home. Although their assumption about his family life was correct, they were wrong when they thought it was a look of anticipation. Rather, it was a look of memory. Because the home he was thinking of was not his present house forty-five minutes out of London, but an old, white-walled house in Jaffna.

Mr. Nadarajah spent most of his free time lost in memories of the Jaffna house. When he was feeling particularly good, he had a tendency to move his legs rapidly, the knees going back and forth sideways like an accordion. This was what he was doing on the train that day in 2002 when he read the *London Times* report about the ceasefire in Sri Lanka. The article reported that the fighting in Jaffna was over, that goods were being shipped there again, and that there were even plans to reopen the road into Jaffna.

Mr. Nadarajah was in his house for hardly two minutes before he announced what he had been thinking of all day. 'In three weeks, we're going back to Jaffna,' he said while he took off his layers of coats and sweaters. He threw the last sweater on the pile that was already in his wife's arms and beamed at her. She was looking at him with a blank face.

He turned to his mother, who was sitting on the sofa, swinging her legs like a child, her heavy, silk sari and wrinkled skin incongruous next to her attitude. 'Ma, we're returning home,' he repeated.

His wife's face had changed by now. Her eyebrows were raised as she asked, 'What are you talking about? How can we go back to that war zone?'

'It's not a war zone,' Mr. Nadarajah said and whipped out the *London Times*. 'Look. The war is over. They've signed a peace deal.'

'A peace deal?' his wife looked up at the ceiling. 'How many of those have there been? They never stay for very long.'

'Well, this one is different,' Mr. Nadarajah replied and settled in a chair. 'This one is going to last. And we're returning.'

His fourteen-year-old daughter, Anitha, came into the room to catch the last words. 'Returning?' she asked. 'Oh god, are we moving again?' In the sixteen years the Nadarajahs had been in England, they had lived in six different homes. The first two years had been spent in a small two-roomed flat in London. But as the loan firm that Mr. Nadarajah started when he arrived in the city began to make profits, they moved out of the flat and into rented houses, which changed every few years, but only became more magnificent in proportions and luxuries.

'Yes, we're moving,' Mr. Nadarajah now answered his daughter and beamed again. 'We're moving home to Jaffna.'

'Jaffna?' Anitha looked horrified. 'You mean Sri Lanka? No way, dad!'

'Yes, Sri Lanka,' Mr. Nadarajah replied. 'The war is over. We're going back to where we belong.'

'He's not serious, is he, mum?' Anitha asked looking at her mother.

'Of course he's serious,' her mother snapped. 'Don't start back-talking now!'

'Back-talking?' Anitha slumped into a chair, her short skirt splayed all over her knees. 'Are you mad, mum? Dad's trying to ruin my life and you start about how to talk.'

Mrs. Nadarajah turned to her husband. 'We do need to go back to Jaffna,' she said. 'They're growing up not knowing how to talk to their elders.' She walked over to her daughter and straightened the skirt so it covered more of Anitha's thighs. 'Sit properly when your father's here at least,' she muttered.

'Sitting properly! Talking properly!' Anitha cried as she rose from her seat. 'Is that all that matters to you people? This is not fair. Dad can't suddenly decide to make all of us leave London. I'm not going to Jaffna!' She stalked out of the room.

Mr. and Mrs. Nadarajah stared after her silently. Mr. Nadarajah shook his head. 'She'll realize when she's older the good of returning,' he said. 'She'll be thankful to us then for taking her back to where she belonged. Where we belong.'

Mr. Nadarajah's mother's voice rose. 'The tortoise only ever returns to the shore to lay its eggs,' she said, her eyes staring at the far wall and her legs still swinging. Since the old lady had a habit of saying random things, which never seemed to have any context to the conversation, neither Mr. nor Mrs. Nadarajah paid much attention to her.

Mr. Nadarajah returned to the newspaper and reread the article on the ceasefire. At last, he could leave this country, where he would never be anything more than a wrong-skinned immigrant. However rich he became, however he dressed and acted, or however he talked, it was always the same. Just yesterday—why, was it just yesterday?—he had the bad luck of tripping over a white man's legs on the train home. 'Watch out where you going, Paki,' the man had said and the only people around who did not have dirty looks on their faces were the ones who were laughing at his seeming immigrant clumsiness.

Now he could leave all this. This land, where even the grandest houses that money could rent always seemed so cold and hollow he had to move his family out of them every two or three years. He would be able to wake up every day in the house of his childhood and youth. He would again be able to walk barefoot in his *dhoti* and shirt to the Buddhist temple nearby to start each day with rituals to the Hindu gods, whose *devalas* took up half of the temple grounds. And each evening, he would be able to take the copper path again to say a few more prayers and then spend a few hours with the priest, Soma Thera, discussing Gandhi's interpretation of *The Bhagavad Gita* or debating on the sixteen *samskars* or comparing the truths of Buddhism and Hinduism.

Mr. Nadarajah was quick in his actions. He put his vice-chairman in charge of the firm, gave up the house to its owner, and withdrew his kids from their school. Two months after the ceasefire agreement was signed, Mr. Nadarajah and his family were on a plane from London to Colombo.

The flight was full of Tamils returning to Sri Lanka, the saris of the women and the sober black of the men's trousers contrasting with Anitha's orange Capri pants and pink tank top and her twelve-year-old brother's red Beckham football shirt. At the start of the flight, Mr. Nadarajah tried to talk to his son about Mr. Nadarajah's Jaffna childhood days, but after first getting silent treatment, seemingly deaf ears, and a blank face from Ravi, and later, a British-accented, 'I don't care, Dad. I don't want to listen to these daft stories,' Mr. Nadarajah returned to just eavesdropping on the conversations around him, happier because it was all in Tamil, rather than because of all the gossip he garnered.

As the taxi drove the family through the streets of Colombo to their hotel, Mr. Nadarajah could only stare around him. He had visited this city a few times when the family lived in Jaffna, but now the memories and pictures he had of Colombo seemed to be those of another place. The roads were still tree-lined, narrow, and bumpy, but that was all he recognized. The taxi went at hardly thirty miles per hour as traffic jammed the roads. On either side, houses hugged each other with no gardens in sight. Remains of abandoned road blocks made of painted bags of sand stood in places, empty security huts behind them. People crowded the streets, walking or standing on the pavement, on the open road, and in the bus stops. And as they neared their hotel, the skyline turned as city-like as any modern city in other parts of the world.

Mr. Nadarajah sat in the passenger seat, his knees silent. All afternoon, while his kids shrieked in the hotel pool and his mother and wife slept, he sat in front of the television, his back slumped against the cane chair. He spent the hours switching between the channels until he came across the six o'clock Tamil news, which featured a special report on Jaffna. While the newscaster spoke in the background and a reporter led the camera through Jaffna, Mr. Nadarajah gradually sat up in his seat.

The report was focusing on how Jaffna had not changed over the years of the war. It showed the old methods of trade that were still practised in the market, walked into people's homes to show their black-and-white televisions, and into their kitchens to show the lack of any western appliances. The report did not show any of the damaged buildings or mined fields. Mr. Nadarajah started to move his knees. Jaffna had not modernized like Colombo; the war had kept his peninsula just the way it was.

A flight service run by a private telecommunications firm trying to cash in on the ceasefire took the family from Colombo to Jaffna. The plane landed in an airfield next to an army camp and Anitha's 'It's so hot here, I'm going to die' was the first thing Mr. Nadarajah heard. He tried to keep calm; he had heard the same words from his daughter too many times in the past two days.

'Dad, I want a coke,' Ravi said.

'What coke?' Mr. Nadarajah said. 'You think they have coke here?'

'No coke?' Anitha asked. 'What kind of uncivilized place is this?'

'Uncivilized?' Mr. Nadarajah said. 'Do you think coke means civilization? Do you have any understanding of what this place is?'

'Some stupid, backward place,' Anitha muttered, but too quietly for her father to hear. Mr. Nadarajah turned away to talk to the man who was to process their papers and followed him to a one-roomed building with unpainted cement walls. Near the entrance to the building, a man leaned over a decrepit cart with a heated iron platter, using his one good arm to scrape the platter clean. 'Sir, a *godamba roti*, sir?' the man said when he saw Mr. Nadarajah. 'I can make you one fresh now. With vegetable mix or eggs? Take some for your family, sir.'

Mr. Nadarajah waved him away, trying to keep his eyes off the three-inch stump, which was all that was left of the man's right arm. But on the way back to his family who were still standing on the edge of the airfield, he stopped at the cart. The front of it was lined with coloured drinks in bright shades of orange, pink, and green. He bought one and took it back to his children.

Ravi's face lit up when he saw the drink in his father's hands, but 'Ew. We're supposed to drink this?' was the only comment Anitha had.

'What do you think?' Mr. Nadarajah asked. 'Weren't you complaining about the heat just now and wanting drinks?'

'A civilized drink; not one that's hot pink,' she replied. 'I'm not drinking this.'

Mr. Nadarajah held out the bottle to his son, but now Ravi just shook his head and looked away. 'Fine, then just be thirsty by yourselves,' Mr. Nadarajah said, putting the straw to his mouth. The first gulp almost came back up his throat, but he finished the drink before the family crammed into a battered, black Morris Minor, the taxi Mr. Nadarajah had reserved from his Colombo hotel room the day before.

'Have we returned to the Middle Ages?' Anitha asked, but Mr. Nadarajah just beamed at the taxi driver and shook his hand energetically. He sat in the passenger seat, shaking his knees and gazing out the window the whole drive from the airfield to the house, which lay a few miles out of Jaffna town. The landscape was the green he remembered it to be, the colour more striking because of the dusty ground. But while Mr. Nadarajah's memories painted Jaffna as arid, now it seemed a leafier, thicker place. Mr. Nadarajah felt suddenly as if he were in the middle of a jungle.

But everything else was the same.

On the sides of the road, the thatched palm-fronds fences rose almost without a gap. A tinge of copper shone on the dust that settled on the car. The palm trees grew high above the ground. And the green grass of Jaffna waved all over the bare fields. Gazing at the old familiarities, Mr. Nadarajah thought of Siva, one of their manservants from the long-ago Jaffna days. Old Siva who been more of a mother to Mr. Nadarajah than his own mother had been. While she would be wandering around the gardens of the house, plucking flowers and singing verses from the *Kurunthokai* love anthology, Siva would get Mr. Nadarajah ready for school and take him there. It would be Siva to whom Mr. Nadarajah would always run to get a cut elbow bathed or break a piece of news. And it had been Siva who had first taken Mr. Nadarajah to the Buddhist temple near their house and taught him the truths of both religions. Mr. Nadarajah had sent Siva the first bit of money he had been able to spare after he left Jaffna, but he had not heard back from the old servant then or when he wrote countless letters over the passing years.

The taxi drove into Jaffna town. The roads were deserted and piles of brick and rubble lined them. Mr. Nadarajah craned his eyes, trying to catch a glimpse of his old primary school on the square, of the two-storied brick building that housed T. M. Tailors, where he had always gone to get his clothes sewn, of the old post office built by the British. But he saw only damaged walls and piles of twisted metal. The only crowded place in the town was the old market square, men and women crouched over piles of produce, home-made clothes, or mats and rugs made of woven palm-fronds.

Then they drove out of the town and through a few miles of deserted, green countryside up to the house. The palm-frond fences of the house were still in pristine condition. The bushes of jasmine that bordered the fences peeped above them. And once Mr. Nadarajah got out of the car and walked into the compound, he saw the house with its walls still painted in white and the wooden doors and windows in brown. Mr. Nadarajah walked up to the front steps, forgetting his family, which stood huddled together in the fence opening. In front of the steps, he lowered his hand to the ground and touched his forehead.

Mr. Nadarajah climbed the steps and took the old, rusted key out of his pocket. He stood for a moment, looking down at the brass key, which took up his entire palm. He remembered how he had locked this door that night the family had fled the peninsula, crossing the Palk Straits on a fisher boat. He reached out to insert the key in the door and realized there was no keyhole. The entire iron block that held the keyhole and the lock had been ripped off the door and only a gaping hole remained in the wood. Mr. Nadarajah reached out and pushed against the door and it creaked open. He drew back his hand with a hiss and stuck a finger in his mouth. One of the splinters from where the keyhole used to be had wedged deep in his skin.

The inside of the house reeked of human piss and animal smells. All the old teak furniture was gone. In the living room, a rattan chair leaned crookedly on three legs. An upturned brass table rusted in the corner. In the bedrooms, cardboard and paper littered the floors. The walls were streaked from the dirty water that ran down them when the rain got through the leaky roof. And even the outside walls, which at the beginning had looked just like the old ones Mr. Nadarajah remembered, were actually only a faded, yellowish-white.

Nevertheless, all of this was really okay for Mr. Nadarajah. It was only his children who ran out of the house screaming it smelled and only his wife who went about with a drawn face. Mr. Nadarajah did an inspection tour of his house and standing in the garden, he said, 'We can get this place fixed up in no time. With a little money, it'll be no problem. All it needs is for us to live in it and then it'll be just like the old times.' His mother plucked a flower from a jasmine bush and took a deep sniff of it. 'The cat, which cannot catch a mouse, plays with its food,' she said. Mrs. Nadarajah only glanced at the kids who were silently sitting close to each other on the front steps.

That afternoon, while his family took naps inside the house, Mr. Nadarajah washed himself at the well and walked down to the temple. He returned looking more tired than what the short walk should have made him.

When his wife came out to the verandah, he was sitting on the rattan chair, which was propped up by a few bricks. 'How was the temple?' she asked. 'Soma Thera was there?'

Mr. Nadarajah did not answer for a few seconds. When he did, she could hardly hear him. 'The old priest wasn't there,' he said. 'Nobody was there. In fact, there was no temple there.'

'No temple?' his wife asked. 'You mean what?'

'The temple was bombed out during the war,' he replied. 'Where it used to be, there's only a pile of rubble now.'

'They bombed out the temple?' she asked, a hand at her cheek. 'Who'd do such a thing? I didn't think it even of the army.'

'Met a man when I was wandering around the rubble. I asked who bombed the place and he said they never knew who the bombs came from. Sometimes it was the army, sometimes it was the terrorists, all they knew was that the bombs fell from planes in the sky.'

'How did this house not get destroyed?' she asked.

'The man said that the terrorists used it as their headquarters for this area,' he replied. 'And then when the army took over again, they had their troops staying here.'

'That must be where all the bathroom-smell comes from,' she said. 'Troops! What do they know of the value of a house like this?'

'I guess that's why whoever bombed the area avoided the house—they had a use for it in mind,' he continued. 'The bombs destroyed everything around.'

'Everything around?' she asked. 'Has everything been destroyed?'

'He said most of the buildings big enough to be seen from the sky were gone. The people who're still around live in small huts and cottages. He said it was a miracle this house had been saved.'

'It is a miracle,' she agreed.

'I think it's a sign that we should stay,' he said, starting to move his knees.

'You still think that?' she asked. 'Haven't you seen how it all is? Can't you see that we can't stay here? The house is in shambles. The temple is gone. There's no one around.'

Mr. Nadarajah waved his hand as if to get rid of her words. 'These are all things we can fix. Why, renovating and furnishing this house isn't going to be any problem. We have the money to do it. And I'm going to have the temple rebuilt. We can find people to do these things.'

Mr. Nadarajah was up with the dawn the next morning as the uncurtained and unshuttered windows let in the rays of the sunrise. He lay still on the palm-frond mat, which they had bought in Jaffna town the previous afternoon. He stared at the ceiling and listened to the sounds outside his window. But the ceiling was not a blank white any more; it was covered in patches of green mildew and seemed to sag in places. Only the muted sound of bird calls drifted in through the windows. No dogs barked or cats meowed. No water splashed as the bucket was let down into the well. No servants called to each other. No rhythmic bang-bang echoed through the house as the cook prepared the flour to make the morning's *roti*.

He heard his wife's voice calling to his son. Mr. Nadarajah almost sprang off the mat with a smile on his face. He would get started today itself. He would go into town and talk to some of the sellers at the market. They would probably be able to help him find some workers to renovate the house.

However Mr. Nadarajah never made it into town that day. While the family was sitting on the verandah, eating the breakfast Mrs. Nadarajah had prepared from cans, a motorcycle roared into the compound. The two men on the bike were in all black and the one in the passenger seat held an AK-47 by his side. Mr. Nadarajah rose and walked to the top of the steps as the men got off the bike. They pulled off their helmets and slowly hung them on the bike handles. They turned around and stared at him for a couple of minutes before walking towards the house.

'So. You have come back?' the man with the gun asked, holding his weapon casually pointed to the ground.

'Do I know you?' Mr. Nadarajah asked.

'You can't even recognize me, can you?' the man gave a bitter laugh. 'You could use us when you were here and then you just went away, didn't you?'

'Who are you?' Mr. Nadarajah repeated. 'Do I know you?'

'You can't remember old Siva?' the man asked. 'Can't you remember how he used to take the two of us to school on his bike?'

'My god,' Mr. Nadarajah rushed down the stairs. 'Yoga, is that you?' He reached out to touch the man who stepped back. Mr. Nadarajah paused. 'My god, I've always wondered what you were doing.'

'You always wondered?' Yoga repeated his bitter laugh. 'Wondering's easy, isn't it? You didn't wonder much when you ran away without looking back at the people who worked in this house?'

'How could I, Yoga?' Mr. Nadarajah said. 'Those times, they were mad. We had no time to arrange anything for any of you.'

'No time; no time for us. Plenty of time to arrange things for you,' Yoga said. 'I heard you went to England. England! Had time to arrange that, didn't you?'

Mr. Nadarajah looked down and then at the other man. 'I didn't go straight there, you know,' he said, 'We had to stay in India for a few years while I arranged that.' He looked back at Yoga and took a deep breath. 'How is old Siva? Is your father still alive?'

'You have no shame to ask that? Yes, he's alive, but now he's a sickly man with the poverty we suffered after you took your family and ran.'

Mr. Nadarajah looked down.

'He suffered, you know, trying to earn money to keep up my mother and sisters,' Yoga continued. 'He wouldn't even let me sell the furniture in this house. He was so loyal to you, my father the fool!'

'I wish he'd let you do that,' Mr. Nadarajah said. 'It was the least you deserved.'

'The least?' the bitter laugh again, but then Yoga's face changed. He stared into the distance. 'We struggled because we had nothing to live on, but you know the reason we really suffered was because you were gone,' he said. 'Do you know how much I missed those walks to the temple? Our conversations at the pond over the fields? You took that with you. After you left, there was no one to talk to.'

Mr. Nadarajah remembered the gangly, scruffy-haired boy who would follow him everywhere, his eyes always upturned to Mr. Nadarajah's face. That boy had disappeared within the heavy-set, thick-mustached man who now stood in front of him. 'What are you doing now?' Mr. Nadarajah asked, trying to smile into the man's eyes.

'What am I doing?' Yoga brought his eyes back from the horizon and straightened his shoulders. 'I'm doing real well, huh? I have great power in this area now. Great power, you know?' He lifted his arm and placed the gun on his shoulder.

'I'm moving my family here permanently,' Mr. Nadarajah said. 'We're going to renovate and live here.'

'Live here?' Yoga's friend suddenly put in. 'Over our dead bodies. You think you can go away and live a great life in England and then come back when you want to?'

'This is still our house,' Mr. Nadarajah said.

'Maybe the deeds say that, but nothing else,' the man replied. 'You won't stay here, man, if you value your life. If you value the lives of those very prosperous, fat-armed children there.'

Mr. Nadarajah glanced back at his family. His wife and children had risen from their seats and were standing at the edge of the verandah, but his mother was smiling to herself while she looked at the far horizon and munched on her food. Mr. Nadarajah stepped forward, his finger raised to the man's face. 'Don't you come here threatening me,' he said. 'Just because you call yourselves powerful, don't think I'm going to be scared of you. Don't you forget who we are and don't you dare forget your place.'

The man swiped at Mr. Nadarajah's hand and Mr. Nadarajah hit out at him. Suddenly Anitha had jumped off the verandah and leaped across the garden to land on the man's back. 'Don't you hit my father,' she screamed as she hammered the man's back with her fists. Before Mr. Nadarajah could pull her off the man, Ravi had joined her and with both children's weight on him, the man fell to the ground. Mrs. Nadarajah came running down the front steps and with her and Yoga's help, Mr. Nadarajah pulled the children off the man. While the parents tried to calm down the children and Yoga helped the other man get up and brushed him off, an old man in white shuffled into the compound. His shuffle breaking into almost a run, he came towards Mr. Nadarajah.

'*Baba*, my *baba* has returned,' he said grabbing Mr. Nadarajah's face, tears running down his own blackened, wrinkled cheeks.

'Siva,' Mr. Nadarajah said as if it were still the old times and was about to clap the man on the back. But as he stared at Siva's wizened eyes and white stubble, Mr. Nadarajah changed his mind. He put his hands palm to palm in front of his chest and said in a respectful greeting, '*Vanakkam*, Siva *ji*.'

The old man, Siva, might have looked weak and Yoga, the strong young man with the gun, but when Mr. Nadarajah mentioned what the men had said about their living in the house, the old man took his son by the scruff of his collar and dragged him to the motorcycle while yelling filth. Mr. Nadarajah felt transported back twenty years as he watched Yoga cowering the way he had when his father had beaten him as a child and even a youth. And just like the old days, Mr. Nadarajah went running to Siva and grabbed him to save Yoga.

'Get out! Get out of here!' Siva yelled at his son even as Mr. Nadarajah held him by the arms. 'Take that black gun of yours and disappear.'

Yoga got on the motorcycle without even pausing to put on his helmet.

'Don't you come back here!' his father yelled. 'Have you no shame? Can't you remember that these were our masters? They're still our masters! And you make threats to them!'

The other man looked like he was about to retaliate, but Yoga pulled him to the bike with urgent whispers. They revved up the engine and the bike turned and streaked out of the compound.

Mr. Nadarajah and Siva sat on the porch talking about the old days. The old man promised to bring some workers with him the next day so they could start renovating the house straight away.

When Siva got up to leave, Mr. Nadarajah walked with him to the compound entrance. 'Siva *ji*,' he said. 'Remember the old Buddhist temple you used to take me to?'

'Yes, yes,' Siva replied. 'It was bombed out. Serve them right!'

'Serve them right?' Mr. Nadarajah asked. 'What do you mean? You were such friends with Soma Thera there! He must've been killed?'

'Yes, he was killed,' Siva replied. 'But that was no more than he deserved—preaching his great dhamma and ruining our lives!'

'Siva!' Mr. Nadarajah said. 'You were such a proponent of Buddhism. Even if you always stayed a Hindu, you made sure to worship the Buddha too. You showed me how Buddhism is a version of Hinduism—a cleaned-up version. And it was you who taught me the truths that Buddhism tells.'

'Truths?' Siva laughed. 'There are no truths there—only lies. Lies that have been fed to these Sinhala people.'

'That's not true,' Mr. Nadarajah said. 'In London, I have many Sinhala friends. They aren't out to ruin Tamils. They just don't understand us. Like we don't understand them.'

'*Baba*, you might've gone to London and not understand anything,' Siva said pausing at the entrance in the palm-fronds fence. 'But I understand perfectly now. Do you know my nieces disappeared after they were arrested at an army checkpoint? Maybe you even remember them, their mother used to bring them here when she had no food to feed them. They were such beautiful, innocent girls. Only sixteen when they disappeared. Their mother died from a broken heart. Their mother: my little sister. The only way for us Tamils to get anywhere is to carve out a piece of this island for ourselves.'

Mr. Nadarajah was silent.

'The Tigers are our only hope, *baba*,' Siva continued. 'It was one of their planes that bombed out the temple. After the government forces destroyed so many things all over the peninsula. Those Sinhala Buddhist thugs, coming in their aeroplanes and throwing down their bombs. Don't even have the stomach to come fight face to face.'

Siva walked out of the compound and Mr. Nadarajah stared after the old servant for a few minutes before he turned to find his mother standing a few feet from him. When she caught his eye, she came over and patted his shoulder absently. 'The fish, which has had a narrow escape from the heron, fears all that is white,' she said, her eyes already drifting away in another direction.

The next morning, without waiting for Siva's return with the workers, Mr. Nadarajah took his family and left Jaffna. In Colombo, he handed the deeds of his house to the chairman of an organization that was looking to open care homes in the north for orphans of the war.

The family returned to London and Mr. Nadarajah bought a house, re-enrolled his kids in their old school, and stepped back into the chairmanship of his firm. However, now his knees were always motionless. Because when Mr. Nadarajah woke up with the dawn again that last morning in Jaffna and lay on his mat and stared at the ceiling, some thoughts had come to him. Yes, he would be able to get rid of the patches of green mildew on the ceiling and even fix the sagging. And yes, he could buy furniture for the house and rebuild the temple so he could walk to it twice a day. But that splash of the bucket being let down into the well, it would never be quite the same splash because the hands that let it down were now too different. And more than that, the ears that lay in bed and listened to that splash were too different. Mildew could be taken away from ceilings, but never from hearts and minds.

Cousin

Cheran

When my cousin speaks
of enduring six displacements
within nine years
the wrinkles gather and droop
along her face.

The single electric light above
merely deepens the darkness.
A sense of loss prevails
always
like a lamp keeping vigil
at a dead man's head.

Her words are not punctuated
by sobs; they are taut
with sorrow.

Stirred by old memories
of providing shelter, so often,
to those who escaped the patrolling guards

Translated by Lakshmi Holmström

and travelled secretly, by night,
she glances towards the threshold
from time to time.
She leaves her backdoor open.

When her children, grown up now,
smile at her, in an instant
the legendary milk-ocean materialises.

Her house was on the road
which stretched all the way to the sea
from the front of the temple.
Not a sign of it now.

We went to take a look, in the morning,
accompanied by soldiers
into the high security zone.
Not even a single parrot left
nesting in the holes of palmyra palms
which still stand upright
although their crowns are shorn.

Upon ripped and fragmented land,
men who hold no attachment to it
nor kinship,
squat, holding weapons.

We return through the ruins,
the south wind that sprang up yesterday
scattering the dust ahead of us,
the heat burning us up with fury.

Only headless shadows follow us.

We whose hearts were moved with love
not only for humankind
but also for plants and trees and homes
endure in our time
only the scourge of human arrogance.

Love in the Tsunami

Passion and loss are the themes of this section suggested by the 'love' and cataclysmic 'tsunami' of the title. The initial pieces are about various forms of passion and sensual pleasure, be it for a lover, for cricket, or rambuttangs. As the section proceeds, the tone darkens to be almost exclusively about loss, often loss caused by Sri Lanka's civil war. The final two poems provide an antidote to samsara, the first poem an ironic holding up of the buffalo as an example to mankind, the last poem about the Lord Buddha.

Letter from Welimada

U. Karunatilake

August. These South West winds
Have blown themselves out
I never thought, love,
I would welcome this silence.

Now the lull has come, and it is sweet
After three months of sound,
That at the start was music
The flutter in the fresh Eucalyptus branches
The swish and moan in the tall grass
The roar in the pale moonlight
Through the silhouettes of agitated trees,
But it went on too long
With this unending boom in the far hills.

Now August tiptoes in and the Eucalyptus boughs
Are a dry exhausted green
And all the slopes are a slither with dry grass.
The rice fields crackle softly

With the promise of less hunger in the village
Though September's yield looks meagre.

What shall I write, love,
In this new, sweet silence
That the house on the *patana* is almost ready
And the valley window waits to frame you
Letting down your hair?

Pradeep Mathew
(From *Chinaman: The Legend of Pradeep Mathew*)
Shehan Karunatilaka

This excerpt from Karunatilaka's award-winning novel brings vividly to life the national passion for cricket, where daily life in Sri Lanka virtually stops, and a nation holds its breath in anticipation of victory or defeat. What I admire about Karunatilaka is his bold and innovative approach to the game, filling his book with trivia about cricket, and even including diagrams.

Pradeep Who?

Begin with a question. An obvious one. So obvious it has already crossed your mind. Why have I not heard of this so-called Pradeep Mathew?

This subject has been researched lengthwise and breadthwise. I have analysed every match our man has played in. Why, you ask, has no one heard of our nation's greatest cricketer?

Here, in no particular order. Wrong place, wrong time, money, and laziness. Politics, racism, power cuts, and plain bad luck. If you are unwilling to follow me on the next God-knows-how-many pages, re-read the last two sentences. They are as good a summary as I can give from this side of the bottle.

Deadline

I made my decision after the 1996 World Cup. The last years of my worthless life would be dedicated to a worthy cause. Not world peace or cancer cures or saving whales. God, if he exists, can look into those. No. In my humble opinion, what the world needs most is a halfway decent documentary on Sri Lankan cricket.

No one knows about this visit to Nawasiri Hospital. Not Sheila, who has begun to notice my falling hair, my swollen fingers, and the rings under my eyes. Not Ari, who has remarked on how my hand shakes as I pour. Not even Kusuma, the servant, who wakes up every other morning to clean up my acidic, bloodstained vomit.

The doctor is younger than my son and has a put-on smile that does not soften the blow. 'Mr Karunasena, your liver is being destroyed. And it will get worse.'

'At least I have my heart.'

My giggle is as pathetic as my attempt at humour. He ignores it and begins scribbling.

'Can't you give me pills?'

'I can give you pills for the nausea and the fever. I can also refer you to our alcohol counsellor.' The doctor tears off a chit branded by a pharmaceutical company I have not heard of. 'The rest, Uncle, is up to you.'

'How much time?' I keep my tone even and my eyes fixed, hoping the pup won't see that the old dog is ruffled.

'If you stop drinking and start eating, exercising, Uncle can bat on for another ten, twenty years.'

The things they don't teach you at school. How to love. How to die. How to stage a dramatic comeback.

Is it possible to hammer 3 goals in extra time after trailing 2–0? Or to land a knockout punch at the end of the 12th? Is it too late to score at 10 an over and turn a paltry 170 into a magnificent 300?

In my life I have seen beauty only twice. I'm not talking *Tharuniya* magazine front-cover beauty. I'm talking staggering beauty. Something so beautiful it can make you cry. Sixty-four years, two things of beauty. One I have failed to cherish, the other I may yet be able to.

Sheila at the Galle Face Hotel, 31st Nite Dinner Dance, 1963.

PS Mathew vs New Zealand, at Asgiriya, 1987.

'What if I cut down to two drinks a day?'

He doesn't look surprised. But at least he lets go of the smile. 'A year or two. Maybe more.'

Thus it was settled. I would attempt to do a halfway decent documentary on Sri Lankan cricket. There is nothing more inspiring than a solid deadline.

Sheila

'I don't mind you writing as long as you don't depress people.'

My beloved wife is making me sweep the kitchen. The last time I held a broom, Diego Maradona was a thin, teetotalling teenager.

'You used to be a poet, Gamini. Now you're just a grumpus.'

She says I cannot spend my retirement in my room reading about cricket and drinking. So I have chores, which at sixty-four, I find abominable. But as long as I am helping around the house, we are not talking about my drinking, and in my retirement such mercies are welcome.

'Don't talk rot, Sheila. When we were young anger was fashionable. Angry young man and all. Now I'm a grumpus?'

'That's not a cricket bat, Gamini. Sweep properly.'

It is true. The world has changed and I have not. As with everything, my fault entirely.

'Heard from Garfield?'

'Just go, men.' Sheila is cutting onions and not crying. She keeps jabbering. 'He's doing well. You better stop this business and talk to him. He's calling tonight.'

'Tonight I will be writing.'

'Do whatever the hell you want.'

She adds the red chilli to the dry fish.

I say nothing, keep sweeping, and decide to do just that.

Pradeep Why?

Another question. Why am I chasing a man who played only four Test matches for Sri Lanka? A man who denied me interviews, delighted me on occasion, disappointed those he played with, and disappeared three years ago. A man whose name is remembered by a minority smaller than our tribal Veddah population.

I ask myself this right after my bath and my morning tea. My tea is taken milk-less with three teaspoons of sugar and five tablespoons of Old Reserve. As you will soon see, I take arrack with a lot of things.

So when did Pradeep Mathew stop being just another Lankan spinner of the 1980s? When did he become something worth obsessing over? A cause I would champion? To answer that I will take you to a boxing match between two men in dinner jackets. One was my dearest friend; the other, my oldest enemy.

Wicket

The word wicket can refer to the three stumps that the bowler attempts to hit. 'The ball almost hit the wicket there.'

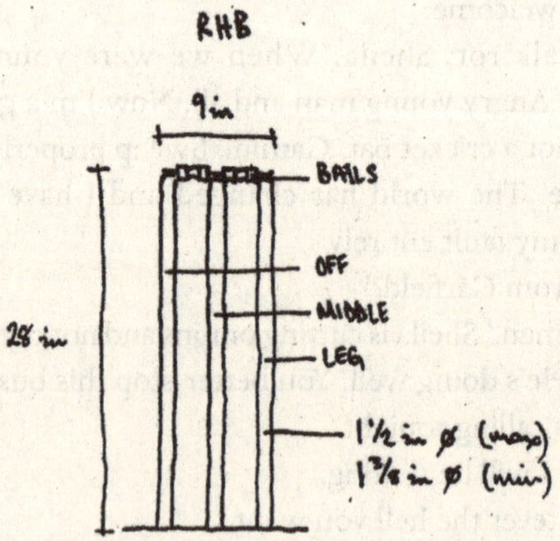

The surface they are playing on. 'The Eden Gardens wicket is dry and difficult to bat on.'

The bowler's performance. 'Laker's taken 7 wickets in this match so far.'

The batting line-up's mortality. 'South Africa lose 5 quick wickets.'

Its versatility is bettered only by a four-letter word that serves as noun, verb, adjective, adverb, and expletive.

Clean Bowled

The simplest dismissal is when the bowler knocks over the batsman's wickets. Mathew did this with most of his victims. He sent left-arm chinamen, googlies, armballs, and darters through pads and feet. Here is a not-so-random sample of batsmen whose bails he dislodged. Border. Chappell. Crowe. Gatting. Gavaskar. Gower. Greenidge. Hadlee. Imran. Kapil. Lloyd. Miandad.

You are shaking your head. You are closing the book and frowning at the cover. Rereading the blurb at the back. Wondering if a refund is out of the question.

Punch-up at a Wedding

In the buffet corner, weighing over 100 kilos, from the bridegroom's hometown of Matara, sports journo, talent broker, amateur coach: Newton 'I came to eat, not to be insulted' Rodrigo.

In the champagne corner, weighing under 180 lbs, teacher, preacher, video fixer, uninvited guest: Ariyaratne 'I have watched every Test match since 1948' Byrd.

Ari is my neighbour and my drinking partner. I have smuggled him in and he has smuggled in a bottle. The Oberoi wasn't Ari's usual watering hole. He has tanked up already at somewhere far less plush. I should have expected trouble.

We are at the wedding of the Great Lankan Opening Batsman, or the GLOB as we shall call him. The GLOB is a man of the people and has invited to his wedding members of the press, ground staff, and a sprinkling of international cricketing celebrities.

Thirty tables away, Graham Snow and Mohinder Binny are swooning over a gaggle of girls. Both were former players who became commentators and then became players. The buffet table has seven types of buriyani. Next to vats of chicken, Tyronne Cooray, the Minister for Sports and Recreation, is laughing with Tom Whatmore, the then coach of the Sri Lanka cricket team.

And this is where it begins. At the Lanka Oberoi in 1994. With Ari Byrd, Thomian blazer torn along the creases, pressing a chicken drumstick into the face of Newton, shrieking, 'You came to eat, no? Ithing kaapang! Eat!'

I have seen many fights. Boxing bouts in Kurunegala, barroom brawls in Maradana. Never have the combatants been less skilled, more drunk, or better dressed.

A waiter guards the buffet table as the men in torn suits roll against empty chairs.

Newton takes a hard bite on the chicken, chomping down on two of Ari's fingers.

'Ah-wa!'

Ari's scream is high and girlish. Our table, composed of inebriated journalists like myself, chuckles, sips, and gazes around with pleasure at sari-clad women, exotic dancers, and international celebrities, who, thanks to Ari's scream, are gazing back, though perhaps not with as much pleasure.

Most observe from the dance floor. Disapproving aunties and jolly uncles push through the has-beens and never-will-bes. Hand on mouth in mock shock. 'This is what happens when you invite the riff-raff,' cackles a crow in a sari. No one for a moment considers stopping the fight just then. Not even us.

Two reasons: (a) Sports journalists rarely see anything in the way of entertainment, especially these days, especially on the cricket field. (b) We all dislike Newton and feel he deserved this bludgeoning with buriyani chicken.

Newton has made a lot more money than any of us. 'For me, of course, journalism is a hobby. A calling. Pocket money.' Newton brings young cricketers to Colombo and sells them to clubs; he also studies race sheets, politically and literally backing the right horses always. I know this pudgy man as well as I know the gentleman who was dousing him in gravy.

'Shall we do something?' asks Brian Gomez, TV presenter and prankster. Brian once typed a letter on Oxford stationery asking Newton to visit the British High Commission to receive his Queen's scholarship. The next day Newton wore a suit to work.

'Let them be,' says Renganathan, Tamil cricket writer. Renga is a good bugger, but unhealthily obsessed with Roy Dias. When he was editor at the *Weekend*, he ran one issue with seventeen articles on this wristy batsman of the 1980s.

Newton gains the upper hand. He smears rice in Ari's eyes and crawls under the table. Elmo Tawfeeq of the *Daily News* tries to separate them, gets elbowed twice, and decides to sit down. Elmo once told us that he hit Imran Khan for a 6. In actuality, he played club cricket with a Bangladeshi who Imran once hammered for 6.

These are the men I have spent my years with and they are all drunk. Failed artists, scholars, and idealists who now hate all artists, scholars, and idealists. The band has stopped playing and I hear raised voices in the distance. Newton and Ari knock into veteran scribes Palitha Epasekera and Rex Palipane and I decide to intervene.

I gulp down the last of my rum, but before I can offer my services, the bride of the GLOB enters, shining under yellow lights. A delicate petal, bouquet in hands, tears in eyes.

In the distance, her husband advances with concern smeared across his brow, thinking what I am thinking: that these animals would tear his flower apart. The flower drops her bouquet and screams in an accent that sounds like Sydney but could be Melbourne, in a voice that is anything but petal-like: 'Get the fuck out of my wedding! You fucking arseholes!'

We can take a fist from a brute, but not a curse from a bride. The waiters assist us in packing up the fight. Released from Ari's gin-powered grip, Newton picks up a mutton curry with intent.

'Put that down!' The GLOB descends on the scene. 'Yanawa methaning! Get out!' Both Newton and Ari heed the great man. With the GLOB is Ravi de Mel, has-been fast bowler. He looks for the softest target, finds it, and snarls. 'Ah, Karunasena. Who else? Kindly take your friends and bugger off.'

Fearing unfavourable press, the GLOB puts on his man-of-the-people smile and pats me on the back. 'Don't get angry, Mr Karuna. Wife is bit upset. Don't you know?'

As we are led out, I see a dark man with a crew cut. He is leaning on table 151, surrounded by sycophants. Indian captain Azharuddin is chatting to him, though the man doesn't appear to be listening. Our eyes meet and he raises his hand. I return the wave, but he has already averted his gaze.

That may or may not have been the moment that started what you are about to read. But it was most certainly the last time I ever saw Pradeep Sivanathan Mathew.

Slide Show

Today Newton looks like a hippo, those days he was more like a rhino. Mathew may have caused the fight, but it was started by Newton. He had issues with me that went beyond cricket and provoked me knowing I would not respond. He didn't count on noble, smashed-on-stolen-gin Ari leaping, quite literally, to my defence.

The ballroom smells of flowers, buriyani, and thousands of clashing perfumes. Strategic buffet tables separated cricket refugees from social parasites. The deluxe section features the national team, some minor celebs, film stars, models, and people wealthy enough to own film stars and models.

The middle section is filled with aunties and uncles, media and business types. They have the best view of the dance floor and the band, neither of which seems to interest them. And then there are us. The journalists, coaches, ground staff, B-grade cricketers, C-grade friends.

Our table sits ten: me, Ari, Newton, Brian, Renga, Elmo, a Pakistani from the Associated Press, his friend, and a young couple who look lost. At the other end of the room, there is a bar serving scotch, vodka, and champagne. Our table has a bottle of arrack and several glasses of passion fruit cordial. We are men of simple tastes: anything, or even with nothing, with arrack will do.

'I should be drinking Chivas with Snow and Sobers,' says Newton. 'They must've misprinted my ticket.'

'So go, will you,' says Ari. 'Maybe Mohinder Binny will ask you to dance.'

The band plays a synthetic love song and the happy couple hold each other and move from side to side. We make quick work of the booze. Everyone whacks two shots, Ari and I whack four. The Pakistanis, Allah be praised, do not drink. As the lights dim, I explore unoccupied tables for bottles to steal. When I return with gin, the conversation has turned to cricket.

Brian Gomez, ever the patriot, proclaims that this Sri Lankan team could be our greatest. Ari says they are OK, but nowhere near the true greats like Lloyd's Windies or Bradman's Invincibles. 'Clive Lloyd's team is the best I've ever seen,' proclaims Renga. We hide our smirks. Every time Renga sees a film or witnesses a cover drive, he proclaims it to be 'the best he's ever seen'.

The Pakistani journalist talks of an all-time football XI featuring Zico, Best, and Maradona. We sip stolen booze and begin fantasizing. What if Ali fought Tyson? Or Navratilova played Billie Jean? It's a good way to pass the time. Better than staring at the dance floor, pretending to grin.

We agree that Lloyd's team were literally head and shoulders above the rest. Elmo offers that Bradman's Invincibles were invincible only because of Bradman. 'You eliminate him, good team. Invincible? That I don't know.' We all drink a toast to Clive Lloyd. The young couple slink off to another table.

Newton is petulant throughout. 'Our team couldn't even draw a two-day match with Bradman.'

'Don't say that,' says Brian. 'We beat New Zealand.'

The dance floor writhes with famous names and dolled-up women who do not belong to them. From the roar of the house band and the machinations of the dancers, it is evident that the alcohol denied to our table has been flowing freely on the other side of the room. Understandable. Dolled-up women prefer to have their bottoms pinched by international cricketers and not by those who write about them.

The Pakistani journalist begins scribbling on napkins. As the only man at the table with an education outside of Asia, he convinces us with diagrams and eloquence that the perfect cricket team should be composed as such:

Two solid openers
Three aggressive batsmen
Two genuine all-rounders
One agile wicketkeeper
Two unplayable fast bowlers
One genius spinner

Seduced by his Parthan lilt and logical arguments, we nod collectively. The Windies were great, but not perfect. No spinner. No all-rounder. Lloyd had four types of hurricanes at his disposal: the elegant Holding, the belligerent Roberts, the towering Garner, and the fiery Marshall. Who needs spinners, counters an argumentative Newton.

Booze flows and conversation splinters. Graham Snow toasts the GLOB and his bride, who begin doing the rounds of the ballroom. Ari and the Pakistani journalist whisper and scribble on napkins. The rest of us charge our glasses and clap as the band switches to traditional baila and a bald man with a moustache commandeers the mic from a bearded man in a hat. Both are middle-aged, pot-bellied, and wearing leather trousers.

Ari and the Pakistani journo silence the table with an announcement. Elmo, Brian, and Renga listen while wiggling their bellies to the bajaw beat.

'Gentlemen. We have constructed the world's greatest cricket team.'

Ari and the Pakistani have prepared a slide show of napkins. Dinner arrives at the table, but is pushed aside for the presentation. 'Of course, I don't agree with some choices,' says the Pakistani.

First slide:

Openers

- Jack Hobbs (Eng-20s)
- Sunil Gavaskar (Ind-80s)

Newton raises his glass. There is much nodding. 'The masters,' says Elmo.

Next slide:

Middle Order

- Don Bradman (Aus-40s)
- Viv Richards (WI-80s)
- Allan Border (Aus-80s)

There is applause. We grin at each other with appreciation. 'How about Zaheer Abbas?' says the quiet friend of the Pakistani journo. We all glare at him and he pipes down into his passion fruit.

Next slide:

All-rounders

- Garfield Sobers (WI-60s)
- Wasim Akram (Pak-90s)

I mention the word Hadlee. Ari and the Pakistani inform me that sadly there are no New Zealanders on this team. 'What about Sri Lankans?' asks Brian and we all snigger. This was 1994. We were drunk, but not stupid.

Next slide:
Wicketkeeper

- Denis Lindsay (SA-60s)

And here the group erupts. Denis Lindsay over Tallon? Knott? Bari? Madness. Newton calls the list pathetic. The rest of the critics hurl their knives. Not me.

I saw Lindsay tour Sri Lanka as part of a Commonwealth side in the 1960s and keep wickets to the fire of Wes Hall and Freddie Trueman and the wiles of Chandrasekhar and Prasanna. I have never seen that level of agility in anyone outside of a cartoon film. Apartheid was responsible for many tragedies. Somewhere at the bottom of a long list would be the short careers of Graeme Pollock, Barry Richards, and Denis Lindsay.

Next slide:
Fast Bowlers

- Sidney Barnes (Eng-10s)
- Dennis Lillee (Aus-70s)

Some say ooh. Some say aah. Some say Sidney who? I mention that the great Lillee took all his wickets in England, Australia, and New Zealand. That over a twelve-year career he never took a wicket in India or the West Indies. No one listens to me.

The clatter of plates and chatter of guests replace baila as the dominant noise. Across the ballroom everyone digs into the roast chicken and richly flavoured rice. But our table is undivided in its attention.

Who could the genius spinner be? A leggie like Grimmet or Qadir? An offie like Laker or Gibbs? A left-armer like Bedi or Underwood?

Final slide:
Spinner

- Pradeep Mathew (SL-80s)

And pandemonium begins. The Pakistani shakes his head and says he had nothing to do with it. Renga, Brian, and Elmo hoot with laughter.

'Y'all are cocked, ah?' Newton launches into a tirade. 'If you want to put a Lankan, put Aravinda or Duleep. Pradeep Mathew? How can you call yourselves sports journalists? Bloody fools.'

Ari puts up his hand. 'This list is based on stats and natural ability. Both Mathew and Lindsay have strike rates and averages that rank them with the greats.'

I step in. 'I saw Lindsay in '63. Maara reflexes. Jonty Rhodes is nowhere. He jumped in front of the batsman to take a catch at silly mid-off.'

'You bloody drunkard, it was '66,' says Newton. 'Y'all are idiots. Mathew can't even make the current side.'

And in the economy section of the crystal ballroom, gobbling chicken buriyani amidst famous acquaintances, Ari and I begin telling them. About the multiple variations, the prize scalps, the balls that defied physics, and that legendary spell at Asgiriya. No one believes us.

Newton calls me a drunk a few more times. I call him a bribe-taking pimp. The rest of the table retreat, while Ari begins slurring.

And as the temperature rises, I look around and see the man himself in a circle of people, looking lost. At his side is a pretty girl, whispering in his ear is the Indian skipper, hanging on each syllable are career reserve Charith Silva and Sri Lankan cheerleader Reggie Ranwala.

Mathew is glaring at me, as if he knows his name is about to cause a brawl. As if he knows I will spend the next five years searching for him. As if he knows he will never be found.

And then, Newton calls me a talentless illiterate who should be writing women's features. And then, Ari stuffs a chicken into Newton's open mouth. And then, all is noise.

Willow and Leather

The ball is made of leather with a hard seam running its circumference. The bat is made of willow. The sound of one hitting the other is music.

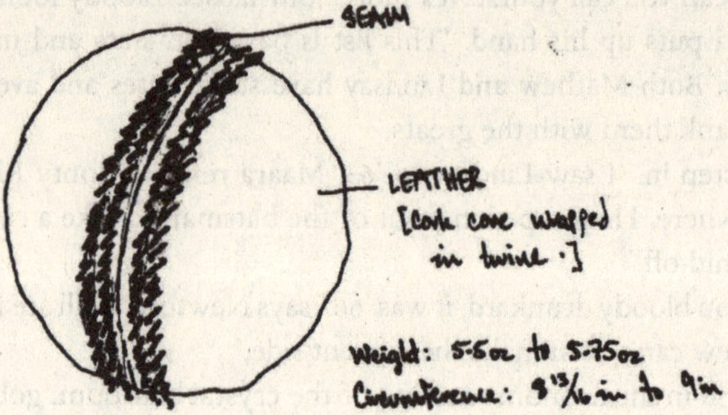

Rambuttangs

Anne Ranasinghe

This time the harvest was good.
In strung-out piles
Of crimson, red, orange and yellow
They burn along the city pavement—
So much fertility against the sterile stone.

The hawkers laugh and jest—richly,
For trade is good.
Buyers, shelling the bitter spiked
Skin with sharp white teeth
Experimentally, also laugh

Because
The rambuttang fruit is juicy
And sweet—mas galavena—
It comes off complete
From the central seed.

Love in the Tsunami

Ashok Ferrey

They found themselves washed up together on the beach by the mighty wave, that mighty wave of NGOs and newspapermen, well-wishers and ghouls that swirled into the country in the wake of the Boxing Day tsunami.

'A broom for you,' said the woman. Veena noticed the fair, thick hair that hung over the woman's face, her very dark eyebrows that seemed almost painted on. Interesting, she thought. They worked side by side for a while, cleaning the beach. The woman, Veena noticed, worked better than any man, pulling heavy chunks of debris out of the way, throwing back her head every once in a while and laughing silently at some private unshared joke. It made a change anyway from the sort of glum, I'm-here-with-the-tsunami type of face people were beginning to cultivate around them. A channel of sweat flowed over the woman's shoulder blades, drenching her short khaki T-shirt, flowing down like a great river between the well-formed globes of her buttocks. The locals watched astounded, standing about in silence. It didn't seem to have occurred to them to lend a hand. Help us out here, Veena wanted to say. It's *your* beach after all.

When the sheer shock of the disaster had worn off and the roads were once more passable, Veena had driven south with nothing more in mind than a vague desire to help out.

'Leave all that to the professionals,' Mrs Patel had cautioned her. 'There are people better qualified than you. You just stick to your designing.'

'You mean there are people out there with PhDs in Tsunami Studies?' Veena shot back. She ignored her mother as she did most times and headed down; and here she was, broom in hand.

The woman said, 'My name is Deborah, but you can call me Debs.' And by the end of the day Veena was well and truly smitten.

Veena's grandfather was Gujarati, one of that small band of buccaneers who had landed in Colombo before World War II in search of trade. Conditions were so good he had immediately called his kinsmen over. First they established themselves in teakwood and steel; then came paper and gemstones. Now there were garments and electronics.

They settled in Kotahena and Grandpass—the industrial heart of the capital adjacent to the port, with its warehouses, its whining saw-mills, its thundering container traffic. They formed a small community, discreet, powerful and immensely wealthy, the almost invisible twill running through the fabric of Sri Lankan society. Nevertheless, they kept unshakeably to their own customs and beliefs. For their dussehra festival in the month before New Year, Gujjus all over India gathered at the crossroads of their villages: they formed concentric circles, men and women, presenting sticks to each other in a courtly and ceremonial dance. And the Gujjus of Colombo did likewise: gathering together on the furry carpet of the Intercontinental ballroom, clashing their sticks in a frenzy of goodwill.

But Veena had rather gone and spoilt it all by wanting to become a designer. Bad form. Awkward too, since she was an only child destined to inherit.

'Go to America,' her father said. 'Design all you want.' Then come back and take over the family business, he wanted to add. America was where you went to work out all your youthful aberrations, get them out of your system, purge yourself. You came back cleansed, hopefully, and ready for your dose of Real Life.

But it hadn't quite worked out that way. Virtually all Veena could remember about America was the boat she and her friends crewed that belonged to Mies Van der Rohe's grandson. She remembered it through a Pimmsfuelled, alcoholic haze: maybe that, not the wind, was what had made the boat go so fast.

Once back she continued to design. First there was the wickedly cantilevered stainless steel staircase leading up to the room Haramanis occupied over the garage, Haramanis their live-in domestic. It was probably too good even for a Los Angeles Art Gallery. Unfortunately it was sadly below par for Haramanis, who cursed loudly as he skittered down its dew-laden steps every morning. Then there were the teak and titanium kitchen cupboards she designed for her mother, on their spindly metal legs. (Wretched girl, said Mrs Patel, how on earth does she expect me to clean underneath?)

But Veena was not unhappy being back. One of the joys of living in Colombo was that you lived many lives simultaneously, in different time zones. For a start there was your home life, which had basically remained unchanged since the eighteenth century. This was in stark contrast to your work life, which had zoomed off well into the twenty-first. And if that wasn't enough, there was the life out there on the streets, stuck somewhere back in the middle of the twentieth. Nowhere exemplified this better than Kotahena, with its throbbing arteries, its teeming in-your-face ugliness. It gave an excitement, an added depth to her designs not easy to achieve abroad. She had come to understand it wasn't the staircase alone that was beautiful: it was the staircase with Haramanis on it, cussing roundly in the eighteenth-century manner. That juxtaposition of old and new was immensely satisfying, like the single cracked-gilt chair in the all-white minimalist room.

Every weekend the tsunami workers came up to Colombo. Mostly young, mostly good-looking, they worked hard, they played hard. Wine sales soared. Restaurants boomed. Colombo took on the tinselled hanky-tonk glamour of a frontier town during the gold rush.

Veena and Debs met up at Barefoot for the jazz. That normally sublime walled garden was packed with so many foreign bodies, it was a positive epidemic. You had to look hard to spot the odd—very odd—native brown face. They pushed their way to a corner table with their pints, and there was such a racket going on it was easy to get personal.

Debs worked for an American NGO which concentrated on the world's trouble spots. It was extremely well-funded and could move man and machinery around the world with incredible speed.

'I have to be prepared to go wherever I am needed at a moment's notice,' she said, putting her beautifully square-cut, man-size hands over Veena's, looking into her eyes with the urgent intensity of a soldier about to go off to war. Veena could see how well she wore her battered, wounded weaknesses on the outside, with careless ease, unashamed. But inside was that silent laughing confidence, that assured strength so often lacking in Sri Lankan men. At least the ones they were forever trying to fix *her* up with.

The latest candidate on this list was Kamal, son of Mrs Ratnam who took her early morning walks with Mrs Patel. Mrs Ratnam stood for property development with a capital P. Colombo had recently broken out in a rash of tower blocks, Ratnam Court, Ratnam Towers, Ratnam Residencies. There were even Ratnam Cottages for the less fortunate.

'One day,' sighed Mrs Ratnam pointing to various carbuncles in the middle distance, 'one day all this will be Kamal's.' She made it sound as if this was a matter of some regret.

Veena's mother quickened her pace, saying nothing.

Veena was brought back to the present by the sound of Deb's voice.

'It's the truth we are all after.' she was saying. 'When I find it, I just go get it.' She looked at Veena. 'If I really want something I go straight for it, the *direct* route.'

Veena shifted uncomfortably in her seat.

'The shortest distance between two points: the straight line. Don't you agree?'

But Veena wanted to ask in reply, 'What if the truth is a moving target, so your route to it becomes a series of zigzags? Isn't *that* then the shortest distance?' But she didn't want to spoil the mood. Instead she continued looking into the eyes of her new-found friend, deep as seas.

'Come with me,' Debs said. 'Come with me to Darfur, come with me to Aceh. You're wasted here.'

'First you'd better come with *me*,' Veena replied. 'Come up next weekend and meet my mother.'

They spent the rest of that week texting each other uncontrollably. Veena took to shutting herself up in the bedroom straight after dinner so she could get in a full three hours of texting, before she fell back exhausted on the bed. God, that Debs woman never slept! Sometimes the phone rang even at two in the morning. Veena's thumb ached from the sheer physical exertion of this homotextual relationship.

She came down to breakfast, face bloated and bleary eyed.

'These early nights are killing me,' she complained. 'My daughter is designing something *big*,' said Mrs Patel to Mrs Ratnam. 'Something to do with tsunami. She's up all hours.'

'She's looking like a tsunami victim herself,' said Mrs Ratnam, a little acidly.

Debs was coming to dinner that Saturday night, driving up from the south straight after work. Early morning found Veena in the kitchen.

'To what do we owe this honour?' asked Mrs Patel.

'I'm cooking dinner for Debs.'

Mrs Patel had to sit down, the shock was so great.

'I'm making Gujarati food.'

Mrs Patel covered her face with her hand. She began to heave uncontrollably.

'Oh, Ma, stop being so dramatic. You'll like her. She's such an easy-going person. I thought I'd make kachori.'

'*Kachori?*' The word escaped Mrs Patel like an ill wind.

'Oh, Ma, go practise the harmonium or something. Go clash a few sticks. And *don't* come back till I'm finished.'

But by the end of the afternoon Veena could understand what her mother meant about Gujarati food. She was exhausted. She felt like she had done the work of the entire cast and crew of *Guess Who's Coming to Dinner?*

So when the bell rang at six she half expected Sidney Poitier on the doorstep. It was Mrs Ratnam with her grandson Raju.

'Your mother invited us for dinner.'

They pushed past her into the living room, sitting down, making themselves at home, and Raju began the exhaustive business of taking the house apart.

Veena looked at them. 'Come in, take a seat, make yourselves at home,' she said. 'Don't mind *me*.'

Veena couldn't stand children, particularly Raju. In a Hindu household this sentiment was about as popular as a steak dinner.

She smiled sweetly at him. 'Go on,' she said, 'play with those fragile crystal ornaments. They're my mother's favourite.'

When Debs arrived Veena showed her the staircase, then the kitchen.

'You're wasted,' Debs repeated. 'You should be designing in LA.'

Veena remembered wandering around Beverly Hills during her time in the US, looking at houses greedily, absorbing every detail. She had decided to walk, something quite unheard of, quite un-American. Horrors! Nobody walked in LA! There were beautiful brick sidewalks bordering perfect patches of grass, planted with discreet signboards that read: 'Armed Response'. But nobody had come running out at her, guns blazing, rather to her disappointment.

'They thought you were the cleaning lady,' her friends remarked, and Veena was secretly quite pleased.

She traversed acre upon acre of silently manicured perfection under a cloudless blue sky. Then, turning a corner, she saw a house being remodelled: and she realized with a shock it was all plywood and chicken-wire, no bricks or mortar anywhere, the sort of construction even a tsunami victim back home would have turned his nose up at. The beauty was, literally, skin deep.

Nothing had brought home more clearly to her the difference between design and decoration, architecture and pastiche. Veena had felt strangely let down by America after that.

Debs was explaining to the dinner guests that work was not going well down south. They were being obstructed at every turn by bureaucracy. Some of the homeless people were even asking for money to help rebuild their *own* houses. Others preferred to stand around and watch. It wasn't easy figuring out their mindset.

Veena's Gujju dishes were arranged on the Lazy Susan around which they all sat. Raju was expert at spinning the disc away from you just when you needed it to stay put, so you reached out to spear a forkful of mango and ended up with a pickled aubergine in your face.

Veena and Debs had polished off the major part of a bottle of red and were playing footsie under the table. Mrs Ratnam watched in horrified fascination, a snake mesmerized by two charmers.

A phone rang somewhere in the house. Debs patted her pocket and looked around.

'It's mine,' she said. 'Now where did I leave it?'

Mrs Patel came in from the kitchen with a plate of parathas in one hand and a mobile in the other. She put the plate down and handed Debs the mobile.

'Crank caller for you,' she said. 'Some woman in LA. *Says she's your wife!*'

They sat in rigid silence, straining to hear every word. Debs was murmuring endearments in the kitchen where she had vanished with the phone. Then she came back in. She put her beautiful, square-cut hands on the table and leant forward, beaming at them. She might have been at a board meeting.

'Shit happens,' she said. Then she left.

Veena felt as if a large block of concrete had fallen on her head from a great height. Mrs Ratnam sat transfixed, refusing all further food. (The halwa lay uneaten in the kitchen.) Really this was better than any dessert.

Raju had the last word as he left with his grandmother.

'I wonder,' he mused, 'do I say Auntie Debs? Or do I say Uncle Debs?'

And now, complete radio silence. Veena waited and waited for the call that never came, the call that might hopefully explain that it was all some ghastly mistake. Her now disused thumb throbbed with the ache of textual frustration. On the bright side she was now getting her full eight hours a night. Even Mrs Ratnam had to admit Veena had got her face back, and was looking quite lovely, *really*.

And then the following Friday, when Veena had just about given up all hope, a message came. 'Meet me at Barefoot, same time, same table.' When she arrived, there was a woman in kaftan and mirrored glasses sitting at their table drinking a pot of Earl Grey, so she hovered till Debs arrived.

'Married!' she exclaimed when they were out of earshot. '*Married*.'

Debs put up her hand as if to ward off these blows. 'It was a mistake. Anyway, it's not as if it's recognized in many places in the world.'

'What does that matter?' Veena asked tearfully. 'You made a choice. Where does that leave me?'

'Listen to me.' Debs gripped Veena's arm tight. 'What was right for me *there*, at that time, is not necessarily what's right for *us* here and now. I have many different lives, Aceh, Darfur, LA. It's very complicated. I can't be expected to reconcile them all, so don't ask me. The reality for us is what is *here*, what is *now*.'

'So what you see is what you get,' said Veena. She added in a small voice, 'And what you don't see is what you don't get.' She thought of the houses in Beverly Hills.

'Don't you think,' said Debs fiercely, 'that what we have together, you and me, is the truth?'

'And a month, a year later, when you get tired, or the job moves you on, will the truth move also? And what do I do then, sit around like a war bride cherishing fond memories of the white hero who showed me the way?'

She had gone too far with that word *white*, though, and she was sorry the moment she said it. There was a small contained explosion.

'Oh you make me sick, the whole bloody lot of you!' Debs shouted. 'You stand about open-mouthed for all this tsunami aid to get your life back. You can't do a thing for yourself, not even sweep a goddamned beach! We tell you what needs to be done, the right thing, and you curl up and get all complicated. It's intellectual laziness. You just can't be bothered to think things through. If you did you'd realize the way to the truth is the obvious way, the shortcut.'

But Veena's mind was still on what Debs had said earlier. 'We're all forced to lead many lives simultaneously,' she countered gently. 'We do it out of necessity, not choice. We don't make a virtue of it.'

Debs wasn't ready to listen. She got up. 'I'm asking you one last time, are you in, or are you out?'

Veena slowly shook her head. To tell the truth, she didn't really know what she wanted, whether she wanted in or out. She knew for sure the way for her wasn't up the lift to the penthouse of Ratnam Towers. But it occurred to her that there was some distance from the point at which she was now to where the truth might lie. And the shortest route between them wasn't necessarily a straight line.

The Fisherman Mourned by His Wife

Patrick Fernando

When you were not quite thirty and the sun
had not yet tanned you into old-boat brown,
when you were not quite thirty and had not begun
to be embittered like the rest, nor grown
obsessed with death, then would you come
hot with continence upon the sea
chaste as a gull flying pointed home,
in haste to be with me!

Now that, being dead, you are beyond detection,
and I need not be discreet, let us confess
it was not love that married us nor affection
but elders' persuasion, not even loneliness.
Recall how first you were so impatient and afraid,
my eyes were open in the dark unlike in love,
trembling, lest in fear, you'd let me go a maid,
trembling on the other hand for my virginity

Three months the monsoon thrashed the sea, and you
remained at home; the sky cracked like a shell
in thunder, and the rain broke through.
At last when pouring ceased and storm winds fell,

when gulls returned new-plumed and wild
when in our wind-torn flamboyante
new buds broke, I was with child.

My face was wan while telling you and voice fell low,
and you seemed full of guilt and not to know
whether to repent or rejoice over the situation.
You nodded at the ground and went to sea.
But soon I was to you more than God or temptation,
and so were you to me.

Men come and go, some say they understand,
our children weep, the youngest thinks you're fast asleep:
theirs is fear and wonderment.
You had grown so familiar as my hand
that I cannot with simple grief
assuage dismemberment.
Outside the wind despoils of leaf
trees that it used to nurse;
once more the flamboyante is torn,
the sky cracks like a shell again,
so someone practical has gone
to make them bring the hearse
before the rain.

Through a Mist

Ajit Tilakasena

Recently, a few writers in Sinhala have started to experiment with magic realism, drawing on their own cultural store of myths and ghost figures. Tilakasena's story is the only translation that I came across. In this story, the levels of loss are personal but also national, embodied in the mass grave of suspected JVP youth. All this loss is captured through the ghosts that form an important part of this story—spirits that come from a Sinhala folk tradition of ghosts. The presence of the Jataka stories adds another dimension of the folk tradition. The structure and tone of the story is elliptical with abrupt shifts in time and points of view, creating a surreal quality and erasing the boundaries between the real and spectral worlds.

As Nimal and his friend, Ratnatilaka entered the bar, Padmadasa, a soldier in the army was inside, seated at a corner table, a quarter full glass near him. There were three others around him listening quietly to what he was saying. There was a plate of prawn *wade* on the table in front of them.

There was a foul smell from the stagnant water in the drain in the rear of the building.

Translated by Vijita Fernando

Nimal took a cigarette from the cashier's desk and lit it from the burning end of the coir coil hanging from a nail there. He came back with the cigarette between his lips, sending out smoke and, for a moment, stood aside watching with the corner of his eye Padmadasa's manner of narrating and his body movements.

Nimal and his friend sat at the table next to Padmadasa's table, close together sharing the ash tray.

Padmadasa didn't see them.

He went on talking, addressing the three who were listening to him, wide eyed.

'That fellow—whoever he is, I say, whoever he is—he has painted a beautiful world to that girl and bewitched her!'

Padmadasa looked at the floor through his entwined fingers, shaking his head from side to side.

'Everything went wrong . . . ! Went wrong . . . !' he exclaimed. As he raised his glass and emptied it in one gulp, a few drops trickled on his chin. He wiped his mouth with the back of his palm and placed his head on the edge of the table.

Then another person came, half a dram from the bar in his hand, and drawing an aluminium chair, joined the others.

As Padmadasa raised his head there was a trace of sweat on his neck. He looked straight at the fourth man.

'You think I am drunk?' He asked the fourth man. 'Huh, I am just about to start. The twenty perches the old man left me is not enough even for my drinks!'

The bar boy came to the table where the two men were sitting. As he wiped the table with a damp cloth, he looked at Ratnatilaka.

'Two beers and something to bite,' Ratnatilaka ordered.

They could hear Padmadasa talking at length.

'. . . every time I go to the village I used to step into that house. One day she was not at home. They said she had gone to bathe. Then I walked to the edge of the garden and went to the stream. I saw the dress she was wearing spread out to dry on the grass. Then it was shady there. I saw her through the *dunuke* bushes near the edge of the stream: she soaped herself and jumped into the stream. Then I slept on the dress she had put out in the sun to dry. She came out and wiped herself and wrapped her hair in the towel. I quickly jumped aside before she could see me! She wore that dress still warm with the warmth of my body . . .'

Suddenly his shoulder muscles sprang as if a spring had snapped. He raised the glass and signalled the boy to bring him another half.

'It was like that, a fragile association . . . I didn't tell her any of the things that were in my head, not even that day inside the house. . . . I didn't give her even a hint . . . I thought of love as something colossal.'

He raised his head and stared vacantly at the roof.

'Everything went wrong. . . . Went wrong. . . . !' he said and shook his head from side to side once again.

'In short, I wanted to settle down because of her. I meant marriage . . . this freedom is not such a sweet thing . . .'

The boy brought the two bottles of beer to the table where the two were sitting, opened the bottles and kept two tall glasses and a plate of potato chips on the table.

'. . . she didn't like my joining the army at all. She said that when she sees my face she thinks of a chopping block. That was after she read of an incident in the newspapers, an incident which had received much publicity. Apart from what she read in the papers, she had got some other news as well. What to do? I told her that I would leave the army. I faltered when I spoke to her. When I went I felt my steps faltering . . .'

Nimal emptied the first glass. Ratnatilaka gradually lifted his head in the trail of smoke which came out of Nimal's mouth. He turned his head and observed the roof forming an obtuse angle at the top and resting on the six pillars.

'. . . On the road, not allowing vehicles to pass, examining inside culverts, poking into the bushes by the roadside, crawling on one's knees along drains . . . one dies a thousand times in these exercises and is born again. I had this fear that I would step on a johnny mine and lose a leg. It is not so with claymores and landmines; then one can lose even the head in one blast in just a fraction of a second! Don't you think that it is some consolation that it happens with no pain?'

Nimal turned his chair and went on listening to Padmadasa. He winked at Ratnatilaka. With the cigarette dangling from the fingers of his left hand, he half emptied the second glass and flung a handful of potato chips into his mouth. As the chips were crunching among his teeth, he settled uncomfortably in his chair, sending clouds of smoke through his nose and started tapping on the table with one finger.

'. . . there is no time, I think, to publish in the evening papers the news of the morning's train crash. Isn't that so?' Padmadasa asked turning towards the four others.

'It was not long since we heard the news and I was there. The two carriages that were derailed were in the stream. I looked everywhere, every corner in the midst of all that crowd. By that time the people in the area had taken down some of the injured. In that confusion a groups of ruffians were taking jewellery off the injured women. The examination of pockets was going on post-haste. The next group was taking everything, even the hair clips, believe me. Some had examined the heel of a shoe of a gentleman crying in pain with his knee broken, to see if there was money in his shoe. I saw two fellows carrying an injured woman and vanishing into the jungle. I knew one of those two chaps. I walked from the engine to the guard's carriage and then followed them into the jungle. I saw the fellow I knew who had gone to the jungle coming out buttoning his trousers, his shirt in his hand. I talked to him. When the first fellow finished, it had been this fellow's turn. He had sat by the woman. The woman was still in the same position, stretched out, staring at the sky as if she didn't see anything. That means the woman had not protested. He had hurried and had stroked her hair and kept his hand on her chest. There was not a stir. He stood up and then only he understood that he had been screwing a dead body!'

'Will even the police do this?' the fourth man asked.

Nimal quickly finished his drink and shaking his feet about, got his slippers on.

When he got up in such haste, Padmadasa who was pouring soda into his empty glass, turned and looked at him. As he saw Nimal he was startled and stumbled out of his chair.

'Nimal aiya! Nimal aiya!'

'Yes, Padme malli, why are your legs shaking?'

The four held their breath, their hands clasping half-filled glasses, and their voices turned to stone.

Padmadasa turned around automatically and steadied himself with his hand on the wall. He looked at Nimal with wild eyes.

Nimal jumped forward and caught him by his hair.

'Padme malli, too much talk. Give it to me straight!'

'Yes, yes, Nimal aiya . . . Mangalika . . .'

'So?'

'Mangalika . . . has run away . . . with some fellow . . . this morning . . . she has left a letter. I came here to tell you . . .'

Nimal took him by the scruff of his neck and flung him aside. He was thrown to the corner of the room.

Nimal and Ratnatilaka went to the cashier's table, and stepping on to the road, each one went his own way.

Nimal went home and stood at the door. He leant towards the inside of the house, his uncertainty tying him up in knots. He went near his sister's room and peered into her room for no reason at all.

It was still not time for her to come home from school. That morning, her school bag slung on her shoulder, she had smiled at the mirror, rushed out of the room, knocking against him. Her bed was still unmade. Her room was untidy.

He walked slowly out of the back door. He could see his mother at the well washing clothes.

He went towards the sitting room.

The light was still burning under the statue of the Buddha in the triangular frame. He stared at the flame till he saw double.

Pouring a glass of water from the clay goblet, he sat on the settee and again stared at the flame. He pressed the glass to his forehead and saw through the engravings a series of lights . . . and as if he had woken from a dream, he saw his mother's figure.

His mother came in with a pot of water on her hip. She took a deep breath and raised the pot on to the shelf and kept her hands on her waist.

'I haven't the strength to lift these things now . . . *Aney* I don't know. . . . Isn't there a girl you like even in that place you work . . . or in any of these places you go to . . .? Or tell me and then I can speak to the clerk at the depot and arrange something. It was he who arranged that marriage for Rathne's sister. So what is wrong with that? They are fine!'

It was that morning that Nimal met Ratnatilaka. When he got off the bus at the junction by the quarry, Ratnatilaka had passed him on his bicycle. He had not seen Nimal. Nimal shouted to him and he had come back and taken Nimal on to his cycle bar.

When they went to Ratnatilaka's house they uprooted some manioc and ate the boiled manioc with a dhal curry and some hot *sambol*. Then they bathed at the well where the storks were making a din.

Towards noon they walked to the market area.

When they came close to the bridge they saw upstream the Bollatota ferry with its huge boulders, but no one was bathing there. Nimal watched the reflections of the range of hills trembling in the water. A light came on to his face as if he had felt a spur of enthusiasm in his mind.

'The river princess is stretched out naked, shaking her hips, twisting and turning . . . I feel like jumping from here itself,' he said.

He took a deep breath and placed one leg on the concrete wall of the bridge.

Ratnatilaka in the twinkling of an eye opened his hand and slapped his leg and Nimal took his leg away.

'Oh, so you are a poet. I always knew it,' Ratnatilaka said.

'No. I remembered:

Sitodakaṁpokkharaṇiṁ yuttam kiñjakkhareṇuna
Nāgo ghamābhitatto'va ogāhe te thanūdaram

—'Just as an elephant who is tired with the heat will jump into a cool pond scattered with the pollen of flowers, so I will jump in between your breasts.'

'That's what I said!' Ratnatilaka said. 'See, I couldn't think of something like that?'

They walked ahead.

'Ratne, haven't you still got hitched to a girl?'

Ratnatilaka's eyes widened. But he said nothing and walked on, looking straight ahead.

'. . . that means that however much our singers have spouted about love, you have not yet experienced it?'

Ratnatilaka stopped and with his hand resting on the concrete wall, he turned.

'Girls are like the water that flows in that stream under that railbridge. That means they are shallow. Not like you and me,' he said and turning, kept on looking at the deep end of the river.

'Since we did not go to work today . . . come let us go and have a beer,' Ratnatilaka said suddenly.

Nimal was suddenly brought back to the real world from his reverie when he heard the sound of the bucket. He was startled as if a thunder bolt had struck.

When he went to the back door, he saw his mother in the rear garden hanging out the clothes. There was still a numbness on his forehead above the eyebrow. He kept the glass on the window sill. He followed his mother as she went to the kitchen to serve his meal. As she opened the pot of rice he told his mother what Padmadasa had told him.

His mother, with the plate in one hand and the wooden spoon in the other, waited for the steam to settle from the rice. She was thinking.

'Whatever the elders do . . .' she swallowed her words. 'Whatever has happened, she is your aunt's daughter. Go there. Go soon after you have your meal. Go and see what has happened.'

The road stretched like a straight line through the jungle. The bus was driven at a monotonous speed. A pot-bellied man was in the driver's seat. One could see no movement in his hands or feet.

The dust which had been disturbed by trucks carrying loads of soil now clung on to the wheels of the bus and blew inside the bus. There was no bird sound. It was as if the birds had all flown away.

People were seated in ones and twos in the seats. In the seat in front of Nimal was a fat woman nursing her struggling baby. She wiped the dust from her face with a piece of cloth.

'What a lot of potholes! Every time the bus lurches I feel like vomiting,' she told her husband seated by her side.

The bus now came out of the jungle to a cleared area and the heat got worse. Nimal felt as if he was travelling directly into the heat.

The woman's husband looked out of the window and saw a darkening cloud in the eastern sky.

''There is water still in the sky. Is there no way to get it down to the earth?' He looked at the middle-aged man with his head swathed in a towel seated opposite him.

''The chilli plants are near death,' he said again.

The middle-aged man was chewing some betel. He spat out of the window and did not reply.

The bus clattered on the wooden bridge and came to journey's end.

Alighting, Nimal walked to the Nugagahamula junction to take the next bus. He saw then that the only bus that plied on this road was being washed on the banks of the stream.

He wondered what to do to spend the time he had to wait. There was not a house to be seen. He walked for a short distance on the cart track leading to the village. He saw a small shack which looked as if it could be a tea boutique. He stopped there. From there he could see the bus being washed.

From where he stood he had a good view of the cinnamon cultivated upland area where it is said that there was a secret grave and where supernatural activities were taking place.

Beyond that small boutique was a precipice. The cart track was alongside, leading to the village. At the bottom of the precipice were paddy fields. Beyond was the upland area planted with cinnamon, and a range of hills.

The sun shone above that range.

There were rumours that the secret grave was a mass grave.

'I can't see a thing, amma,' a little boy of about seven clinging to his mother's hand, said. He was standing on a stone just beyond the tea boutique.

'Let's go, let's go,' she said dragging him along with her towards the junction.

'You can't see it all the time,' the boutique keeper said, turning towards them as they left. Then he turned towards Nimal.

'The ghost can be seen only at noon, then at sunset and again at dawn.' Nimal bought a cigarette and lit it.

'Give me two hundred and fifty grams of *bombili* dry fish,' an emaciated middle-aged woman in a cloth and jacket said, stepping into the boutique. She stepped out and looking in every direction, sat on the bench, shifting her chew of betel in her mouth from one jaw to the other.

'Have you seen it?' Nimal asked the man as he was making a cover for the goods he was going to sell to the woman.

He had seen, as the sun was about to set, the phantoms amid multifarious hooting appearing suddenly and floating upwards. They were all young men. At those times if you place your ear to the ground you can hear a noise like a pot of water bubbling in the heat. In the middle of the night the sound is like the wailing of parents going in search of their children.

One morning when he was opening the door of his boutique a dog had rushed in, barking, and chasing a lizard. The lizard turned into a rock wall and a tangle of creepers, rushed down the precipice and escaped. He had rushed to the rock wall and seen the paddy plants bending in waves towards the land.

One morning when he was returning after his meal at the tea boutique at the junction, a young man had joined him and started a conversation.

'Where are you going?'

'I am going to bring a procession,' the young man had replied.

As the young man opened his mouth to say something more, a leaf from a nearby tree fell into his mouth. He coughed, and put his finger inside his throat to take it out; but it got lodged further and further inside his throat. The boutique keeper had got excited and run to the water pot and brought water in a coconut shell. At that time he was being enveloped in a mist and as a whiff of air drove away the mist, the young man had disappeared.

The boutique keeper had been alone after his mother's death the previous year, he said. As he couldn't attend to the boutique and also cook, he was in the habit of going to the junction for his breakfast and lunch. At night when he closed the boutique and went home he cooked something for his dinner.

One afternoon, he said, he saw a young woman coming towards the boutique along the cart track. She came with head bowed, turned near the boutique and crossing the stile entered his house. When he went to see what was happening, he saw her squatting behind his kitchen and washing the pots and pans. He came back. At night when he closed the boutique and went home the lamp had been lit. His dinner was on the table. The two of them sat side by side and ate the meal and he helped her to wash up. He spread a new mat on the bed and placed two pillows side by side. She came and lay on the bed. He locked up, blew the lamp off and came to bed. He turned towards her and stretched out his hand. But his hand touched only the mat. As he stood up, the mat coiled round from the feet end and hit against his elbow. He lit the lamp and looked around. She was not to be seen. But he could see the impression of her head on the pillow.

'Can you weigh my two hundred and fifty grams of *bombili* dry fish . . .' said the woman and got up from the bench where she had been sitting all this time.

Nimal, while smoking his cigarette, looked towards where they were washing the bus.

'Whatever we say, sister, there is the power of the flesh. The avarice that comes from it is not temporary. It grows with age. The difference is that when one gets old it is easy to reduce it. It is difficult when it comes with immaturity. This is a decision that has been taken at such a time,' Mangalika's aunt—her mother's sister—said, sitting in the verandah and sipping her tea.

'Little nangi, you can't imagine how much I cried this morning . . . so much that I developed a hiccup,' Mangalika's mother said.

'Must I talk about what my man's sister's younger daughter did? She has given her gold necklace worth about ten or twelve thousand rupees to that boyfriend of hers and made a huge fuss at home saying that it was lost. She had given him an earring and said that it got lost at the bazaar. She gave everything she has in her passbook till now it is empty. Then when there was nothing more he could get from her he vanished!'

'We had arranged a marriage for her from a place suited to her. They had agreed to the proposal. I had saved money to get her a pair of gold earrings . . . but if she had some other marriage in mind, little nangi, she could have told us. I can't even think with whom she has gone!'

'When a man starts haunting the mind of a young woman, a gap is made there, because she can't get the one she wants in flesh and blood. To fill that with someone else, sister, can be very dangerous.'

Mangalika's father came to the verandah lighting a cigarette from the kitchen fire. With him was Mangalika's younger uncle. The uncle sat in the easy chair and kept the tray of betel on the arm of the chair.

'When she sighs deeply once or twice and sheds a few tears the fellow melts like butter. Then he does whatever she says,' he said.

'Our child was not used to tricks. She was always obedient . . . What surprises me is, after having been like that. . . .'

'Her body was mature for her age. She walked straight, isn't that so, sister? Her nose was fine . . . that is where the attraction was.'

'In the morning while brushing her teeth she talks with the pet *mynah*. I peeped into her room because there was no sound today. . . .'

The clock in the sitting room began to strike. Mangalika's aunt and uncle realized that it was getting late. The buggy cart in which they had come was untethered near the woodshed, the bull was lying under the breadfruit tree, after grazing there.

A few bulls were coming towards the shed, one by one.

Mangalika's aunt looked over the fence and exclaimed.

'Ah, here comes Nimal putha!'

Mangalika's mother, her eyes wide, turned towards the garden.

Nimal took one step to the verandah.

'We had no way of sending you a message. Padmadasa came early in the morning and he said he will give you the news. Was it from him that you heard?' she asked.

Nimal climbed up the steps.

'Sirimal also came early and Sena came in the evening. They both sighed and looked disturbed. Maybe our child did not know what each of them had kept secret in their minds. Padmadasa had been contemplating leaving the army and training as an estate superintendent. We didn't know. Padmadasa also has had an idea about our child. Very seriously.'

'Maybe because she was pleasant and friendly, many have been having expectations about her,' Mangalika's aunt said.

'But she has never behaved badly with anyone, nor has she been staring from the balcony,' Mangalika's father said.

'We heard very early about the train derailment,' Mangalika's mother said. 'As soon as we heard we sent Padmadasa to see if they were in it.'

'Now is there any use looking for her? The girl is past twenty one . . .' Mangalika's uncle said.

Nimal went into the house.

Soon after the clock struck seven the buggy cart came to the front door, its lantern lit. Mangalika's aunt and uncle left in it, to the sound of the bull's jingling bells.

After dinner Nimal went through the courtyard to the back door, from there to the rear garden, but as it was muddied came back for his rubber slippers. Then he stepped into the garden again.

There was a half moon and in its light and the light of the stars, he walked round the house and came to the woodshed. The shapeless bundle crouching there got up as he approached and he saw that it was the person who worked in the garden and the vegetable plot. That person lowered the sarong he had hitched up and walked towards Nimal.

He told Nimal that Sirimal and Sena had both been unhappy. Sena had been aimlessly walking about the garden and looking up as if to find a strong branch. Then in the afternoon he had said he was going to bring a rope and had gone. Sirimal had been lying on the planks in the shed, with his legs stretched out, like a corpse. He had rummaged among the things in the shed and found an empty bottle. He had taken the bottle and left in the afternoon saying he was going to buy insecticide. Padmadasa had left in the morning itself saying he was going for a drink.

So the three had gone at three different times, in three different directions.

'The garbage heap over there is still burning. I'll come back lighting this cigar in it,' the person said. Nimal walked round the house again.

Mangalika's mother, tidying the dining room, heard the clatter of his slippers as he walked on the gravel. Arranging the washed plates on the shelf, she swept the dining room and came and stood at the door to the courtyard.

She saw Nimal going towards the wooden stairs, a pillow in one hand and a lighted stub of a candle in the other.

'I don't know why you don't listen to me when I tell you not to sleep there. You always want to sleep upstairs. It is deserted and I don't know when I last cleaned it or broke the cobwebs there.'

Nimal started climbing the stairs.

'There is a broom behind the door and a new mat in the bundle,' she shouted to him from below.

Nimal climbed the creaking steps slowly. Pausing on one, he lit his cigarette in the flame of the candle.

Upstairs there was a box of crockery which was used only on New Year Day. That was all there that could be called valuable. There were some broken down chairs and a table and several broken bits of household goods. There was also an unused almirah and a few door frames placed against it.

Nimal kept the candle on the window sill and looked out of the window. Over the tree tops he saw a clear, star-studded sky. The moonlight fell on the *erabadu* tree and the flowers on it looked like strips of meat. The frogs croaked incessantly. A goat bleated in a human voice.

He saw that there were no cobwebs on the window. He opened out the camp-bed which was against the wall and noticed that there was no dust on it. He went to the corner to get the broom but found that it was under the bundle of mats.

He took out two mats that were on top of the bundle of mats. He placed the bed facing north and laid one mat on it and covered it with the other. As he lay on the bed and turned to a side he could hear a new creaking sound.

The flame of the candle was turning red in its last gasp and emitting a whiff of smoke. A ray of moonlight and starlight from an opening in the roof dispelled some of the darkness. In the semi darkness he took two puffs of the cigarette. The butt he threw went out through the window like a flitting firefly.

He fell asleep lying on a side. He woke two hours before dawn.

It was not a noise outside or a frightening dream that woke him. He felt something soft against his elbow and on his arm, and from his arm towards his pillow.

A mist had crept into the room, through the window and the top of the walls, dimming the moonbeams and the starlight which strained from the glass above. But as he turned his head he saw that the light in the room was from a chimney lamp on the wall shelf. Though his eyes were heavy with sleep he saw a familiar face almost within reach of his hands emerging through the mist like an image, now seeing, now invisible in the ripples of disturbed waters or like an unblown flower bending from its stem. Mangalika. Mangalika dressed in a nightdress, sitting on the side of his bed. Over his body she had draped an arm and was stroking his elbow.

Everything was quiet.

As she moved her lips slightly he saw a soft smile. Then he could see definitely that it was she, Mangalika, from the dimple forming in her cheek.

'Nimal aiya . . .'

It was she. He knew he could not mistake her voice.

The mist blew into the room again and as she became a shadowy form, he drew a sharp breath.

'I was here for one whole day all alone, Nimal aiya. A day and a night. I knew you would come. I knew you would come if not yesterday evening, at least this morning. . . . I think that knowledge is combined with my past birth.'

In the semi darkness he could hear her breathing. A fragrance from her cheeks assailed his nose.

'I took food and water for two days and came here yesterday morning, an hour before dawn.

'Here I counted the number of times the wind blew and thought of plenty of things about the future.

'Nimal aiya, let us go. . . .'

Her hand rested on his elbow.

This was the first time in his life that he had felt the softness of a girl and the fragrance of a girl so close.

'Let us go as we have been aspiring to over so many lives . . . Nimal aiya.

'In our ALAMULA JATAKA I was an anthill between cactus plants. You were close by. You were a *watupalu* creeper. My love was that creeper. You were twined on a *sevalabomi* tree with spreading branches. There was no effort that you spared to come down one of those branches to come to me. During a drought the tender leaves withered and dried up. When it began to grow again during the rains you came down one of the branches that had bent towards the earth and embraced me. You embraced me from head to foot, embraced me entirely. The two of us became one. The farmer came with a stake and a hoe in his cart to break and remove the anthill. He could not see me in your embrace. He saw only the creeper and he looked about and went away, deceived.

'Also, in our BAKABAKA JATAKA I was a female frog and lived in the edge of the garden of an old house. You were a frog in the same compound. As I was hopping about looking for food I fell into an empty well nine fathoms deep. You heard my cries and you came to the edge of the well and seeing me at the bottom on the verge of death, with an all enveloping love you jumped in. We were imprisoned in that deserted well, suffering without food and spent the drought season with great difficulty. Though you were doubtful about our ability to survive and worn out, you would always find me a worm or catch a fly and feed me and it was only then that you ate.

'As the monsoon rains came the well started to fill up gradually and then we swam about happily as the water rose and the whole of night we were chattering *baka baka* in great joy. In the morning the water had come up and we jumped out.

'Also, in our WARAMANDA JATAKA I was a female deer on the edge of a forest and you were a young male deer deep in the forest. It was the dry season and the lakes and streams had dried up. There was water only in one hole. I was used to drinking water from there. Seeing this a Veddah set up a trap of deer skin with a noose. Not knowing anything I went as usual to drink water and I was caught in the trap. Hearing my groans, you sniffed your way from the forest and following on my track, saw the trap I was caught in. Then you trod on one end of the noose again and again the whole night trying to save me and just before the Veddah came, you were able to free me from the trap.'

She got up and from the bundle of mats she took out a long rope. It had knots every two feet.

'Nimal aiya, one hour before dawn the moon will set. Then it will be very dark. Then I will climb on to the window sill and tie the rope to the rafter. I will drop the other end to the ground and I will get down with the help of the knots of the rope. Then you take the bag with my clothes and come down and give the bag to me . . . In our SWARNATANTRI JATAKA I was a maggot entangled in a cobweb. Before the spider could come you came as a beetle sliding down a string which shone like gold with the dew and saved me . . . you too must be remembering those experiences as well.

'I am going in the morning bus and I will get down at the halting place at the banyan tree. I will have breakfast at the all-night tea boutique there and take the other bus to the Bollethota junction. It will be dawn then and I will wash my clothes in the stream there, spread them to dry on the stones and then bathe there.

'You come up to the room along the rope and untie it and put it in the corner where the mats are. Put off the light and go to sleep. Wait till the crows start crowing and then come down. Then my aunt will make you a cup of tea. As soon as you have drunk the tea, don't wait for breakfast but come.'

She half knelt by the camp-bed and placed her chin on the bed.

'Nimal aiya, all that I can hear is the sound of your breathing. . . . Till you come I will be in the water, hugging the water to me. Nimal aiya, we have to be born again and again through many lives.'

She turned her head and looked at the top of the stairs. Then turning again towards him she relaxed her pose with a slight smile.

'How good that no one is listening to us!' she said.

The Mission

S.D.V. Perera

The first clear peals of the single bell of the Anglican church told the villagers that it was Sunday and a quarter to nine. Paul Arasaratnam in his new cassock was walking slowly to the church. He was so glad that the garment was so light, made of cool white cotton, almost as light as his verti. The sky was heavy with cloud and it was very hot. Not a breath of wind stirred the sail-like leaves of the straight, tall palmyra palms. The monsoon should soon break; what a relief that would bring!

A few children were heading for the Sunday school. When he was still some distance from the church, Father Paul, for that was how he was known in the village, heard the sound of running feet behind him, and turned round. It was a young boy of about fourteen years who should be going to Sunday School. He was panting. 'I am sorry to trouble you, Father, on Sunday morning, but Jeyam has disappeared, and mother is in a terrible state. Can you come home now, Father, and speak to her, please?'

Father Paul stopped, thought a while, pulled out a little pad from the pocket of his cassock, wrote a few words, and handed the note over to the boy. 'Take this to Brother James: he'll be at the back of the Church. And bring me a reply; I'll be at your place.' The boy dashed away and Father Paul changed direction.

He walked between the high palmyra-leaf fences that concealed the houses from the street, and stood at the doorway of Jeyam's house. He could hear the suppressed sobbing coming from inside. He knocked and waited.

After a brief silence the boy's mother opened the door, wiping her tear-stained face with the fall of her sari. 'Now please sit down,' he said, 'and tell me what has happened.' There was little to tell. Jeyam had gone to school for soccer practice on Saturday afternoon. He had not returned at 6.30 as he usually did. She had sent the younger son, Thambi, to inquire at his friends' homes but they had no news of him. They had sat up late thinking he had gone to a late night movie. They had then informed the police, who had not done anything except take the particulars down and say that so many young boys were disappearing that it was difficult to keep track of them all.

'What do you think has happened?' asked Father Paul.

Through her tear-filled eyes she looked at him in consternation. 'Can't you guess, Father?'

As he remained silent she burst out, 'You know quite well the guerillas have taken him.' The helplessness she had displayed when he came in was replaced by a strength which seemed to tell him that if he was not able to help, she would seek out the boy herself. In a slow, even tone she asked, 'Will you find him, Father, and bring him back to me?

There was a long pause as Father Paul pondered the request. It was broken by the arrival of Thambi with the reply from Brother James. He took a quick glance at the note and put it in his pocket. He looked at the boy and his mother long and thoughtfully and said, 'Yes, I will do my best to find him and bring him back: but keep this to yourselves.' He then prayed over them briefly, stepped out of the house and turned homewards.

Jeyam was one of the brightest boys in the Anglican high school of the area. Hc was in the university entrance form and was hoping to do a degree in engineering. After the boy's father's death two years previously the family's hopes had been centred on him. Father

Paul recalled that his people were far more ambitious for their children than his Sinhala friends in the South.

Father Paul knew a little about the guerillas. A good number of them had been killed recently and they were increasingly recruiting young people from the top forms of the schools. It was an advantage, he was given to understand, to take young boys as they were single-minded and easier to train. The nick-name 'the boys' given to the guerillas seemed particularly appropriate now—they *were* boys!

The local guerilla leader was, to the public, a shadowy figure known as Hanuman; but Father Paul knew him to be a former school teacher, Sittampalam, whom he had known at the University of Ceylon in Colombo. The thing was to discover his hide-out.

When he got home he changed into shirt and longs, got on his bike and began riding through the back roads to the provincial capital, Jaffna. As he neared the town he could hear the sounds of war that seemed all-pervading these days—the occasional lobbing of mortar shells into the Fort of Jaffna, where some of the Government forces were trapped, and the roar of helicopters bringing supplies to the beleaguered soldiers.

When he reached the town centre he dismounted and wheeled his bike through the crowds bargaining near the stalls and spilling over into the open market. He got across to the main street which was relatively quiet and knocked at the closed door of a barber saloon. A boy came running out of the alleyway by the side of the shop and said, 'I'll tell the master. Please wait.' A minute later the barber himself came out. 'Good morning, Father,' he said looking both pleased and puzzled. 'Siva,' said Father Paul, 'I am truly sorry to disturb you like this; you can see I have not come for the usual.' He smiled and the barber said, 'Come to the back of the shop, Father.'

They went to a little room where there was a whole line of coloured pictures of the gods and goddesses of the Hindu pantheon with a little oil lamp burning below them. They sat and the boy brought out two cups of steaming black coffee. The air was oppressive with the fragrance of sandalwood mingling with the faint odour of 'Jaffna' cigars.

'I have come, Siva,' began Father Paul, 'to get your advice and help for an errand of mercy. You can see how important it is—I am here instead of at the Church on a Sunday morning.'

The barber was frankly surprised as he said, 'How can I help a person of your standing, Father, except perhaps by giving you a good haircut.' He smiled, trying to ease the tension that had suddenly come into the room.

'You can by giving me some information.' Father Paul took out his pad, tore out a sheet, wrote the name, 'Hanuman,' and passed the paper to the barber, saying, 'Can you tell me where I can contact him?'

The barber was visibly agitated but said, 'Who is he, and what makes you think I know him or his whereabouts?'

'If anyone in Jaffna knows his whereabouts, it has to be you. I know how well-informed you are. Any information you give me will be kept secret.'

'For what purpose do you need to contact him, Father,' he asked and Father Paul then knew he had the information.

'It is to help a poor widow who wants to know her son's whereabouts. She is in my Church. The boy disappeared yesterday.'

The barber suddenly became very tense as if he remembered something. 'Father,' he whispered, 'were you followed here?'

'No, Siva. I decided to come here about an hour ago and cycled here through the back roads.'

'You have put me and yourself into some danger by calling here on a Sunday morning when you would be easily spotted. However I know, Father, how concerned you are about your flock as you call them and I'll do what I can.'

He rose and took the paper in his hand. 'First let us consign this to the flames.' He held the paper over the flame of the oil lamp till it was quite charred.

There was a long silence while Siva weighed matters in his mind. At last he spoke. 'Don't be angry, Father, but I have to ask if you are an agent of the Government.'

'Siva,' said Father Paul, 'you know me better than that; I am an agent for nobody but God.'

'I believe you, Father.' said Siva, 'When will you come for the usual?'

'On Wednesday.'

'I'll have news for you by then possibly. I can't promise anything except that I'll do my best. And Father, if you are not what you seem, the guerillas will not have any mercy on me or you.'

'I understand that very well. Thank you very much for your trust.'

Coming out of the alleyway and changing to his casual tone the barber said, 'I've got a good quantity of old newspapers for you, Father.' He called out to the boy who returned with a big bundle of newspapers which they tied on to the pillion of the bicycle.

When Father Paul arrived at the barber shop the following Wednesday there was a customer there already. The barber gave him a warm welcome. 'Ah, Father, you have come for the usual. Please sit down. I won't be long.' While putting the finishing touches to the job he was doing, he threw casual questions and comments to Father Paul to keep the conversation flowing.

When the customer had left, Father Paul took his place for 'the usual'. Above the mirror appeared the usual array of gods, but on one side was a picture of the British Royal family, and on the other one of Nehru.

As the barber trimmed his hair to a pleasing tonsure he spoke quietly. 'You've come on a very good day. We'll talk a little later.' When he finished he called the boy and asked him to attend to any customers who might come. If anyone asked for him he was out.

They went to the same room at the back. Siva said, 'He is here and he will see you at the back of the alleyway on the side of Suppiah Pillai's cloth shop about 12 o'clock. You should not wait here. Spend some time in the market or in the shops and then go there. You know the place?'

'Yes, I do,' said Father Paul. 'You mean to tell me he is here in the heart of Jaffna?'

The barber smiled. 'It is the safest place—among the people. Finding him here is more difficult than in the jungles of the Wanni.'

When he arrived at the back of the alleyway there was a small crowd milling around a pedlar who had displayed a collection of gold bangles and chains on a wooden carton and was calling out, 'Gold, genuine gold! A wise investment!' There was no sign of Hanuman among the crowd and Father Paul began to take an interest in the reactions of the crowd to the gold articles. One man wondered whether it was stolen property. An old woman took one of the bangles in her hand and looked at it closely. The pedlar did not like this very much and she sensed as much. She returned to her friends in the crowd and whispered, 'I don't think it is very high quality.' The pedlar was getting exasperated. 'Look,' he said, 'If you think the stuff is not genuine or the price is too high, why are you crowding around and suffocating me? Try your luck at the jewellers' shop.'

Three or four young men turned up from nowhere and one of them asked, 'How do we know these are not smuggled from India?' The pedlar took a step towards him. 'Are you accusing me?' he asked. 'No,' said the young man, 'I am asking you.' Another young man took a chain into his hand. 'I don't think this is genuine gold.' 'It is 9-carat gold,' said the pedlar. 'I don't think it is gold at all,' said another, 'it is a cheap alloy, gold-plated.' The pedlar pulled off the chain from the man who had taken it. Suddenly there was a flurry of hands round the wooden carton. It overturned and a free-for-all began. Father Paul stepped back from the edge of the circle and felt a tap on his shoulder. He turned and there was Sittampalam, smiling. The smile was unmistakable in spite of his new moustache. He was dressed in a verti and looked very different from the stylish figure he cut in Colombo in his University days.

'Come, Arasa,' he said, 'we have more important things to do than watching a street fight.'

They walked towards the open market and wandered between the stalls, lingering here and there, and walking again and talking. 'What's the trouble, Arasa?'

'Sittam, I have come to speak to you about a boy whom your men have taken.'

'Come, Arasa, we don't take people; they join us. Let's have a sherbet.' They sat on a bench outside the drinks shop sipping the sherbet.

'I am sure he would have not joined unless he had been subjected to some strong, even physical, pressure.' said Father Paul.

'I dare say some of our men get carried away sometimes, but I'll tell you this, Arasa, our men will never approach anyone who has not shown support for the cause.'

'But, this boy was heading for the University and a bright career,' said Father Paul.

'Are you suggesting, Arasa, that we should recruit the more stupid members in our community?'

'No. I am not suggesting that. I am suggesting that it is not fair to involve young boys prematurely in politics, train them to carry out acts of violence and expose them to injury and death.'

Sittampalam got up, returned the glasses to the drinks shop. He got behind an empty bus and leaned on it, and Father Paul joined him.

'Look, Arasa,' began Sittampalam, 'these boys at the top of the schools are far more mature than we were at that age; they are avidly political and know exactly what they are doing. As for the risk to their lives, we never send recruits to the firing line—it will be many months before Jeyam (I know that it is of him you are speaking) will see any fighting.'

Father Paul realized the futility of argument and simply asked, 'Is there no possibility of your releasing him to enable him to at least finish his schooling?'

They started walking back to the alleyway where Father Paul had asked a boy to look after his bike.

'It is not a question of our releasing him. I will send him to your place in a few days, and he will tell you himself what he wishes to do. Is that fair?'

'Yes,' said Father Paul, 'but he might come when I am out.'

'He'll come when you are in, Arasa. Don't worry about that.'

They reached the bike and Father Paul gave the boy 50 cents. He wheeled the bike away from the wall on which he had leaned it and said, 'Thank you, Sittam, for giving me your time and for listening to me.'

'Goodbye, Arasa, Look after yourself,' said Sittampala. 'And Arasa, don't get involved in these matters. Let events take their course. Just pray for us and the people we are fighting for. Also, don't try to contact me again. It is not safe for you or for us. Goodbye!' He smiled and disappeared into another crowd that had gathered around another pedlar who had set himself up in the same place and was selling imported razor blades.

Seeing a man who had been with the previous crowd, Father Paul asked him, 'What happened to the man selling jewellery?' 'He dropped everything and ran away. You know those young fellows who roughed him up were collecting gold for the guerillas.'

When he saw Jeyam's mother he said, 'I am in touch with him and will let you know very soon whether I have been successful or not. You must not ask me anything more now.' Quite unexpectedly she received the news with stoical clam. 'Thank you, Father, you took a great risk for my sake. Also I now think they did not take him; he went of his own accord.' Father Paul was taken by surprise. 'How do you know that?' he asked. 'After you left that day I was thinking and remembered that several times recently he had been telling me and Thambi about the inevitability of the struggle. I then thought that he was talking in general terms. I was mistaken. It was his way of preparing me for this. It is his fate.' The family were devoutly Christian, but in times of crisis the Hindu concept of Karma seemed to come up from deep within them to support them. Impersonal fate seemed easier to turn to in trouble than a personal god of love. So the words of consolation which Father Paul had in mind were left unspoken.

As the weeks went by, the inevitability of the struggle was brought home to the village. The distant sound of mortar fire reached them more frequently, and from uncertain directions came spasmodic machine gun fire. While some degree of fear had been seeping into the village from the time the Government forces first appeared in the peninsula about two years previously, now it was palpable. Curiously enough it manifested itself, not in panic, but in an excessive coolness and deliberation with which the villagers went about their business as if nothing unusual was going on around them. Then quite suddenly it became quiet again and so it remained for many weeks.

Father Paul went about his duties, visiting the sick and the old and paying visits to his parishioners. He found himself more on his knees than before as he sought guidance for his work as pastor to his flock.

He recalled the wonderfully happy years he had spent in the South with friends of all ethnic origins—Tamils, Sinhala, Muslim and Burgher—in boarding school, university and most of all at Theological College. Why had such bitter hatred developed between the Tamils and the Sinhalese? As Christians the members of his parish could not be allowed to develop such hatred, for there were many Sinhala people who were brothers and sisters in Christ; nor could they be allowed to hate Sinhala Buddhists when they had to love even their enemies. How difficult that was, especially for those whose loved ones had suffered at their hands.

He considered the Liberation Theology adopted by some of the Catholic clergy in the South and Central American countries. In all sincerity he could not say that the position of the Tamils in Sri Lanka was comparable to the masses in those lands where armed struggle seemed the only means of survival.

The guerillas known locally as 'the boys' was another problem. His attitude towards them was ambivalent; he admired their readiness to sacrifice their careers, the well-being of their families and even their lives for a cause they believed in. He doubted that if he was in their place he would be prepared for such sacrifice. On the other hand he was repelled by the ruthlessness with which they treated those whom they considered collaborators: he recalled the revulsion to the point of nausea he had experienced when he came across a small crowd slinking away from a young man who had been shot and tied with barbed wire to a lamp post.

What was his role in all this? Could he take a neutral position, rendering to Caesar the things that were Caesar's and to God the things that were God's? But who was Caesar here in Jaffna? The Government of the country or the Guerilla High Command who held sway over whole areas of the peninsula?

The guerillas were making door to door calls to collect money for their needs, and one of the children at the top of the Sunday school had asked her teacher whether it was right for the Christians to give money to people who might use the money to buy guns to kill people. The teacher had told the girl he would have to think about it and asked Father Paul. He had said, 'No, if we knew that the money would be so used.' He felt it was not a very straightforward answer, but what else could he say? The whole ethics of war was too big a subject to discuss with young people; in any case he was himself unsure of his own position in the conflict.

So, he was on his kness more than ever before, seeking answers to the perplexing question, that assailed him—not only for his own salvation, but also for the guidance he had to give his flock: for he could see in the eyes of his parishioners the unspoken plea for leadership.

It was when he was praying near midnight that he heard a knock on the door of his house. Someone must be very sick to call at this time, he thought, and put on his cassock. When he opened the door he saw Jeyam. 'I am very sorry to disturb you at this time, but it is the safest time,' he said.

They went in and Jeyam began to talk. 'I am so sorry to have caused you so much trouble, Father.'

'It is not me you have to consider, Jeyam, it is your mother and brother.'

'I realize that, Father. Would you please give this letter to her. I have explained everything and I hope she and Thambi will understand.'

'So, you have decided to stay with the guerillas?'

'Yes, Father.'

'Are you sure about what you are doing?'

'Yes, Father.'

'Did they force you to join? Were you under pressure?'

'No, Father. One of them came to the school some weeks ago when we were at soccer practice and asked us individually, if there was a need would we be willing to join them, and I said "yes". It appeared that they needed me and when he came the next time I went with him. I had to go without telling mother or Thambi, because you know, Father, if I stayed to say "goodbye" to them I would never have gone.'

'Hanuman said it is still open for you to change your mind; to return to your family, go to University and serve your people when peace returns.'

'Yes, Father. It is open to me even now, but I have made up my mind. These are extraordinary times, Father, and you have to make extraordinary decisions.' Those words would normally sound rhetorical and even pretentious; but Jeyam spoke them with such simple conviction and naturalness that Father Paul had no further words of persuasion to offer.

'Give me the letter; I'll take it to your mother first thing in the morning. Try to send even brief messages to her from time to time if you can do so safely.'

'Yes, Father. I must go now. Thank you for looking after my family. Take good care of yourself, Father, and do not leave the village, except in an emergency.'

As he turned to go, Father Paul said, 'Give me a minute or two,' and he took him in again. 'You will be trained to kill, Jeyam. Do so only if it is absolutely necessary. Take every opportunity to be merciful. Don't let them brutalize you. Keep the goodness in your heart intact. Remember your prayers.' He embraced the boy, prayed over him and said, 'God keep you safe, my son.'

Jeyam's mother heard the news of her son's midnight visit and his decision to remain with the guerillas with quiet resignation. The promise of messages from him was welcome, but now her life seemed to be centred on Thambi and his future. She had extracted a promise from him that he would never join the guerillas and that he would go into University either in Sri Lanka or in India.

Father Paul visited the family from time to time. He was pleased to learn that Jeyam had kept his promise to write: once a month or so a letter would come. No one knew who had brought it but in the morning it would be slipped under the door. It appeared that he had now finished his training and was very fit. There was no indication where he was but these notes cheered the mother, and Father Paul detected in her tone a certain pride in the fact that her son was a grown man and a soldier. She did not seem to realize that the end of his training also meant the beginning of fighting. And when he raised the matter delicately, she surprised him yet again by saying, 'If he is destined to live, he will live.' Clearly it was her fatalism that gave her strength, not her Christian faith.

She longed to get a letter across to him, but Jeyam, in his first note had asked her not to try to contact him as it would not be safe. Then letters from Jeyam stopped coming altogether. His mother was now greatly distressed. She envisaged the worst and only wanted to know whether he was alive. She approached Father Paul, but he pointed out to her that it would not be safe not only for himself but for Jeyam too. Reluctantly the mother accepted this.

Some weeks went by and word got round that nearly the whole of the peninsula was in the hands of the boys. The only sound of war was the occasional, distant sound of mortar shells coming from the direction of Jaffna. It looked like almost complete victory and Father Paul wondered whether it would be safe now to make inquiries about Jeyam. So he was in the right frame of mind when the boy's mother approached him again. He agreed to make inquiries but when she gave him a letter, saying, 'If you get a chance see that he gets this letter,' he hesitated. However, when he saw the appealing look on her face and considered that the fighting was almost over, he agreed and took the letter.

This time he got on to the main Chunnakam–Jaffna road and rode along in the humid heat under a vast, darkening rain cloud. He hoped the delayed monsoon had come at last to bring the cool weather. He wouldn't mind one bit if he arrived in the pouring rain. As he neared the city he could hear the thud of mortar shells but he knew the town itself was safe.

And then the storm broke. From the low, black sky flashed forks of lightning and the rain poured. The thunder drowned the sound of the mortars. With the cool rain pouring down his head and face and arms, Father Paul rode on relishing the refreshing coolness and the sense of security the storm seemed to give. However, as he rode he felt the soaked trouser legs clinging to his calves and slowing down his pedalling.

Then much to his surprise he saw four or five cyclists racing towards him. As he swung to a side they whizzed past him, their shoulders bent over the handlebars. At the same time he heard the sound of small arms fire. A bigger group of cyclists was approaching. The one at the head shouted to the others above the howling storm, 'You boys go ahead, I'll see who this idiot is.' He jumped off his bike, gripped Father Paul by the front of his shirt and wheeling the bike with his other hand pulled him away from the road into the vegetation on the side of the road.

'What the hell do you think you are doing?' he asked in a hoarse whisper, 'Do you want to get killed? Are you a collaborator? Quick, answer me!' Father Paul was shivering with the cold and with fear.

'I am just a Christian priest,' he managed to say. 'I am carrying a letter to a boy who has joined the guerillas. It is from his mother.'

'Are you mad?' he asked. 'Where are you taking the letter?'

'To Sivalingam's barber shop.'

'You fool give me the letter.'

He was reaching for the letter in his hip pocket when he heard another burst of fire above the storm. He felt a stab of pain on his shoulder and fell on his knees. The guerilla lay sprawled in front of him. Paralyzed with the shock all he could do was to gaze at the young man's body and see the blood from his chest and head trickling down very red and then becoming watery as it merged with the rainwater coming down along the sides of his body and forming a pink stream that joined the brown muddy puddle under the bushes.

Father Paul was still on his knees when the Government troops came running across the road. One of the soldiers jabbed him in his chest with his rifle butt and asked, 'Who are you? What are you doing here?' He couldn't speak. Somebody jabbed him again and then an officer came up. Father Paul felt a warm dampness spreading from his shoulder to his shirt front, then he slumped forward, his head falling on the body of the dead guerilla.

When Father Paul came to, he found himself on the floor of some sort of vehicle. The sides were green and as greater awareness came to him he realized he was in an army jeep. There was a soldier behind the steering wheel. Father Paul turned on his side to sit up, but felt a shooting pain on his shoulder and fell back with a moan. He then noticed a large bandage which covered his left shoulder and upper arm.

His stirring had alerted the soldier who turned around and was now looking at him. Through the pain that was now increasing he felt that the face that was turned towards him was known to him. He puckered his brows in an effort to recall the name and tried again to raise himself up to get a better view of the face but fell back and nearly passed out with the pain.

He was saved the trouble when the officer came around to the back of the jeep and sat in full view of him. The officer smiled slightly and Father Paul, half remembered the name. It began with R . . . He was with him in boarding school in Kandy. When they went up to the third form his parents could not afford the fees and he left to join the neighbouring Central School. He had been a very nice chap. He never saw him after that. He remembered going to his place; his mother used to make delicious pancakes filled with coconut treacle. She was a lovely lady, gentle and soft-spoken . . . and then he remembered the name. He passed out with the effort and when he opened his eyes the officer was looking at him. Father Paul opened his mouth to speak the name, but the officer—he was clearly not an ordinary soldier—put his finger to his lip in a warning gesture.

'Yes,' he said, 'I am Ranatunga. Arasa, how did you get caught up in this? Tell me the truth, the whole truth. Speak slowly. You have lost some blood.'

Father Paul started telling him about Jeyam's midnight visit leaving out all references to the barber shop and Hanuman, and when he came to the letter, he suddenly remembered and twisted himself to reach for his hip pocket. The pain was excruciating.

'You are looking for the letter,' said Ranatunga. 'I have it. Please continue with your story.'

'Is that the whole truth?'

And Father Paul nodded.

'If there was the slightest suggestion that you had information of value I would have had to send you to the Regional Commander for questioning and that would not have been a very pleasant experience for you. So thank your lucky stars . . . or your God.'

'I would prefer to thank God,' said Father Paul slowly, 'After all, the stars belong to Him! What about the letter?'

'You have been lucky again,' he said, 'the wording of the letter could have been from any mother to any son who ran away from home. Very sentimental and no mention of guerillas. So another psalm of praise is called for.'

'What are you going to do with me, Rana?'

'I was coming to that. You'll be taken to the hospital to get your wound dressed. It's not a very deep wound and the bullet has been removed. It is a miracle that you survived that hail of gunfire. Your God has been very merciful to you this time; but don't count on Him the next time.'

'I have to count on Him every time, Rana. Whether He lets me live or lets me die is His business.'

Ranatunga smiled. 'I can't take you in this jeep, but another will be here soon and it'll take you to the Chunnakam Hospital.'

'After that?'

'After that you go home.'

'Thank you, Rana,' said Father Paul.

'Don't mention it, Arasa, and I mean it: no one must know that you know me.' And becoming very serious Ranatunga continued. 'Look Arasa, you are a priest. Look after the spiritual needs of your people. Don't get involved in anything to do with the war. Leave that to the people who are fighting, and pray for peace.'

Father Paul asked, 'Rana, how did this terrible hatred between our people arise?' Before Ranatunga could say anything there was a roar and a screech of brakes as another jeep came and stopped alongside. Two men jumped out and saluted the officer.

'Take Father Paul Arasaratnam to the Chunnakam Hospital. He is a Christian priest. You can tell the doctor that he was caught in the crossfire. He has got a wound on his left shoulder. The bullet has been removed. No guard is necessary. When he is discharged he can find his way home.' Turning to Father Paul and with a smile he said, 'Take care of yourself, Father, and be careful where you ride your bike. Hope you'll be o.k. soon.'

They lifted him into the jeep and it raced away. He was being thrown from side to side, and with the pain he felt he was bleeding again. He steadied himself by holding the seat with his other hand. They were passing several foot patrols. Suddenly there was a shout from the roadside and the jeep came to a stop. A soldier came up and began speaking urgently to the officer on the passenger seat. Father Paul could not make out the words at first. After some time he made out the words 'captured', 'commanding officer' and 'questioning'. A few minutes later the gate of the jeep was lowered and a young man, bound hand and foot, was almost flung on the floor of the jeep and the soldier who had stopped the jeep jumped in front.

The jeep started to move and Father Paul adjusted himself into a position from which he would be able to see the young man's face. When he did so their eyes met. It was Jeyam! Father Paul nearly passed out but managed to hold on to consciousness. Far from being in a state of fear, Jeyam seemed to be in a state which could only be described as spiritual exaltation. His eyes were dilated and there was a beatific smile on his lips. 'Don't worry, Father,' he said softly, 'they'll not get anything from me.' With that he rolled over on his side.

When they arrived at the hospital the soldiers jumped off and came to the back of the jeep to help Father Paul out. It was then that they saw that the guerilla was dead. 'Cyanide,' said the officer almost casually. 'But, Sir, there was no capsule on him when we captured him,' said the soldier who had stopped the jeep. 'He must have taken it before, expecting to get caught;' said the officer, 'take the body to the hospital and find out his identity.'

Father Paul looked on as they lowered Jeyam's body on to the grass in the hospital grounds and undid the ropes that bound him. He reflected on the respectful way the soldiers seemed to treat the dead body and recalled how they had flung the living man into the jeep: death seemed to have conferred on Jeyam a solemnity which his enemies seemed to recognize.

One of the soldiers went to the hospital to make inquiries. The officer turned to Father Paul who was still in the jeep and asked him almost casually.

'Father, do you know the man?'

'Yes, I do. He attends a school in my village not far from here.

His mother is a member of my Church. I will probably have to take the funeral service.'

The officer paused and asked more pointedly, 'You are not involved with the guerillas?'

'No, officer, but I have to see to the spiritual wants of families whose sons have run away from home to join the guerillas.'

'That's alright Father, please do not get involved with them. If you do, you will be in great danger.'

'I realize that,' said Father Paul.

The soldier returned from the hospital and confirmed Jeyam's identity and the officer took down the details. The hospital attendants came out with a stretcher, placed the body on it and took it away. Father Paul told the officer that if the body could be kept in the hospital for two days he would be able to break the news to the boy's brother first and then make arrangements for the funeral. The officer said, 'I can arrange that, but, will you be well enough in two days? We'll have to ask the doctor.'

They brought the stretcher for Father Paul and he was carried to the casualty section where they removed the blood-soaked bandage and cleaned and dressed his wound. They also gave him an injection.

'You are very lucky, Father; you'll be alright,' said the young doctor. 'How did this happen?'

Father Paul told him.

'But, Father, didn't you know that no one goes on the Chunnakam Road these days.'

'No. I didn't,' said Father Paul and the doctor looked at the officer in disbelief. 'Can I go now?' asked Father Paul.

'Certainly not,' said the doctor, 'you've lost a good deal of blood and we'll have to give you a transfusion and keep an eye on you tonight and tomorrow at least.'

They took him to a bed in an airy ward and he felt much better. He would be well enough to take the funeral service the day after tomorrow, he thought. After a light meal he fell fast asleep but awoke about midnight. He gazed at the ceiling of the dimly-lit ward and began recalling the events of the day. And then he asked himself how he would break the news to Thambi and what words of comfort he could offer the mother.

The whiteness of the ceiling blurred to red and brown and pink and his eyes closed. He began searching in his mind for one clear light, one clear word by which he could live. One after another scriptural texts flashed in white upon the black screen beneath his eye-lids. 'Come unto me all ye that are heavy-laden', 'Love your enemies', 'Let not your heart be troubled' and many more. They came and went, one after the other. And then came one that stayed on the screen: 'Be ye wise as serpents and harmless as doves.' With that receding into the deep recesses of his mind, Father Paul fell into a dreamless sleep.

It Could Happen Anywhere, Anytime

Thamaraichelvi

Was it really a week since Raghavan had returned from Saudia Arabia. Yes, from last Sunday to this Sunday it was eight days. Gayathri was surprised that the eight days had ended so swiftly.

Her heart had melted when the two children were jumping around their father who had come back after four years. Eight-year-old Parthipan had said more than a hundred times, 'You won't leave us any more and go to Saudi, will you?' Four-year-old Bharani was always cuddling into her father's arms.

'Look, Gayathri, what pain these little ones have gone through because of my leaving them. But I had to go because of our situation here. Why should I have gone if the conditions had been favourable to us? I went because of my frenzy to show the neighbours that we too could live in comfort. Because of this I lost the pleasure of living with these children and watching them grow.'

Gayathri felt his pain.

It was true, they had both married amidst high expectations on both sides. At that time he was working in the Jaffna Kacheri and she was a teacher in a school in Kokuvil.

They had gone to work while living in a rented house. Parthipan

---

Translated by K.S. Sivakumaran

and Bharani were born then. They could just manage with their two salaries.

Then Raghavan had told her about his idea of going abroad. She didn't like it at first. 'We can manage with what we have. If you are gone, who is going to help me and the children?'

'How long can we live in a rented house? We must buy a piece of land for ourselves and build a house. Can we do that with our salaries? That's why, Gayathri, you must let me go for two years. Then we can be secure, and start a business.'

He argued and made her agree to his proposal. He brought a distant aunt, Paackiam, who didn't have any support to live well on her own, and he got her to stay at home, and borrowed money from many and left for Saudi. But he could not get the salary he expected in that country. He had to work hard to get a decent salary. The two years originally intended became four. But within those four years he was able to settle all debts and to buy a three-acre bit of land in Kokuvil, and they were able to build a small house there.

'But don't go anywhere else now. Stay with us. Had I taught here as before, no problems would have arisen. But some teachers were transferred to the Kilinochchi district, and it was my bad time so that I too was transferred. I hated the world at large because I had to leave for Kilinochchi every Monday and return only on Friday. It was terrible travelling, and it was terrible staying there without the children.' She stopped to calm herself before continuing. 'It's not like before. Everything has changed in these four years. In Kilinochchi, I would yearn for Fridays. It was a pity for the children. . . . If the aunt had not been there, what difficulties would I have faced? I had to leave on Mondays before the children awoke or they would cry and I would think I should not leave. But now you can look after the children. I can go and come in peace.'

Raghavan felt the sleeping children fondly with his hands.

'I am thinking of going to the school tomorrow.'

He raised his head in surprise. 'Why Gayathri . . . if leave is available, why don't you stay back?'

'Because you were here I was on leave the whole of last week. It's not nice now to stay back. I have been given the Grade 5 scholarship class. If I don't go, the poor children will suffer. The school is a rural school, hardly any qualified teachers. . . . The Principal gave me this class depending on me. It's not nice to continue to be on leave.'

'What's this . . . when I am back?' He looked at her in a pitiable manner.

'What to do? The coming Friday is a Poya. I will get back on Thursday. OK?' She looked at him pleadingly.

He sighed. 'Be careful. Go and come back as soon as you can. Problems are getting worse everywhere. I heard that in Yakachi there were problems for two days. Don't even know whether buses are running. First find out and then go.'

'Even after you get to Kilinochchi, you have to walk four miles into the interior. There is no transportation available. It's a really arduous journey. With great difficulty I had to go and come every week. But it was not the journey that mattered, it was leaving these children at home and going that gave me pain. I feel like crying when I tell you all this.'

He pressed her hand in support. 'What shall we do? If you could manage for another year, we can try to get a transfer back here,' he said softly.

On the next day, early in the morning at 3.00, she attended to the cooking with the help of the aunt. At 4.30, she went to bathe and got ready to go to Kilinochchi. She wrapped herself in a sari, packed the food in an airtight box, and put that with some clothes in the small bag she had taken every week for the last one year. She kissed her children who were still sleeping but they stirred and seemed to wake. Perhaps they felt something of what she felt. It was somehow harder after the week she had stayed with them.

Raghavan watched her silently through all the different activities and sensed her emotion. He felt sad. 'Parthipan seems to be able to understand the situation, at least to some extent, but Bharani's eyes are full of tears.'

She stroked Bharani's face and was nearly in tears herself.

'What can a four-year-old child understand? It's OK. They've been through this for the last year . . . I'd better go.'

'I'll come to the bus stand and get you into the bus. Shall we go by bike?'

'No, no, let's go by the cross lanes. There is no fear there. Don't I go and come alone every week?'

Raghavan put a shirt over his sarong. They said goodbye to the aunt and left.

It wasn't dawn as yet and there was a faint trace of moonlight in the sky. The lane was quiet. In some houses there were electric lights. Raghavan carried her bag and walked with her.

There were four or five people at the bus stand. The street lamp was dim. The first mini-bus would come only at 5.30. Gayathri looked around. Usually on Monday mornings many teachers teaching in schools in Kilinochchi and Paranthan would be at the bus stand. But there were none of them today.

'I don't know whether no one has come because of the trouble at Elephant Pass yesterday and the day before. If people are not going, you don't need to go, Gayathri.'

'Let's wait for some time and see.'

After ten minutes, two girls came over. Gayathri's face blossomed. 'They too go to Kilinochchi. They're volunteer teachers. No fear now.'

When the two saw her, they said. 'It's good to see you, Miss. We have a companion now.'

Raghavan felt a little at ease, but he was sorry there was no one else.

It was 5.30 and the dawn was breaking slowly. The minibus came.

'I too will come with you up to town,' he said, and got into the bus with them.

'It's OK, we can go by ourselves. These troubles are new to you. That's why you're afraid. We are used to these troubles. There's nothing to fear.'

'No, Gayathri. I will be happier if I come with you.'

In Jaffna red coloured buses were boarding passengers.

'If you go by the CTB bus, you will be crushed. If there's a minibus, we could find a seat.'

He made her get into a minibus along with the others, and waited outside the window looking at her. He pressed his hand over her hand that was resting on the window pane.

'You will come on Thursday, Gayathri. Won't you?'

She laughed. 'Of course I'll come.'

The bus departed. She waved until she could not make him out any more.

The bus was not as crowded as she had expected. She didn't feel tired as she was seated. She felt enthusiastic and excited about the future, thinking about her husband and the children. 'By this time they would have got out of bed. I don't know how he is going to tackle them.'

The bus stopped at Chavakachcheri and started on its journey after a lot of passengers boarded. It was comforting that several of them were known people. When the bus passed Palai, there were a lot of young men standing on the road.

Then some youth stopped the bus at the Yakachchi junction. 'They are coming round and round in the helicopter. It's not advisable to go now. Watch out and then go later, when the sky is clear.'

The bus stayed in the shade of a tree.

'There are always problems now. People shut themselves up when they see anything. But if there is bombing on one side, people can move about on the other side.' Someone in the bus was speaking at length.

Gayathri was looking out of the window of the bus. If it was some time ago, in such a situation the heart would have frozen with fear. There was no need to fear now.

The bus stayed for half an hour and then started moving. There was a lorry plying before the bus. This gave the driver of the bus some boldness. They were now approaching Elephant Pass.

At a distance she could see the wide curve of the sea, as the bus took a turn. Because of the noise of the bus, one couldn't hear the noise of the helicopter at first. But as the helicopter flew low, a feeling of fear got into her for the first time.

The bus jerked and stopped, the driver undecided whether to drive ahead or stay still.

Gayathri looked around at the women who were travelling with her. They too looked worried as they peered through the windows.

In the opposite direction they could see army men marching through the shrubs in the sprawling white sand.

'The Army is going towards Yakachchi. That's why the helicopter is flying over, to guard them. That's why the boys stopped us.'

Everybody's face was now filled with fear and sorrow.

The bus was slowly crawling along the road.

Suddenly they heard a deafening sound. For a moment Gayathri didn't know what was happening. She couldn't even hear her own voice crying 'Aruma', because she had closed her ears with her hands. She came to know that something had happened to her only when the pain in her whole body registered itself in the veins of her brain. . . .

When she opened her eyes with the greatest difficulty, she couldn't see anything in front except smoke all around. A smell of burning, and of hospitals, filled her nostrils. The cries she heard were the cries of the dying. They cut into her heart. Oh my God, what had happened?

She cried without knowing whether she cried for herself or those around her, or those no longer with her. She couldn't move her hands or her legs. Blood everywhere.

'Amma, Aiyo, Amma—am . . . ma . . . ithu . . . ithu (mother, oh mother, this, this).'

As consciousness ebbed, she saw the hands and face of her husband as he waved at her, and then the faces of her children, sleeping in their bed.

The Water Buffalo

Siri Gunasinghe

My beard on fire
in haste,
I was running, running down in the dawn,
bearing the burdens of life
all on my back;
at the edge of the road, in a large clump of grass,
like a fat merchant sprawled on his easy-chair
I saw you lie.

Both eyes closed;
and at the earth-shattering
battering of my feet
you did not even start.
Ears turned down;
my sky-thundering
lightning-like haste
did not surprise you.

Teeth uncleaned
face unwashed,

Translated by Ranjini Obeyesekere

in the mountain's moist lap
of lush marsh grass
mud splashed:
What if, like you,
I too
could laze?

Tell me my buffalo,
you who can't even stand
yes you, Reverend Sir!
Are you observing rites,
contemplating the impermanence of life,
belching with both eyes closed?

Or do you count beads
with each slow puff
of dilated nostril?

Like eye-flies slowly crawling
from a partly opened flower
are the thoughts that seem to teem
from those faintly twitching eyes;
what secret do they hold?

Head half-lifted up
spit drooling, lips that chap
like a toothless mouth chewing betel
all alone;
a lazy past was yours.

The full weight of earth and sky
bundled in one load
like the wisp of a cotton flake
you bear

on those handsome, upturned horns.
How do you do it
oh buffalo?

You do not know of yesterday
nor have yet come to know today.
Tomorrow you know nothing of.
Undying time alone is yours.
You are my only idol
all in stone.

Rahula Is Born

Ariyawansa Ranaweera

Sleep, search for me not my son so tender
A world full of light, unto you I render

Son, the chamber you sleep in, glitters
While darkness gathers outside

You summon me, even in your sleep, my son
Out here it is dark, and you do not know

Raising your feet so tender one day
You will step into this gloom like me

To light up your way on that day
I go in search of light, son, and do not weep

Sleep, search for me not, my son so tender
A world full of bliss, unto you I render

Translated by E.M.G. Edirisinghe
Prince Siddhartha, before he abandoned his family and wealth to pursue Buddhahood, visited his sleeping son, Rahula, and his wife to bid them a silent goodbye.

Healing the Forest

This section is devoted exclusively to the ethnic war from 1983 onward. It draws its title from a poem by Cheran, included here, that speaks of a Tamil ritual called Kaadaatru (the healing of the forest). It is performed to announce or initiate closure.

In my readings, I found it was often poetry that most brought alive the experience of the war. The passion forced on the language by brevity, the intense focus on a moment, makes poetry a great medium through which a reader can experience the cataclysm of the last thirty years. Further, poetry in the Jaffna Tamil milieu, both at home and in the diaspora, has played an important political role in uniting the community, who gather in large numbers for poetry readings called *kaviatanku*. As Cheran, one of the best-known Tamil poets of our time, puts it, 'In our context, poetry is hardly for silent reading or the sole enjoyment of intellectuals. It must appeal to the common person.' But good poetry also comes at the truth at a 'slant', to quote the poet Emily Dickinson. It does not face it head-on, in all its prosaic starkness, but approaches it from the angle of metaphor and idea and image. This has a paradoxical effect: it softens truth's harshness through the beauty of language, while at the same time leaving an indelible impression of the truth in a reader's mind.

The section opens with a prescient poem by Anne Ranasinghe that was written pre-1983. The next few poems capture the 1983 riots, which formed a watershed in the communal conflict, the war in Sri Lanka being dated from July 1983. These poems are followed by 'The Stealing of a Jeweled Lamp' and 'Whose Child Is This?' which take a look at the 1987–89 JVP insurrection. I have included the second insurrection as part of the civil war because it took place during this period, and its goal was not just to overthrow the ruling classes, but to also get rid of the IPKF and the LTTE. What follows next is a series of poems about individuals who were casualties of the conflict, often because they stood up for what they believed in. This series ends with 'Death at Noon' by Vivimarie Vanderpoorten. The remaining poems look at the war in a very personal way, through the eyes of various individuals, or at a specific moment such as the bombing of the Central Bank in 1996.

Cheran's 'Healing the Forest', the last poem in this section, suggests we are very far from healing. Yet, despite my agreement with the sentiments of the poem, I wanted the anthology to end on a note of grace, without diluting the impact of Cheran's poem. The Epilogue, a poem by Ramya Chamalie Jirasinghe, looks at the beauty of nature and the renewal it can offer.

At What Dark Point

Anne Ranasinghe

Every morning I see him
Sitting in the speckled shade
Of my blossom laden araliya tree
Which I planted many years ago
In my garden, and the branches now
Have spread into our lane.
Under my tree in a shadow of silence
He sits, and with long skeletal hands
Sorts strands from at tangle of juten fibres
And twisting twisting twisting makes a rope
That grows. And grows. Each day.

Every morning I pass him. He sits
In the golden-haze brightness under
The white-velvet fragrance of
My tree. Sits
On the edge of his silence twisting
His lengthening rope and
Watching
Me.

And seeing him sit day after day,
Sinister, silent, twisting his rope
To a future purpose of evilness
I sense the charred-wood smell again,
Stained glass exploding in the flames
(A fireworks of fractured glass
Against the black November sky)
The streets deserted, all doors shut
At twelve o'clock at night,
And running with animal fear
Between high houses shuttered tight
The jackboot ringing hard and clear
While stalking with the lust for blood.

I can still hear
The ironed heel—its echoing thud—
And still can taste the cold-winter-taste
Of charred-wood-midnight-fear.
Knowing
That nothing is impossible
That anything is possible
That there is no safety
In words or houses
That boundaries are theoretical
And love is relative
To the choice before you.

I know
That anything is possible
Any time. There is no safety
In poems or music or even in
Philosophy. No safety
In churches or temples
Of any faith. And no one knows

At what dark point the time will come again
Of blood and knives, terror and pain
Of jackboots and the twisted strand
Of rope.
And the impress of a child's small hand
Paroxysmic mark on an oven wall
Scratched death mark on an oven wall
Is my child's hand.

The poet is a German Jew married to a Sri Lankan. Her family died in concentration camps.

Murder

M.A. Nuhman

Last night
I dreamt
Buddha was shot dead
by the police,
guardians of the law.
His body drenched in blood
on the steps
of the Jaffna library!

Under cover of darkness
came the ministers.
'His name is not on our list,
why did you kill him?'
they ask angrily.

'No sirs, no,
there was no mistake.
Without killing him
it was impossible
to harm even a fly—
Therefore . . . ,' they stammered.

Translated by S. Pathmanathan

'Alright, then
hide the corpse.'
The ministers return.

The men in civvies
dragged the corpse
into the library.
They heaped the books
ninety thousand in all,
and lit the pyre
with the Cikalokavadda Sutta.
Thus the remains
of the Compassionate One
were burned to ashes
along with the Dhammapada.

The Jaffna Public Library was burnt down in 1981 by the police and government-sponsored militia. It was one of the biggest in Asia, containing 90,000 books, including many irreplaceable manuscripts, that were all lost in the fire.

Yet Another Incident in July 1983

Basil Fernando

Burying the dead
being an art well developed in our times
(our psycho-analysts have helped us much
to keep balanced minds—whatever
that may mean)
there is no reason really
for this matter to remain so vivid
as if some rare occurrence. I assure you

I am not sentimental, never having
had a 'break down' as they say.
I am as shy of my emotions
As you are. And I attend to my daily
tasks in a very matter of fact way.
Being prudent too, when a government says 'Forget'
I act accordingly. My ability to forget
has never been doubted, never
having had any adverse comments

on that score either. Yet I remember
the way they stopped that car,
the mob. There were four

in that car, a girl, a boy
(between four and five it seemed) and their
parents—I guessed—the man and the woman.
It was in the same way they stopped other cars.
I did not notice any marked

difference. A few questions
in gay mood, not to make a mistake
I suppose, then they proceeded to
action, by then routine. Pouring
petrol and all that stuff.
Then someone, noticing something odd
as it were, opened the two left side
doors, took away the two children, crying and resisting
as they were moved away from their parents.

Children's emotions have sometimes
to be ignored for their own good, the guy must have
thought. Someone practical
was quick, lighting a match
efficiently. An instant
fire followed, adding one more
to many around. Around
the fire they chattered
of some new adventure. A few

scattered. What the two inside
felt or thought was no matter.
Peace loving people were hurrying
towards homes as in a procession. . . .
Then suddenly the man inside
breaking open the door was
out, his shirt already on
fire and hair too. Then bending,

took his two children. Not even
looking around as if executing a calculated
decision, he resolutely
re-entered the car.
Once inside, he closed the door
himself . . . I heard the noise
distinctly.

Still the ruined car
is there, by the road-side
with other such things. Maybe
the Municipality will remove it
one of these days
to the Capital's
garbage pit. The cleanliness of the Capital
receives Authority's top priority.

Big Match, 1983

Yasmine Gooneratne

Glimpsing the headlines in the newspapers,
tourists scuttle for cover, cancel their options
on rooms with views of temple and holy mountain.
'Flash point in Paradise.' 'Racial pot boils over.'
And even the gone away boy
who had hoped to find lost roots, lost lovers,
lost talent even, out among the palms,
makes timely return giving thanks
that Toronto is quite romantic enough
for his purposes.

Powerless this time to shelter or to share
we strive to be objective, try to trace
the match that lit this sacrificial fire.
the steps by which we reached this ravaged place.
We talk of 'Forty Eight 'and 'Fifty Six',
of freedom and the treacherous politics
of language; see the first sparks of this hate
fanned into flame in Nineteen Fifty Eight,
yet find no comfort in our neat solution,
no calm abstraction, and no absolution.
The game's in other hands in any case.

These fires ring factory, and hovel,
and Big Match fever, flaring high and fast,
has both sides in its grip and promises
dizzier scores than any at the oval.

In a tall house dim with old books and pictures
calm hands quiet the clamoring telephone.
'It's a strange life we're leading here just now,
not a dull moment. No one can complain
of boredom, that's for sure. Up all night keeping watch,
and then as curfew ends and your brave lads
dash out at dawn to start another day
of fun, and games, and general jollity,
I send Padmini and the girls to a neighbor's house.

Who, me?—Oh I'm doing fine. I always was
a drinking man you know and nowadays
I'm stepping up my intake quite a bit,
the general idea being that when those torches
come within fifty feet of this house don't you see
it won't be my books that go up first, but me.'

A pause. Then, steady and every bit as clear
as though we are neighbors still as we had been
In Fifty Eight. 'Thanks, by the way for ringing.
There's nothing you can do to help us but
it's good to know some lines haven't yet been cut.'

Out of the palmyra fences of Jaffna
bristle a hundred guns.
Shopfronts in the Pettah, landmarks of our childhood
Curl like old photographs in the flames.
Blood on their khaki uniforms, three boys lie dying;
a crowd looks silently the other way.

Near the wheels of his smashed bicycle
at the corner of Duplication Road a child lies dead
and two policemen look the other way
as a stout man, sweating with fear, falls to his knees
beneath a bo-tree in a shower of sticks and stones
flung by his neighbor's hands.

The joys of childhood, friendships of our youth
ravaged by pieties and politics,
screaming across our screens, her agony
at last exposed, Sri Lanka burns alive.

In the Month of July

Jean Arasanayagam

Childhood is far away
beneath a tree
playing with pebbles
skillfully tossing them from
back of hand
to palm
requiring a certain skill and
magical ritualistic incantations.

As one grows older
the pebbles grow too
into great stones and
rocks hurled with violence
smashed skulls spilled brains
splattering the pavements.

In the month of July
a man fled from his pursuers
he climbed a tree

the mob aimed stones at him
until they got him down
probably fell off, his grasp loosened
slippery with blood, his body already battered
and then they trampled him to death.

The Stealing of a Jeweled Lamp

Buddhadasa Galappatty

Comrades, I need an answer
As to why you killed my husband
When he broke your law, the Law of Darkness
When you forbade the lighting of lamps
To make your point

He is not guilty
He obeyed your law
It was me
Who made him break it

For the offence
Of lighting a lamp
You have put out the lamp
That brought light to my household

It was not he who wanted it lit
But I, to quieten my little son
Who feared the darkness

Translated by Malini Govinnage

I
Asked him to light the lamp

Where is your justice?
Why could you not find out
The reason he broke your law
Before you put out the lamp of my life?

During the second JVP insurrection, the insurgents would order curfews or blackouts with severe punishments for those who disobeyed.

Whose Child Is This?
(From *Nischalai Ratriya*)

Buddhadasa Galappatty

From what distance comes he floating
For what reason does he float?
Though I do not know the reason
It is a fact that he does float.

Woken by the rising sun,
Running quick to the river's edge
The mind, startled as never before
Encounters something never seen before.

Did they abduct him at dead of night?
Kill him after sadistic tortures
Tie his hands and pluck his eyes out
Dump his corpse into the water?

From what distance comes he floating?
For what reason does he float?
Who is left to tell about it
Who is there to listen to it?

Translated by Ranjini Obeyesekere

Stand back. Prod it with a stick
Prod and free it from the bank
Instantly a sharp pain pricks
But how or who am I to claim it?

Now again the river claims it
Once again it floats on down
Shelters at the river's edge
And yet again is prodded out.

No one's come to claim this child
Yet somewhere a mother grieves
Hopes to see his face before she dies
Lives on in that dream.

During the youth insurgencies of 1971 and again in 1989 bodies of young men and women were often found floating down rivers—abducted, tortured or killed by the army and paramilitary forces.

Lines for Richard

Alfreda de Silva

The dreams of many seasons were
woven in your short summer's warp and weft.
The stage that you adorned
is now bereft.

Still in the quiet of that hall
one hears the haunting resonance of your voice,
that brought to life this character
and that in solo theatre.
Children's laughter pealed with wild delight
as they pranced with you through Kipling's jungle land
and youth sat marveling
when you peopled an evening
with the world that Dickens wrote about.

Then again, in different
vein, there were the plays
where you explored some inner dark,
and an audience went
reliving their own lives
in the tragic roles
you made so real.

Yet, for all that restless
energy and camaraderie,
there was in you a stillness
and a transience
and like the dragon-fly
that basks in sunlight a little while
spreading its brilliant wings
for all to wonder at and gaze upon.
one moment you were here, and the next gone.

Richard de Zoysa was a poet, actor, journalist and human rights activist. He was abducted from his home and murdered by, it is widely believed, a death squad formed by members of the government to crush the JVP.

Elegy for Neelan Tiruchelvam

Indran Amirthanayagam

I walked that street as a child, under the mango trees,
Smelling the bushes of white flowers gathered for temples,
My tongue a sweet shop furnished by my grandmother,
Crushed with chilies in coconut fed by her servant,

I belonged to that elite the columnists liked
To attack, for its insularity, its absolute divorce
From the fratricidal reality, there on the corner
Of Rosmead Place and Kynsey Road he died.

I did not know him well, he belonged to that group
Seen from afar fighting so that its fellow citizens
Enjoy a little more of their human rights, someone
Who had a solid knowledge of the recent history

Of peacemakers in other countries who thought
That one can live with dignity, without bothering
A fly, that suddenly the human world would improve
Because of the sweat of writing new and just laws.

He exploded on the corner of Rosmead and Kynsey,
Fell with all of his blood, his ambition, to the end
That waited for him, that named him with another fame,
One more of the human beings who denied

That the nighmare could touch him, as if he had
Some immunity against the barbarians, that letters
Written in laws had the power to absorb
A bullet, to convert its powder into a flower,

Mr. Tiruchelvam, I'll wait for you with a bouquet
Of flowers, all the cars are bottled up, there is no exit,
The corner is the crossing point, destiny, the morning,
You are fifty-five years old, rich, famous

There are other great figures in the country, models
Throughout all the world, we are not going to be sad,
We will push forward, put your name on the lintel
Of a school, the signboard of a street, in the memoirs

Published by the civil cells you founded
So that the country can have places of reflection
Far from the crossing points, the shouting
In congress, the beating in jails, the melancholy

That can bury everybody until the sun rises,
Until its children rise, until the mangos ripen,
Until the crushed chilies return to the tongue,
Even if you are far away on the shore

Of an unknown land, that you write in another
Language to make of this murder an image,
A teaching, so that you can recount these streets,
Rosmead and Kynsey that observed your play,

That now have another meaning, names of a cemetery.

Dr Neelan Tiruchelvam was assassinated by an LTTE suicide bomber in July 1999. He was a Tamil politician who advocated a negotiated settlement to the ethnic conflict, and a critic of the LTTE. Before his assassination, he worked with his friend, President Chandrika Kumaratunga, on a devolution package which he hoped would address the needs of the Tamils.

Krishanthy

Vinothini

Her death occurred
when birds sang
and the sun fell into the sea
at the open space of white sand
without anyone knowing

When she was born as a female child
neither she, nor her mother, could have thought
of such an end

Their looks first pierced her like thorns
then their terrible hands held her arms

Voices were not raised as she fainted
and they raped her senseless body
It happened at the open space of white sand
and they buried her
at the edge of the salty cremation ground

Translated by M.A. Nuhman

When she was born
she would not have thought of such an end

Krishanthy Kumaraswamy was gang-raped and murdered in August 1996 by six Sri Lankan Army soldiers, as she was returning home from school, after sitting her A-Level examination. She became a symbol of the atrocities committed by the Sri Lankan Army against Tamils and Tamil women in particular. The six soldiers were sentenced to death by the Sri Lankan courts.

Death at Noon

for Lasantha

Vivimarie Vanderpoorten

Today dawned
Like any other morning

At the other end of the world
My sister sits nursing a cup of coffee
Her fingers numb
From minus twenty
Mind numb with shock.

Here, I drive to work
Still swear under my breath
at the driver of the truck
that cut into my lane
nearly killing me,
Plan my day
Tick off the list of things to be done:
A listening test to be recorded
A lecture to prepare for
A report to write
A professor to be contacted

Before lunch.
But more than four of my colleagues
Are in black and white
And I realise that includes me.
We stand around the
Water filter
Discussing 'heroism'.
And no one is in a mood to work today
Even those joyous about captured
Territory.

Maybe we are numb too
Though it's warm
and all we have today
is a cloudy sky.

Lasantha Wickrematunge was editor of the *Sunday Leader* and was very critical of the government. He was assassinated in January 2009. In an editorial Wickrematunge wrote shortly before his death, which was published posthumously, he stated, 'When finally I am killed, it will be the government that kills me.' His killer remains unidentified.

A Soldier's Wife Weeps

Kamala Wijeratne

Last Saturday when you went back from leave
I watched until you disappeared over the bend
and long after, until my breast gave a great heave,
and lit the lamp before the Buddha and prayed no end.

On Wednesday when the crow cried on the dead branch
and the sky coloured over with the colour of charcoal
I had no fears, I knew you were safe
I had your horoscope read and there were no malefics

But on Thursday when they bore you home
I did not know what to believe, what to think
it was as if I had slept a long sleep
and saw things in a haze between life and death.

Was it on Saturday that we bathed together at the village well
and you boy-like threw stones at the sneering frogs
and drank deeply of the scent of the giant palm
that had ominously broken in splendrous fragrant flower?

Looking back now I seem to see things I never saw before
the way you hung behind me and touched my hair
the way you leaned against the door
and watched me as I bustled about.

They gave you a hero's burial
with all military honours
the band played
and your body passed from hand to hand

I saw everything from inside a mist
the drone of voices like a plane
making its uncertain way through the clouds.
I think they spoke of the way of life and death.

I think of the bare, barren years
stretching like a road swaying through a desert
and wonder how to preoccupy myself
how to make the days go forward.

On weekends when I have nothing to do
I spread the white wedding sari on the floor
and contemplate how I stood on the poruwa with you
shyly tying the piece of white cloth around my waist.

How wrong the horoscope readers were . . .

Oppressed by Nights of War

Sivaramani

Oppressed
by nights of war
our children
become adults

Across the pathways
of their bright fledgling mornings
faceless and bloodied corpses are flung
their quick laughter
is shattered by crumbling walls
and our little ones are children no longer

Even the faint sound of a lone gun
shattering the silence of a starry night
destroys forever
what children's stories tell

In these foreshortened days
they have long forgotten
to play hopscotch
to make carts from palm-fruit shells

Translated by Lakshmi Holmström

Now they only learn to shut the gate in time
to listen when dogs bark strangely
never to ask questions
to be silent when they get no reply

These they have learnt like dumb animals
they pluck away
the wings of dragonflies
they shoulder sticks for guns
their friends become their foes

Oppressed by nights of war
our children have grown up

Our Folks Are Not Ungrateful

Puthuvai Ratnathurai

The Nallur festival has ended,
even the wind has departed,
leaving the temple street desolate;
twenty-five days of joy,
still fresh in the heart,
with longing eyes, some youth
still wander to see the chariot;
only those who have seen,
would know the pangs
of missing those sparkling eyes;
the different chariots,
now all inside;
the chariot enclosed,
its golden tip hidden
until next year;
the Navalar hall padlocked;
on West street
Muthu Vinayagar remains silent,
a single wick burns inside;

Translated by Chelva Kanaganayakam

at the entrance
of Manonmani temple,
a few stragglers, me
and some dogs;
from where did the crowds gather?
like an empty sea,
where did they disappear?
The crowds on temple street
are beautiful;
thousands around me,
proclaiming,
I am not alone,
a source of joy.
Without seeing the chariot,
the marriage of the gods,
who stood guard at the gates?
while the silk-dressed anklets
came here,
who stood awaiting the enemies?
Like saints free of desire
who stood there to protect?
Those who came to the festival
their possessions locked,
their keys intact, to
whom did they entrust their land?
Unwashed faces and dishevelled hair
these border gods with guns
stood guard;
with scythes stood some others;
Did the silk dresses at the festival,
pray for them too?

Sure they did,
our folks are not ungrateful.

The poet was the official bard of the LTTE. For historical interest, I would have liked to include some of his more polemical poems, but none of those have been translated yet. This poem comes closest to expressing a political opinion.

The Worship-Scar

S. Vilvaratnam

When my friend introduced his father
casually I asked about the scar
to be told it was the worship-scar

The old man stroked his forehead as he spoke
his eyes lighting up
And I bit my tongue
in grief for my ignorance

Calling for Allah
he had bowed until
his native soil had scarred his bowed forehead

And I wondered at my impudence
that had dared chase them away from the soil of their birth
as though I had struck their worship-scarred foreheads
with a hammer?
How thus could I injure myself?

Their worship-scars seared
the guilt-stricken scar of my conscience

Translated by A.J. Canagaratna

Like the third eye
they grilled and drilled my scars from the battle-field too
When, but when, will my scar disappear?
When will my crime
violating the beauty of the soil
that is etched on their foreheads
Be expiated?

If ever from exile
they return home
and full-throatedly
call for Allah
and renew their worship-scars
stroking their foreheads on the soil of their land
the tears dammed up for years and years
will burst the dykes of my eyes
only if I might immerse myself
in that cleansing cataract
will my blemish
recorded by history
be washed clean

That moment alone
will consummate my liberat
ion.
Friend, I have entreated Allah myself
to hasten
that sweet moment of reconciliation.

In 1990, the LTTE, in an act of ethnic cleansing, expelled the Muslim population of 72,000 from the North, because of the refusal of the Muslim leadership to support the LTTE's goals. Also, the creation of a government-sponsored Muslim Home Guard had led to violence between the Muslims and the Tamils.

Nowadays

Shanmugam Sivalingam

Nowadays
cats, at all times,
carry their young in their mouths
prowling through
narrow deserted streets.

Hornets, nowadays,
no longer build against house walls
plastering their nests with clay.
Close to the forest,
they seal their rocky crannies
with molten lead.

Even the weaver bird
these days
broods over its eggs
in holes underground.

Because . . . forgive us
let these at least
survive.

Translated by Lakshmi Holmström

Explosion

Vivimarie Vanderpoorten

On the day the truckload
of explosives
drove into the central bank,
for a long second
time staggered
All sounds of a workday morning
in the city
even the cawing of the crows
merged into a solitary
Boom
Prism of fire and fury

Lives ended
eyes were blinded
retired wage earners
collecting provident funds
were crushed
under brick and glass
the nearby vegetable seller's
hands were severed
like cucumbers,

Women in sari
held their eyeballs in their palms
and blood spattered
the streets,
erasing memory.

Out of the broken window
of a damaged car—
dead driver—
the radio blared, unscathed
on a commercial break
a man's pleasant voice
announced
that big or small, insurance
protects them all.

The Central Bank bombing by the LTTE took place in January 1996.

A Return

Avvai

When he came back to me
His heart had turned to iron
His brain was a gun
His friend, his foe
I was caught off my guard
By love
And other affections disappeared

He had shot his friend
And spoke of bravery
Of sacrifice and weapons
Of killing people on the other side

I was silent, forgetting entirely
About humankind
About liberty

But now I know

I cannot any longer be a mother

Translated by K.S. Sivakumaran

Won't he one day
Believe me to be his enemy
And bury me too?

A Poet's Fearless Death

Puthuvai Ratnathurai

If I am not stricken by disease
or felled by enemies,
if I do not perish by these,
I will thrive even in old age;
my poems
will give me the strength of youth.
To walk apace
to swing my arms
bend to pick up a grain of earth;
if I have the strength
I will ascend and fly,
with the courage to face death;
I will love life
as roots with flowers
and flowers with roots, I will live.
With my poems
I will be born again,
alongside those
fighting injustice
I will blossom;
I will not grow old

Translated by Chelva Kanaganayakam

not be infirm;
my poems will prevent my death.
When the final lines of
my life are written,
do not come close to me;
in the light of a small lamp
a face is all that is needed.
When I was born,
when I was poor
I was alone;
When I give myself to death
I want to be alone;
The sound of Death
ringing in my ears won't agitate me,
I will welcome death;
a mat to lie down
a little water to quench my thirst,
my song in my ears
that is enough,
I will depart.
My body frozen,
when I am a corpse,
do not despair;
when my body lies at home;
sing my songs,
read my poems aloud,
be at peace;
I came
lived
and left;
no, I did my best

The poet is one of the disappeared in the last phase of the war in 2009.

Healing the Forest

Cheran

To heal a still
smoldering land,
we went;
no bird in sight.

An empty sky
above the sparrow-flying
earth.

An ash-covered landless earth
to the edge of that wide expanse;
here, no one knows
how to gather bones.

Yet,

Our libation of milk
the relentless
welling of tears
now mocked with glee

Translated by Chelva Kanaganayakam

with dance and song
by an estranged foe;
what then is the
way ahead?

To cool the burning heart
there is nothing today.

No witness
for the drop of blood
still not dry.

To claim closure
to dissolve ashes in the sea
to scatter in the air
to close one's eyes,
there is no air
there is no sea
there is no way
to heal the forest.

Part of the Kaadaatru ritual involves collecting the remaining bones of the dead relative at the cremation grounds. They are placed in a human shape and milk poured on them.

Epilogue

The Moon at Seenukgala

Ramya Chamalie Jirasinghe

We followed a footpath fading like old ink
on an ancient map
through a crowded forest of trees straining
up, sun-searching;
branches, boughs, pushing leaves lightwards.
Birds, dumbstruck by the morning-dusk
of this shade,
flew noteless from nest to fruit to open mouth.
Butterflies rose from the ground like
crystallised dust
settling, clustered, helter-skelter everywhere.
The forest, all wilderness,
drank our walking sounds and turned footsteps
into leaf-mulch thuds, cracking dry vines
back into earth fodder, when suddenly
it stopped.
The forest pulled its denseness behind us and
pushed us on
to open land, dry grass, where a river thundered
somewhere
everywhere ahead of us.

We stood, shielding ourselves,
sun-shocked-sound-struck.

The river, mad, impatient drove over its bed, a half
bared back, a skinless spine of disparate boulders.
We stepped across this humped liquid ground,
like mariners navigating through exposed icebergs,
but this was tropical journeying,
beneath us the water foamed, plunged, fell,
and unexpectedly, pooled completely still
within a ring of stones.

Night came as suddenly as we had upon the river.
Above us, a full moon touched our heads
and a Scorpio twisted its stingless tail northwards,
pointing us to places we no longer sought.
Someone stoked a small fire and wood-smoke
filled the crystal air, a thin strand, rising
like the desperate signal of the lost traveller.

We stepped into the still water
surrounded by a river
determined to leave as we shuddered,
shocked by the discovery that our roots
grow lush, full, tunnel deep into the Earth's core
at times and places like these.
Every road ever travelled,
every timeless quest for gold, ambrosia,
love, ends here, where our skins become
the scales of fish, our bones crisp boughs of
driftwood, our hair our teeth,
every element every tree every water and every stone.

Knowing we had to return to
where we had come from,
we reached up, plucked out the moon and
put it into our pockets.

Each day, now, as we grope our way through cities
of wide tarred roads,
name-boards marked indelibly,
directions signposted,
we pull out this moon, a white-disk compass,
hold it to our ears and listen to
the sound of the river rushing home,
or twist it, a dial on our palm,
and watch the wood-smoke tumble out,
and singing, laughing, throw this moon back up
into the sky,
and watch the water crash through
every concrete building;
washing our hardened walls,
filling our closed rooms
with lunar rivers boulder forests liquid fires.

This, is the way home.

About the Contributors

Writers

Avvai comes from a distinguished family of poets. She is the daughter of Mahakavi and the sister of Cheran. An anthology of her poems, *Ellai Kadatthal*, appeared in 2000. Some of her plays won national awards in Sri Lanka.

Liyanage Amarakeerthi is a fiction writer, poet and a literary critic, working primarily in Sinhala, with six collections of short stories, three novels and one collection of poems to his credit. 'The Hour When the Moon Weeps' is taken from his 1992 book *Rala* (The Waves), his second book of stories.

Indran Amirthanayagam is a poet, essayist and blogger in English, Spanish, French and Portuguese (http://indranamirthanayagam.blogspot.com). He has published nine poetry collections thus far, including *The Elephants of Reckoning* which won the 1994 Paterson Prize in the US.

Jean Arasanayagam is of Dutch Burgher origin. Married to a Tamil, her poetry and prose often address the ethnic, religious and political turmoil in Sri Lanka. She has published twenty-four collections of poetry, eleven of fiction and a collection of three plays.

Thamaraichelvi worked as a teacher in the Vanni district of the Northern Province of Sri Lanka. Over three decades she has published eight books, including two collections of short stories. In 1993, her novel *Thakam* won an award for best novel of the year.

R. Cheran is one of the best-loved and most influential of Tamil poets in Sri Lanka. Son of the poet Mahakavi, Cheran published his first collection of poetry in 1982 and has published eight collections to date, as well as numerous essays and articles. *In a Time of Burning, You Cannot Turn Away* and *A Second Sunrise* are all collections of his work translated into English.

Michelle de Kretser was born in Sri Lanka and emigrated to Australia when she was fourteen. Her novel *The Hamilton Case* won the Commonwealth Prize (South East Asia and Pacific region) and the UK Encore Prize. *The Lost Dog* won the 2008 New South Wales Premier's Book of the Year Award and was longlisted for the Man Booker Prize and the Orange Prize. Her latest novel, *Questions of Travel*, won the prestigious Miles Franklin Literary Award.

Alfreda de Silva wrote both poetry and prose. Her collections of poetry include *Out of the Dark, the Sun* and *Unpredictable Blood*, as well as a collection of poems for children. She worked as a teacher, freelance journalist, broadcaster and script writer for television.

Nihal de Silva's first book, *The Road from Elephant Pass*, won the Gratiaen Prize as well as the State Literary Award for best novel in 2003. It was also longlisted for the International IMPAC Dublin Literary Award and was made into a popular film in 2008. His other works include *The Ginirälla Conspiracy*. He was killed by a landmine explosion at the Wilpattu National Park.

Wimal Dissanayake is a national award–winning poet and literary critic. He has published seven volumes of poetry in Sinhala. His English poems have been published in several prestigious journals including *Cambridge Review*. He currently teaches at the University of Hawaii and is an honorary professor at the Open University of Hong Kong.

Basil Fernando is a lawyer who worked as a senior UN officer and is a well-known advocate of human rights. He published his first anthology of English poetry in 1972, and thereafter published several English and Sinhala anthologies.

Chitra Fernando was born in Sri Lanka and moved to Australia in the 1960s where she taught English and linguistics as a senior lecturer at Macquarie University. She is the author of several collections of stories for children and two collections for adults, *Three Women* and *Between Worlds*. Her novel *Cousins* was published after her death in 1998.

Patrick Fernando studied Western Classics at the University of Ceylon and worked for the Income Tax Department of the government. His first collection of poems, *The Return of Ulysses and other Poems* was published in the UK. His second collection, *Selected Poems*, was published posthumously by Oxford University Press, New Delhi.

Vijita Fernando is one of Sri Lanka's best-known translators working from Sinhala to English. She has been awarded the Gratiaen Prize, the Ian Goonetilleke Prize and six state literary awards for her translations. She is also a writer in English and has published two collections of short stories, *Eleven Stories* and *Once on a Mountainside*, as well as a novel titled *Somewhere*.

Ashok Ferrey's first collection of short stories, *Colpetty People*, was shortlisted for the Gratiaen Prize and remains a top-selling book in English in Sri Lanka. His other works are *The Good Little Ceylonese Girl*, *Serendipity* and *Love in the Tsunami*, a collection of short stories. His latest novel, *The Professional*, was published by Random House India.

Buddhadasa Galappatty has published eight volumes of poetry and two collections of short stories in Sinhala. He won the Best Poet of the Year Award 1999 at the State Literary Festival for his collection of poetry *Thuruliya Akuru Viya*. Some of his poetry has been translated into English.

Vimala Ganeshananthan, a medical doctor, found her mother's writings in a few school exercise books. Her book *The Yaal Players: Memories of Old Jaffna* combines her mother's writings with her mother's recounting of many events in her life, and the history of Jaffna.

V.V. Ganeshananthan's first novel, *Love Marriage*, was longlisted for the Orange Prize and named one of Washington Post Book World's Best of 2008, as well as a Barnes & Noble Discover Great New Writers pick. She teaches creative writing at the University of Michigan.

Yasmine Gooneratne has won acclaim as a critic and author, and has written volumes of literary essays as well as poems, short stories, a family memoir and three novels. *The Sweet and Simple Kind*, her latest novel, was shortlisted for the 2007 Commonwealth Writers' Prize and nominated for the 2008 International IMPAC Dublin Literary Award.

Sunil Govinnage is a bilingual poet and author, now domiciled in Australia, where he works as a civil servant. He has been writing poetry in Sinhala since 1965, and in English since 1989. Govinnage's first volume of English poetry, entitled *White Mask: A Collection of New Australian Poetry*, was published in 2004.

Siri Gunasinghe is an award-winning Sri Lankan poet, novelist, art historian and film-maker who helped pioneer the free-verse tradition in Sinhala poetry. Two anthologies of his poems have been translated into English under the titles *Beyond Words* and *Sepalika*.

Romesh Gunesekera is the author of seven books. His first novel, *Reef*, was shortlisted for the Guardian Fiction Prize and the Booker Prize, and won the Yorkshire Post Best First Work Award and the Italian Premio Mondello Five Continents Prize. His latest novel is *Noontide Toll*.

Ashley Halpe taught at the University of Peradeniya lecturing in English literature. He is the recipient of the French government's Chevalier de l'Ordre des Palmes Académiques, and the author of three volumes of poetry including *Homing*. He has also translated several works of Sinhala literature into English, including Martin Wickramasinghe's *Viragaya* and *Madol Doova*.

Ameena Hussein is a co-founder of the Perera Hussein Publishing House which has established itself as the front runner for cutting edge Sri Lankan fiction. Her work *The Moon in the Water* was longlisted for the Man Asian Literary Prize and the International IMPAC Dublin Literary Award. Her first short-story collection, *Fifteen*, was shortlisted for the Gratiaen Prize in 1999.

V.I.S. Jayapalan has been writing poetry for over three decades and is a well-known Tamil poet from Sri Lanka. He has also written short stories and two short novels. His poems have been translated into several languages including English, German and Sinhalese. He took to acting in 2011 and played a major role in the Tamil film *Aadukalam*. He won an award at the 58th National Film Awards for his acting. He lives in Norway.

Ramya Chamalie Jirasinghe is the author of *Rhythm of the Sea*, a book on the Asian tsunami, and *Trinity*. Her book of poetry, *There's an Island in the Bone*, won the State Literary Joint-Award for Poetry in 2011. She was longlisted for the Fish Poetry Prize of Ireland in 2011 and was a joint runner-up to the UK Guardian Orange First Words Contest of 2009.

Shehan Karunatilaka's novel *Chinaman: The Legend of Pradeep Mathew* was published to great acclaim internationally. It won the overall Commonwealth Book Prize in 2012, as well as the DSC Prize for South Asian Literature in the same year. It also won the 2008 Gratiaen Prize.

U. Karunatilake, a graduate of science from the University of Ceylon, worked in the pharmaceutical industry. His collections include *Colombo Diary*, *Kandy Revisited* and *Testament in Autumn*. His *Kundasale Love Poems* is about the death of his beloved wife, a loss he struggled to come to terms with.

Isankya Kodithuwakku is a graduate of Kenyon College and Columbia University. Her first book, *The Banana Tree Crisis*, was published in 2006 and won the Gratiaen Prize and the State Literary Award. She is currently at work on a novel.

Parakrama Kodituwakku, recipient of Sri Lanka's prestigious Kala Suri honour, is a notable Sinhala poet and was one of the foremost among a group of poets who led a revival of and experimentations in Sinhala poetry from the 1950s to the 1970s. His books include *Podi Malliye*, *Otunna Himi Kumaraya*, *Rashmi: Bhava Kawya*, *Alut Minihek Avit* and *Rosa Male Hadawatha*.

Mahakavi was the pen name for T. Rudramoorthy, who was born in Alaveddy, Jaffna. One of the pioneers of modern Tamil poetry in Sri Lanka, he introduced the rhythms of ordinary speech into his poems. In addition to his poetry, he wrote five epics, three stage plays in verse and ten radio plays.

Carl Muller is best known for his trilogy about the Burghers of Sri Lanka, who are descendants of the Dutch and Portuguese colonizers: *The Jam Fruit Tree*, *Yakada Yaka* and *Once Upon a Tender Time*. He won the Gratiaen Prize for *The Jam Fruit Tree* and a State Literary Award for his historical novel *Children of the Lion*.

Nayomi Munaweera is a Sri Lankan–American author. Her debut novel, *Island of a Thousand Mirrors*, was longlisted for the Man Asian Literary Prize, shortlisted for the DSC Prize for South Asian Literature and won the Commonwealth Prize for Asia. It will be released internationally by St Martin's Press. She is at work on her second novel.

Appadurai Muttulingam writes in Tamil and has published eight short-story collections, among other works. He has won numerous awards including the Tamil Nadu Government first prize for the book *Vamsa Viruthi* and the Sri Lanka Government Sahitya Academy Award. A selection of his short stories was translated in English under the title *Inauspicious Times* in 2008.

M.A. Nuhman was born in Kalmunai, Eastern Province, Sri Lanka. He is a professor of Tamil at the University of Peradeniya. He is a poet, translator and critic and is the author of several critical works and a book of Tamil translations of Palestinian poetry. His own collections of poetry include *Thaatthaamaarum Perarkalum*, *Azhiyaa Nizhalgal* and *Mazhai Naatkal Varum*.

Michael Ondaatje is the author of six novels, a memoir, a non-fiction book on cinema and several books of poetry. *The English Patient* won the Booker Prize; *Anil's Ghost* won the Irish Times International Fiction Prize, the Giller Prize, and the Prix Médicis. His newest book is *The Cat's Table.* Born in Sri Lanka, he now lives in Toronto.

S.D.V. Perera is the author of *A Schoolteacher's Odyssey, Memoir of a Teaching Career*. His stories have also appeared in *Channels* magazine and *Navasilu*. He received an honorary degree in geography at the London School of Economics and taught in Sri Lanka, the UK, Ghana and Tasmania for many years before retiring.

Puthuvai Ratnathurai published his first collection of writings in 1970 and since then published six collections of poems. Closely allied with the LTTE, he was their official bard and head of the LTTE Cultural and Arts Department. He is one of the disappeared during the final phase of the war in 2009.

N.S.M. Ramaiah was born in Badulla in the hill country of Sri Lanka and his work addresses the lives and struggles of Indian Tamil workers on tea estates—former indentured labourers who continue to function in dismal work and living conditions. His collection of short stories *Oru Koodai Kolunthu* (A Basketful of Tea Leaves) won the Sahitya Academy Award in 1980.

N.K. Ragunathan is one of the pioneering members of the Progressive Writers of Sri Lanka. His first collection of writings, *Nilavile Pesuvom*, was published in 1962 and his second collection, *Thasamankalam*, in 1996. He is also renowned for his play *Kandan Karunai*, based on the traditions of folk theatre.

Anne Ranasinghe escaped from Nazi Germany to England, married a Sri Lankan professor and became a citizen of Sri Lanka in 1956. The Holocaust is a recurring theme in her poetry and is contrasted with Sri Lanka's violent history. Her collections include *At What Dark Point* and *Not Even Shadows*. Her works have been published in seventeen countries and translated into nine languages.

Ariyawansa Ranaweera is a prolific poet, with over twenty titles to his credit. He has also translated many foreign writers into Sinhala. He is highly acclaimed for his deft and simple use of language and his ability to obtain from ordinary landscapes—considered unlikely to yield or inspire poetry—thoughts and lines that are startling, revealing facets of eternal truths.

Ayathurai Santhan published a novel, three collections of short stories and a collection of poems in English, as well as sixteen books in Tamil. Among his work are *The Sparks*, *In Their Own Worlds*, *The Northern Front*, *Survival*, *Simple Things* and *The Whirlwind*. He won the Sri Lankan State Literary Award twice, for his work in English (2000) and in Tamil (1975).

Shanmugam Sivalingam was born in Pandriuppu in the Eastern Province of Sri Lanka. He is considered one of Sri Lanka's major Tamil poets and short-story writers. A collection of his most important poems was published in 1988 under the title *Niir Valaiyangal*. His second collection of poems, *Citaintupona Thecamum Thoornthupona Manakkukaiyum*, was published in 2010.

Regi Siriwardena was a well-known novelist, translator, critic, teacher, playwright and film script writer. His translations of Sinhala poetry and fiction appeared in several journals in Sri Lanka and abroad. He published several collections of poems, including *Waiting for the Soldier, To the Muse of Insomnia, Poems and Selected Translations* and *The Pure Water of Poetry*.

S. Sivaramani was well known for her political and feminist poems, and was one of the founding members of the Women's Study Circle in Jaffna. She graduated from the University of Jaffna where she studied English and drama. A collection of her poems, *Sivaramani Kavithaigal*, was published in Sri Lanka, India and Canada. She committed suicide in 1991.

Ajit Tilakasena has published seventeen books to date, included in which are two volumes of concrete poetry and nine volumes of short stories. He is one of the pioneers of modern Sinhala literature, using the grammar of spoken Sinhalese without descending into colloquialism. A collection of his stories was translated into English under the title *The Pilgrimage*.

Vivimarie Vanderpoorten is an academic and a poet, educated in Sri Lanka and the UK. She has two volumes of published poetry, *Nothing Prepares You* (2007) and *Stitch Your Eyelids Shut* (2010). Her first book won the country's prestigious Gratiaen Prize. She currently teaches English linguistics, language and literature at a Sri Lankan state university.

C.V. Velupillai wrote poignantly about the plight of the Tamil estate workers who laboured in the tea estates of Sri Lanka, drawing attention to the legislation that deprived many of them of citizenship. His collection *Born to Labour* was a compilation of several of his works that appeared in various newspapers in India and Sri Lanka.

S. Vilvaratnam was born in Pungudutivu in the Northern Province. He began writing in the 1970s and came into prominence in the 1980s. His collections of poetry include *Akangalum Mukangalum* and *Nettriman*.

Vinothini was born in Jaffna. Her poetry deals with love, war and the sorrow and frustrations of our times. Her collection *Muhamoodi Seipavan* (The Maker of Masks) was published in India.

Lakdasa Wikkramasinha was a bilingual poet whose interest in Sinhala literature led him to experiment with fusing Western and South Asian traditions in his work. He was considered one of Sri Lanka's finest poets writing in English, whose career was cut short by drowning at sea. His collections include *Lustre, Fifteen Poems, O Regal Blood* and *The Grasshopper Gleaming*.

Martin Wickramasinghe is one of Sri Lanka's most beloved writers, a pioneer of modern Sri Lankan writing in Sinhalese. He is the author of numerous novels and essays but is perhaps best known for his trilogy *Uprooted*. His work has been translated into numerous languages and many of his novels have been made into very popular Sinhala films.

Kamala Wijeratne's poetry collections include *The Smell of Araliya*, *A House Divided*, *The Disinherited* and *Millennium Poems*. She has also published a volume of short stories titled *Ten Stories*. She has won the State Literary Award twice.

Translators

A.J. Canagaratna worked as a teacher, journalist and English instructor at the University of Jaffna before retiring. His English translations of Tamil poems and short stories have appeared in numerous journals and anthologies.

Lakshmi de Silva has translated several major works from Sinhala to English including the works of Martin Wickramasinghe and E.R. Sarachchandra. She also writes poetry in English.

E.M.G. Edirisinghe was a multifaceted man. A tax officer by profession, he was a translator of poetry, fiction and film scripts. He also made his mark as a reputed film critic and a critic of cultural and social issues.

Malini Govinnage is a journalist, translator and literary critic. Among her several translations from English to Sinhala are *Fontamara* by Ignatzio Silone and *The Bolivian Diary* of Ernesto Che Guevara.

Kumari Goonesekere has a BSc Honours in chemistry and holds an MA from Princeton University. Her translations of Liyanage Amarakeerthi's work first appeared in *A Lankan Mosaic*.

Lakshmi Holmström's most prominent works have been her translations of short stories and novels of contemporary Tamil writers. She currently lives in the UK and was appointed Member of the Order of the British Empire (MBE) in 2011.

Chelva Kanaganayakam is a professor in the Department of English at the University of Toronto. He has published and edited several books including several translations of work from Tamil into English.

Ranjini Obeyesekere has taught at the University of Peradeniya, Sri Lanka, as well as at Princeton. She is a well-known translator, working from Sinhala into English. Her publications include modern Sinhala writing as well as older texts.

S. Pathmanathan, a retired principal of Palaly Teacher's Training College, is a poet, literary critic and translator, translating both from and into Tamil. He has also published a collection of his own poems, *Vadakkiruththal*, and a collection of African poems translated into Tamil.

S. Rajasingam taught in Nigeria for several years before returning to Jaffna, where he worked as a lecturer in English at the Technical College. He has translated many works of Tamil into English.

K.S. Sivakumaran writes in both English and Tamil and is a well- known critic and translator. He has introduced Tamil writing to Sri Lanka and the world through his contributions to two Encyclopaedias of World Literature.

Ranga Wickramasinghe is a medical doctor. His father is Martin Wickramasinghe, whose *Gamperaliya* trilogy he has co-translated into English, with Lakshmi de Silva. He is secretary of the Martin Wickramasinghe Trust.

Copyright Acknowledgements

Grateful acknowledgement is made to the writers, translators and publishers who granted permission for the work that appears in this anthology:

The Chariot and the Moon

Mahakavi. 'The Chariot and the Moon'. *Veedum Veliyum.* Translated by S. Pathmanathan. Sri Lanka: 1972.

Martin Wickramasinghe. 'The Mahagedara'. *Uprooted.* Translated by Lakshmi de Silva and Ranga Wickramasinghe. Sri Lanka: Sarasa, 2009.

Vimala Ganeshananthan. 'Our Valavu'. *The Yaal Players: Memories of Old Jaffna.* Sri Lanka: Kumaran Book House, 2013.

Carl Muller. 'The Jam Fruit Tree'. *The Jam Fruit Tree.* India: Penguin Books India, 1993.

Wimal Dissanayake. 'The Walauwa'. Translated by Ranjini Obeyesekere. *An Anthology of Modern Writing from Sri Lanka.* Edited by Ranjini Obeyesekere and Chitra Fernando. Tuscan, Arizona: The University of Arizona Press, 1981.

Michelle de Kretser. 'The Hamilton Case'. *The Hamilton Case.* Australia: Knopf, 2003.

Regi Siriwardena. 'Colonial Cameo'. *Selected Writings of Regi Siriwardena, Volume 1.* Edited by A.J. Canagaratna. Sri Lanka: International Centre for Ethnic Studies, 2005.

Lakdasa Wikkramasinha. 'Stones of Akuratiye Walauva'. *Fifteen Poems.* Sri Lanka: Kandy Printers Limited, 1970.

N.K. Ragunathan. 'Let's Chat in the Moonlight'. Translated by A.J. Canagaratna. *Lutesong and Lament: Tamil Writing in Sri Lanka*. Edited by Chelva Kanaganayakam. Toronto: TSAR Publications, 2001.

Chitra Fernando. 'The Perfection of Giving'. First published as 'Action and Reaction', in *Three Women*. Sri Lanka: Lake House Investments Ltd Book Publishers, 1983.

Nayomi Munaweera. 'A House Divided'. *Island of a Thousand Mirrors*. Sri Lanka: Perera Hussein Publishing House, 2013.

N.S.M. Ramaiah. 'Among the Hills'. Translated by Chelva Kanaganayakam. *Lutesong and Lament: Tamil Writing in Sri Lanka*. Edited by Chelva Kanaganayakam. Toronto: TSAR Publications, 2001.

Ameena Hussein. 'Guava Green and Mango Ripe: Field Trip Memories'. *Fifteen*. Sri Lanka: International Centre for Ethnic Studies, 1999.

Ashley Halpe. 'April, 1971'. *Contemporary Sri Lankan Poetry in English*. Edited by Rajiva Wijesinha. Sri Lanka: British Council Sri Lanka, 1988.

Parakrama Kodituwakku. 'Court Inquiry of a Revolutionary'. Translated by Ranjini Obeyesekere. *An Anthology of Modern Writing from Sri Lanka*. Edited by Ranjini Obeyesekere and Chitra Fernando. Tuscan, Arizona: The University of Arizona Press, 1981.

Liyanage Amarakeerthi. 'The Hour When the Moon Weeps'. *The Hour When the Moon Weeps*. Translated by Kumari Goonesekere. Sri Lanka: Vijitha Yapa Publications, 2007.

Nihal de Silva. 'The Rag'. *The Ginirälla Conspiracy*. Sri Lanka: Vijitha Yapa Publications, 2005.

No State, No Dog

Jean Arasanayagam. 'Inheritance'. *Colonizer/Colonized*. Sri Lanka: Writers Workshop, 2000.

C.V. Velupillai. 'No State, No Dog'. *Born to Labour*. Sri Lanka: M.D. Gunasena & Co., 1970.

Ayathurai Santhan. 'The Whirlwind'. *The Whirlwind*. India: V.U.S. Pathippagam, 2010.

Michael Ondaatje. 'The Cat's Table'. *The New Yorker*, 16 May 2011. From *The Cat's Table*. Canada: McClelland and Stewart, 2011.

Yasmine Gooneratne. 'Migrant Poet'. *The Penguin New Writing in Sri Lanka*. Edited by D.C.R.A. Goonetilleke. India: Penguin Books India, 1992.

V.V. Ganeshananthan. 'Hole-in-the-Heart'. *Love Marriage*. USA: Random House, 2008.

V.I.S. Jayapalan. 'A Night in Frankfurt'. Translated by S. Rajasingam. *Lutesong and Lament: Tamil Writing in Sri Lanka.* Edited by Chelva Kanaganayakam. Toronto: TSAR Publications, 2001.

A. Muttulingam. 'The American Girl'. Translated by Lakshmi Holmström. Unpublished. Reprinted with permission from the author and translator.

Sunil Govinnage. 'That Innocent Smile'. Translated by Ranjini Obeyesekere. Unpublished. Reprinted with permission from the author and translator.

Romesh Gunesekera. 'A House in the Country'. *Monkfish Moon*. Great Britain: Granta Books, 1992.

Vijita Fernando. 'The Homecoming'. *Once, on a Mountainside.* Sri Lanka: Tharanji Prints, 1995.

Isankya Kodithuwakku. 'The House in Jaffna'. *The Banana Tree Crisis.* Sri Lanka: Vijitha Yapa Publications, 2006.

Cheran. 'Cousin'. Translated by Lakshmi Holmström. *In a Time of Burning.* Todmorden UK: Arc Publications, 2013.

Love in the Tsunami

U. Karunatilake. 'Letter from Welimada'. *The Kundasale Love Poems.* Sri Lanka: Sarasavi Publishers, 1999.

Shehan Karunatilaka. 'Pradeep Mathew'. *Chinaman: The Legend of Pradeep Mathew.* India: Random House India, 2012.

Anne Ranasinghe. 'Rambuttangs'. *Mascot and Symbol.* Sri Lanka: English Writers Cooperative of Sri Lanka, 1997.

Ashok Ferrey. 'Love in the Tsunami'. *Love in the Tsunami.* India: Penguin Books India, 2012.

Patrick Fernando. 'The Fisherman Mourned by His Wife'. *Selected Poems.* India: Oxford University Press, 1985.

Ajit Tilakasena. 'Through a Mist'. Translated by Vijita Fernando. *The Pilgrimage.* Sri Lanka: Sarasavi Publisher, 2012.

S.D.V. Perera. 'The Mission'. Navasilu: *Journal of the English Association of Sri Lanka.* Vols 11 and 12, 1994.

Thamaraichelvi. 'It Could Happen Anywhere, Anytime'. Translated by K.S. Sivakumaran. *Bridging Connections: An Anthology of Sri Lankan*

Short Stories. Edited by Rajiva Wijesinha. Sri Lanka: National Book Trust, 2008.

Siri Gunasinghe. 'The Water Buffalo'. Translated by Ranjini Obeyesekere. *An Anthology of Modern Writing from Sri Lanka*. Edited by Ranjini Obeyesekere and Chitra Fernando. Tuscan, Arizona: The University of Arizona Press, 1981.

Ariyawansa Ranaweera. 'Rahula Is Born'. Translated by E.M.G. Edirisinghe. *Echoing Ethos: Selected Poems*. Sri Lanka: Vidarshana, 2001.

Healing the Forest

Anne Ranasinghe. 'At What Dark Point'. *At What Dark Point*. Sri Lanka: English Writers Cooperative of Sri Lanka, 1991.

M.A. Nuhman. 'Murder'. Translated by S. Pathmanathan. *Lutesong and Lament: Tamil Writing in Sri Lanka*. Edited by Chelva Kanaganayakam. Toronto: TSAR Publications, 2001.

Basil Fernando. 'Yet Another Incident in July 1983'. *Contemporary Sri Lankan Poetry in English*. Edited by Rajiva Wijesinha. Sri Lanka: British Council Sri Lanka, 1988.

Yasmine Gooneratne. 'Big Match, 1983'. *Contemporary Sri Lankan Poetry in English*. Edited by Rajiva Wijesinha. Sri Lanka: British Council Sri Lanka, 1988.

Jean Arasanayagam. 'In the Month of July'. Navasilu: *Journal of the English Association of Sri Lanka*. Vols 7 and 8, March 1987.

Buddhadasa Galappatty. 'The Stealing of a Jeweled Lamp'. Translated by Malini Govinnage. *The Valley Below*. Sri Lanka: Sarasavi Publishers, 2008.

Buddhadasa Galappatty. 'Whose Child Is This?' Translated by Ranjini Obeyesekere from *Nischalai Ratriya*. Translation unpublished. Reprinted with permission from the author and translator.

Alfreda de Silva. 'Lines for Richard'. *Mirroring Images: An Anthology of Sri Lankan Poetry*. Compiled by Rajiva Wijesinha. India: National Book Trust, 2012.

Indran Amirthanayagam. 'Elegy for Neelan Tiruchelvam'. *Uncivil War*. Toronto; TSAR Publications, 2013.

Vinothini. 'Krishanthy'. Translated by M.A. Nuhman. *Mirroring Images: An Anthology of Sri Lankan Poetry*. Compiled by Rajiva Wijesinha. India: National Book Trust, 2012.

Vivimarie Vanderpoorten. 'Death at Noon'. *Stitch Your Eyelids Shut*. Sri Lanka: Akna Publishers, 2010.

Kamala Wijeratne. 'A Soldier's Wife Weeps'. *A House Divided*. Sri Lanka: Privately published, 1985.

Sivaramani. 'Oppressed by Nights of War'. Translated by Lakshmi Holmström. *The Rapids of a Great River: the Penguin Book of Tamil Poetry*. Edited by Lakshmi Holmström, Subashree Krishnaswamy and K. Srilata. India: Penguin Books India, 2009.

Puthuvai Ratnathurai. 'Our Folks Are Not Ungrateful'. Translated by Chelva Kanaganayakam. *Wilting Laughter: Three Tamil Poets*. Translated and edited by Chelva Kanaganayakam. Toronto: TSAR Publications, 2009.

S. Vilvaratnam. 'The Worship-Scar'. Translated by A.J. Canagaratna. *Mirroring Images: An Anthology of Sri Lankan Poetry*. Compiled by Rajiva Wijesinha. India: National Book Trust, 2012.

Shanmugam Sivalingam. 'Nowadays'. Translated by Lakshmi Holmström. *The Rapids of a Great River: the Penguin Book of Tamil Poetry*. Edited by Lakshmi Holmström, Subashree Krishnaswamy and K. Srilata. India: Penguin Books India, 2009.

Vivimarie Vanderpoorten. 'Explosion'. *nothing prepares you*. Sri Lanka: Zeus Paperbacks, 2007.

Avvai. 'A Return'. Translated by K.S. Sivakumaran. *Mirroring Images: An Anthology of Sri Lankan Poetry*. Compiled by Rajiva Wijesinha. India: National Book Trust, 2012.

Puthuvai Ratnathurai. 'A Poet's Fearless Death'. Translated by Chelva Kanaganayakam. *Wilting Laughter: Three Tamil Poets*. Translated and edited by Chelva Kanaganayakam. Toronto: TSAR Publications, 2009.

Cheran. 'Healing the Forest'. Translated by Chelva Kanaganayakam. *You Cannot Turn Away*. Toronto: TSAR Publications, 2011.

Epilogue

Ramya Chamalie Jirasinghe. 'The Moon at Seenukgala'. *There's an Island in the Bone*. Sri Lanka: Yara Press, 2010.

